D0821401

THE OXFORD HISTORY OF
ENGLISH LITERATURE

General Editors
JOHN BUXTON, NORMAN DAVIS,
BONAMY DOBRÉE, *and* F. P. WILSON

XI

THE OXFORD HISTORY OF
ENGLISH LITERATURE

Certain volumes originally appeared under different titles (see title-page versos).
Their original volume-numbers are given below.

THE RISE OF
THE ROMANTICS
1789–1815

*Wordsworth, Coleridge,
and Jane Austen*

W. L. RENWICK

CLARENDON PRESS · OXFORD

Oxford University Press, Walton Street, Oxford OX2 6DP

Oxford New York Toronto
Delhi Bombay Calcutta Madras Karachi
Petaling Jaya Singapore Hong Kong Tokyo
Nairobi Dar es Salaam Cape Town
Melbourne Auckland

and associated companies in
Berlin Ibadan

Oxford is a trade mark of Oxford University Press

Published in the United States by
Oxford University Press, New York

© Oxford University Press 1963

First published 1963
Reprinted 1967, 1974, 1990

Originally published as volume IX with the title English Literature
1789–1815 (ISBN 0-19-812206-3)

All rights reserved. No part of this publication may be reproduced,
stored in a retrieval system, or transmitted, in any form or by any means,
electronic, mechanical, photocopying, recording, or otherwise, without
the prior permission of Oxford University Press

British Library Cataloguing in Publication Data
Renwick, W. L. (William Lindsay)
English literature, 1789–1815—(The Oxford history of
English literature; V. 11).
1. English literature, 1745–1837—Critical studies
I. Title
820.9'006
ISBN 0-19-812237-3

Library of Congress Cataloging in Publication Data
data available

Printed in Great Britain by
Courier International
Tiptree, Essex

To my students in
Newcastle upon Tyne and Edinburgh
1921–1959

PREFACE

L IKE other writers in this series, I have to acknowledge my difficulty in keeping proportion. It is inevitable in any history of literature, and especially in a period when so many different things were happening at the same time to distract men's minds, and which is by now so heavily anthologized and diagrammatized. No disproportion is deliberate. I have neither indulged nor disguised my own tastes, but I have no thesis to force on the reader. My affair here is with people— what they were doing, and, so far as I can observe or deduce or guess it, how and why.

Twenty-five years is short of the dignity of a 'Period', and indeed there are themes for which it is too short; but the editorial division is implicit testimony to the complexity of the time. My pragmatical rule has been, to include authors whose most characteristic work was published between 1789 and 1815 though their roots were in the past—such as Gilbert White and James Bruce; to consider the whole working life of such as Coleridge and Wordsworth, who made themselves before 1815 and thenceforth continued on the same lines; and to leave over, not without regret, the later work of some like Landor and Scott, who changed much of their practice about 1815. If I have poached, as in Burns, it is because I thought it useful in marking the course of things as I saw it.

To contrive some sort of order, certain kinds and processes of writing have been separated, though not strictly, into chapters. They must not be regarded as insulated from one another: they were contemporaneous, and most intelligent people were interested in most of them. The reader must do the adding-up for himself. Scotland has been considered separately, and at what some readers may think excessive length, in order to define certain conditions which have operated in the two kingdoms throughout the generations and become conspicuous in the time.

I have to thank many friends, but especially Mrs. J. T.

Stevenson for generous help with the chronological table. And I must add my stone to the cairn which all contributors to this series are in bounden duty to erect to the general editors, Professor F. P. Wilson and Professor Bonamy Dobrée.

W. L. R.

Edinburgh
November 1961

CONTENTS

I

OPENING

THIS volume covers only twenty-five years, but they are the years from the destruction of the Bastille to the battle of Waterloo—years during which successive shocks and reversals excited men's minds and imaginations, from that first picturesque and symbolic action, through victory and disaster, the expansion of strained attention over all Europe from Russia to Portugal, the vacillation of allies and the spasmodic excursions from Egypt to the West Indies, to the dizzy whirlabout of the Hundred Days. The time's changes involved a greater change. The great actions took place on the Continent; that was nothing new, but the old continental wars had not engaged the hearts and emotions of whole communities and the deepest faiths of convinced political parties. The new wars were conflicts of societies as well as of dynasties. Even where our study seems remote from politics, the swirl of political excitement, the turbulence of suspicions, hopes, fears, prejudices, and sympathies, must be present in our mind throughout, as they were present in men's lives.

The 14th of July 1789 is one of the great birthdays of the world. However violent the birth-throes, the National Assembly seemed to be bringing forth a fair child, but its growth was so rapid and so strange that the twenty-five years divide into brief periods as general opinion—in this country, with which we are concerned—followed its phases of development. For a year or two English observers might well feel a friendly interest, none the less real for a touch of patronage, the happier face of the traditional view of the French so brightly and brutally expressed by Smollett in *Peregrine Pickle* and by Hogarth in his picture of Calais Gate. Not only exponents of popular Whiggism, not only students of Voltaire and Rousseau, but anyone who read the descriptions of French political and agrarian conditions by Arthur Young, Dr. Moore, and the many other tourists knew that the distribution of power, the system of finance, and the tenures of land needed drastic readjustment. Now the

French were modernizing their affairs at last, which was all to the good in the eyes of believers in constitutional monarchy, and of political economists and agriculturists both professional and gentlemanly.

All too soon the revolution of Mirabeau became the revolution of Marat, of Robespierre. London knew the mob, and English politicians knew how to use it, but the Parisian mob seemed to be getting out of hand. The fate of Charles I was bathed in mists of historical sentiment; that of King Louis was an actuality, the more shocking that the slaughter of his whole family proved it a matter of personal hatred which their personal characters seemed not to deserve. Then, as since, the English, unaware of the peculiarity of their own political nature, were horrified by the spectacle of political debate that ended at the guillotine. Thousands of honest Britons might have written as one solid northern Whig, George Dempster, did in January 1794:

When France began its reformation and limited its monarch and stipended its clergy, I thought I saw philosophy at last in its proper station on the globe providing by its wisdom and goodness for the happiness of mankind. But alas—our philosophers only open'd the gates of the police to let in a band of ruffians to cut their throats, and now in the levity and savageness of the French character, in their rigour and folly, my judgment is quite bewilder'd.

A year earlier a less sophisticated politician, Robert Burns, had written, 'As to France, I was her enthusiastic votary at the beginning of the business: When she came to show her old avidity for conquest, in annexing Savoy, etc., to her dominions, and invading the rights of Holland, I altered my sentiments.' Other enthusiasts who had crossed the Channel to assist in the creation of the new Utopia had more personal reasons for disillusionment as they reflected in the gaols of Paris on the course of things.

As the 1790's drew on, opinion veered and fluctuated. The government that fought the republic in 1793 had its opposition, old radicals who had cheered for Wilkes and Liberty in their time, and younger men—and women—who had learned from their fathers 'the homely beauty of the good old cause', whom the French excitement might rouse but to whom it brought no blindingly new light, for indeed they were carrying forward to the Revolution ideas and emotions engendered by the American

War of Independence. For them the breaking-point was 1794 and the trial of Hardy, Horne Tooke, and Thelwall for high treason. Though the jury staunchly acquitted them, they took warning; and in any case, the confusion of their reforming campaign with Jacobin extremism put them in a false position. Less enthusiastic votaries might well grow not only sceptical but weary of following the internal convulsions of Parisian parties and the rapid succession of new careers, each seeming, at this distance, only another spasm of eloquence and another violent death: until they found a more consecutive interest in the rise of General Bonaparte, a political phenomenon of more endurance, masterly rather than partisan, a brilliant individual in an individualistic age, a superb technician, and the liveliest sporting spectacle of all time.

By 1798 William Taylor of Norwich, an old friend of the revolution, could write to Southey, 'I grow very antigallican. I dislike the cause of national ambition and aggrandizement as much as I liked the cause of national representation and liberty.' But France now was Bonaparte, and interest and opinion gathered round him rather than round any variant of political theory, and were concentrated in the rush to France after the Peace of Amiens in 1802. It was a curious and significant episode. The agelong instinct of the islanders to escape the confines of the seas was momentarily liberated, and the flood of *Tours, Travels, Observations,* duly swollen. Enough of the old social sentiment for France still survived to make the visit a social duty, for the dreadful disappearance of old personal connexions was a horror of the Jacobin chaos which Bonaparte had ended. Romantic admiration for the marvellous superman was gratified, and his profile, his eyes, his uniforms, were duly commented upon. Curiosity examined the sites of the twelve-years' drama. Artists, including young Hazlitt and even Crome of Norwich, found inspiration in the greatest collection of masterpieces ever brought together in one place, amateurs infuriated the painter Martin Shee by setting up for connoisseurs on the strength of 'a pop visit to the Louvre', and the scientifically minded, amateur and professional, brought themselves up to date in laboratories and factories. When the peace was broken, the resultant solidarity of the national feeling against Napoleon was the stronger that these delights were withdrawn, and that the imprisonment of visitors and tourists in Verdun

symbolized the abrogation by the upstart dictator of the old
social relations which had persisted through and in spite of the
eighteenth-century wars. France and Britain were now set
against one another more profoundly and more comprehensively than they had ever been in their long history, and settled
down to the grim struggle that was fought to a finish in 1815.

Such momentous happenings were bound to work changes,
but in any case the country was ripe for changes. Energy was
stimulated, but energy already existed in plenty. The French
Revolution and the wars it bred were indeed badly timed
for Britain. The native movement for political reform was
strangled between revolutionary violence and governmental
repression, and had to wait till 1832. The question at issue
in the trials of 1794 was less the propriety of Englishmen's
sympathizing with the ideas of the French Convention than
the preservation of the traditional right of Englishmen to
disagree with the English government, but a harassed and
nervous government saw nothing but danger in disagreement.
Pitt, the hope of reform within the constitution, became Pitt
the war-monger, the source of corruption, and the hammer of
taxation. He had to shelve the abolition of colonial slavery
for fear of alienating Bristol and Liverpool, and Catholic
emancipation because any dissension might open a breach in
the national ranks. The problem of Ireland was complicated
once more by entanglement in foreign policies. Scientific farming was speeded up with an eye to increased production alone;
and it was a tragedy for Britain, and consequently for all the
world that was to learn from Britain, that foreign revolutions
distracted attention from the revolution being wrought at home
by rapid technological and scientific advance. Thinking was
too much political thinking to help men to grasp and manage
the new industrial relationships, so that habits were formed,
vested interests created, and antagonisms developed that were
not faced for a hundred years and remain unsolved to this day.

By its very nature, the French Revolution broke the ancient
social connexions between the two countries, and with them
much of the old intellectual and cultural commerce. French
music, never much admired in England, was dead; and though
English painters recognized the value of the French tradition
of drawing, they believed, and with reason, that they were
working on more hopeful lines. Contemporary France had

indeed nothing to offer in philosophy, and was barren of literature as never before or since. Political excitement played its
unhappy part in the estrangement of the two cultures to a
degree which no earlier wars had approached. Wordsworth
knew the Abbé Delille, but he derived too much from England
to be useful. Wordsworth was too much involved in new experiences and new political interests to use such opportunities as
he may have had, and the course of events in France disappointed him so deeply that France became an enemy instead
of an inspiration. Coleridge, ever excessive, refused to admit
that anything tolerable could possibly come out of France.
Landor was as bad and Southey no better; and as loss of
interest and positive rancour became general even among less
excitable people, England, though perhaps gaining in the confidence needed to work out her own modes, lost the valuable
discipline which French example had exercised over the centuries. Italian literature, unaffected as yet by political feeling,
continued in favour among cultivated amateurs. Wordsworth
learned some Italian at Cambridge from Agostino Isola, whose
granddaughter Charles Lamb adopted in later years; Scott was
not alone in enjoying Ariosto, nor Hoole in translating him;
Petrarch was widely read, and occasional sonnets were translated. William Roscoe[1] set an excellent example to historians,
in his *Life of Lorenzo de' Medici* (1795) and *Life and Pontificate of
Leo the Tenth* (1805), of the treatment of politics and culture as
a unity in time—a complete specimen, indeed, of the change in
historical method which the historians of literature and the arts
were slowly bringing about; and H. F. Cary's[2] translation of
Dante (1805–8; 1814) is a recognized masterpiece. But Italian
was too much an outgrowth of the Grand Tour and eighteenth-
century taste to exert creative or critical influence until later,
when Frere and Byron rediscovered the comic poets. German
was new, lacking the old prestige of French and Italian but
gaining by its novelty, none the less for its acknowledged debts
to Bishop Percy and Shakespeare and Shaftesbury. It was promul-

[1] 1753–1831. Attorney in Liverpool; banker, ruined by a run on his bank, 1820.
M.P. 1806–7. Botanist, collector of books and prints, and versifier. Centre of Whig
and cultural interests in Liverpool, and well known and liked elsewhere.

[2] 1772–1844. Born at Gibraltar; educated Birmingham and Christ Church,
Oxford; M.A. 1796. Held two livings in Staffordshire and Warwickshire; non-
resident 1807. Assistant librarian British Museum 1826–37. Translated *Inferno*
1805, *Purgatorio* and *Paradiso* 1812; also Aristophanes *The Birds*, and Pindar.

gated by dispersed enthusiasts, of whom William Taylor[1] of Norwich was the chief, and in the 1790's it was rather fashionable among young men. As usually happens, they were attracted by the striking rather than the solid, and soon tired of the extravagances of the Teutonic imagination. Coleridge, who came to it later, might have done more if he had persisted in his good intentions: he found much on which to exercise his metaphysical bent, though whether he had a true and profound understanding of Kant and the German philosophers is doubtful. It was after 1820 that German systems really influenced thought in this country. During the wars only science, which does not touch the deeper springs of thought, feeling and action, maintained the intellectual link with France; and it was a great age of science in both countries.

Scientific, technological, and industrial developments are not our immediate affair, but they had profound effects on intellectual developments. For one thing, they forced a regrouping of the country's intelligence. Some of the older regional centres still enjoyed their provincial importance. Communications were improving rapidly, but the railways had not yet drained the provinces and enabled the advertising power of the London press to stunt local activities and local reputations. In Norwich, for instance, a closely-knit society of middle-class families, divided in worship between the Cathedral, the Octagon Chapel, and the Friends' Meeting House but united by a strong local attachment and solid burgess hospitality, carried on a tradition of good works, reformist politics, and unprofessional learning, and organized what came to be important musical institutions, while a whole school of painters headed by John Crome and John Sell Cotman, if less regarded socially, formed one wing of England's original contribution to the art of painting.

It is curious [wrote Miss Anna Seward in her *Life* of Erasmus Darwin] that in Dr. Johnson's various letters to Mrs. Thrale, now Mrs. Piozzi, published by that lady after his death, many of them, at different periods, dated from Lichfield, the name of Darwin cannot be found; nor, indeed, that of the ingenious and *lettered* people who lived there; while of its mere common-life characters

---

[1] 1765–1836. Became interested in German literature during business residence in Germany. In Paris 1790, and interested in Revolution. First of many translators of Bürger's *Lenore*; also Lessing's *Nathan the Wise* and Goethe's *Iphigenia*. A good, broadminded critic on *The Monthly Review*, *The Monthly Magazine*, &c. Published various works, including a *Historic Survey of German Poetry*, 1828.

there is frequent mention, with many hints of Lichfield's intellectual barrenness, while it could boast a Darwin, and other men of classical learning, poetic talents, and liberal information.

But indeed Dr. Darwin had left Lichfield for Derby, and his intellectual affinities lay significantly in Birmingham.

For towns like Birmingham, Manchester, Newcastle, attracted brains as well as hands, produced intellectual concepts as well as money, and created new organs of co-operation and propagation in the Literary and Philosophical Institutions which, from the late 1780's onwards, nurtured the intellectual life of generations of good citizens. There the new problems were discussed, the new discoveries announced. Free from academic routine as from responsibility to ratepayers or stockholders, expressing and developing the local interests of their members, they performed functions which Oxford and Cambridge could not or would not perform. (The Scottish universities have a different history, as may appear later.) They brought into the main stream of national activity the values of the non-conformist academies; and if science was largely kept at the service of the industrialists, it is safer with them than with politicians. Even the obsession of efficiency was less dangerous in terms of the ventilation of mines and the coupling of looms than when assumed as the dominant principle of human life by Malthus in his *Thoughts on Population* (1808). These societies, built up by men like Watt and Priestley, and offering a livelihood to men like Dalton and Humphry Davy and Faraday, crowned the eighteenth-century doctrine of Reason as did the French Revolution itself. Nor was science merely industrialized, witness Dalton's work in the Manchester Institution, and Lord Cockburn's reminiscence that 'Grown-up people talked at this time of nothing but the French Revolution, and its supposed consequences; younger men of good education were immersed in chemistry and political economy'. The societies also brought together the devotees of natural history and antiquarianism, the inveterate amateur studies of this island, and, by stimulating co-operative field-work and publication, made solid contributions to both.

By lectures, and still more by collections of books more solid and more extensive than the commercial 'circulating libraries', the Institutions ministered to the new generation whose new energy exercised itself in wider fields than their elders cared to explore, and created a society more various in character and

interests than that which had mirrored itself in the literature of
the previous age. Nor was literature neglected. The flood of
minor poetry that flowed from provincial presses may be negligible in quality, but the quantity is impressive. Men do not
indulge in such pursuits unless they maintain their respect in
the community by, or at least in spite of, them. The new interests
were imposed upon a tradition of classical learning, and if they
drew off much energy from the classics it was but to produce a
better balance. And with men like Dr. Parr[1] and Dr. Charles
Burney—who shared little of the liveliness and charm of his
father the musician and his brother the sailor—the studies that
had given the older generation a training in art, philosophy,
and civic virtue became a mere pedagogic exercise. Porson is
saved by his services to textual criticism and his eccentric
legend, but the 'Greek play bishops' lowered the classics as well
as the Church in the esteem of men who were thinking about
more living issues, and pedants, like Dr. Burney who 'broke
out' at a dinner-party 'into a discourse upon the properties of
the conjunction *quam*' until Southey found 'it was a relief to
leave him', imperilled the influence of the classics by sheer
weight of boredom. Fox's delight in Homer and Horace was
part of his charm, his personal legend, but it belonged to an
earlier generation, rather than with the younger and more
variously minded part of the nation.

The situation in the sister arts must also be noticed. They
were unbalanced and changing with the rest, no less significantly. One great eighteenth-century poet remained at work
till 1796—Robert Burns;[2] and he had changed his practice.
He had made a splendid and immediate success with his social
poems of the current tradition, but had not repeated it. It is
unnecessary here to discuss all the possible reasons. He had
done that kind of poetry. He had done it brilliantly, but it was
not the only kind of poetry. He had to progress to something
more nearly absolute and autonomous. The change in his
desires and ambitions cannot be attributed to the French
Revolution, for it happened before the Bastille fell. He sympa-

[1] 1747-1828. Born at Harrow; educated Harrow and Emmanuel, Cambridge.
Taught at Harrow, Colchester, and Norwich. Curate at Hatton, Warwick; prebendary of St. Paul's 1783. Friend of Priestley, and praised by Landor. Strong in
Latin, unreadable in English. Called 'The Whig Dr. Johnson' but, apart from
fluency in talk, resembled him mainly in his worse characteristics.
[2] 1759-96. See the previous volume.

thized strongly with the insurgent people of France, but so did others; and though his habit of emphatic speech, and one characteristically impulsive action, roused suspicion at a time when the emphatic expression of such sympathies was easily misconstrued—especially in the servant of an acutely nervous government—his sentiments ran in the common course. His ephemeral election squibs add nothing to his stature, and whatever force political feelings and political circumstances may have had in his daily business, they had no force in his poetry, for the current of his poetic power was running in directions over which they could have no control.

Nor need we seek an explanation in the mysterious operations of a metaphysical entity called 'Romanticism'. It was not a change of creed or allegiance, but his own development. The *Epistle to Dr. Blacklock* (1789) and the *Elegy on Captain Matthew Henderson* (1790), if not in his best, are in his old vein. But *Tam o' Shanter* (1790), his one important long poem after 1787, is his most original poem because it is his most independent poem, owing nothing to social behaviour or extraneous personalities, but existing freely as a brilliantly conceived and brilliantly executed effort of the imagination. It matters little that it is localized, for however the topographical setting may have assisted the poet's imagination, it is not requisite to ours, any more than the lakeside where Wordsworth (or his sister) saw the daffodils, or the little hill upon which Keats stood tip-toe. The story has a local habitation because a story must have some locality: it does not depend on that locality. A good story does not depend on anything but how it is told. He told this good one, and never told another. For Burns never thought of poetry as a career, like Tennyson, or as a scheme of life, like Spenser. Once the Edinburgh edition was off his hands he pursued a new notion without thought of gain or reputation, following his impulse in poetry as he did, for good and evil, in life.

Burns had begun with songs, and why he did not include more than four of them in the Kilmarnock Poems (1786) we do not know: he had written some forty, and these four are not the best of them. He probably thought them trifles, compared with epistles and satires. In Edinburgh he revalued them, and made song-writing his life-work, for there he met musicians who shared his passion for the native music—James Johnson, who was compiling a *Scots Musical Museum* (published in parts, 1787–1803), and George Thomson, editor of *Scottish Airs with Poetry* from 1792 onwards—and was seized with the positive ambition to provide a corpus of verses for the corpus of tunes they were collecting. The patriotic motive was honourable and natural, but not purely poetic; and it was putting a strain on any poetic power, however great, to maintain continuously and at length the inspiration that had visited many Scottish men and women fitfully and for brief intervals, and to keep it in time with arranger, engraver, printer, and publisher. The comedy of daily life could be run straight into the moulds of traditional social poetry; the process of lyrical distillation is less direct and less under control, and the product, denuded of the varied interests which may compensate by partial strength for partial weakness in social poetry, must come clear and unclouded. He held to his purpose, in sickness and health, to the end of his life. Altogether he gave the publishers over 250 songs. On the happy day when the tune in his head and the mood in his heart and the subject in his eye came in consonance together, he wrote masterpieces; at other times he hammered out copies of verses no better than the next man. Most of the best loved are the better for being filtered through the tact and taste of generations of singers—a process he would not complain of, since it is the next stage in the longer process of which his work was but a part.

Music was the inspiration, and the danger, for a good tune may carry off poor verse; but this traditional music is the important music at the time, for however the music of the concert-room might contribute to the cultivation of its devotees, it was practically ineffective among men of letters. Traditional music —let us avoid the question-begging term 'folk-song'—the music that was part of the culture preserved by memory and not in books, was not yet destroyed in England by the combined forces of industrial migration and official education, but it was ignored along with the rest of English music by a society brought up in the eighteenth-century cult of subservience to the foreigner, and now at the feet of Haydn: which did it no harm, but left the recording precariously late. In Scotland it was cherished in all ranks of society. The enterprise of Burns and Johnson was not the resuscitation of a lost tradition but the consolidation of a living one. Later on, Tom Moore undertook the same task for the traditional music of Ireland, with less power but with considerable verbal and rhythmical skill and a pretty vein of sentiment. But major English poetry had forgotten Milton's lesson of how to nourish itself on music. As it happened, the greatest of the new poets, Wordsworth, came from the part of the country poorest in traditional music, and with all its new energy, England produced no composer to take his place with the men of letters, so that the arts were unbalanced and were to be even more unbalanced in the next two or three generations. There was still singing in England, but it was to be found in the minor theatres where the ballad-opera was decaying— although Samuel Arnold is credited in *Public Characters of 1799–1800* with forty-six 'operas' and Thomas Shield with thirty, and the Dibdin family produced such things unendingly, with Charles exploiting a quasi-popular type in his sea songs—and in the glee clubs which kept alive the tradition of amateur singing in harmony and handed on something, for greater choral composers to work upon. These had their virtues, but they too were insulated from major poetry, by social circumstance and social habit as much as by difference of artistic ambition, just as church music, with its fine eighteenth-century tradition of hymn and anthem still upheld by the Wesley brothers, was separated by its special function.

If music was thus in shadow, the visual arts were receiving a good share of the time's energy. Sculpture, as usual in England, was confined largely to portraiture and sepulchral monuments, but painting was developing significantly, within a strong society of artists and patrons to which the Diary of Joseph Farington, R.A.,[1] gives us entry. Farington is not one of the great diarists, but he knew everybody, and his addiction to gossip and professional politics, joined with the curious passion of his type for putting everything on paper, makes him an invaluable witness both to historical detail and, cumulatively, to the growth of the profession in numbers, in social importance, and in self-confidence. He is so occupied, however, with the personalities and personal relations of his colleagues that it is with difficulty, and only in anecdote and casual criticism, that we can observe the cross-currents of their artistic motives and ambitions. That might be expected from a practitioner of social instincts, an Englishman and therefore not given to manifestoes

[1] 1747–1821. Pupil of Richard Wilson. R.A. 1785. Diary published 1922–28.

and proclamations. No one tried to oppose a new canon of painting to the only formulated body of doctrine, which is to be found in the professorial lectures of the Royal Academy.

There is nothing to compare with the great *Discourses* of Reynolds: West, the second President, ventured only one. Instead, we have James Barry's[1] solid instruction to young painters, full of observation and memory of pictures, and honourably informed by professional zeal. His successor Henry Fuseli,[2] the proud receptacle of a classical education, exalted the Greeks with much citation of literary evidence—there being no other —and this may have balanced the hag-ridden Teutonic imagination that lends at least psychological interest to some of his paintings and drawings. For him, the painter is concerned with gods, or at least demigods, not with ordinary men or mere natural appearances. He conveys an excited conception of largeness and elevation rather than a sense of sublimity, but with immense vitality of conviction. John Opie,[3] whose education was scanty and whose uneven style suggests the assistance of his novelist wife, continued the line with nervous propriety, supported by a few borrowed quotations. He died before he had acquired the experience or the confidence to give utterance to the native faith that can be felt behind his orthodoxy; meanwhile he had betrayed the whole situation.

When beauty is said to be the proper end of art, it must . . . be understood . . . as meaning the perfection of each subject in it's kind, in regard to form, colour, and all it's other associated and consistent attributes. . . . The discovery or conception of this great and perfect idea of things, of nature in it's purest and most essential form, unimpaired by disease, unmutilated by accident, and unsophisticated by local habits and temporary fashions, and the exemplification of it in practice, by getting above individual imitation, rising from the species to the genus, and uniting, in every subject, all the perfection of which it is capable in it's kind, is the highest and ultimate exertion of human genius.

This is third-hand Aristotle, exhausted by literary critics a

[1] 1741–1806. Born in Ireland. Pupil of West in Dublin. R.A. 1773. Professor of Painting 1782. Expelled from Academy 1799 after many quarrels.
[2] 1741–1825. Originally Füssli. Born in Zurich. In England 1763; Rome 1770–8. R.A. 1790. Professor of Painting 1799, and Keeper 1804. Edited Pilkington's *Dictionary of Painters*. Friend of Blake.
[3] 1761–1807. Born in Cornwall. Self-taught. Helped by Wolcot. R.A. 1788. Professor of Painting 1807. A portrait painter. For his wife, see Chap. IV.

hundred years earlier; with a little half-understood Burke and some orthodox Reynolds, it provides the aesthetic basis: the rest is the tradition of the Roman studios and the *Caffe Greco*.

Serious painting meant the 'historical', 'epic', 'ideal', 'heroic': the terms mean much the same—figure composition on the grand scale, a literary or legendary reminiscence embodying an emotional situation with an elevated moral content, looking to Michelangelo and Raphael as the great exemplars. It broke the hearts of Mortimer, Barry, and Haydon, and if it may claim to have produced one master, William Blake, he was decidedly a by-product, and the whole stream of English social habit ran against it. The grand style is for urban palaces, and Englishmen were losing what little taste they ever had for living in urban palaces; nor did their theology require such decoration in their churches. The minor form, *genre*, wherein figure composition embodies emotions and interests of ordinary life, could be absorbed, though high academic superiority ranked Hogarth with the vulgar Dutchmen and the superficial French. As for portrait, unless the sitter was elevated above the ordinary social being, it was, for such as Fuseli, a mere trade.

It was in landscape that the new energy, the new vision, appeared. Here the painters rode the main current, along with the natural scientists and the new philosophical poets: already, in the words of Sir Kenneth Clark, 'almost every Englishman, if asked what he meant by "beauty", would begin to describe a landscape'. Fuseli could admit generalized landscape to the extent of a paragraph.

To portrait-painting . . . we subjoin, as the last branch of uninteresting subjects, that kind of landscape which is entirely occupied with the tame delineation of a given spot . . . what is commonly called views. These if not assisted by nature, dictated by taste, or chosen for character, may delight the owner of the acres they enclose, the inhabitants of the spot, perhaps the antiquary or the traveller, but to every other eye they are little more than topography. The landscape of Titian, of Mola, of Salvator, of the Poussins, Claude, Rubens, Elzheimer, Rembrandt, and Wilson, spurns all relation with this kind of map-work.

Yet it was from such interests that the great English school of landscape developed. The landscape gardeners and the amateur theorists, for all their occasional citation of Claude, thought in realities, not representations, and they worked out their ideas on the ground. The 'gentleman improver', the county historians, the tourists at home and abroad, employed the water-colourists until they made themselves valued for their own sake and for the peculiar emotions they fixed on paper. The whole process can be seen in the history of Turner. Conversely, the strong local attachments of Crome[1] and Constable[2] engender spiritual values apparent in their works. Even the scientists and manufacturers had their Wright of Derby, whose portrait of Sir Brooke Boothby so deliciously summarizes the dilettante romanticism of the late eighteenth century. They too, in their fashion, were working on realities, on things seen, not on intellectual concepts. The rusticity of Morland and Bewick[3] owed nothing to the pastoral tradition.

They were not, therefore, concerned to write down their principles, or even to formulate them professionally, and they left the Sublime, the Beautiful, and the Picturesque to the amateurs. It was not until 1833, at the age of fifty-seven, that Constable lectured on landscape, and he did it extempore, commenting on examples exhibited to the audience. He knew what he called 'the moral feeling of a landscape', but when 'the amiable but eccentric Blake, looking through one of Constable's sketch books, said of a beautiful drawing of an avenue of fir trees on Hampstead Heath, "Why, this is not drawing, but inspiration" ', the single-minded Constable 'replied, "I never knew it before; I meant it for drawing." ' Ten years after Constable, a non-professional, John Ruskin, unhampered by literary documentation and founding on Turner's pictures and his own vision, began to thrash it out; but the painter's business is painting. Martin Shee's *Rhymes on Art* (1805) contain little more, either in his couplets or in his voluminous footnotes, than professional invectives against connoisseurs and dealers— though there is more in his *Elements of Art* (1809)—and the same themes fill too much of Prince Hoare's periodical *The Artist* (1809-10), wherein, however, James Northcote, R.A.,[4]

---

[1] 1768-1821. Sign painter, and self-taught artist.
[2] 1776-1837. Born and educated in Essex. Studied in London. R.A. 1829. A devoted painter, recognized late in life.
[3] 1753-1828. Born at Ovingham, Northumberland. Apprenticed in Newcastle. His delightful autobiography published by his daughter, 1822, is the basis of a *Life*, M. Weekley, Oxford, 1953.
[4] 1746-1831. Assistant to Reynolds, whose *Memoir* he published 1813. R.A. 1787. *Fables* 1828. See Hazlitt, *Conversations with N.*, 1830.

asserts the autonomy of 'the art' against literature and the theatre. Hazlitt was right in haunting the biographer of Reynolds, though he was too old by the date of the *Conversations* (1830) and there is too much of Hazlitt in them, for he expressed the new energy as well as remembering the old gossip; but his *Fables* (1828) is a desirable possession for his charming designs rather than his verse, though that is better than the feeble efforts of Richard Westall, R.A. Shee,[1] when Sir Martin and P.R.A., wrote lively Irish novels of which the second, *Cecil Hyde* (1834), is readable, and is credited with a play in specialized bibliographies. Judging by the fragments he printed in catalogues, it is well that Turner's epic, evidently founded on his favourites Milton and Thomson, is not extant. If Farington's anecdote is true, one can sympathize with Wilkie when he was 'offended with *Wordsworth* who offered to *propose* subjects to him to paint, and gave him to understand that when He could not think of subjects as well as paint them He would come to Him'. We can see the parallel interests in their work, just as we can fancy a parallel between the 'historical' school and the long poems of Southey and Landor; but 'the art' was freed, to make its separate contribution to the perceptual and emotional content of the imagination in the new generations.

For change was at hand, French Revolution or no French Revolution. The eighteenth century had done its work, and by the law that fruition is death, was due to disappear. The physical generations mark the course. Dr. Johnson had died in 1784, and few of the old Literary Club had lived to hear the end of the Bastille. Sir Joshua Reynolds delivered his last Discourse to the Royal Academy in 1791, and died in 1792, but blindness had already stopped his painting in 1790, the year in which John Wilkes retired from politics to his comfortable city office. The last part of *The Decline and Fall of the Roman Empire* appeared in 1788, but Gibbon, surviving in physical decay till 1794, belonged to the Enlightenment, an international type destroyed in France by the practical revolutionaries and represented in England—where faith and joy in the revolution was founded on evangelical sentiment rather than philosophic scepticism—in legal and administrative disquisition, with Bentham and Austin and the Utilitarians, not in political principle or activity. Horace Walpole could not stop writing letters; but

[1] 1769–1850. R.A. 1800; P.R.A. 1830.

even if nature had spared his body and spared the friends who had best inspired his incomparable art, what could he write, until he died in 1797 at the age of eighty, but curses on the men whose indiscriminate ferocity was destroying so much of the world which had so long been his study and his delight? Boswell gave Dr. Johnson his new and greater avatar in 1791, and himself died in 1795. Cowper's translation of Homer was published in 1791, *The Castaway* written in 1798, and his mortal frame persisted till 1800, but except for rare glimmerings of reason, he had been lost to the world since 1787. All these were recent. Their books lay on people's tables and their sayings passed in conversation. But they were the latest generation of the century, with all the prestige of their century's achievement still bright in men's eyes, but themselves disappearing fast.

II

THE DESTINY OF NATIONS

IN times of violent action and rapid change, compendious treatises of political philosophy can scarcely be expected. The political habit of mind of such a one as Dr. John Moore[1] is clear enough: it is that of a decent Whig who had seen much to criticize under the old régime, but his *Journal during a residence in France, from the beginning of August to the middle of December 1792*, published in 1793–4, and his *View of the Causes and Progress of the French Revolution* (1795) are, as the titles suggest, intentionally informative and not argumentative. Moore was a shrewd and practised observer. He describes men and scenes—notably meetings of the Convention—as he saw them, and from his vantage-point in an official household had access to the available sources; nor does he indulge in speculation or prophecy. In his remarks on French military organization and discipline, here and in the earlier tours of the 1770's on which his son accompanied him, we may find some origins of Sir John's famous Light Division, as well as his early friendliness to the French and his appreciation of economic motives, unusual in a professional soldier: 'As a man, I wish the French success, and as a soldier also. We shall have no war till they have established a good government—and begin to think that we have usurped a greater share of trade than they will think us entitled to.' Dr. Moore tried to give facts, with no more commentary than he could help, and more objectively than, for instance, Helen Maria Williams[2] in her *Letters containing a sketch of the Politics of France* (1795–6). Commentary, however, abounds in orations imperfectly transmitted in the record and necessarily shorn of all the circumstances of time and place that prescribed tone and form and the kind of immediate effect for which they were designed, and in pamphlets which partake of the same

[1] 1729–1802. Studied medicine in Glasgow, later in Paris and London. Army surgeon 1747. Practised Glasgow 1751–72. Travelled with Duke of Hamilton 1772–8. In France 1792.
[2] 1762–1827. Published verse and prose, but more conspicuous in politics, joining Girondist party in Paris and just escaping guillotine.

nature and the same disability. Apart from their value as evidence of bodies of opinion and the clash between them, and perhaps of permanent differences in human temperament, their interest rests more in incidental felicities or profundities than in any general vision of humanity or affairs. In *The Example of France a Warning to Britain* (1795) Arthur Young[1] gives the practical man's view:

We have had, on the one hand, panegyrics on Gallic freedom, with enthusiastic calls to pursue the same system in order to arrive at the same happiness; on the other hand, every circumstance of the Revolution, from the original wish for liberty, has been condemned and satirised with more wit than truth.

The Revolution before the 10th of August [the rising of the Paris Commune and attack on the Tuileries] was as different from the Revolution after that day as light from darkness; as clearly distinct in principle and practice as liberty and slavery.

In effect,

I am inclined to think the application of theory in matters of government, a surprising imbecility in the human mind.

The reply by Daniel Stuart, joint secretary with his brother-in-law James Mackintosh of the Society of Friends of the People, is the usual journalistic statement of the negative; its title is the significant thing: *Peace and Reform, against War and Corruption*— that is, against Pitt. This is the usual party pamphlet, one of hundreds.

The central figure of controversy was Edmund Burke.[2] When the standard-bearer of liberty, who had upheld the American colonists' right to rebel, threw the weight of his authority against the French, his old sympathizers were naturally perturbed and even shocked. Burke was sixty when the Bastille fell, and past his best. For some four years of laborious preparation he had been carrying the burden of the impeachment of Warren Hastings,

---

[1] 1741–1820. Apprenticed at Lynn, but began farming 1763. Many works on agriculture. F.R.S. 1773. Tour in France 1787, 1788, 1789: *Travels in France* 1792. Secretary to Board of Agriculture 1793.

[2] 1729–97. Trinity College, Dublin, 1743–8, and the Middle Temple 1750. First works *A Vindication of Natural Society* and *On the Sublime and Beautiful* 1756. Began *Annual Register* 1759. M.P. 1765; in Parliament till 1794, but not in office after 1783. Visited Paris 1773 and disliked the French. Began attacks on Hastings 1783 which ended in his impeachment 1787: trial Feb. 1788–95. Quarrelled with Fox and the Whigs 1791. Voted against parliamentary reform, supported war with France. See Vol. VIII in this series.

with ever-diminishing support from his fellow directors. The business was dragging, and it was to drag for six more years until its somewhat ignominious failure. His speeches against Hastings display all his unrivalled power of marshalling facts, his gift—stimulated here by romantic visions of the gorgeous East—for conjuring up elaborate imagery, and his Irish birthright of sustained invective. For these they are worth study, and they are a quarry for anthologists of prose. But they were unsuccessful: his facts did not convince, his imagery faded as the argument halted, his invective palled as invective does. Sympathy veered to Hastings in his long ordeal, if only because it was too long, and newer and nearer excitements competed with the stale drama in Westminster Hall. The long labour, the long uncertainty, the strain of keeping the affair from collapsing altogether, were bound to tell on a man of the nervous temper so clearly visible in Reynolds's portrait of him, whose personal activity was his only claim on society.

The real anxiety behind the *Reflections on the Revolution in France* (1790) was over—to quote the rest of his title—the *Proceedings in Certain Societies in London Relative to that Event*: and that anxiety may have its roots deep in his own situation. For Burke was never secure, either in his involved finances or his very dubious family or his position in the Whig party. He had made his place in the world by service to one Whig faction. The death of his patron Rockingham had already made that place insecure enough, but any attack on the existing political organization threatened its very foundations as well as the more conscious assumptions of his whole career. This eighteenth-century personage held paramount the cohesive instincts of humanity. His political philosophy rested on a mystical conception of institutions and a profound distrust of the individual. Power cannot inhere in or be attracted to or altered by a mere arithmetical aggregation. There must be a unity, and, according to contemporary theory, such unity implied a contract. Apart from all the other difficulties of that conception, Burke's profession and experience could allow for only one contract: that made by the Whig nobles in 1688. Between whom it was made, for what purpose and with what degree of rigidity, was never clear and was sufficiently disputed, but for Burke it was absolute. *An Appeal from the New to the Old Whigs* (1791) was an appeal to that mystical understanding against such other contracts as that advanced by James Mackintosh in *Vindiciae Gallicae*, a contract between the representative and his constituents. Burke had dealt with the limitations of such a contract in his *Letter to . . . the Sheriffs of Bristol* (1777), but now he was on more dangerous ground, and a candid reader might conclude that the real importance of Burke's interpretation of the settlement of 1688 lay in its defence of the permanent power of the Whig oligarchy which he had served and upon which his whole career had depended. That would not be entirely true, but it would not be completely false. With all his intellectual comprehensiveness, he lacked the intuitive comprehensiveness called tact; and his brilliant weft of imagination, rhetoric, and political wisdom was woven into a hard, rigid warp of Whiggish superiority and exclusiveness. The Old Whig was appealing to an accomplished fact sanctified by long acceptance, against the New Whig concept of an active principle still capable of controlling human relations and modifying them in new ways.

It is impossible to read the *Reflections*, the *Appeal*, and the *Thoughts on a Regicide Peace* (1796) without admiration or with conviction. There is something dead at the heart of them. Yet none of his opponents carried his power or his armament. He could fire salvoes—emotion, eloquence, sagacity, imagination, experience, insight, broadside in one paragraph—where they fired single guns. In a *Letter . . . in Reply . . . by a Member of the Revolution Society* (1790) the clever if erratic Earl Stanhope[1] defended the Society, of which he was actually chairman, largely by repetition of its declarations and an attack on Burke's treatment of Hastings, which, he contended, proved the fallibility of Burke's judgement. A greater man, Dr. Priestley,[2] in his *Letters to . . . Burke* (1791), is deflected too much by the dissenting interest into the antiprelatical, even anticlerical line. The notion of the Church as a necessary part of the corporative State made it part of the target, as it remained up to 1832 and even after the Oxford Movement reasserted its peculiar right

---

[1] 1753–1816. Third Earl. Married Pitt's sister Hester. Lifelong Whig; opposed war and Irish union. Invented rotary printing press and other improvements. F.R.S. 1772.

[2] 1733–1804. Educated for presbyterian ministry; tutor in languages at Warrington Academy 1761. F.R.S. 1766. Published religious, political, and scientific works. His home wrecked by Birmingham mob 1791. Emigrated to New York 1794. Heretic in religion and revolutionary in politics but his permanent work is in science. Discovered oxygen 1774 but did not understand its importance.

and status, but Priestley's line was less effective; and his prose
is gritty. John Thelwall probably did more harm by teaching
rhetoric than by preaching revolution, if his pupils copied his
self-indulgence in Apostrophe and other unreliably explosive
figures, but Coleridge and Wordsworth liked him; if Horne
Tooke posed somewhat awkwardly as injured innocence, he
was too old to do more; even a respectable and ineffective
busybody, Capel Lofft, could score a hit on Burke's conservatism. The one man who met Burke most fairly in his own
waters was James Mackintosh.[1] *Vindiciae Gallicae* is a light
cruiser to Burke's battleship, but Mackintosh manœuvred with
skill and coolness, refusing warily to conform to Burke's decep-
tive tactics—for Burke's discursive conduct of an argument is
much more controlled than appears at first sight—and arranged
his matter to suit his own methods. He saw the Revolution of
1688 as an historical transaction and not as the delivery of
Whig tables upon a political Sinai, avoided side-issues, and
avoided too the deadly weakness of Burke, the recurrent over-
reach that sets even the sympathetic reader at odds with his
author. Mackintosh's withdrawal of sympathy from the French
after 1793 does not require Hazlitt's explanation in *The Spirit
of the Age* that he was converted by a week-end talk with Burke:
it means only that in 1794, as in 1791, he represented a large
and respectable body of British opinion. His later career, both
legal and public, was that of an honourable lover of liberty and
justice. There is nothing much to detain one in his histories or
Miscellaneous Works, but by his intelligence, good sense, good
taste, and good nature, Mackintosh stands a little above what
he himself describes as 'That large body of literary men who
are destined to minister to the general curiosity; to keep up the
stock of public information; to compile, to abridge, to translate;—a body of importance in a great country, being necessary
to maintain, though they cannot advance, its literature.' A
commentator on the central Books of *The Prelude* could find
good parallels in the *Vindiciae*, and it is always a pleasure to
watch him at work, as it apparently was to meet him at dinner
—except to Coleridge, whose monologues he enjoyed interrupting.

[1] 1765–1832. Educated Aberdeen and Edinburgh, Lincoln's Inn 1795. Recorder
of Bombay 1804–6 and judge 1806–11. M.P. 1813. Professor of Law, Haileybury,
1818–24. Published historical and philosophical works.

The real clash of convictions comes with Thomas Paine.[1] To read *The Rights of Man* is to inspect the armoury of democracy. The visitor finds little beauty or subtlety or expansiveness of mind or spirit; but here are weapons, hard, sharp, well arranged and ready to the hand. For Paine's was no improvised enthusiasm. A man of fifty-two when the Bastille fell, his Quaker directness of mind and plainness of speech trained and exercised in the debating societies, he had done valuable, and recognized, service to the American cause between 1776 and 1780, especially with *Common Sense* (1776), in which he had, like a good debater, summed up the sense of his side. He had been in Paris in the early days of revolutionary idealism, and when Burke's *Reflections* appeared in 1790 he was ready to answer with *The Rights of Man*, followed in 1792 by a second part in reply to the *Appeal from the New to the Old Whigs*. In so far as he defended the French and disputed Burke's version of events and his high Whig interpretation of history, he was in line, as we have seen, with others; in attacking English abuses and calling for reforms he might be approved in part by Burke himself and still more by Pitt; to preach red revolution was another matter. 'Let the axe be laid to the root'—there were those among the people very ready to rise to the old watchwords of Cade and Ket now recalled in American and French terms, Levellers and Clubmen by instinct and tradition and with plentiful cause for present discontent. Such a peremptory challenge demanded a peremptory reply. Pitt had to condone subversion or prosecute. To escape prosecution Paine crossed to France, became a member of the Convention in association with the Girondins, debating-society products like himself, and was imprisoned by that other embodiment of peremptory force, Robespierre. His anomalous nationality exemplifies the temper of the time. Apparently he could be an American citizen, a French citoyen, and a British subject all at once: in fact he belonged to a peculiar eighteenth-century country of the mind, a notional debating-society far from the actuality of any true political institution.

That detachment was his strength and his weakness. Because of it he is a lesser man than Cobbett, who is sometimes regarded

[1] 1737–1809. Born Thetford. Excise officer 1761. America 1774. Published *Common Sense* 1776. France 1781 as secretary to American envoy. Member of French Convention September 1792. Returned to America 1802, but became unpopular. Died in New York. Extreme radical by faith and temperament.

as his successor. His emotional deficiency, insensibility to the natural pieties and failure to understand their force or even existence in other men, account for much of the instinctive hostility aroused, along with more thoughtful enmities, by *The Age of Reason* (1794). To attack the churches which seemed to be everywhere in alliance with the states he wished to overthrow was a natural instinct, authorized by French precedent, and plausible tactics. But where Priestley was a dissenter at odds with the Establishment, Paine was a thorough-paced eighteenth-century deist, and the result read like an attack on all religion. Also, by the time this deification of Reason was published, men were hearing what was happening in Parisian churches in that sacred name. Even his American friends were revolted. By 1795, indeed, Paine was out of date. The policy of the clean slate rests on the pathetic optimism that expects the slate to stay clean of itself. The debating-society phase was over, and Paine had nothing more to say.

Yet the works stand. Paine was too single-minded to be an interesting person, but he put a jagged cutting edge on eighteenth-century rationalism, and he cannot be denied the respect due to honesty and conviction. Turning back to the others after reading in *The Rights of Man*, one feels anew Burke's richness of mind and imagination but also his fatigue and worry and the basic falsity of his position, Mackintosh's balance and humanity but also his excess of suavity and lack of resonance; and the Irish orators, with all their passion and volubility, look just the dexterous duellists they were. It seems absurd that anyone should pit against this formidable figure the erstwhile ornament of Dr. Johnson's circle, the genteel moralist Miss Hannah More. Her tracts, like other tracts, had probably more success with the distributors than with the receivers. Yet the simple pieties exist, and the simple sense of right and wrong, and she was wise in appealing to the humbler motives of good conduct of which the Paines of this world are commonly oblivious. She kept out of the debating society, and though her practical religion perturbed some parsons, it never hardened into moral intellectualism. Wordsworth made poetry out of similar matter, but that was his own discovery; and it is curious that he, and Shelley after him, were caught by the next example of the untempered rationalism of which Paine was the most forcible exponent.

The works of such men as Burke and Mackintosh arose out of a contemporary situation, but in *An Enquiry Concerning Political Justice* (1793) William Godwin[1] attempted what Burke declared abhorrent, the settlement of political principles—that is, a moral system of the public relations of men—by purely intellectual process in the endeavour to give the world a completely fresh start. Godwin had been an efficient student in the strict training for the Calvinistic ministry, and might have made an orthodox divine if only he had had one spark of religion in him. As it was, he applied the procedure of his seminary to the secular ends of the time, seeking not salvation, but justice. He translates the basic tenets of Puritanism into secular terms:

The nature of happiness and misery, pleasure and pain, is independent of all positive institution: that is, it is immutably true that whatever tends to procure a balance of the latter is to be rejected. In like manner the promulgation of virtue, truth and political justice must always be right. There is perhaps no action of a rational being that has not some tendency to promote these objects, and consequently that has not a moral tendency founded in the abstract nature of things.

This is common in all English democratic movements from Milton to the trades unions—which is why governments, and reverted democrats like Coleridge and Wordsworth, were suspicious of Dissent—but Godwin eliminates not only the intuitive forces of religion but the human forces of emotion in order to ground his system on the presumably calculable processes of the intellect. Here also the unconscious parallel persists. Man's thought must be innately right, since 'To a rational being there can be but one rule of conduct, justice, and one mode of ascertaining that rule, the exercise of his understanding.' There must be a principle of evil, though when and how the intellectual Fall occurred does not appear, since 'All vice is nothing more than error and mistake reduced into practice, and adopted as the principle of our conduct.' Yet man can be reclaimed by returning to the primal grace within him, through 'that admirable principle of which we should never lose sight, the uncontrolled exercise of private judgment.'

Godwin may be praised for avoiding the re-erection of a

[1] 1756–1836. Dissenting minister, but turned atheist until converted by Coleridge Married Mary Wollstonecraft 1797; and Mrs. Clairmont. Publisher 1805, failed 1822. Made Yeoman Usher of the Exchequer 1833.

personal Devil, but he comes near to it in his rejection of authority. 'Government by its very nature counteracts the improvement of individual mind.' Mackintosh had denied what Burke assumed, the validity of 'corporations'—a nobility, clergy, and so on, as entities existing by right of prescription—and allowed nothing but the elector and his representative. Godwin advanced from this in asserting that 'Society is nothing more than an aggregation of individuals.' 'Those numerous passages in poets, divines and philosophers, which have placed our unalterable duty in the strongest contrast with the precarious authority of a superior, and have taught us to disclaim all subordination to the latter, have always been received by the ingenuous mind with a tumult of applause', 'our unalterable duty' being arrived at by that same 'admirable principle', 'the uncontrolled exercise of private judgment'. It might plausibly be argued that, as so often happens when men revolt, Godwin was reversing the basic assumption of his training, the dominion of God as reinforced by the precepts of Calvinism, but indeed Godwin did not combat the axioms of religion: he merely ignored them. Yet he remains as rigid in his puritanism. His is not the genial creed of *Fay ce que vouldras*. King Solomon said, 'Every way of a man is right in his own eyes: but the Lord pondereth the hearts.' Godwin accepted the first clause, but sank the second. When he says 'A virtuous disposition is principally generated by the uncontrolled exercise of private judgment, and the rigid conformity of every man to the dictates of his own conscience', we must take the term *conscience* in a sense obsolete in English but preserved in French, or regard it as a secularized version of the doctrine of the Inner Light so important among dissenting sects; for if not from the inner light of the individual, whence do 'virtue, truth and political justice' derive? Godwin holds them as trump cards outside the face values of the cards played in the sequence of human action, we are never sure what suit they belong to, and are left with a mystical concept of ethics, a refrigerated version of the old Catharist heresy that the Elect are sinless, springing here out of Calvin's purer doctrine of Election, grafted on Rousseau's dogma of the primitive virtue of mankind and made independent of divine sanction, as if all unperverted men were Elect and therefore incapable of wrong whatever they did. But indeed the mind is helpless before such a statement as this: 'If every man could with perfect facility obtain the necessaries of life, and obtaining them feel no uneasy craving after its superfluities, temptation would lose its power. Private interest would visibly accord with public good; and civil society become all that poets have feigned of the golden age.' That is, if everybody were perfect, everything would be perfect. This ingenuousness, breaking into the selfconscious priggishness of his logical precision, saves Godwin from our worst feelings, just as the naïve ineptitude of some of his illustrations betrays the idealistic simplicity of the maxim they are supposed to illustrate; but the real coldness and poverty of his conception of ethics appears in his enthronement of justice as 'the sum of moral and political duty'. Even Spenser could make little of justice, and indeed Godwin saw for himself before long that it would not do. He could only tamper with, rather than modify in any useful direction, the later editions (1796 and 1798) of *Political Justice*. Its interest, for the modern inquirer, and its power, for fresh minds like those of Wordsworth and Shelley, lie in the eagerness for some sort of solution of the human problem that informs its unconscionable logic.

One may suspect that it was *Political Justice* that completed Wordsworth's mental confusion until he 'yielded up moral questions in despair'. That passage of *The Prelude*, Book XI, 298–305, might well describe the experience of an anxious and inquiring reader such as Wordsworth was and Shelley was not. Equal frustration follows the attempt to disentangle the ethics of *Caleb Williams* (1794), that long illustration of the principles of *Political Justice* or (as it may be) second assault upon its basic problem. The justification for the novel as a vehicle is contained in *Political Justice*:

There is indeed no species of composition, in which the seeds of a morality too perfect for our present improvements in science, may more reasonably be expected to discover themselves, than in works of the imagination. When the mind shakes off the fetters of prescription and prejudice, when it boldly takes a flight into the world unknown, and employs itself in search of those grand and interesting principles which shall tend to impart to every reader the glow of enthusiasm, it is at such moments that the enquiring and philosophical reader may expect to be presented with the materials and rude sketches of intellectual improvement.

Caleb Williams is a readable, even absorbing, novel to this day, by virtue of the intrusion of just those qualities of *imagination* and *enthusiasm*, for it is kept alive by its emotional qualities— fear, resentment, the suspense of the chase, the cross-currents of desire and will, the duel of man and man. If it be true, as Godwin says in *Political Justice*, that 'Literature and disquisition cannot of themselves be rendered sufficiently general; it will be only the cruder and grosser parts that can be expected to descend in their genuine form to the multitude; while those abstract and bold speculations, in which the value of literature principally consists, must necessarily continue the portion of the favoured few', then we must accept our lowly place among the multitude.

Yet we may allow that it is the energy of *Political Justice* persisting in Godwin's mind and projected into *Caleb Williams* that gives his improbable story the power it indubitably possesses. Godwin wrote other novels in which that energy, that imagination, and the glow of enthusiasm, however aroused, are merely absent. They are dead; *Caleb Williams* is not; nor, oddly enough, is *Political Justice*. He was thirty-seven when his masterwork was published in 1793, but he had to come up a long way to reach that level. It was really his first effort, for his earlier works are negligible, and in it, and in *Caleb Williams*, he expended himself. Of the long tale of later novels, histories, biographies, only one piece holds that energy: *Memoirs of the Author of a Vindication of the Rights of Woman* (1798), his first wife, Mary Wollstonecraft. Only in that tragic episode did life contain anything appropriate to 'the author of *Political Justice*'. Otherwise he was the rather futile, rather likeable creature, admired in a sort of retrospective fashion, kept alive for us in the letters of Charles Lamb and somewhat shabbily gilded in the reflected rays of Shelley.

Such notable bodies of political thought as these belong to the first phases of the Revolution. After 1793 there was little to express but concern and emotion, for fair discussion of sources, sanctions, and forms of government was silenced by successive demonstrations of will-power, with which there is no arguing. Burke continued to reiterate his unaltered views, but he died in 1797, and what he would have thought of Bonaparte's restoration of order, and still more of his reconstruction of the state of France, no man can tell. Napoleon's usurpation could be justified by as good reasoning as that of William III; but Burke was

too old for new ideas, and the spectacle of Fox attending the
First Consul's drawing-rooms in 1802 would probably have
confirmed his prejudice for legitimacy. The English never fight
on theory, and Bonaparte was something they could understand. Men rejoiced at victories at sea and were depressed by
defeats on land; but deeper feelings were stirred only by the
Spanish uprising in 1807. When Napoleon invaded Spain,
most Whigs would agree with Wordsworth's landlord Mr.
Crump: ' "Well, Mr. W., is there no good to come of this? What
do you say to rooting out the Friars, abolishing the Inquisition,
sweeping away the feudal tenures?" in short, though he did not
mean to defend Bonaparte, "Oh no, on no account: yet certainly he would be a great benefactor to the Spaniards: they
were such vile slaves." ' Among such liberals as Mrs. Inchbald
similar opinions took the form that English arrogance takes
among the lesser intelligentsia, the assumption that everything
that happens anywhere is the fault of the English, no other
breed having will, desire, or initiative: 'No doubt (Napoleon's)
reign would have been a blessing to them, would they at first
have submitted. But now the avenger is the character he must
take, and we shall have to lament another nation, added to
the number of those, on whom we have forced him to draw the
sword.' Most men hailed the news with delight. Governments
had failed, and now a people was taking over the war against
tyranny. It was the true answer to the perversion of revolutionary force among the French; the reception of it in Britain
reflects the common impatience with official incompetence and
hesitation. This enthusiasm excited Landor to his three-man
expedition to Spain, though its main result was to give him a
violent dislike for the English diplomatists in that country and
an unusual understanding of the difficulties that hindered Sir
John Moore. These difficulties Wordsworth brushed aside,
along with the topography, the climate, and the formidable
French armies and their experienced generals. Here was another
people rising against tyranny, to be welcomed all the more that
the tyrant was the traitor of that earlier 'exercise of hope and
joy' which he had shared and lost. This emotional response was
deeper than that of Coleridge, or of Scott, who inherited from
Scottish history a sounder instinct about such matters.

Wordsworth had felt for himself, in Calais in 1802 and again
during the threats of invasion, 'the solemn fraternity which a

great Nation composes, gathered together, in a stormy season, under the shade of ancestral feeling', and that sentiment, the sentiment of liberty, a deadly hatred of Bonaparte and the French, and typical English generosity towards anyone except English generals who fight against the common enemy, make up the whole content of his tract (1809) on the Convention of Cintra, as noble a piece of scolding as any in the language. Burrard and Dalrymple might well be blamed for over-caution, for behaving like the eighteenth-century professional soldiers they were instead of recognizing the new kind of war in which they were faced by the new kind of army forged at Valmy and Jemappes; but after all they did shift Junot's troops out of Portugal, which is what they were sent to do, and the only alternative to their over-generous terms discoverable in Wordsworth's diatribe was to hand them over to the Spanish guerrillas to have their throats cut. This civilian ferocity, however, merely means that Wordsworth was out of touch with things. He had neither the knowledge nor the logic for such work. Like a true scion of an unmilitary people whose warlike instincts always favour irregular operations and refuse preparation, he could not remember that wars are won by hardheaded soldiers manipulating elaborate organizations; and like a true Englishman could not imagine that the Spaniards were Spaniards and not quasi-English. Even if the slow movement of Wordsworth's mind and hand, and the fussiness of de Quincey, had not delayed it beyond the moment at which alone it might have been effective, the tract would have fallen flat, and deservedly. It fails as the 1815 Ode and the Thanksgiving Ode fail, because Wordsworth—the Bard of the egregious sonnet 'occasioned by the Battle of Waterloo'—was not on the level of his subject but floated in a cloud of moral sentiment too far away to see its outlines.

If, at the cost of further delay, the Cintra tract had awaited the publication of Captain C. W. Pasley's[1] *Essay on the Military Policy and Institutions of the British Empire* (1810), a refreshingly direct contribution by an efficient, intelligent, well-read soldier, it might have been improved. In a letter to Pasley Wordsworth rightly rebuked him for some arguments which, though understandable in a practical man who had witnessed the incom-

[1] 1780–1861. Served in actions 1799–1809. Captain 1807. F.R.S. 1816. Organized military engineering training; director at Chatham 1812–41. K.C.B. 1846. General 1860.

petence and corruption of some allies and the unreliability of all, were politically and diplomatically unsound and even morally dubious, but the fact that he wrote to a stranger suggests that he was impressed. The military policy Pasley advocated was that which prevailed after 1811. Whether that fact, and the fact that a downright critic in a junior rank, incapacitated by wounds from active service, was forthwith entrusted with the reorganization of the Corps of Royal Engineers and received steady promotion, indicate that he had some connexion with the Wellesley party, or that he was the mouthpiece of the younger generation of soldiers, is not relevant here, but the *Essay* went into several editions. Coleridge, who had met Pasley in Malta, found in it useful ammunition for Daniel Stuart's newspaper campaign, and Jane Austen admired it perhaps because Pasley contrasted the failures of the army with the success of the navy. Certainly the greater part of it, paraphrased with the requisite alteration of proper names, would have made any modern publicist's reputation for shrewdness and imagination; which is why it is worth including here, though it is a technical rather than a political disquisition. But indeed political ideas, like political satire, came in season again only after the final convulsion of Waterloo.

It seems strange at first sight that a time of such political excitement produced so little political satire. It may be accident that none of the greater minds had gifts that way, as Wordsworth's heavy-handed efforts prove, but in any case great events stirred men's moral, imaginative, and emotional natures too deeply for satire. The temperature was too high for the arts of ridicule to be practised with the control they require, and the stakes were too heavy for its pleasures to be enjoyed: after 1792 another *Rolliad* was impossible, a *Vision of Judgment* possible only after 1815. The serious poems in the weekly *Anti-Jacobin* (Nov. 1797–July 1798) may well be forgotten along with its serious prose; but where political feeling was crossed with literary criticism the scale and spirit were right for satire. The method adopted was parody, which might seem trivial but is immediately effective because the object of satire is kept continuously in the reader's sight. William Gifford,[1] the editor of

---

[1] 1756–1826. Shoemaker's apprentice. Helped to enter Exeter College, Oxford; B.A. 1782. Editor of *Anti-Jacobin* 1797–8, of *Quarterly Review* 1809–24. Edited works of Massinger, Ford, and Ben Jonson.

the *Anti-Jacobin*, had already two satires to his name. In *The Baviad* (1794) he devastated an English Florentine coterie whose leader usurped the academic title Della Crusca. It was perhaps natural for a man who had had to fight his way from a miserable boyhood to a recognized position in scholarly literature to be irritated by the poses of comfortable aesthetes—Gifford's brief autobiography ranks with Holcroft's among the records of self-emancipation—but Robert Merry and his friends Jerningham, Greatheed, and 'Anna Matilda' Cowley were too feeble a folk to be worth the expense of skill or to arouse the bitterness of *The Baviad*; and if it be the actors' tragedy that their triumphs do not survive beyond the memories of their audiences, neither do such attacks as *The Maeviad* (1795). Gifford is at least an effective executioner compared with his fellow Tory and admirer Thomas James Mathias.[1] Many a reader has opened *The Pursuits of Literature* (1794-7) with curiosity and soon closed it with boredom—possibly assuaged with such desultory calculation as that it averages 4.55 lines of verse to the page (in the 9th edition, 1799, *plus* or *minus* in the other 15), solidly encased in footnotes and prefatory matter. As a piece of book-making it is so astonishingly inefficient that the physical effort of reading it makes too great a demand on human attention. The author is a political and academic Tory of the most high-and-dry description; beyond that, his satire has no direction and no movement. Warton, the antiquarian commentators on Shakespeare, a college election in Cambridge, the immorality of Lewis's *The Monk*, Geddes's 'sacrilegious' translation of the Bible, Jacobinism, various translations of Gray's *Elegy* into Greek, all arouse much the same quantity and quality of indignation; he approves equally of Burke, of 'the mighty magician of THE MYSTERIES OF UDOLPHO', Jacob Bryant the mythologist, Roscoe's *Life* of Lorenzo de' Medici—Liverpool being too far away, presumably, for echoes of Roscoe's politics to have reached him—and various bishops and Cambridge dons whose names may be found in university lists but nowhere else.

The best of the *Anti-Jacobin* parodies, however, live by their

---

[1] 1754?-1835. Trinity College, Cambridge; M.A. 1777. Treasurer to Queen; librarian at Buckingham Palace 1812. F.R.S. 1795. Italy 1817. Translated English poets into Italian and Italian into English. Excellent Italian scholar, but made many enemies by his satires.

comic force, directed by keen intelligence and sharpened by sheer cleverness, aimed at single targets each in turn. Canning, Frere, Ellis, and the others who contributed lines or passages— for the composite authorship is uncertain in detail—chose these targets for political reasons, which are temporary, but directed their attack on permanent critical weaknesses. The parody of Southey's *Inscription . . . in Chepstow Castle* is plain travesty; but that of his *The Widow* exploits the discrepancy between his simple ballad-matter and the artificial sapphics in which he frames it; and the result is funny by exaggeration of the same discrepancy:

> Was it the squire, for killing of his game? or
> Covetous parson, for his tithes distraining?
> Or roguish lawyer, made you lose your little
>   All in a lawsuit? . . .
>
> I should be glad to drink your Honour's health in
> A pot of beer, if you will give me sixpence;
> But for my part, I never love to meddle
>   With politics, sir . . .

That sort of thing is funny in itself, as a comedian's dance is funny with no need of external reference: but one can never read Southey's quantitative verses again without remembering it. So also Baron Macdonald's jibes at the Dukes of Bedford and Northumberland for their attempts to evade taxation amuse by setting antique ballad-style against technical phrasing, but that game is simple and common. *The Loves of the Triangles*, however, is a rapid, economical, and valid criticism of the inherent weakness of Erasmus Darwin, and successful both as such and in its own right by the skilful handling of the verse.

> Stay your rude steps, or e'er your feet invade
> The Muses' haunts, ye Sons of War and Trade!
> Nor you, ye legion fiends of Church and Law,
> Pollute these pages with unhallow'd paw!
> Debased, corrupted, grovelling, and confined
> No DEFINITIONS touch *your* senseless mind;
> To *you* no POSTULATES prefer their claim,
> No ardent AXIOMS *your* dull souls inflame;
> For *you*, no TANGENTS touch, no ANGLES meet,
> No CIRCLES join in osculation sweet! . . .
>
> 'Twas thine alone, O youth of giant frame,
> Isosceles! that rebel heart to tame!

> In vain coy Mathesis thy presence flies:
> Still turn her fond hallucinating eyes;
> Thrills with *Galvanic* fires each tortuous nerve,
> Throb her blue veins, and dies her cold reserve.
> —Yet strives the fair, till in the giant's breast
> She sees the mutual passion's flame confessed:
> Where'er he moves, she sees his tall limbs trace
> *Internal Angles equal at the base;*
> Again she doubts him: but *produced at will*
> She sees *th' external Angles equal still.* . . .

It is so skilful that even Darwin could not be angry. What Mrs. Inchbald or Coleridge thought of *The Rovers* we cannot guess, but it is indubitably a masterpiece, kept alive by the same gift for nonsense as *The Progress of Man* which parodies Payne Knight.

The strength of this hybrid of politics and criticism becomes more obvious when the results are compared with the popular *Rejected Addresses* of James and Horace Smith.[1] True, political feelings had changed between 1797 and 1812, but the Smiths were not concerned about them, and little about critical values. They were exploiting the celebrations over the reopening of Drury Lane theatre after the fire of 1809, to raise a laugh and turn an honest penny. The *Anti-Jacobin* men were cleverer and better trained, and, what is even more important, they were in the centre of affairs and ideas. Too strict a comparison is scarcely fair, because nowadays we look back to the great 'Romantics' first and almost exclusively, and the Smiths' parodies of them are not their best. To make their effects they relied on the commonest and weakest charge against Wordsworth, that of childishness, on verbal reminiscence of Scott, though the active scene is rightly chosen, and on little else for Byron; and they could make nothing of Coleridge. They were happier when they rested on long-established critical notions, as they could with Crabbe, Cobbett's prose harangue, or Tom Moore's lyrical vein, or the Lucretian translator's style of 'Dr. B.'. But even if they had had the sharpness and the weight of the earlier group, their simpler motives could not give the thrust required for deeper penetration.

The reader who turns to Cobbett[2] for satire will find some

---

[1] 1779–1849; 1775–1839. A clever pair of humorous journalists.

[2] 1762–1835. Born Farnham, Surrey, son of a labourer. Soldier 1783–92. America 1792; bookseller and publisher in Philadelphia; prosecuted for libel 1797. London 1800, Tory journalist, but became radical about 1804. Farmed

rough sarcasm but little else: Cobbett always kept something of the sergeant-major he had been, and New England was not the place wherein to acquire the finer strokes in journalism. After his return to England in 1800 he employed himself regularly in his parliamentary reports, and if an over-anxious government had handled him better his aggressive royalism might not have changed into such aggressive radicalism, for he was something better than a mere politician, and the few outbursts of indignation for which he suffered were over temporary affairs. It was after 1815 that the Cobbett appeared who stands as a permanent testimony to one element in the English nature. Sydney Smith[1] was, on the other hand, too much of a party politician, and found in politics an outlet for the wit which otherwise would have been exercised only at dinner tables. If he had been allowed to follow his early inclination for law, he would have grown into a successful barrister of the most admired and detestable kind; in the Church of England his native good humour, goodwill, and practical charity had opportunity to develop, but he was always advocate rather than thinker— the philosophical lectures by which he brought himself before the London public are compiled from textbooks, with some fragmentary memories of what he learned from Dugald Stewart and Thomas Brown in Edinburgh. The subject of his longest effort, *The Letters of Peter Plymley* (1807–8), brought out his strength and his weakness. A sensible good-natured man protests against political disabilities suffered by fellow countrymen, in the name of liberty, and as a measure of common sense. He has no love for Catholic doctrine or practice, but it is irrelevant, for politics and religion are two different things. This is admirable, and the exercise of wit is appropriate to a cause which could be debated and agreed in parliaments; it could not, however, be settled there: to persuade King George III to do something which he regarded—however wrongheadedly—as contrary to his coronation oath was beyond the power of wit or

from 1804. America 1817–19. M.P. 1832. Began *Cobbett's Weekly Political Register* 1802 and continued it till death. For his best-remembered work, see Vol. X of this series.

[1] 1771–1848. Winchester and New College, Oxford; fellow 1791. Tutor to Michael Hicks Beach in Edinburgh; hence his part in *The Edinburgh Review* 1802. London 1803. Settled in his living of Foston, Yorkshire, 1808; prebendary in Bristol 1828, canon of St. Paul's, London, 1831. His religion purely cerebral, but his kindliness and wit made him popular, not only in Whig circles.

argument. Pitt resigned in protest, but to suggest as Smith does that the King should be coerced by paralysing the government of the country, was, especially at such a time, irresponsible. Catholic emancipation was not a party tenet, but the frivolous suggestion could come from a Whig because many Whigs despaired of the defence against Napoleon and were prepared to let him enjoy his conquests. Smith imagined that it would appease the Irish, or at least cancel the attraction of a French empire now (speciously enough) reconciled with the Pope, if Roman Catholics were empowered to sit in Parliament and to hold certain offices from which they were excluded: Southey exposed the superficiality of such ideas. The principle that civic status is a birthright would have been theme enough; when he deals with it as a practical need of the time Smith betrays his insularity. Whether remorseless jibing at Canning, who also believed in Catholic emancipation, was the best policy, and whether continuous jibing at him—for Smith, like a true Eng-lishman, believed that a joke is the better for repetition—as the joker of the *Anti-Jacobin* did not invite a devastating *tu quoque*, is dubious. Whether Peter Plymley was effective is equally dubious, for it was twenty years before the cause was won. The general effect of the *Letters*, however, is sympathetic, if taken as they were issued, one at a time. The wit and humour are enjoyable; and the apologue of Mrs. Partington and her mop, in a speech on the Reform Bill of 1832, gave a familiar image to succeeding generations. Smith and Cobbett are necessary to any analyst of the English mind and character.

There is, then, little enough that can be called satire, but most—such as it is—on the Tory side. It was only after 1812, when the Prince of Wales disappointed the Whigs who had expected that his assumption of the full powers of regency would mean their immediate accession to power, that the light verse of Tom Moore played about his Royal Highness's morals, habits, and physical conformation: and that was the beginning of a new age.

It would be wrong to leave this subject without mention of the growing importance of the newspapers. Their condition was low enough. Many of them lived on borrowed matter. Copy-right seems to have been understood in easy-going fashion— even Wordsworth, strict and even suspicious in his dealings with publishers, seems not to have cared about the unauthorized reprinting of poems from paper to paper. There were, however, a few notable editors. Their work was not easy. Besides the occasional hindrances which governments could place in the way of journalists they disliked as insufficiently subservient or amenable to bribery and intimidation, two standing difficulties limited the energies of the newspaper men: the stamp duty which added at one time as much as fourpence to the price of copies, and the incalculable law of libel, an astonishingly futile protection for individuals by modern standards but, in default of powers of arbitrary arrest, a ready weapon against independent opinion. James Perry[1] of *The Morning Chronicle* was prosecuted several times, and John Walter[2] of *The Times* at least thrice. Walter's[3] son John lost all government advertising as well as the Customs printing contract for his outspoken opposition. It is to their honour that they refused to be deterred. Daniel Stuart, who owned *The Morning Post* from 1795 till 1803 and, later, *The Courier*, an evening paper like his brother Peter's *The Star*—the first regular evening paper—changed like so many others from early sympathy with the Revolution to moderate Toryism, but remained, again like many others, an inveterate anti-Pittite. Stuart, according to Lamb 'one of the finest tempered of editors', had the closest connexion with literature, since he not only employed journalists like Arthur Young and James Mackintosh and less convinced professionals like Coleridge, Southey, and even Lamb, but also printed poems of Moore and Wordsworth. His guineas were a godsend to these struggling writers, and all his life he was ready with a twenty-pound note when Coleridge asked for it. Perry too had a wide circle of literary and learned friends, and earned a word of tribute from Lamb in his inaccurate but amusing essay on 'Newspapers Thirty-five Years Ago' (1831).

The younger Walter, however, is the most important figure

---

[1] 1756–1821. Educated Marischal College, Aberdeen. After some time as an actor, founded *The European Magazine* 1782. Of radical opinions but, according to Lamb, 'with a dash, no slight one either, of the courtier' in his manners.

[2] 1739–1812. Born London. Coal-merchant, and underwriter ruined by the American war. Began printing 1784. Founded *The Daily Universal Register* 1785; changed title to *The Times* 1788. Handed over management to his son Henry, 1795.

[3] 1776–1847. Educated Merchant Taylors' School and Trinity College, Oxford. Joint manager with his brother of *The Times* from 1797 and sole manager 1803. Editor 1803–10; joint editor with Sir John Stoddard (see Chap. III) 1811–15. M.P. 1822–7, 1841.

in English journalistic history, not for his literary connexions but for his professional zeal and competence. For one thing, he maintained a fierce and determined independence in the face of all threats and proffers. The press of this country owes its freedom more to his courage and integrity than to any political theory or social agency. In the second place, when he was denied proper access to the foreign news which, since communications were largely under government control, were in practice a perquisite of the Foreign Office clerks, he organized his own system, sending his men abroad to wherever important action was to be expected. Thus Crabb Robinson[1] was special correspondent in Germany and in Spain and Portugal—including Corunna—in 1808-9, and Edward Sterling, afterwards one of the new breed of leader-writers who earned for *The Times* its nickname 'The Thunderer', was correspondent in Paris in 1814. By such means Walter secured more information, more detailed and more reliable, and also more recent, until business firms and even ministers of state came to him for the latest intelligence. This was more than a display of imaginative organization, since good information is a greater contribution to the liberty of the public mind than the most efficient indoctrination. The third essential of journalism, speed of distribution, was attended to as carefully. The elder Walter had begun his career by acquiring 'logographic' type in which whole words were cast instead of single letters. The younger acquired the stronger and faster iron press invented by Lord Stanhope, and, in 1814, the first press powered by steam, which multiplied the hourly output of copies. This remarkable combination of character and technical efficiency, together with its continuity in one family, set standards for the whole press of the country as well as setting their own paper on a solid foundation as part of the new public power, 'the fourth estate of the realm'.

Meanwhile, far from the surge of debate and battle, immune alike from the sentiment of history, the suffering of the poor, and the pomp of armies, Jeremy Bentham[2] brooded over the

[1] 1775–1867. Born Bury St. Edmunds, son of a tanner. Solicitor in London 1796. Barrister, Middle Temple, 1813; on Norfolk circuit till 1828. Helped to found University College, London, and the Athenaeum Club. Notable for good sense, good nature, wide interests, and conversation, but devoid of creative capacity. His diaries are indispensable.

[2] 1748–1832. Westminster and Queen's College, Oxford; M.A. 1766. Called to the bar, Lincoln's Inn, but did not practise. His first published work was

pure science of government and jurisprudence. It was ominous that the only scheme he carried to completion was a project for a model prison: it was creditable to the powers that, to his infinite disappointment, the project remained on paper. Its only merit was the efficiency with which the prisoners could be dominated, for the theory of retribution and the theory of reclamation both assume the moral nature of the delinquent, and that was too far a fetch for his disinterested intellect. He would not have understood, if he heard it, the reply of Mount-stuart Elphinstone, administrator, soldier, and humanist, to one who recommended the application of Bentham's theoretical jurisprudence to his Indian province: 'I shall think I have done a great service to this country if I can prevent people making laws for it until they see whether it wants them.'

Yet Bentham wrought in fields that needed him—the chaos of corrupt administration and the chaotic accumulation of disparate laws. He was the progenitor of all those eminent civil servants whose labours men accept and admire without gratitude. He had a mind like a mechanical coal-cutter, emitting clanking, ill-tempered noises as it moved along, and requiring the services of two or three labourers to shovel its products into trucks for conveyance to consumers. Even so, these products became profitable only when processed by Malthus, Austin, James Mill, and other disciples, and that removes his effect and significance to later volumes of this history. He stands here as a portent rather than as a force, a cold light above the turbulence of the time.

A *Fragment on Government* 1776. Very influential in later jurisprudence, and in ethics as leader of the Utilitarians. Supported the foundation of London University.

III

THE FACE OF THE EARTH

If the labours of Men of science should ever create any material revolution, direct or indirect, in our condition, and in the impressions which we habitually receive, the Poet will sleep then no more than at present; he will be ready to follow the steps of the Man of science, not only in those general indirect effects, but he will be at his side, carrying sensation into the midst of the objects of the science itself. The remotest discoveries of the Chemist, the Botanist, or Mineralogist, will be as proper objects of the Poet's art as any upon which it can be employed, if the time should ever come when these things shall be familiar to us, and the relations under which they are contemplated by the followers of these respective sciences shall be manifestly and palpably material to us as enjoying and suffering beings.

So said Wordsworth in 1800, in the Preface to the second edition of *Lyrical Ballads*. He must have heard of Lavoisier in France and Priestley in England—though more as politician than as scientist, perhaps—and in Bristol he must have seen Dr. Beddoes, whose assistant Humphry Davy had administered 'laughing gas' to Coleridge and Southey, was consulted by Wordsworth on punctuation in the very year in which these words were published, and was to become a friend of his household. Most great poets have been interested in science, and Wordsworth, as an intelligent man, knew what was going on in his time. But no chemist or physicist even in that great age of physical science constructed a new scheme of things as Newton had done, to which constructive artists in other kinds could respond as Thomson had responded to Newton's. While Wordsworth was writing his Preface, Dalton was arriving at his idea of atomic structure and bringing a semblance of order by the tabulation of atomic weights, but that was, and remains, even for the amateurs, an affair of the laboratories, carried out as a specialized activity with specialized apparatus and recorded in a specialized dialect. The laboratory workers did not disturb the common course of thought as the

older astronomers had done, for their work was too particular
and remote to affect the imagination until Shelley, whose own
imagination was particular and remote, made poetic imagery
out of some of their more elementary fragments. James Hutton
was founding modern geology in the 1790's; and geology, like
astronomy, concerns the impressions a man habitually per-
ceives in his daily walk; but the theological and philosophical
landscapes had not yet suffered the eruptions and inundations
that were to come, and for such as Wordsworth, mineralogy
was still an affair of cabinets and collections. Natural history
was another matter, neither remote nor untouched with emotion, by reason of that inveterate English habit—which indeed
balances Newtonian physics in *The Seasons*—of loving daily observation of the living beings that share our earth with us. The
greatest monument of that habit, Gilbert White's *Natural History of Selborne*, was published in 1789.

White[1] is not an exciting figure, but he stands for a conspicuous English culture-type that has had subtler and more
serious influences on our poetry and painting than our critics,
for whom it is too common for remark, have allowed; and it is
for this reason, rather than any peculiar literary grace, that he
must be noticed here. It is in the nature of things that the letters
which compose his work cover more than twenty years. Custom
and the kindly touch of time are of the essence of the mild
emotions that related him to his surroundings. He was sixty-
nine when they were published: a good Oxford scholar and
orthodox parson, who resigned his Oriel fellowship and held no
cure of souls, for he merely acted as curate in the neighbourhood of his inherited home. It was perhaps natural that the
only political comment of a man of seventy-four should be the
laconic postscript to a private letter: 'Sad work in France!!';
but White had long since accepted his parish as his world, one
of the innumerable diary-keepers and contributors of Nature
Notes to periodicals and local societies to be met anywhere in
England at any time. He was no great biologist and no sys-
tematizer, saw no visions and refrained from moralizing or
philosophizing, but he had the sceptical common sense of the
scientist—his attitude to the problem of the summer migrants,
for instance, might be that of Sir Thomas Browne. Nor did he

---

[1] 1720–93. Born Selborne, Hampshire. Educated with the Wartons at their
father's school, and at Oriel College, Oxford. Settled in Selborne 1755.

'carry sensation into the midst of the objects of the science itself',
for he was no poet. Soil, climate, vegetation, birds and animals,
local history, especially such as changed the aspect of the place
or the habits of its people, and the antiquities that witnessed
to its ancient life: these sufficed to fill his abundant leisure and
provide the discursive commentaries sent to Thomas Pennant
and Daines Barrington. White would be good company for any
of our poets except the townsmen Donne and Blake, or for
Virgil or Horace. At the other end of England, William Bewick,
in different circumstances and with other endowments, shared
the same temper, and Constable wrote to his friend Fisher, 'The
mind that produced the "Selborne" is such a one as I have often
envied. . . . This book is an addition to my estate.' What Constable envied was a mind so completely on terms with its surroundings; the addition to his estate was its testimony to one
of the stabilizing factors in our island temperament. Its virtue,
like the virtue of Constable's own art, is not in flashes. Quotation will not reveal it; the whole book is needed, for understanding comes with acquaintance, between the reader and
Gilbert White as between Gilbert White and the inhabitants of
coppice and downland and garden and cottage; and though we
must not exaggerate his literary achievement, he is an acquaintance worth having.

It was for the benefit of this widespread community of
amateur scientists that, while the eighteenth-century Goddess
Reason was enjoying her brief and disastrous political avatar,
her putative offspring the Didactic Muse responded for the last
time to mortal invocation in the guise of the

> BOTANIC MUSE! Who in this latter age
> Led by your airy hand the Swedish sage. . . .

In colder if less appropriate diction, Dr. Erasmus Darwin[1] published in 1789 *The Loves of the Plants*, an exposition of the
Linnaean system of botanical classification, which reappeared
as Part II of *The Botanic Garden*, with *The Economy of Vegetation*
as Part I, in 1791. 'The general design . . . is to enlist imagination under the banner of Science; and to lead her votaries from
the looser analogies, which dress out the imagery of poetry, to

---

[1] 1731–1802. Born Elston, Northamptonshire; educated Cambridge and Edinburgh. Practised medicine in Lichfield; refused appointment as physician to
George III. Founded Philosophical Society in Derby 1784.

the stricter ones which form the ratiocination of philosophy'—
exactly the opposite of Wordsworth's notion, and, on Blake's
principles, atrocious blasphemy. The botanist's enthusiasm
might, one thinks, have carried off a popular dissertation in
prose, with all the elegances proper to a scientific demonstration
and calculated to recommend his theme to the judicious reader.
If a man of fifty-eight could scarcely be expected to anticipate
the higher philosophic ambitions of the new poets who were
about to return to the high themes of Spenser and Milton, it
was a long cast back, beyond the discursive method of Blair,
Young, Akenside, to the informative-didactic schemation of
Dyer and Garth and Grainger. Part of the reason may be
sought in Darwin's earlier life in Lichfield, within that old-
fashioned society of provincial *literati*, sufficiently intelligent
and self-consciously cultivated, based on the cathedral close
with outposts in country houses of the neighbourhood, and
sharing the fate of such communities in losing its intellectual
ascendancy to the newer centres. By 1789 Darwin had deserted
it for the more exciting company to be found in Derby and
Birmingham and found his natural place in the 'Lunar Society'
in which, when the full moon made night journeys easier, he
met James Watt, Boulton, Keir, and Priestley to discuss
scientific papers; but he had lived in it long enough to be
immersed in its habits and assumptions. His prose notes represent the interests of technologists; the verse represents Lichfield,
his literary friends and his much-loved garden there.

Verse was one emphatic way of indicating that Darwin's
exposition of the physiology and classification of plants was
intended for the non-professional social being, and verse allowed
the infiltration of the socially desirable qualities of elegance and
sentiment into an intellectual exercise. Darwin may have been
misguided in imposing upon this sufficiently satisfactory botany
an anthropomorphic sentiment—suggested indeed by Linnaeus's tabulation of the genera by their sexual characteristics
but by the same token distorting it—and a synthetic lacquer
of style, but he was not wrong about his public. The contemporary social being accepted it. Horace Walpole was delighted;
and if the younger generation scoffed, Darwin himself acknowledged good-humouredly the accuracy of Canning's parody in
The Anti-Jacobin. Nor was it all factitious. Wordsworth must
have hated much of it, but he read Darwin and acknowledged

his borrowings. The reader might be flattered to recognize himself as one

> Whose mind the well-attemper'd ray
> Of Taste and Virtue lights with purer day;
> Whose finer sense each soft vibration owns
> With sweet responsive sympathy of tones. . . .

Here at least scientist and non-scientist could, and can, meet. Edward Tighe, Esq., no doubt exemplifies amateurism rather than either agriculture or poetry in his Latin poem on the Cultivation of Broccoli partly translated in *Phytologia*, but on the scientists' side Robert John Thornton,[1] Darwin's disciple and an expositor of Linnaeus, adorned his unlucky *British Flora* with poetic quotations and with specially-commissioned poems— though he was less fortunate with his poets than with his artists —and, on the side of the poets, such names as Crabbe and Tennyson, not to mention Wordsworth himself and some modern poets, can be cited as keen field observers.

Darwin's choice of verse as his medium might grow from a deeper and more relevant instinct. *The Botanic Garden* was followed in 1794–6 by the prose *Zoonomia*—in which, incidentally, Wordsworth found the story of Goody Blake and Harry Gill—and *Phytologia, or, the Philosophy of Agriculture and Gardening*, 1800. *The Botanic Garden* was a piece of straightforward exposition, and the prose parts were filled out with Darwin's various scientific observations both 'pure' and 'applied'; but just as Newton had imposed order on the scientific thought by the application of universal principles, so Darwin sought a unifying principle, which for him, as a biologist, must take the form not of law, but of history. Having discussed the question of generation in animals and plants, he ventures the speculation for which he is best remembered:

Would it be too bold to imagine that, in the great length of time, since the earth began to exist, perhaps millions of years before the commencement of the history of mankind, would it be too bold to imagine, that all warm-blooded animals have arisen from one living filament, which THE GREAT FIRST CAUSE endued with animality, with the power of acquiring new parts, attended with new propensities, directed by irritations, sensations, volitions, and associations;

[1] 1768?–1839. Qualified in medicine at Cambridge and Guy's Hospital; practised in London. *New Illustration of the Sexual System of Linnaeus* 1797–1807; *Temple of Flora* 1812, which ruined him financially.

and—thus possessing the faculty of continuing to improve by its own inherent activity, and of delivering down these improvements by generation to its posterity, world without end?

And, since 'Vegetables are in reality an inferior sort of animals',

Shall we then say that the vegetable living filament was originally different from that of each tribe of animals above described? And that the productive living filament of each of those tribes was different originally from the other? Or, as the earth and ocean were probably peopled with vegetable productions long before the existence of animals; and many families of these animals long before other families of them, shall we conjecture that one and the same kind of living filaments is and has been the cause of all organic life?

Darwin could not prove it; it was something suggested by the growth of animal and vegetable embryos, advanced tentatively —all the more tentatively, perhaps, because he knew it was flagrant heresy. It passed unnoticed until Charles Darwin set forth something like it in the strength of accumulated examples, and earned the theological odium his grandfather largely though not entirely escaped. What was important was his insistence—for he repeated himself freely—on the unity of all living things as partaking in one life-principle. The living being is not a machine actuated by external forces. Pleasure and pain, volition, psychological activity, are of its essence. 'The loves of the plants' is not a mere literary trick. Plants have all that animals have.

Vegetable life seems to possess an organ of sense to distinguish the variations of heat, another to distinguish the varying degrees of moisture, another of light, another of touch, and probably another analogous to our sense of smell. To these must be added the indubitable evidence of their passion of love, and I think we may truly conclude, that they are furnished with a common sensorium belonging to each bud, and that they must occasionally repeat those perceptions either in their dreams or waking hours, and consequently possess ideas of so many of the properties of the external world, and of their own existence.

This may be an evening dream in the garden; but if he too might say

> 'Tis my faith that every flower
> Enjoys the air it breathes,

why deny him his poetry? He refused metaphysics and referred back constantly to the body. He did not extend his theories and observations to criticism of the activities of the living thing, which is ethics, but to the proper business of his own profession of medicine in the second volume of *Zoonomia*, and, in *Phytologia*, to agriculture and horticulture. His medical system was not advanced, and his agricultural theories are dwarfed to insignificance by the brilliant succession of empirical agriculturists. He shared the common scientist's confusion of classification with explanation. His notion of poetry was vicious enough:

Nature may be seen in the market-place, or at the card-table; but we expect something more than this in the play-house or picture-room. The farther the artist recedes from nature, the greater novelty he is likely to produce.

The principal part of the language of poetry consists of those words, which are expressive of the ideas which we receive from the organ of sight.

His views on metre are unintelligible. But he was, as Coleridge found him, 'a wonderfully entertaining and instructive old man', who believed in life and a living universe, and passed on something of his faith. In the strength of that faith he exposes Wordsworth's limitation as compared with the lesser poet Thomson. It is unnecessary to 'carry sensation into the midst of the objects of the science itself': it is there already. His verse, his style, his anthropomorphism, were dangerous devices, for they distract attention from the native force that set him to work and set him to 'vulgarize' his theories—the fascination of the objects themselves and the passion to comprehend their modes of existence apart altogether from our human desires and contrivances, for which he may be honoured.

Neither garden nor laboratory, however, nor the isle of Britain itself, could contain such strongly developed interests, especially among peoples of inveterate wandering habit. In glancing at the works of travellers and explorers we must be content only to indicate some types and motives, and within each to note some that stand out in relief by the nature of the curiosity and excitement passed by writer to reader, the way strange things and peoples are seen and felt, the more or less unconscious revelation of personality and the technical-aesthetic enjoyment of the handling. The notable voyages of the eighteenth century were often made by the Royal Navy, and two naval officers may come first, since they continue the work of their seniors in the service. Captain William Bligh[1] told a plain tale plainly, but his *Narrative of the Mutiny on Board the Bounty* (1790) and *A Voyage to the South Sea* (1792) disclose a dozen classical themes: the drama of the mutiny, the long hazard of the open-boat voyage, the recurrent individual tragedies and the privations and contrivances that brought the survivors to land. The teller is a recognizable type: the professional naval officer with a scientific bent, not attractive but a man to be respected, overcharged with the one idea of carrying out the special duty for which he is detailed. In telling his tale he had the advantage of knowing his duty, which was to give a clear account of occurrences, report on the behaviour of his subordinates, and record such observations as might add to the hydrographical, meteorological, and medical files of the Admiralty, with notes on his special botanical mission, for the use and profit of the service; and he writes his professional report with that professional formality which, rising at times to a restrained elegance, gives so much character and quality to naval papers and by communication lends additional grace to Southey's excellent prose in his *Life of Nelson*. This candid and unstudied professional style gives character also to George Vancouver's *Voyage to the North Pacific Ocean* (1798). Vancouver[2] writes like an officer and a gentleman, with a touch of unobtrusive cultivation and a tolerant humorous humanity. He did what he was sent to do—he was, obviously, not the sort of man to have mutinies aboard his ships—and he had the topographer's eye for landscape, for the description of landmarks is an important duty of the compiler of sailing directions: the marginal sketches appear on the chart along with the figures of soundings and currents. And if he notes such phenomena as the thievishness of Pacific Islanders or the shyness of Nootka natives in much the same tone as he records barometer readings or the appearance of whales, that is proper to his purpose and office, does not

---

[1] 1754–1817. Born Tinten, Cornwall. Sailing master in *Resolution* on Cook's second voyage 1772–4. Commanded *Bounty* 1789, on voyage to Otaheite for breadfruit plants; cast off in open boat by mutineers, landed at Timor, 1789. F.R.S. 1801. Governor of New South Wales 1805; deposed 1808. Rear-admiral 1811, Vice-admiral 1814.

[2] 1758–98. Seaman in Cook's second and third voyages. Lieutenant 1781, captain 1794. Surveyed south-east Australian and New Zealand coasts, and Pacific coast of North America.

preclude an undertone of quiet amusement, and does avoid ill-timed censoriousness. These two may stand for their type; there were others, both amateur and professional.

It was the excellent Daines Barrington, the recipient of Gilbert White's second series of letters, who encouraged James Bruce of Kinnaird[1] to publish his *Travels to Discover the Source of the Nile* in 1790: a far cry from Selborne, but not so opposed in its interests as might appear. The topography, antiquities, and natural history which Bruce recorded were of strange places and strange peoples; he had harsh things to tell, refused to mitigate or romanticize them, and was received with so much scepticism, distaste, and even anger that he has not yet had his due. 'Peter Pindar', the grand mouthpiece of English vulgarity, displayed his usual shrewdness in comparing Bruce with Boswell. They were of the same breed of lowland Scots lairds, though Bruce was the better specimen. After the manner of his kind, he was seized by an irrational and fantastic notion—too extreme to be called 'romantick' by his contemporaries but describable, not unsympathetically, by his compatriots as 'daft'—followed it with careful efficiency, and recorded his proceedings and observations soberly, in competent colloquial prose and highly competent drawings.

During a business tour of Spain, mere intellectual curiosity made him add Arabic and Geez, the classical language of Abyssinia, to his useful stock of languages. Arabic gained him the British Consulship in Algiers, where he learned how to deal with piratical potentates, and Geez, presumably, turned his fancy eastward. Bruce might stand as the complete traveller, unprofessional in outlook—though he worked for usefulness as in his series of soundings in the Red Sea—well equipped in arms and instruments and by preparatory study of astronomy, navigation, history, cookery, tropical medicine, botany, and draughtsmanship. As a humanist and a man of the world he saw people as individuals. He had the rare and valuable gift of being able to accept *difference*. Treachery and ferocity abounded, but those treacherous and ferocious people were not to be summed up in these epithets; they had other characteristics. He made friends of some and enemies of others, treated the

---

[1] 1730–94. Born Kinnaird, Stirlingshire, educated Harrow and Edinburgh. Wine merchant in London. Consul in Algiers 1763; studied antiquities in North Africa. Explored in Abyssinia 1769–72. Died of a fall in his own house of Kinnaird.

powers diplomatically or with argument or a judicious show of force as need arose, and flattered the ladies, without losing his own standards in civilized aversion or romantic admiration, impressing himself and his status by his bearing, horsemanship, and marksmanship, since he went without disguise and not only his purpose but his life depended on the impression he made upon people who judged men by their own crude but aristocratic values. He was thus well aware of himself; and his own feelings of elation, fear, dejection, pride, anger, though never obtrusive, are constantly present, and included among the objects of his humour.

The Welled Omran, a lawless, plundering tribe, inquieted me much in the eight days I staid at Spaitla. It was a fair match between coward and coward. . . . These plunderers would have come in to me, but were afraid of my firearms; and I would have run away from them, had I not been afraid of meeting their horse in the plain.

Wild oats also grow up spontaneously . . . the taste is perfectly good. I often made the meal into cakes in remembrance of Scotland. The Abyssinians never could relish these cakes.

Self-revelation was not his hobby as it was Boswell's. His survival depended too often upon sheer pride and fortitude to permit of much indulgence of feeling, but he could recognize the interest of his own emotions when a moment of relaxation allowed, as when he encamped at last by the source of the Blue Nile which he had come so far to find.

The night of the 4th, that very night of my arrival, melancholy reflections upon my present state, the doubtfulness of my return in safety, were I permitted to make the attempt, and the fears that even this would be refused, according to the rule observed in Abyssinia with all travellers who have once entered the kingdom; the consciousness of the pain I was occasioning to many worthy individuals, expecting daily that information concerning my situation which it was not in my power to give them; some other thoughts, perhaps, still nearer the heart than those, crowded upon my mind, and forbade all approach of sleep.

I was, at that very moment, in possession of what had, for many years, been the principal object of my ambition and wishes: indifference, which from the usual infirmity of human nature follows, at least for a time, complete enjoyment, had taken the place of it. The marsh, and the fountains, upon comparison with the rise of many of our rivers, became now a trifling object in my sight. I remembered that magnificent scene in my own native country, where the Tweed, Clyde, and Annan rise in one hill; three rivers, as I now thought, not inferior to the Nile in beauty, preferable to it in the cultivation of those countries through which they flow; superior, vastly superior to it in the virtues and qualities of the inhabitants, and in the beauty of its flocks; crowding its pastures in peace, without fear of violence from man or beast. I had seen the rise of the Rhine and the Rhone, and the more magnificent sources of the Saône; I began, in my sorrow, to treat the inquiry about the source of the Nile as a violent effort of a distempered fancy:—

> What's Hecuba to him, or he to Hecuba,
> That he should weep for her?—

Grief or despondency now rolling upon me like a torrent; relaxed not refreshed, by unquiet and imperfect sleep, I started from my bed in the utmost agony; I went to the door of my tent; every thing was still; the Nile, at whose head I stood, was not capable either to promote or to interrupt my slumbers, but the coolness and serenity of the night braced my nerves, and chased away those phantoms that, while in bed, had oppressed and tormented me.

It was true, that numerous dangers, hardships, and sorrows had beset me through this half of my excursion; but it was still as true, that another Guide, more powerful than my own courage, health, or understanding, if any of these can be called man's own, had uniformly protected me in all that tedious half; I found my confidence not abated, that still the same Guide was able to conduct me to my now wished-for home: I immediately resumed my former fortitude, considered the Nile indeed as no more than rising from springs, as all other rivers do, but widely different in this, that it was the palm for three thousand years held out to all the nations of the world as a 'detur dignissimo', which, in my cool hours, I had thought was worth the attempting at the risk of my life, which I had long either resolved to lose, or lay this discovery, a trophy in which I could have no competitor, for the honour of my country, at the feet of my sovereign, whose servant I was.

This is honest and convincing in its unforced mingling of feeling and reflection and the recognition of the concomitant physical symptoms. Bruce does not indulge this strain, but some twenty years after his return Mungo Park,[1] another lowland Scot equally possessed by a remote and irrational idea,

---

[1] 1771–1806. Born near Selkirk, studied medicine Edinburgh. Surgeon on an East Indiaman; visited Sumatra 1792. Sent by African Association to explore Niger 1795, returning 1799. Practised medicine at Peebles. Second expedition 1805. Drowned in Niger with all his crew.

penetrated the other side of Africa and unconsciously provoked in the readers of his *Travels in Africa* (1799) the overflowing sympathy that Bruce did not invite and would have regarded as intrusive. Bruce was a laird, and succeeded by his pride. He stood no bullying and permitted no interference with his scientific pursuits. Park was a cottar, and succeeded by his peasant stoicism, his endurance of wrong, violence, and indignity, holding to his fixed idea and gathering his scientific observations as his forebears gathered their crops through all the wars and oppressions of border history. Formally he was an employee of the African Society, one of the agencies through which Sir Joseph Banks, erstwhile companion of Captain Cook and now œcumenical pontiff of all science, organized the furtherance of this branch of human knowledge; in himself, he was one of those who cast themselves upon opportunity to wander and find out.

We follow his fortunes as we follow those of Oliver Twist. A plain good soul wanders alone among perils, cheated and robbed by rapacious bedouin, guided casually by indifferent companions, succoured in dire stress by kind black women. The horror of slavery, the African shame that contaminated European traders as the oriental vice of opium did elsewhere, hangs over the whole landscape. We are relieved when he finds one secure village where he may rest until at last he is convoyed to the threshold of the intelligible world. Bruce would have faced these savage Moors as a chieftain among chieftains, beaten them at their own sports, flirted with the women among whom Park figures like Gulliver among the Brobdingnagians, and produced a lucid account of their hunting techniques illustrated with drawings of the local species of fox and gazelle. Vancouver would have moved confidently among those unreliable tribes, a King's officer with a couple of stolid ratings at his back to see there was no nonsense. Park's is a lonely, desperate, helpless heroism. He drifts as chance allows among wild beasts in disease-ridden forests at the mercy of savage kings. Yet this is no waif. He can make do with what the robbers have left him, keep alive on what food the charitable women can spare him, rise from his fever and struggle a little farther. He scarcely seems to resent ill-treatment. It is what an explorer might expect, like malaria or snakebite, to be avoided or endured but not a reason for abandoning the work or interrupting

it as long as a man can stand up and see. All the time, on the
last edge of consciousness and in the path of destroying armies,
he keeps on doing what Sir Joseph Banks sent him to do—
plotting the course of the River Niger. It is useful to buy a
handful of corn with a brass button from his coat, to recover a
hat or coat that seemed lost: the real positive gain is a compass
bearing on a river-reach, or even a glimpse between trees of
the current running in a verifiable if unexpected direction. It is
necessary to keep alive, to reach the trading-post, because
otherwise the Royal Society will not get those damp-stained
notes and will be unable to mark those few ascertained points
on the blank map of West Africa. So in his simplicity he writes
down what happened to him, 'who robbed him, who helped
him, and who passed by', and he does not fail of response. Yet
that response is emotional rather than imaginative, the emotion
too personal and too uniform, and the picture too chaotic, for
the creative intellect to fasten upon and turn to its own purposes. The painful drama is self-contained, to receive its only
possible addition in the tragedy of the second expedition when
the Niger drowned him.

After the tragedy, a comedy, in one of the first North American books to make a real contribution to the English imagination. William Bartram's[1] *Travels through North and South Carolina,
Georgia, East and West Florida . . . containing an Account of the Soil and
Natural Productions of those Regions, together with Observations on the
Manners of the Indians* (Philadelphia, 1791; London, 1792) is a
plant-collector's description of his professional tours, but his
solitary boat-trips affect us like a Shelleyan dream of peace and
beauty. Physical contacts are more difficult to convey in words
than sights and sounds, so we are not affected by the frantic
irritation of biting insects. Even the wretched results are only
medical symptoms, not present sensations. All is caught up in
the spirit of delight. In his bursts of fine writing where every
noun has its inevitable adjective, the absurdity is delightful
because it is the record of his delight in the landscape, the
flowers, birds, and beasts. Bartram provides a map, but there is
a pleasing sense of uncertainty about our exact position at any
one moment. His professional assurance about his plants gives

[1] 1729–1823. Born at his father's botanical garden, Philadelphia. Travelled in
search of plants in 1770's, and published *Travels* 1791. Plantsman rather than
systematic botanist, a good observer and a delightful character.

us an irrational confidence in him: however menacing the
ferocious alligators, we know they will not harm us, and that
he will duly conduct us to the hospitable dwelling of his good
friend L. McIntosh esq. In any case it does not matter very
much, while *Magnolia grandiflora* is so stately and *Carica papaya*
so elegant, the agile roebuck bounds lightly over the extensive
savannah, and the shining fish rove and figure in the clear
water.

What a beautiful retreat is here! blessed unviolated spot of earth,
rising from the limpid waters of the lake: its fragrant groves and
blooming lawns invested and protected by encircling ranks of
Yucca gloriosa. A fascinating atmosphere surrounds this blissful
garden! the balmy Lantana, ambrosial Citra, perfumed Crinum
perspiring their mingled odours, wafted through Zanthoxylon groves.

He is all absurd and charming, this academic naturalist so
fondly in love with all beautiful things.

As with flowers and beasts, so is he with men. His gentle
Quaker spirit inhibits criticism of his neighbours, white men
whose brutal behaviour pained him and red men who were, by
his own calmly-stated evidence, treacherous and bloodthirsty.

However strange it may appear to us, the same moral duties
which with us form the amiable, virtuous character, so difficult to
maintain, there, without compulsion of visible restraint, operate like
instinct, with a surprising harmony and natural ease, insomuch that
it seems impossible for them to act out of the common high road to
virtue.

They seem to be free from want or desires. No cruel enemy to
dread; nothing to give them disquietude, but the gradual encroach-
ment of the white people. Thus contented and undisturbed they
appear as blithe and free as the birds of the air, and like them as
volatile and active, tuneful and vociferous. The visage, action, and
deportment of the Siminoles, form the most striking picture of
happiness, in this life; joy, contentment, love and friendship, without
guile or affectation, seem inherent in them, or predominant in their
vital principle, for it leaves them but with the last breath of life. It
even seems imposing a constraint upon their ancient chiefs and
senators, to maintain a necessary decorum and solemnity, in their
public councils; not even the debility and decrepitude of extreme
old age, is sufficient to erase from their visages, this youthful, joyous
simplicity; but like the gray eve of a serene and calm day, a gladden-
ing, cheering blush remains on the Western horizon after the sun is set.

He has just informed us that these paragons had only recently invaded the region, expropriating or exterminating the former inhabitants; but that was yesterday, and time has no power in Bartram's paradise. It may prove him the poorer thinker, the lesser scientist, reducing all to the sentiment of the immediate impression; but if the tradition of the Noble Savage has merged with the tradition of the Golden Age and the softer side of quakerish Deism to form an idyll that is largely reflection of his own happy soul, what matter?

What an elysium it is! where the wandering Siminole, the naked red warrior, roams at large, and after vigorous chase retires from the scorching heat of the meridian sun. Here he reclines, and reposes under the odoriferous shades of Zanthoxylon, his verdant couch guarded by the Deity: Liberty, and the Muses, inspiring him with wisdom and valour, whilst the balmy zephyrs fan him to sleep.

It is a boy's daydream, which became the young Coleridge's.

Meanwhile, Canada was producing a type-specimen of a different kind of traveller. Alexander Mackenzie,[1] one of those hard-headed Scottish highlanders who have left such a deep mark on trade and politics in the Dominion, was no solitary or sentimental wanderer, but the determined and efficient leader of a team working with well-established skills to open up trade-routes for the North-Western Company in its bitter and not always scrupulous competition with the Hudson Bay Company. There were others, but Mackenzie had larger ideas than most, and drove himself and his *voyageurs* to the northern shores in 1789 and, in 1793, to the western, where he just missed meeting Vancouver. In preparing for the press his *Voyage from Montreal . . . to the Frozen and Pacific Oceans* (1801) he seems to have thought that an occasional bit of fine writing was expected of a traveller, to judge by a few awkward patches that may well have been furnished by a literary friend; it is not for them that we read his *Voyage*, but for its record of hard going and for its facts. He notes the topography and products of the country, the appearance, dress, dispositions, and languages of the Indian peoples, the quantities and qualities of the furs they produced, and the water-ways and the possible trading-posts by which the new territories might be exploited: all useful information for the Company's board of directors. He looked for landmarks rather

[1] 1755?–1820. Explored north-west Canada 1789; to Pacific coast 1792. Knighted 1802. Member of Canadian provincial parliament.

than landscapes—indeed the severity of his dangerous passages left little leisure for aesthetic disquisition—and leaves the strongest impression of one kind of excellence in that the reader feels that with the *Voyage* in his canoe he might find the way for himself. It is all strange country, but we now know what to expect, and the trails are marked—all the more clearly that the pioneer was a business man.

These are tales of the wilderness. Other travellers had preceded Bruce in Abyssinia—Dr. Johnson disbelieved him on the strength of having translated one—and the country, however strange, had a recognizable political system, a history (one chronicle of which fills a whole volume of the *Travels*) and religions positively oriented on Jerusalem and Mecca. Those members of Lord Macartney's staff who made profit out of the first British Embassy to Pekin in 1792 were in the curious position that few writers on China have been able to change. The best were (Sir) George Staunton[1] and (Sir) John Barrow.[2] In his *Authentic Account of an Embassy to China* (1797) Staunton was more concerned with official movements and delays, and Barrow, in *Travels in China*, which he published in 1804, with scientific observation; they both write like efficient civil servants. They observed shrewdly and accurately, with interest and good sense, not uncritically but unhampered either by romantic presuppositions or by missionary zeal, all they could or were allowed to; and they kept within the bounds of their observations, swayed only by the conflict between the sympathetic interest felt by eighteenth-century thinkers, the irritation of trading concerns whose operations were hindered by Chinese authority, and curiosity about the source of so much attractive bric-à-brac. Barrow learned some Chinese—Staunton's son stayed in the country and produced in 1810 the first translation from Chinese into English—but these valuable memoranda, in the nature of things, can carry little of the imaginative excite-

---

[1] 1737–1801. M.D., Montpellier. Friend of Dr. Johnson and Burke. Practice in West Indies involved him in public affairs. Secretary to Lord Macartney in Madras, where he did useful diplomatic work for East India Company. Baronet 1785; F.R.S. 1787. Secretary to Macartney's embassy to Peking 1792. His son Sir George Thomas Staunton (1781–1859) accompanied him and continued work in China; F.R.S. 1803; M.P. 1818.

[2] 1764–1848. Ironfounder in Liverpool, then in household of Lord Macartney, later as private secretary. With him at Cape of Good Hope 1800–2; second secretary of Admiralty 1804–45. Baronet 1835. Founded the Royal Geographical Society.

ment of Marco Polo or the philosophical stimulus Voltaire caught from Matteo Ricci and the Jesuit Relations. At least they are free from the sentimental exoticism of later generations. Sir Joseph Banks, once more, did well to commission Barrow, then on government service at the Cape, to collect information on South Africa. *Travels to the Interior of South Africa* (1801–4) contains his clear firm statements of observed facts regarding land-surfaces, flora, fauna, and peoples. His very intelligence isolates his matter in a white light, so that though his description of Bushman paintings, for instance, shows real and enlightened interest, we should enjoy some tincture of amateurish enthusiasm. Still, he gave Sir Joseph specific answers to specific questions; the inquirer will find them there, and he will respect their author.

One might expect interest of the same kind from travellers to and within India, and it can be found in plenty. George Forster describes a long hard *Journey from Bengal to England, through the Northern Part of India, Kashmire, Afghanistan, and Persia, and into Russia, by the Caspian Sea* (1798) in letters to a friend, a form which should admit of the personal quality both of the writer and of the recipient whose place the reader to some extent occupies, and which does make for ease and directness in the writing. Unfortunately, he divides the interests so unhappily that he is worth mentioning mainly as exemplifying the travellers' personal and factual values in conflict. He is not readily enthusiastic, but one feels he might have been if he had forgotten his position 'in the Civil Service of the Honourable the East India Company' and said like one habitual reader of travels,

> A traveller I am,
> Whose only tale is of himself.

But just as one is becoming involved he breaks off with an apology and turns into the other kind of traveller, dealing out geographical and historical information. Of this other kind is E. D. Clarke, a Cambridge don whose *Travels* in Russia and the Near East (1810) leave a strong impression of intelligence but little of personality except his extreme dislike of Russians, which may be attributed to his misfortune in seeing Russia under the half-crazy rule of the Tsar Paul I—he has nothing but admiration for the Cossacks and other non-Russian peoples of the south over whom the Russians were extending their empire. If the reader's interests lie in topography, botany, antiquities, climatology, or manners and customs, he can gather miscellaneous facts from Clarke and from Clarke's quotations from the unpublished travel-diaries of Reginald Heber, and be led to other works of that excellent man—though mediocre poet—who became Bishop of Calcutta. But the writers on India were addressing a public whose minds were seldom free. Trade, war, international politics, the home politics entangled in the status of the East India Company and such affairs as the trial of Warren Hastings, all imported associations into men's minds and feelings, so that expectations and prejudices, the side-issues of topicality, prevented the detachment with which the travel-book should, ideally, be read if it is to arouse the creative imagination. There were social satires and comic illustrations to set alongside the aquatints of the brothers Daniel and the other prints so useful to Southey in *Kehama*. Charles Lamb could not have written to anyone in India as he wrote to Manning in China; Wordsworth, Coleridge, Scott, like thousands of their compatriots, had relatives and friends in the services, and the common idea of India must have been formed by gossip, scandal, and table-talk more than by books. Thus Elizabeth Hamilton made her *Letters of a Hindoo Rajah* (1796) out of the table-talk of her brother, an East India Company officer on leave, and Scott incorporated in *The Surgeon's Daughter* (1827) the descriptive notes contributed by his neighbour Colonel Fergusson, who had held a command in Delhi. Oriental scholarship, too, much cultivated among officials, had already caught the attention of the amateur reader along with the many —and often exciting—histories. But Southey's *Curse of Kehama*, the only large-scale treatment of an Indian theme, was a very deliberate move in a poetic campaign. India never caught the imagination of our poets as America did. The springs were contaminated; too much was known, in too many directions, and anything from India approached the nature of tourist literature, the literature that appeals less by the fresh strangeness of its imagery than by its relation to an existing body of thought and knowledge in the book-buying library-using public.

There would be little profit here in examining in detail the piles of *Tours to* and *Letters from* the Lakes, Wales, Scotland, and the Continent, produced too often for the sake of social prestige rather than out of any true excitement of thought or feeling. Curiosity may make a reader look up descriptions of places he knows, but anyone who cares to turn over the various Tours of, for instance, Sir John Carr may console his boredom by absolving himself from reading the many others who remarked on much the same things in much the same way. As Dr. Stoddart said in *Remarks on the Local Scenery and Manners in Scotland* (1801), '*Tours* are the mushroom product of every summer. . . . In fact, tours are read, as much as any other ephemeral product; and some of them live.' The works of travellers like Forster and Clarke are dead because the valuable information has long ago been digested in the relevant geographical and other text-books; most of the Tours are dead because they contained nothing worth keeping alive. Dr. Stoddart's own is remembered only for what he does not record—his recitation of the un-published *Christabel* that acted so rewardingly on Walter Scott. In his *Letters from Spain and Portugal* (1797) Southey destroys the effect of his pleasure in beautiful scenery by dreary complaints of dirt and bad food, and drearier diatribes against monks, shrines, church observances, and Roman Catholicism in general.

The tolerable Tours are those whose authors pursued a definite interest, as Arthur Young did in his agricultural and economic observations, which had a positive bearing on con-temporary politics and now have an equivalent historical value. Of the many Tours satirized by William Combe in *Dr. Syntax in Search of the Picturesque* (1810), those of the master, William Gilpin,[1] become almost endearing by virtue of the reverend gentleman's delighted absorption in the principles he loved and propagated, as the genial reader recreates the mixture of innocence and sophistication, rigid pictorial theory and sheer visual enjoyment. It is easier to return to him than to Payne Knight[2] and Uvedale Price,[3] in whom the theory dominates and who argue indefatigably over definition and interpretation

---

[1] 1724–1804. M.A. Queen's College, Oxford, 1748. Schoolmaster of advanced ideas; vicar of Boldre in the New Forest 1777. Also published biographies and religious works. His brother Sawrey G., R.A., was a noted painter of horses.

[2] 1747–1829. Educated Eton and Christ Church, Oxford. Baronet 1828. Opposed the methods of Humphrey Repton 1794–5, and improved his own estate on his own lines, exercising some influence accordingly.

[3] 1750–1824. In Italy 1777. Collected coins and bronzes, bequeathed to the British Museum, landscape being episodic in his mainly classical interests.

until all aesthetic pleasure is lost in disquisition. In *An Essay on the Picturesque, as compared with the Sublime and the Beautiful* (1794), Uvedale Price set out to add another chapter to Burke's *Philosophical Enquiry into the Origin of our Ideas of the Sublime and Beautiful.*

The principles of these two leading characters in nature, the sublime and the beautiful, have been fully illustrated and discriminated by a great master; but even when I first read that most original work, I felt that there were numberless objects which give great delight to the eye, and yet differ as widely from the beautiful as from the sublime. The reflections I have since been led to make have convinced me that these objects form a distinct class, and belong to what may properly be called the picturesque.

His main distinction was already formulated by Gilpin. 'According to Mr. Burke, one of the most essential qualities of beauty is smoothness', but Gilpin rightly states that 'roughness forms the most essential point of difference between the beautiful and the picturesque'. Gilpin, however, does not discriminate firmly enough, and Price wishes to establish the absolute discreteness of the two concepts. Whatever his intention, he was incapable of philosophical inquiry, and merely pursues his theory through some classes of natural objects. Nor is his basis adequate, for 'the picturesque' remains a critical, not a psychological term. There are experiences in which the mind abdicates, among the Alps, in the Thames valley, in Touraine, or again in Glencoe or Yarrow; in the company of such as Price one must keep it alive, to be permitted to approve of Bettws-y-Coed, and even perhaps to suggest a few improvements in Borrowdale. The picturesque is a matter of interest and enjoyment; while it is— or was—capable of arousing the enthusiasm of amateurs—in both French and English senses of the word—it does not touch the deeper springs of motive or exert any compulsive or controlling power over philosophers or poets or painters. The picturesque enthusiast is indeed on the same level as the tourist. Gilpin, Knight, Price are to Constable, Turner, Towne, on one hand, and Wordsworth and Coleridge on the other, as Carr and Stoddart and the rest are to Bruce and Park, Vancouver and Mackenzie. Yet the efforts of neither the picturesque-hunters nor the general tourists were lost. They taught people to look at things around them—trees and streams, animals and the lie of country, their textures and colours—and also to look at other peoples, their costumes, habits, houses, dances, tempers, and morals. It may have helped to create habits of observation and tolerance; in any case the historian must note the existence of this large body of letterpress and aquatint, and its contribution to the culture—that is, the fused knowledge, imagination, and habit—of the English-speaking people at large.

IV

VIEWS OF MEN, MANNERS, AND SOCIETY

IT is useful to examine the novels of any past time at an early stage in the imaginative effort to comprehend it, because they offer direct access to the intelligent general public in its more relaxed moods—the public that provides the novelists' audience and, for the most part, sets their themes, so that both deliberately and by accident they represent its habits, desires, and norms of judgement. With this public at this time novels held a somewhat equivocal position. Novel-reading could only be condescended to as an indulgence, condemned by many good people as a danger to morals. The great eighteenth-century novelists offended the sense of propriety of the later generation; even Richardson, though certainly on the side of the moral angels, could be embarrassing, and *The Vicar of Wakefield* and *Rasselas* were solitary efforts and limited in scope. The serious literary public had never admitted Fielding's claim that Novel was a Kind bred between Epic and Comedy, nor had it given proper value to Smollett's endless vitality or to the subtlety of Sterne. Meanwhile novels poured from the presses and through the circulating libraries, articles of commerce which anyone with any discrimination could see were negligible not only by the standard of Dr. Johnson but by any standard at all. The curious inquirer who samples the commercial novels may find, at long intervals, an amusing phrase or touch of observation, but he will soon be content to leave them to the economist, the sociologist, and the bibliographer, and accept the few writers who enjoy established reputations by virtue of some individual significance which cannot be diminished by the mob who exploited the vogues they created.

Here, as in politics, Dr. John Moore[1] is a transitional figure. Moore had a double link with Smollett in that he followed him as apprentice to Dr. Gordon in Glasgow and edited his works with a memoir attached, and his unexacting conduct of a novel

[1] See Chap. II, p. 18.

derives from his fellow townsman and fellow practitioner. There is little story and less plot in 'Moore's novels; the intention and the interest are declared in the subtitles: *Zeluco, Various Views of Human Nature taken from Life and Manners, Foreign and Domestic* (1786); *Edward, Various Views of Human Nature taken from Life and Manners, Chiefly in England* (1796); and *Mordaunt, Sketches of Life, Characters, and Manners in Various Countries* (1800). *Zeluco*, the life-story of a Sicilian scoundrel, has its moral—how evil propensities are fostered by early indulgence and bring men and women to wretchedness—but the interest is in the exotic variety of character and incident, and it never descends into mere horror or deliberate indulgence in crime. In *Edward* Moore handicapped himself with a type of male perfection in the leading role, an error he largely overcame in *Mordaunt*, but he surrounded it with such lively pictures of English oddity that it almost escapes the condemnation of Sir Charles Grandison. In *Mordaunt*, at the age of seventy-one, he looked back over his five-year tour on the Continent with the Duke of Hamilton in the 1770's and his stay in Paris in 1792–3 with the Earl of Lauderdale, and worked up, with some contemporary history, sketches of English behaviour abroad, lighter than those in *Zeluco* but such as he could not with propriety have included in his serious *Views of Society and Manners in France, Switzerland, and Germany* (1779) and *in Italy* (1781). The experiences of a French émigrée make a transition, and the rest is placed in England. It is considered the weakest of the three, partly through the eternal difficulty of the epistolary form, but something depends on the reader. If any 'lesson' is to be drawn, he must do it for himself: the morals are sound but not insisted on. He will not be thrilled or dazzled, but will find himself in direct contact with a shrewd, mature, and observant professional man accustomed to good company, from whom he can expect a succession of character-sketches and scraps of conversation both natural and witty. Moore was a man of the pre-revolutionary eighteenth-century world, and he describes that world, and the irruption into it of revolutionary types, with few prejudices and few illusions but with a sustained dry humour and a crisp ironical touch which we meet again only in Jane Austen. He makes his transitions from anecdote to anecdote with social adroitness; and he has one unusual gift: he can describe good people without making them either tiresome or insipid—the kind

Mrs. Barnet in *Edward*, for instance, and that agreeable young man Travers in *Mordaunt*—and actions of charity without mawkishness. Miss Edgeworth represents the same eighteenth-century pattern of behaviour. She had more to say, but Dr. Moore had no designs for our improvement, and had a masculine frankness she could not assume and which no later novelist could quite recover.

It may be fortuitous that the significant novelists are, from the death of Smollett to the rise of Scott, women. It may be that men were too much concerned with the urgent public causes of the time. 'Committed' artists are committed to contemporary causes whose interest evaporates, and all the more quickly if these causes are successful. If such artists survive at all, it is by virtue of qualities to which the causes are irrelevant even if, as with Godwin, their commitment generates an urgency which communicates itself to the reader. In *Caleb Williams* Godwin's[1] philosophy generated such urgency of excited thought as to create theme and story together in a unity of interest and produce an original work. Once he had lost faith in his own doctrine he found no substitute, and attempted themes which other novelists were making fashionable: in *St. Leon* (1799), Gothic marvels; in *Fleetwood* (1805), modern society; in *Mandeville* (1817), a vague historical setting. But though he had realized that his negation of humane emotion invalidated *Political Justice*, he had not lost his logical habit nor transformed his cold intellectual temperament. These denied him the necessary modicum of sensibility to the feelings and relations of real men and women, or to the aesthetic values of the outside world, the sensations of travel, or even horror, out of which the novels he followed were created. Nor could he recommend the forced efforts of a crude and violent invention by skill and tact in the writing. On the other hand, Robert Bage,[2] a survivor from the older generation, is disappointing because his native liveliness has to compete with his intention to promulgate the political and moral liberalism in which he believed. Certain characters recur in his novels—an emancipated young woman for whose counterpart, except for a coarser version by Richard Cumberland, we have to go back to Aphra Behn; a liberal young hero

[1] See Chap. II, p. 24.
[2] 1728–1801. Born in Derbyshire, son of a paper-maker, whom he succeeded. A Quaker, and friend of the Revolution, he began writing at 53.

who is more convincing in *L'Ingénu* of Voltaire, especially as
Bage is so hampered by tradition that he can symbolize his
hero's triumph, in *Hermsprong*, only by discovering him to be
the lost heir to a baronetcy. Thomas Holcroft,[1] though unlike
Bage a professional writer, appears to better advantage in
drama, where the demands of stage and actors can rectify
intellectual overweighting, than in his slow and heavy novels,
where it is uncompensated by the reader's divination of any
engaging qualities in the writer such as almost save the novels
of Bage. Serious purpose there must be, but permanence is
granted only to such purpose as arises from the permanent
interests: deep concern with human behaviour or the exercise
of the free imagination—morality or romance.

This appropriate moral seriousness remained with the women.
Leaving aside, with relief, the many flat moral fables whose
literary values are as scant as those of the commercial romance,
we find it in the two novels of Mrs. Elizabeth Inchbald,
A Simple Story (1791), and *Nature and Art* (1796). Mrs. Inchbald,[2]
the wife of an actor, was herself a practising actress and dramatist. When at the age of thirty-eight, after twenty years' mixed
experience of the workaday world, she turned her hand to the
lucrative form of the novel, her imagination still worked in
terms of the theatre. The original theme of *A Simple Story*, the
relations between Miss Milner and Dorriforth, a high-spirited
worldly young woman and a strong-willed priest, is soon
dropped, perhaps as too difficult to sustain, perhaps as too
delicate for a Roman Catholic writer, probably because a novel
ought to end in a marriage and Dorriforth so occupied the
author's imagination that it could not create another dominant
male. On inheriting a peerage, the priest is absolved of his
vows, and takes over the part of leading man, leaving that of
the religious director to another priest, Father Sandford. The
theme then becomes the love-conflict of Miss Milner and Lord
Elmwood, as Dorriforth now is, and the proper submission of

[1] 1745–1809. Born in London, son of a shoemaker. Pedlar, stableboy at New-
market, schoolmaster, and, from 1770, actor. His first play, *Duplicity*, 1781.
Journalist at Rome and in France (1783) and Germany. Indicted for treason but
acquitted 1794. Besides plays, novels, and verses, produced translations from
French and German. Friend of Godwin and Lamb.

[2] 1753–1821. *Née* Simpson; born near Bury St. Edmunds. Left home at 18, and
married an actor 1772, who died 1779. Actress till about 1790; thereafter lived in
London by writing. A pretty, respectable woman, and a devout Catholic.

a wife to the better principles of a husband. But *A Simple Story* is really two stories. A violently compressed interlude informs the reader that Lady Elmwood's imperfect nature led her into unfaithfulness and remorseful death, a tragic motive which merely links the comedy of character to the romantic comedy of the second part, in which Lord Elmwood, having rejected his daughter Matilda in resentment at her mother's conduct, is reconciled by her sweet and simple nature. The only other characters are a devoted *confidante*, a minor libertine, and a noble young lover for the Lady Matilda. In *Nature and Art* she exploits the old device of contrast, useful in drama but, as even Jane Austen found, too rigid for the slower processes of novel. The graphs of action are obvious: generous honesty moving through poverty to happiness, and self-seeking unscrupulousness through worldly success to spiritual misery. In both novels the actions are insulated in a *lieu théatral*; time is, in essence, the arbitrary time of drama, and narrative sequence, the logic of the story-teller, is reduced to such statements of circumstance as a dramatist is forced to make in order to explain how the characters come to be in the situations presented, or is a substitute for the expression, gesture, and intonations of the stage. The confusion of the two arts affects the style accordingly: it varies from breathless exposition to forcible speech, with much of stage direction alternating—an irritating trick—between the past tense of narrative and the present tense of the theatre.

The first impression, then, is of Mrs. Inchbald's incompetence. Hints of genuine religious themes, such as no contemporary contains, fade into the common social themes of self-control, worldly vanity, romantic simplicity, and the importance of moral training. What might be accepted or condoned by the insulated audience in the theatre, concentrated in the intense awareness of watching an action, does not survive in the relaxed mood of a reader and the less direct transference from the printed page. If, however, the reader turns, for instance, to Holcroft, or the later novels of Godwin, his respect for her and his opinion of her contribution to a still imperfect art rise as he labours through their endless statements of fact and descriptions —not revelations—of character. She leaves, somehow, the impression of an honest and truly respectable if humourless woman where they remain merely industrious professional writers; and she convinces the reader of the intensity, even the passionate reality, of her characters' emotions however transitory and uncertain they may be. Something of dramatic method was needed to turn historical disquisition and the débris of poetry into novel: Mrs. Inchbald gave the example. Two quotations may make the contrast clearer, especially as the second is a quotation from a letter:

When she arrived at the door of the study, she opened it with a trepidation she could hardly account for, and entered to Dorriforth the altered woman she has been represented. His heart had taken the most decided part against her, and his face had assumed the most severe aspect of reproach; but her appearance gave an instantaneous change to his whole mind, and countenance.

She halted, as if she feared to approach—he hesitated, as if he knew not how to speak. Instead of the anger with which he was prepared to begin, his voice involuntarily softened, and without knowing what he said, he began,

'My dear Miss Milner.'—

She expected he was angry, and in her confusion his gentleness was lost upon her. She imagined that what he said might be censure, and she continued to tremble, though he repeatedly assured her, that he meant only to advise, not upbraid her.

'For as to all those little disputes between Mr. Sandford and you,' said he, 'I should be partial if I blamed you more than him—indeed, when you take the liberty to condemn him, his character makes the freedom appear in a more serious light than when he complains of you—and yet, if he provokes your retorts, he alone must answer for them; nor will I undertake to decide betwixt you. But I have a question to ask you, and to which I require a serious and unequivocal answer. Do you expect Lord Frederick in the country?'

Without hesitation she replied, 'I do.'

'One more question I have to ask, madam, and to which I expect a reply equally unreserved. Is Lord Frederick the man you approve for your husband?'

Upon this close interrogation she discovered an embarrassment, beyond any she had ever yet betrayed, and faintly replied,

'No, he is not.'

'Your words tell me one thing,' answered Dorriforth, 'but your looks declare another—which am I to believe?'

'Which you please,' was her answer, while she discovered an insulted dignity, that astonished, without convincing him.

'But then why encourage him to follow you hither, Miss Milner?'

'Why commit a thousand follies (she replied in tears) every hour of my life?'   (*A Simple Story*, ch. xi.)

. . .; Frank came after me, and with some reluctance, foreboding a repulse, asked whether he should have the pleasure to dance with me. His manner and the foregone circumstances made me guess his question before he spoke. My answer was—'I have just made a promise to myself that I will dance with Mr. Clifton.' It was true: the thought had passed through my mind.

Mr. Clifton, madam!

Yes—

You—you—

I have not seen Mr. Clifton? Right— But I said I had made the promise to *myself*.

Poor Frank cóuld contain no longer! I see, madam, said he, I am despised; and I deserve contempt; I crouch to it, I invite it, and have obtained a full portion of it—Yet why?—What have I done? —Why is this sudden change?—The false glitter that deceives mankind then is irresistible!—But surely, madam, justice is as much my due as if my name were Clifton. Spurn me, trample on me, when I sully myself by vice and infamy! But till then I should once have hoped to have escaped being humbled in the dust, by one whom I regarded as the most benignant, as well as the most deserving and equitable of earthly creatures!

This is indeed a heavy charge: and I am afraid much of it is too true. Here is company coming. I am sorry I cannot answer it immediately.

I can suffer any thing rather than exist under my present tortures.

(Holcroft, *Anna St. Ives*, vol. iii, letter xli.)

Mrs. Inchbald sees and hears; Holcroft merely writes.

If Mrs. Inchbald's novels derive from the theatre and fail by incomplete transformation into the narrative medium, Miss Hannah More's[1] one effort, *Coelebs in Search of a Wife*, derives from the periodical essay, and would also be held to fail in the same way if it were a novel at all. The full title declares its nature: *Coelebs in Search of a Wife, comprehending Observations on Domestic Habits and Manners, Religion and Morals*. In earlier days when her cheerful youth brightened Dr. Johnson and his circle, she had written plays of no quality; in 1809, when *Coelebs* was published, she was sixty-four, the authoress of *Thoughts on the Importance of the Manners of the Great, An Estimate of the Religion of the Fashionable World*, the political tracts alluded to earlier, and *On the Modern System of Female Education*, and had now retired

---

[1] 1745–1833. Born in Gloucestershire, daughter of a schoolmaster. Lived in Bristol and London; settled with her sisters near Cheddar, occupied with education and good works.

to a west-country parish. The general theme, then, was that of the essayists from Addison to Dr. Johnson. The audience she addressed was theirs, and so was the method, introducing and discussing the particular themes by character-sketches, anecdotes, and conversations among a group of representative figures, and adding some attractiveness, for the young ladies to whom most of it was addressed, by a slight tale of love and marriage diversified only by a faint ruffle of jealousy. The aim is the maintenance of order in society, in religion, in individual moral and emotional life. There is something of Rousseau in the advocacy of household education and rural retirement; the suggestion of anything of Rousseau beyond those prevalent notions would horrify. Miss More believes in culture: that is, in literature, including such poetry as makes for edification but not novels, especially those French and German ones which make for indiscipline in feeling and behaviour; drawing as a pastime for children and an elegant amusement for their elders; the simplest of music, of which, though a friend of the Burneys, she is deeply suspicious as an emotional extravagance and a pretext for vain display. These, with strict non-evangelical religion, good works dictated by the heart and performed in person (but not the direction of organized charities which employs only the head and engenders self-importance), gardening, and good manners, make up the formula of the good life. With individual modifications, it is that of all the women novelists. It is conveyed in *Coelebs* in lucid good-humoured eighteenth-century prose, with some lively observation, an interest in human motives, some humour, much shrewdness, considerable wisdom, and solid determination. Miss More's is a slight addition to the tradition of the novel, but it counterpoises that of Mrs. Inchbald. It all remains within the sphere of society; and the method proved its intrinsic value in the hands of Thomas Love Peacock.

Mrs. Charlotte Smith[1] wrote unhampered by any notions derived from drama or moral essay, or, for that matter, any theories about the nature and conduct of narrative. Having married, and parted from, the wastrel son of a rich merchant who left his fortune so strictly tied up that it could not be touched, she had one purpose in attacking 'so trifling a Compo-

[1] 1749–1806. *Née* Turner; born in London. Married 1765. Her improvident husband imprisoned for debt 1782. Lived a hard life in France and England.

sition as a novel'—to earn money to keep herself and her eight children. She therefore wasted little time on subtleties of construction, character, or motive, but having an idea for a story, began, and went on as things came into her head to add to it, her strong sense of grievance dictating her theme—the tribulations of virtue surrounded by persecutions and treacheries. There are few criticisms from which she could be absolved. Her narratives proceed without balance, proportion, or economy, perfunctory at real turns of action and at other times unnecessarily particular in details, full of elaborate but obviously contrived coincidences, and sometimes impeded by interpolated histories which at best merely add to the general gloom and at worst are merely intrusive. Conversation varies from literary-stilted to colloquial and even dialectal. Character, where it exists, is black or white; and goodness is strictly rationed to one shiningly virtuous character in a family, the rest being villainous or foolish or dissipated. Rich merchants are vulgar and heartless and lawyers rascally as one might expect from her own history—except that one fortuitously honest one is needed to assist the happy ending that saves herself from despair and leaves the gentle reader pleased. This is the third-rate novel of any age. But that does not dispose of it. Mrs. Smith was an intelligent woman with a reputation, by no means undeserved, for her poetry; she was close on forty when she began, had been married for some twenty-five unhappy years, and had seen much of the world, not always in its more pleasant aspects. Though the suggestion would have horrified her, she, alone among these women novelists, reminds one of Smollett—many characters pursuing their own interests, an endless flow of incidents, much movement, and few illusions about human nature.

Like anyone who writes for money, she had to catch the interests of the middle-class public, and this she could do because she belonged to it and had no mission either moral or artistic. In her third novel *Celestina* (1791) the plot turns on the mystery of the heroine's parentage; it is solved in the last chapters after a picturesque excursion to the Pyrénées. The vogue of tourist literature is exploited in her other novels by whisking away various characters to Skye, the Scottish Highlands, and various parts of England. So also, in *The Old Manor House*, an episode in Canada admits a somewhat random description of arboreal vegetation on the banks of the St. Lawrence. *Desmond* (1791) gave a favourable view of the French Revolution, but events and change of opinion turned against its popularity, and *The Banished Man* (1794) reports fairly directly the experiences of French *émigrés* of 1793 in France, Germany, and England, as recounted by one to whom Mrs. Smith had given hospitality; it is a competent sympathetic study of types and emotions among 'displaced persons', and strongly anti-revolutionary. In *The Old Manor House* (1793) the date is prudently set back in the 1770's. Mrs. Smith's favourite patterns of an inheritance withheld from the immaculate hero and the persecution of the immaculate heroine are ingeniously combined but less ingeniously worked out. To separate Orlando and his Monimia still further, he is made to serve in the American War of Independence against 'the American soldiers, fighting in defence of their liberties (of all those *rights* which his campaign as a British officer had not made him forget were the most sacred to an *Englishman*)'; his doubts of the justice of his cause preserve the sympathy of the liberal public and make his presumed death the more affecting. *The Young Philosopher* (1798) exploits the image, common to Whig enthusiasts and contributory to the disillusion of critical travellers and emigrants for two or three generations to come, of America as the land innocent of the oppression, dishonesty, class distinction, and all other social and political evils of Europe. All this made for variety as well as number of characters, from bad baronets and presuming tradesmen to boorish yokels (and one good-hearted smuggler), dishonest servants, ferocious but (to the hero) well-disposed American Indians, raffish officers, dissolute Oxonians, bloodthirsty Jacobins, and one honest British naval officer, with all their female consorts and counterparts. It is a busy world, much of it probably recognizable to contemporaries, like the General Tracy in *The Old Manor House* who might be a caricature of Tarleton or Burgoyne; no one could miss the lampoon on Burke in *The Banished Man*, or the personal spite in the irrelevant introduction of Orlando to a 'modern Centlivre', author of 'dramas (the productions of writers of the sixteenth and seventeenth centuries modernised)' in whose air there was 'a conviction of self-consequence, which predominated over the tender languor she affected—indeed it was towards the gentlemen only that this soft sensibility was apparently exhibited':

apparently Mrs. Inchbald had not exhibited it to Mrs. Charlotte Smith. None of it is 'important', but it gives the historian
a fair idea of what average liberal middle-class people talked
about in the leisure moments of the 1790's. By virtue of its very
lack of deliberation it has a life of its own, which is missing
from Mrs. Opie[1] (*Father and Daughter*, 1801; *Adeline Mowbray*,
1804) who interlards morality with pathos—Sydney Smith told
her, rightly, 'Tenderness is your forte, and carelessness your
fault'—Elizabeth Hamilton,[2] who combines religion, sentiment,
and criticism of housing and husbandry in the Highlands in
The Cottagers of Glenburnie (1808), and Mrs. Mary Brunton[3]
(*Self Control*, 1811; *Discipline*, 1814) who combines morality and
satire, redeeming herself occasionally by scraps of realistic conversation and some clear aquatint pictures of contemporary
Scotland. To combine moral lessons with good novel-writing
was left for Maria Edgeworth[4] to accomplish.

It was reported that Madame de Staël said, 'que Miss Edgeworth était digne d'enthousiasme, mais qu'elle s'est perdue
dans la triste utilité'. Her daughter, Madame de Broglie, denied
the report, but most readers will agree, and regret the truth of
it. All her work was intended to inculcate the admirable ideas
in which her father trained her—morality, integrity, good sense
and good feeling, education, and the creation of living conditions conducive to their development—but she had many other
virtues, and they were so often restrained and even distorted by
her serious purposes as to cast doubt on her critical sense.
Certainly she never regarded the writing of novels as an art
worthy of pursuit for its own sake; and indeed she was no great
contriver of stories, but was content with a few commonplaces
—the lost heir with its variant the lost or rejected daughter—
the Lady Matilda motive—and its further variant the doubt-

[1] 1769–1853. Born in Norwich, daughter of Dr. Alderson, a prominent local
liberal. Married John Opie, R.A., 1798. Became a Quaker, and did much phil-
anthropic work.
[2] 1758–1816. Born in Belfast; brought up by a farmer uncle in Stirlingshire. In
England 1788–1804, then Edinburgh. Died in Harrogate. Unmarried, but in later
life commonly called 'Mrs H.' of her own choice.
[3] 1778–1818. Born in Orkney, daughter of Col. Balfour of Burray. Lived from
1803 in Edinburgh, where she married the Professor of Oriental Languages.
[4] 1767–1849. Born in Oxfordshire. Companion, housekeeper, and general
manager of her father Richard, M.P., in France, England, and at home in Edgeworthstown, Co. Longford in Ireland, and governess of his children by successive
wives, but was able to see much of intelligent society, scientific and literary.

fully legitimate young man or woman—the Evelina motive—adventitious reversals of fortune, and the inevitable mating of eligible young ladies and gentlemen. There is no passion in her love-affairs: though the assessment of eligibility supplies what little plot there is, marriage is a formula of narrative. Thus *Harrington*, an apology prompted by an American Jewess for the ugly figures cut by Jews—especially in *The Absentee*—begins well with a piece of child psychology, but ends with the hero's marriage to the daughter of the chief among her admirable Jews, a consummation made possible by the discovery that her Christian mother had brought her up a good Protestant. In *Ivanhoe*, a couple of years later, Scott displayed better manners as well as better art. Even where we suspect personal feeling, as in the figure of Count Altenberg (in *Patronage*) who may be reminiscent of her lover the Swedish Chevalier Edelcrantz whom she met and dismissed in Paris in 1802, the emotional temperature is low. But she cared little for the train of a story. We are invited to look at this person or incident or description, then at that, with little more than temporal connexion; purpose and story do not combine into plot. At worst, as in *Almeria* or *The Dun* in *Tales of Fashionable Life*, we have an overdone specimen of the essay in story form that was passable in the *Spectator* or *Rambler* because it was short; *Manœuvring* and still more *Ennui* in the same series are almost saved by social observation, even as *The Parent's Assistant* indeed proves her love of children as well as her notions of education; but at best the reader is continually conscious of the intrusion of the theme, checking the story as an outcrop of rock in a field checks the plough. Yet we understand why Walter Scott, the best of critics, said that 'her true and vivid pictures of modern life contain the only sketches reminding us of human beings whom, secluded as we are, we have actually seen and conversed with in various parts of this great metropolis'. The vivid truth may appear only in occasional anecdote and character-sketch, but it is never entirely absent.

Miss Edgeworth had unusual opportunities. Her father's daughter was free of society in England, France, and Ireland. The range of society, however, differed in each country. In France her father's circle was liberal and enlightened, but not revolutionary nor Bonapartist, the society of the later and less worldly salons, deep in *belles-lettres*, science, and good works.

The young woman saw the best of polite behaviour, heard correct cultivated conversation, and read the books the good ladies approved. Here she met the works of Marmontel from which, as has often been observed, she learned to frame her *contes moraux* and to break up a lucid flat narrative style with a realistic dialogue. She was a greater writer with a wider range and more acute observation, and no one was needed to teach her the dry touches which must have caught the fancy of Jane Austen, as when the heroine of *Patronage* entered a fashionable assembly 'without any prepared grace or practised smile, but merely as if she was coming into a room'. Yet in *Belinda* she pointedly alludes to Marmontel's story *La Femme comme il n'y en a peu*, and the main plot of *Belinda* is an elaborate variation on that *conte moral*. Fortunately, temperament and other influences saved her from the formalized emotionalism of her model, and the diluted Rousseauism of educational theory and the cult of simplicity could reach her from many other sources. English society, though wider, was similarly limited by her father's interests to scientists like Dr. Darwin and the members of the Lunar Society, educational theorists who argued about Rousseau and Dr. Bell and Dr. Lancaster, progressive agriculturists, scholars, and literary figures, no sportsmen and few artists. Her cultivated gentlemen, equally versed in literature and science, possess—it is the mark of this amateur culture—astonishing quantities of miscellaneous information; her young ladies, besides a sufficiency of French and English *belles-lettres*, are accomplished musicians and painters, but her only sketch of a professional painter (in *Patronage*, chapter xv), though recognizably of the time, is heavily satirical, and though she is highly conscious of furniture and decoration, and even of dress, her only interest in landscape is to discriminate the well-cultivated from the neglected. Here too the literary influences correspond. Except for *Sir Charles Grandison*, the great novels of the earlier generation presented an England she scarcely knew and from most of which she was carefully protected. The essayists, Dr. Johnson, the Whig intelligentsia, the bluestockings, and—most importantly—Miss Burney, gave her her standards and procedures, and especially the formal styles of conversation and letter-writing that contrast so oddly with the familiar and realistic that—since they appear in all novels down to the 1840's—they must have authenticity of some kind, if only as symbolic of the social and moral quality of those characters who use them.

It is not true that, as is often said, only her Irish characters are interesting and successful; even allowing for these limitations she added something new to Society's awareness of itself: but Ireland held two advantages over France and England. In the first place, her knowledge of Irish society was more complete and natural, that of a neighbourhood with all its claims and chances, not that of a selective cultural group. So she could accept and depict an equivocal figure like Sir Terence O'Fay in *The Absentee* and an earthy one like King Corny in *Ormond*. Where their English counterparts would have been a low intriguer and a boorish squire, they are persons, as is Count O'Halloran (in *The Absentee*), who in an English avatar would be an admirable but rather grotesque specimen of Anglo-French culture. She heard something of the facts of English political life, but met political figures only in agreeable drawing-rooms; she was nearer to the truth of Dublin: hence the difference, in scale and in destiny, between the Lord Oldborough of *Patronage* and the Sir Ulick O'Shane of *Ormond*. Her Irish society added even fresher pictures than her English—her French ones are merely those of a polite visitor—to the literary record; and, most notably, her pictures of the lower-class Irish opened a new volume, the importance of which may be measured not only in later Irish writing but, as Scott testified, abroad. She knew them as she did not know the lower-class English, and still less the French, and they gave her—as did some of her upper-class acquaintance but less emphatically—the other advantage of a rich, highly coloured and copious speech unhampered by literary precedent. Personal relations with these people, closer than mere observation, gave her an effective command of this fresh speech; she wisely did not attempt that of her few English country-folk, for it was not a question of anecdotal verisimilitude but something better and more creditable to her, an artist's appreciation of language and style. The *Essay on Irish Bulls* proves that she and her father studied and discussed it; her lively use of it in the novels, compared with the dullness of the *Essay*, proves her sense of its quality as well as her acute ear.

The trick of italicizing words and pronunciations that an Englishman would find comic or anomalous betrays, however, her consciousness of the strangeness of Ireland. Scott felt no need of such condescending tricks; his people spoke in their own way and required no apology. The social traditions of Scotland, as well as his own nature, made it easy for him to be on personal terms with all classes as an Edgeworth could not be. Her peasants have not the individuality and dignity of Scott's; they are the tenantry and servants, living in a fixed relation to the great house—an alien people, indeed, for the time had not come for such as she to be aware of Gaelic history or culture. They were all Irish together, of course, and none of her Irish characters of whatever degree could dwindle into such puppets as some of her English, but all her love of home and all her appreciation of Irish generosity, impulsiveness, and warmth of personal attachment could not change the attitudes and standards, inherited and acquired, proper to her status, education, and experience. She had comparative standards always in her mind, and saw critically as well as sympathetically. The lower Irish required the protection of their superiors against their native improvidence and sluttishness, and even from the futile or dangerous roguery into which their native cunning could degenerate. *Ormond* in particular exposed their weaknesses. Severer criticism was reserved for their betters who failed in their duty and those middlemen who turned the failure to their own advantage. There is nothing edifying in the Memoirs of the Rackrent family. It succeeds by the device of the single narrator, which focuses and unifies the annals of 'the drunken Sir Patrick, the litigious Sir Murtagh, the fighting Sir Kit, and the slovenly Sir Condy' by force of form and style, precludes the intrusion of any pseudo-romantic mechanism such as spoils *The Absentee*, and makes the criticism the more powerful by its transmutation into the enveloping emotion of the faithful retainer. Her main targets are irresponsibility and extravagance, not only in her Irish tales. The practical woman who had to take charge first of her father's and then of her brother's accounts was acutely aware of the economic side of life and included it among her themes as few novelists have done. The possession of a certain income is necessary to Jane Austen's characters, to keep them within the range to which, for her own artistic ends, she chose to restrict herself; the handling of money is another matter. Honourable and dishonourable ways of getting money give the scheme of *Patronage*; the wise and reckless spending of it makes those of *Ormond* and *Castle Rackrent*, sets in motion the plot of *The Absentee*, and is the starting-point of *Belinda*, her best novel of English society.

In this novel she included several themes: the reclamation and reunion of a frivolous wife and a dissolute husband who are not so heartless as they seem, through the efforts of Belinda; the re-establishment of their neglected daughter who remains unspoiled through the influence of a united family whose home education she shares; Belinda's two attractive suitors, one rejected because of his addiction to gambling, the other's acceptance delayed by imputations of an immoral connexion which turns out to his credit and meanwhile exhibits a curious romantic commonplace—an allusion to Bernardin de St. Pierre as the first theme is to Marmontel, and the discovery of yet another lost child: these, with the various antitypes to Belinda's virtues of sincerity, disinterestedness, judgement, and good taste, and her lover's accomplishments, delicacy, and so on, make up a more complex tale than the original moral purpose promises. Here, and again in *Patronage*, the combination of several themes, their comparative congruity as compared with those of *The Absentee*, and the maintenance of the balance of interest between them, are notable successes, and with little precedent, for Miss Burney, and even Richardson, could handle only one at a time. In *Evelina*, again, the social theme is the contrast of politeness and vulgarity, but Miss Edgeworth moved familiarly enough in polite society to find deeper moral contrasts between figures who are by no means devoid of politeness and cultivation. This complexity of interest makes *Belinda*—though not Caroline in *Patronage*—a more agreeable young woman than the recital of her virtues might suggest; and, along with some ingenious turns of plotting and many well-observed additions of personality to both major and minor characters, it advances the reality, the complexity, and density, as well as the craftsmanship of the novel. Miss Burney invented the social novel; Miss Edgeworth made it. In most respects she has been outdone by later novelists, but she stands with Smollett as one who set generations of them on their way.

Younger Irish novelists, however, did not follow up Miss Edgeworth's lessons in responsibility and rural economics. Sydney Owenson[1]—better known by her married name of

---

[1] 1776?–1859. Born in Dublin, daughter of Robert Owenson, an actor. Married Sir Thomas Morgan, a surgeon, 1812.

Lady Morgan—began her literary career in 1803 with *St. Clair*, followed in 1805 by *The Novice of St. Dominick*, the main purpose of which seems to be the filling of four duodecimo volumes for the common market. In the following year she made her reputation with *The Wild Irish Girl*, the exotic charms of which, now that the most serious of Irish rebellions was safely over, the English were prepared to welcome. It may best be compared with *The Absentee*, which, coming two years after, might be read as a criticism of it, for both turn on the same situation, the un-announced visit of a young heir to the family estates which he has never seen. Miss Edgeworth's novel is much better written and arranged, but it does not annul the very divergent values of Miss Owenson's. As her title suggests, she abandons the sobriety of the elder generation in favour of the uncontrolled exuberance of native—and of course generous—temperament. In the second place, she draws upon the rising enthusiasm for Irish history, antiquities, and literature, which was to reach its strength later but had already begun, in Ireland as earlier in Scotland, to provide an outlet for offended nationality. Joseph Walker's[1] *Historical Memoirs of Irish Bards* (1786) treated of matters somewhat recondite technically and linguistically, but his *Historical Essay on the Dress of the Ancient and Modern Irish* (1788) nourished the visual imagination and, in particular, provided picturesque details for such a figure as the Prince of Inismore, a survival who represents the Golden Age when, in Landor's mocking epigram,

> Tara rose so high
> That her turrets split the sky,
> And about her courts were seen
> Liveried Angels robed in green,
> Wearing, by St. Patrick's bounty,
> Emeralds big as half a county.

Miss Owenson belonged to an early stage; she blames Macpherson for thinking Ossian a Scottish Gael, but praises his spirit and intention. Later generations elaborated an idealized past till it became a matter of faith; it was alien to Miss Edgeworth, for the Enlightenment looked forward, and was apt to regard history, in the words of its last poet Shelley, as 'that record of crimes and abuses'. Lady Morgan's later novels, *O'Donnell*

---

[1] 1761–1810. Born and educated in Dublin. An original member of the Royal Irish Academy, and a notable student of Italian literature.

(1814) and *Florence Macarthy* (1818), considerably higher in literary quality, would face the same barrier. Her most useful innovation, though English novel-readers might not see the force of it, was her acceptance of native habits and feelings of which Miss Edgeworth might be cognizant but into which she could not enter. The comparable figures are the chaise-drivers who act as guides to the two young men. Both are full of cheerful good will, but Miss Owenson's Murtach is also a notable singer, dancer, and story-teller, accomplished in arts which, though relegated to a peasantry, form none the less an authentic and living culture. Miss Edgeworth's theme was the discovery by a young landlord of his responsibility to the land and the tenantry; Miss Owenson's was the discovery of a mode of life which a European like Miss Edgeworth could, at best, only patronize as amiable eccentricity. Both themes were useful and honourable.

C. R. Maturin,[1] who was never quite original, took something from both. *The Wild Irish Boy* (1808), less derivative than its title suggests, mingles romantic love and criticism of society. His old Chieftain de Lacy, though less out of this world, owes much—even a scarlet cloak—to the Prince of Inismore, and his household 'was a castle rackrent, a house of disorder and riot'. Disorder and riot are indeed his theme. He looked back in *The Milesian Chief*, but the historical type he dwells upon is the embodiment of disorder, the rapparee, the outlaw, rebel, and lawbreaker, and the figures he draws at full length are old women whose wild aspect symbolizes their ferocity and venom. He darkens Miss Edgeworth's pictures of shiftless neglect into scenes of desolation and savagery, not for the sake of reformation or moralizing, but for their own sakes, to indulge his own delight in gloom and destruction. The two women each have something positive and pass it on to later writers; he is negative and can be better placed with the school from which also he derived and with which his reputation faded, that of Matthew Lewis and the 'horrific' romance.

We may believe that Mrs. Radcliffe had no more idea than her most simple-minded reader of what was behind the black veil until the moment came when it had to be raised in order to let the story end; but something had to be there, and

---

[1] 1782–1824. Born in Dublin; educated at Trinity College; B.A. 1800. Clergyman and schoolmaster with no great success.

unfortunately a real physical horror—since supernatural objects were not in her *métier*—might cause only disgust; a poor ending, incongruous with the spirit of her tale and unpleasing to her own aesthetic sensibility. We may believe also that as young Matthew Lewis[1] was writing *The Monk* (1796), the 'horror' novel *par excellence*, he had no clear idea of how it was to build up, but proceeded by a series of improvisations, on the single principle that one shock must be succeeded by another, and perforce a heavier. In his melodrama *The Castle Spectre*, even if the 'comic relief' is none too diverting, an audience would have at least the movements of the actors to watch; a reader of *The Monk* is allowed neither relief nor relaxation. It begins with bright social satire—a fashionable congregation listening to a popular preacher, halfway between Hogarth and Rowlandson, and a pair of libertines out of Restoration comedy—but Lewis is soon led off into a long interpolation into which he tips a collection of traditional horrors—brigands, jealousy, necromancy and exorcism, the Bleeding Nun, the Wandering Jew— a morass from which he never contrives to extricate himself. The popular preacher is Ambrosio the wicked Monk, and what might have been satire becomes mere vulgar ultra-protestant anticlericalism; thence to sorcery, raising a devil, and a gathering of ghosts. The scene of vol. iii is a convent, developed in the heaviest-handed Germanic style from Diderot's *La Religieuse*; after a murder or so, the action descends, via a mechanical statue, to the vaults wherein a wretched prisoner is raped in a sepulchre and murdered. The Monk being himself incarcerated at last, the devil is raised once more, buys another soul, carries the Monk out of prison by the hair and drops him from a tremendous height upon an inaccessible mountain where— rather tamely, in the absence of flames and sulphur—he dies of injuries and exposure. A reader who had to wait his turn to get all this from the circulating library a volume at a time might persevere to the end; but what made it notorious was the widespread denunciation of the strong sexual vein running

---

[1] 1775–1818. Born in London, son of a deputy secretary in the War Office. Educated at Westminster and Christ Church, Oxford. In Weimar 1792–3; attaché, British Embassy, The Hague, where he wrote *The Monk*. M.P. 1796–1802. Inherited family property in West Indies, which he visited 1815–16 and 1817; died of yellow fever on the voyage home. A kindly little man, interested in slaves, whose conditions he tried to improve, he mixed in high society and among men of letters, including Scott, Byron, and Shelley.

through it. The vogue of *The Monk*, if not its notoriety, was short-lived; even after expurgation it was not kept in print beyond 1800, and Lewis's versions of two German romancès, and his dozen tragedies, were readily forgotten. Only his verses lasted a little longer, by association with the early efforts of Scott in which connexion they may be noticed later.

He had really exhausted his repertory of horrors in *The Monk*, and his readers also. It is noticeable mainly as the most extreme example of horror-romance, and that largely by Lewis's knack of handling English prose. It seems odd to find him writing a good-humoured comedy, *The East Indian*, and the humane *Journal of a West Indian Proprietor*; they seem more natural to the little man whose cheerful company Scott and Byron enjoyed, but they only emphasize the unreality of the whole business. It was a personal freak, a game of little imaginative importance even for its author. Mrs. Radcliffe invites her readers to participate in the apprehensions of her characters; Lewis invites his to be horrified at the actions and experiences of his. C. R. Maturin invites his to share the temperamental melancholy in which he envelops characters, actions, and scenes. He cannot be taxed with the sexual inclination of Lewis; but the omission of Luxuria—conspicuously in *Women, or, le Pour et le Contre*—somehow makes the operation of the other six Deadly Sins more arbitrary. He damns them as becomes a clergyman, but his destructive temper makes that damnation his end, with no hint of triumph, and only faint suggestion of the survival, of the Virtues. *Fatal Revenge*, a wordy tale of 'ambitious wickedness' and 'vengeance as atrocious as the crime that provoked it', shows how 'they who desired the knowledge of things concealed from man, found their pursuit accompanied by guilt, and terminated by misery and punishment'. In *Melmoth the Wanderer* the eponymous hero-villain attests, in italics, '*I have traversed the world in the search, and no one, to gain that world, would lose his own soul!*' but that is in the huddled conclusion of four long volumes of studies in hopelessness and despair. *Melmoth*, however, is his best. The connecting theme, an ingenious variant of the Wandering Jew, opening and closing in contemporary Ireland, is worked out in five episodes, two of them in seventeenth-century England, three in eighteenth-century Spain with excursions to Germany and a highly coloured Southeyan India; but this effort at variety fails to relieve the monotony of tone and motive: what is vainly offered in exchange for souls is always escape from misery, and the piling-up of miseries occupies the interest. Melmoth's glittering eyes are too uniformly baleful, and his victims too uniformly powerless. Maturin does communicate some sensation, but less by his heavy descriptions than by exploiting oppression and claustrophobia, the most easily communicated of physical sensations. His violent embodiments of passion are impressive but not memorable. His is a cold violence, and his hostility, as a good son of the Church of Ireland, to Puritans, Methodists, and the Church of Rome, and as a good Irishman to native dirt and disorder, breeds coarse and often clumsy description that cannot be dignified as satire. It is perhaps proper that he should be best remembered by Coleridge's chapter in *Biographia Literaria* on his tragedy *Bertram*, except for an uneasy feeling that Coleridge's wrath was kindled less by contempt for the themes and emotions of *Bertram* than by annoyance at a heavy-footed intrusion on ground he considered his own property. The romances at least have a solidity and weight of their own, and Maturin, however devoid of poetry, idealism, wit, or humour, testifies to something in the spirit of the age that was not to die until Byron and Shelley had redeemed it.

If Miss Edgeworth stands for sense and responsibility, Mrs. Ann Radcliffe[1] stands for the legitimate irresponsibility of the free imagination and for sensibility—not the irresponsible social sensibility which is sentimentalism, but certain kinds of sensibility of which Miss Edgeworth was not capable and would not care to be. The young Ann Ward was a favourite in the house of her uncle Thomas Bentley, partner of Josiah Wedgwood and director of their London factories of decorative pottery, who was in close touch with artists and the art collectors then growing conspicuous in society. From the first she shows a strong visual imagination cultivated by familiarity with pictures, especially the landscapes of Salvator Rosa, Claude, and Claude's English followers headed by Richard Wilson, and by the literary example of Gilpin. The cult of emotional susceptibility to natural scenery was not only a painters' fashion, and Mrs. Radcliffe knew and quoted Thomson, Gray, Mason,

[1] 1764–1823. Born in London, daughter of William Ward. Married William Radcliffe, editor-proprietor of the weekly *English Chronicle*, 1787. Lived quietly in London except for holiday tours together.

Collins. She learned, however, more than the common amateur cant that amused Jane Austen, and went beyond the bare naming of objects for their associative value that too often suffices for the pupils of Akenside and the Wartons. Colour and light created emotion by direct impact on her senses, along with natural sounds and music; and she attempted to convey her responses by the most powerful and best controlled method, that of organized composition. This is clear in her third novel, *The Romance of the Forest*, in which she found herself:

His château stood on the borders of a small lake that was almost environed by mountains of stupendous height, which, shooting into a variety of grotesque forms, composed a scenery singularly solemn and sublime. Dark woods intermingled with bold projections of rock, sometimes barren, and sometimes covered with the purple bloom of wild flowers, impended over the lake, and were seen in the clear mirror of its waters. The wild and Alpine heights which rose above were either crowned with perpetual snows, or exhibited tremendous crags and masses of solid rock, whose appearance was continually changing as the rays of light were variously reflected on their surface, and whose summits were often wrapt in impenetrable mists. Some cottages and hamlets, scattered on the margin of the lake, or seated in picturesque points of view on the rocks above, were the only objects that reminded the beholder of humanity.

On the side of the lake, nearly opposite to the château, the mountains receded, and a long chain of Alps were seen in perspective. Their innumerable tints and shades, some veiled in blue mists, some tinged with rich purple, and others glittering in partial light, gave luxurious colouring to the scene.

(Chapter xv.)

This might be derived entirely from pictures, but in 1794, two years after the publication of the *Romance*, her susceptibility was increased, and her visual memory stored, by a tour in Holland, Germany, and the north of England; and in the writing of *A Journey through Holland and the Western Frontier of Germany*, published in 1795, her method was reinforced by the effort to convey from her mind to the reader's a complete concept of the things perceived as they are related in space. This is conscious and deliberate, born of the artistic experience in which, as she says in *A Journey*, 'a wish to present the picture, and a consciousness of the impossibility of doing so, except by the pencil, meet and oppose each other', and far beyond the normal tourists' catalogues of what was visible. It is also her own, earlier than the elaborate descriptions of the Beckfords in their records of travel. She now encountered 'picturesque' and 'romantic' scenery in its reality, and she set it down in painter's style:

About half-way to Andernach, the western rocks suddenly recede from the river, and, rising to greater height, form a grand sweep round a plain cultivated with orchards, garden-fields, corn and vine-yards. The valley here spreads to a breadth of nearly a mile and a half, and exhibits grandeur, beauty and barren sublimity, united in a singular manner. The abrupt steeps, that rise over this plain, are entirely covered with wood, except that here and there the ravage of a winter torrent appeared, which could sometimes be traced from the very summit of the acclivity to the base. Near the centre, this noble amphitheatre opens to a glen, that shews only wooded mountains, point above point, in long perspective; such sylvan pomp we had seldom seen! But though the tuftings of the nearer woods were beautifully luxuriant, there seemed to be few timber trees amongst them. The opposite shore exhibited only a range of rocks, variegated like marble, of which purple was the predominating tint, and uniformly disposed in vast, oblique strata. But even here, little green patches of vines peeped among the cliffs, and were led up crevices where it seemed as if no human foot could rest. Along the base of this tremendous wall, and on the points above, villages, with each its tall, grey steeple, were thickly strewn, thus mingling in striking contrast the cheerfulness of populous in-habitation with the horrors of untamed nature. A few monasteries, resembling castles in their extent, and known from such only by their spires, were distinguishable; and, in the widening perspective of the Rhine, an old castle itself, now and then, appeared on the summit of a mountain somewhat remote from the shore; an object rendered sweetly picturesque, as the sun's rays lighted up its towers and fortified terraces, while the shrubby steeps below were in shade.

The music had not ceased, when we returned to the inn: and the mellowness of French horns, mingled with the tenderness of haut-boys, gave a kind of enchantment to the scenery, which we con-tinued to watch from our windows. The opposite mountains of the Rhine were gradually vanishing in twilight and then as gradually re-appearing, as the rising moon threw her light upon their broken surfaces. The perspective in the east received a silvery softness, which made its heights appear like shadowy illusions, while the nearer mountains were distinguished by their colouring as much as by their forms. The broad Rhine, at their feet, rolled a stream of light for their boundary, on this side. But the first exquisite tint of beauty soon began to fade; the mountains became misty underneath the moon, and, as she ascended, these mists thickened, till they veiled the landscape from view.

The effects are noticeable in her next novel, her most popular work, *The Mysteries of Udolpho*, published in 1794. The landscapes in that restless work may be labelled Pyrennean or Apennine, and adorned with incongruous vegetation, but they are solid. Such subjective terms as 'romantic' and 'sublime', scattered freely through *The Romance of the Forest*, occur sparsely and with more precise connotations, and the emotional effect is created by direct means, without recourse to figures of speech.

Behind the spot where they stood, the rock rose perpendicularly in a massy wall to a considerable height, and then branched out into overhanging crags. Their grey tints were well contrasted by the bright hues of the plants and wild flowers, that grew in their fractured sides, and were deepened by the gloom of the pines and cedars, that waved above. The steeps below, over which the eye passed abruptly to the valley, were fringed with thickets of alpine shrubs; and, lower still appeared the tufted tops of the chestnut woods, that clothed their base, among which peeped forth the shepherd's cottage, just left by the travellers, with its bluish smoke curling high in the air. On every side appeared the majestic summits of the Pyrénées; some exhibiting tremendous crags of marble, whose appearance was changing every instant as the varying lights fell upon their surface; others, still higher, displaying only snowy points, while their lower steeps were covered almost invariably with forests of pine, larch, and oak, that stretched down to the vale. This was one of the narrow vallies, that open from the Pyrenées into the country of Rousillon, and whose green pastures, and cultivated beauty, form a decided and wonderful contrast to the romantic grandeur that environs it. Through a vista of the mountains appeared the lowlands of Rousillon, tinted with the blue haze of distance, as they united with the waters of the Mediterranean; where, on a promontory, which marked the boundary of the shore, stood a lonely beacon, over which were seen circling flights of seafowl. Beyond, appeared, now and then, a stealing sail, white with the sun beam, and whose progress was perceivable by its approach to the light-house. Sometimes, too, was seen a sail so distant, that it served only to mark the line of separation between the sky and the waves.

The extract from the *Journey* serves to explain the improvement in pictorial composition between the *Romance* and *Udolpho*:

indeed one might guess that she had written the first half of *Udolpho* before the tour and the rest after it. Fancy landscapes could be loosely sketched, but the conscientious tourist had to give an orderly account of the things seen, and the habit remained. The tour, however, gave more than landscapes. Much of the country traversed was a theatre of recent war. While the journalist husband recorded the history and statistics, the romancer saw, in truth of fact, the ruined buildings, the trees damaged by gunfire—a detail few men and fewer women in England could have visualized—the homeless refugees, the 'emaciated figures and ghastly countenances' of the wounded, the fiercely mustachioed soldiers and how 'as they stood singly on the ramparts, or in groups at the gates, their bronze faces and Roman helmets seemed of a deeper hue, than the gloom, which partly concealed their figures'. She heard them 'at the gates . . . chanting martial songs in parts and chorus; a sonorous music in severe unison with the solemnity of the hour and the imperfect forms, that meet the eye, of sentinels keeping watch beneath the dusky gateways'. The fateful import of such scenes touched more than her aesthetic sensibilities, and she knew the tension and uncertainty of a countryside in danger. The union of sensuous and emotional impressions is the working mode of the romantic imagination, and she was one in whom the unified sensation formulates itself in fictitious narrative. She might say, with Stevenson, that 'Some places speak distinctly.' Action does not intrude upon the scene, but is evoked from it.

The river, expanding into a vast bay, seems nearly surrounded by mountains, that assume all shapes, as they aspire above each other; shooting into cliffs of naked rock, which impend over the water, or, covered with forests, retiring in multiplied steeps into regions whither fancy only can follow. At their base, a few miserable cabins, and half-famished vineyards, are all, that diversify the savageness of the scene. Here two Capuchins, belonging probably to the convent above, as they walked along the shore, beneath the dark cliffs of Boppart, wrapt in the long black drapery of their order, and their heads shrowded in cowls, that half concealed their faces, were interesting figures in a picture, always gloomily sublime.

That is 'the dismal old town of Boppart . . . still surrounded with venerable walls', as seen from the river. Here is the first appearance of the sinister figure that weaves the dark plot of *The Italian*:

As he emerged from the dark arch of a ruin that extended over the road, his steps were crossed by a person in the habit of a monk whose face was shrowded by his cowl still more than by the twilight. The stranger, addressing him by his name, said, 'Signior, your steps are watched; beware how you revisit Altieri!' Having uttered this he disappeared before Vivaldi could return the sword he had half drawn into the scabbard, or demand an explanation of the words he had heard. He called loudly and repeatedly, conjuring the unknown person to appear, and lingered near the spot for a considerable time: but the vision came no more.

Monks, monasteries, convents, constitute one of the stock incantations of the School of Terror. It might derive a little of its power from folk-memory of the unpopularity, already inveterate in Chaucer's time, of the regular orders; the vulgar 'rationalist' scandals came in Victorian times and drew something from the School itself. Some vague touch of French anticlericalism might be suspected, but there was no poison in the English blood to breed any comparable venom. More than two centuries after they had disappeared, such figures and institutions were outlandish images. A plain Protestant Englishwoman like Mrs. Radcliffe might disapprove on grounds of reason or humanity, but with little or no theological implication. In an open society, isolation from the community was anomalous; and, again, the barred door always provokes curiosity if not suspicion. It was their exoticism that gave value to the images. The cheerful brother who showed the Radcliffes round the monastery Sanctae Crucis 'drew a ludicrous picture of the effect that would be produced by the appearance of a capuchin in London, and laughed immoderately at it'. Boppart prompted quotation from one of the main well-springs of the whole concept, the *Eloisa to Abelard* of Alexander Pope, the amateur painter to whom also a convent was only an idea. Mrs. Radcliffe's villainous Italian Schedoni was not villainous in being a monk, nor was he corrupted by monasticism; he was a bad man, who, for the romancer's purposes, could be moved, black-draped and cowled, through the arched and vaulted shadows that were the monastery.

The other romantic incantation, the Castle, is less obsessive in effect. Later in life she wrote *Gaston de Blondeville, or the Court of Henry III keeping Festival in Ardenne*, which was printed only by her biographer in 1826. This was written to amuse her husband, now Rouge Croix Pursuivant in the College of Heralds and Fellow of the Society of Antiquaries, and to commemorate their holiday jaunts, especially to their favourite St. Albans and Kenilworth. Except for an unusual ghost whose activities suggest an Icelandic rather than an English ancestry, it is all heavily architectural and antiquarian, compiled out of county histories and *Archaeologia* with little attempt at assimilation. At least she used raw material, not the second-hand history which Miss Jane Porter[1] combined with the novel of sensibility all too readily in *Thaddeus of Warsaw* and *The Scottish Chiefs*, though these indeed are fair specimens of their common type. The failure to fuse invention and information—the central problem of historical and documentary novel—passes almost unnoticed in Mrs. Radcliffe's first romance *The Castles of Athlin and Dunbayne*, a mixture of Clara Reeve and Home's *Douglas*, for there, as in most of the lesser contemporaries, the only value of the setting in 'old times' is to legitimize violent attitudes and absolve the writer from the reader's expectation of some sequence and likelihood in the behaviour of the characters, and to admit some surface coloration of antique detail while motives and sentiments are those fashionable and current. In her better romances the Castle contains gentlemen rather than knights, and if there are robber barons, they are casual aberrations of society, not misgrowths of a political constitution like those she heard of in the Rhineland. With her husband she clambered through the dungeons of Brougham Castle with all the appropriate feelings; when with the help of Piranesi she reconstructed them, she peopled them, not with Cliffords and de Vaux, but with familiars of the Inquisition. That institution was already imaged in English memory and literature as a hostile monster. In *The Italian* it is a harsh but efficient tribunal, no mere nightmare but so alien to the English as to be almost inexplicable.

Vivaldi almost believed himself in the infernal regions; the dismal aspect of this place, the horrible preparation for punishment, and, above all, the disposition and appearance of the persons that were ready to inflict it, confirmed the resemblance. That any human being should willingly afflict a fellow-being who had never injured or even offended him; that, unswayed by passion, he should de-

---

[1] 1776–1850. Born in Durham, daughter of an Irish army surgeon; educated in Edinburgh. Lived with her sister Anna (1780–1832) in London after 1790, and in Esher. Both wrote copiously.

liberately become the means of torturing him, appeared to Vivaldi nearly incredible. But, when he looked at the three persons who composed the tribunal, and considered that they had not only voluntarily undertaken the cruel office they fulfilled, but had probably long regarded it as the summit of their ambition, his astonishment and indignation were unbounded.

That is the normal English view of the Parisian tribunals of the Terror, the news of which was doubtless amplified by the French *émigrés* with whom the Radcliffes talked in Germany, and some of whom may have owed their unexpected escapes, like Paolo in *The Italian*, to one who 'thought that to be a guard over prisoners was nearly as miserable as being a prisoner himself. "I see no difference between them," said he, "except that the prisoner watches on one side of the door, and the sentinel on the other."' Such serious reflections might seem out of place in a romance; they were aroused, not by medieval day-dreams, but by contemporary realities. This modern intrusion on the imaginary past of the action-time may account in some measure for what all her critics have condemned, the painfully mechanical explanation of the mysteries with which the author has teased her readers. 'Oh! I would not tell you what is behind the black veil for the world!' exclaimed Miss Isabella Thorpe, kindly; even the impressionable Miss Catherine Morland might share, after reading the fourth volume of *Udolpho*, 'the contempt awakened by so pitiful a contrivance' felt by Walter Scott. Ten years later, having himself suffered it twelve times, Scott knew 'the torment of romance-writers, those necessary evils, the concluding chapters'. Mrs. Radcliffe had to face the necessary evil, and her modern intelligence could not smother in clouds of superstition or occultism or historical sentiment the difficulties which invention, that capricious power, had created for it. Perhaps it is as well that *Christabel* is unfinished.

In his admirable introduction to the novels in Ballantyne's Novelists' Library, however, Scott shows, without retracting his criticism, how little *Udolpho* depends on that unlucky contrivance. Ever since Walpole, tiring of 'the cold and well-disciplined merit of Addison' and 'the sober and correct march of Pope', began to fidget and 'thought that a god, or at least a ghost, was absolutely necessary to frighten us out of too much sense', a secure society had taken pleasure in imaginative insecurity, enjoyed the novelty of irrational fear and horror.

Walpole depended, however, on startling his readers, and *The Castle of Otranto* fails because the shock of alarm occurs at the beginning, and, since acute fear is evanescent, the reader's emotions have subsided long before the end. Lesser writers, and notably Maturin, tried to overcome this basic difficulty by successive attacks on the reader's nerves, but, as Scott remarked, the feelings become hardened, so that more and more powerful shocks are necessary, until the reason, hitherto in willing abeyance, revolts against the extravagance of the images and the whole thing falls to pieces. The women novelists, however, left the extremes of sentimentalism and horror to the less practical sex. Mrs. Radcliffe plays on the longer-lived strain of apprehension. Her ways have been well noticed, especially by Scott; she captures the reader's attention through her four volumes by a broad appeal to all his senses, in their aesthetic extension as well as their primitive being. She attempts even to compensate for the absence of music: her heroines have the habit of composing verses at suitable or unsuitable moments. They are bad verses, but they represent the missing element in the unified sensation as she had felt it when the landscape at Godesberg at sunset 'was to the eye, what the finest strains of Paisiello are to the heart, or the poetry of Collins is to the fancy'. She may have heard it as she wrote, for such a rhythm as this in *Udolpho* is clearly a musical reminiscence:

> How pleasant is the green-wood's deep-matted shade
> On a mid-summer's eve, when the fresh rain is o'er;
> When the yellow beams slope, and sparkle thro' the glade,
> And swiftly in the thin air the light swallows soar!

There are no verses in *The Italian*, for the lyrical mood is lost and music would be out of place. In Stevenson's terms, Mrs. Radcliffe had written 'the novel of adventure, which appeals to certain almost sensual and quite illogical tendencies in man'; she never touched 'the novel of character, which appeals to our intellectual appreciation of man's foibles and mingled and inconstant motives', for she needed no characters but only coloured figures; in *The Italian* she approached the third class, 'the dramatic novel, which deals with the same stuff as the serious theatre, and appeals to our emotional nature and moral judgment'. There are degrees of seriousness; the fact that Mrs. Radcliffe wrote nothing more in her remaining twenty-six years of life suggests that *The Italian* brought her to a point beyond which she could not and did not care to go. Criticism and, still more, satire, is out of place in romance. Moral judgement is a responsibility, and she had written for pleasure—her own and her reader's—a pleasure nearer, in nature and quality, to ballet than to drama. Her villain Schedoni is a dramatic—or melo-dramatic—figure, presented dramatically: that is, in action and not as a philosophical or psychological or moral demonstra-tion. The judgement required of the reader is simple enough to keep the book within the realm of romance, but real enough to keep it within the world, so that in his self-dramatization as an anti-Grandison hero, Byron, a worldly romantic, could borrow from the picture of Schedoni, and Shelley could borrow, along with Mrs. Radcliffe's scenery, something of her forlorn wander-ers, Adeline and Emily and Ellena, to soften and beautify the Godwinian victims of social injustice. It was not too long a step from literature to life, from her irresponsibility to theirs. This—and the space given to it here—might seem to be taking too seriously what was only a pastime, yet if Miss Edgeworth's morality is allowed to have some effect, why not Mrs. Radcliffe's imagery?

Much as she enjoyed the fantasies of Mrs. Radcliffe, Jane Austen[1] had no desire to intrude on that province. Her brisk intelligence was active as she read, and too active to allow her to write in that irresponsible vein even if she had been tempted. She had neither the peculiar knowledge nor the queer gift, she did not need to court popularity for money, and she kept to her own theme and her own method. Fanny Burney had set the theme with *Evelina, or, the History of a Young Lady's Entrance Into the World*, and the method, which was Comedy. But, as we have seen, there looms behind Hannah More the shadow of the Moral Essay, behind Mrs. Inchbald the Drama, and in Miss Edgeworth we are conscious always of the Enlightenment. Jane Austen was entirely novelist. For her, the moral structure of the world stood by its own weight, and the novel was a form in its own right. She enjoyed the behaviour of people, and she enjoyed reading novels. The novelists made enjoyable books out

---

[1] 1775–1817. Born at Steventon, Hampshire, sixth child and second daughter of the vicar there. Her annals are simple: lived with her parents in Steventon till her father retired in 1801, then in Bath. Her father died 1805. After various moves, they settled at Chawton, near Alton. She died at Winchester.

of people's behaviour; the women novelists especially made them out of the behaviour of people in relation to young women, so that she could judge as she read; and the romancers made enjoyable books out of imaginary behaviour unrelated to people as she or anyone else ever saw them. That is, she was born with the necessary gifts: human interest, imagination, and the love of writing, and with them the regulative principles of solid morals, realistic common sense, and artistic discrimination.

These she exercised first in her voluminous reading. The true novel, as practised by Miss Burney and Miss Edgeworth, was one thing, the romance another, and the sermon yet another; and they must be kept separate. Mrs. Charlotte Smith may have had reason for her picture of the distressed heroine beset by injustice, but she had little invention, and, not really believing in the novel as a serious medium, drifted into romantic inconsequence: so she is burlesqued in *Catherine* and *Lesley Castle*. Catherine's guardian aunt reproaches her: 'All I wished for, was to breed you up virtuously; I never wanted you to play upon the Harpsichord or draw better than anyone else. . . . I bought you Blair's Sermons and Seccar's explanation of the Catechism'; and so that the point should not be missed, *Coelebs in Search of a Wife* was substituted for Seccar. The novel should not be silly, but it should not be mere 'improving literature' either.

It is a commonplace of criticism that hers are regional novels as truly as Hardy's or Arnold Bennett's, but her restrictions were conscious and deliberate, to maintain the authenticity guaranteed by her own observation and—inseparable from it— the aesthetic unity of her artifacts. The much-canvassed restrictions are those of action, class, and sex. Her own family and friends were not without their tribulations, and in her novels elopements, marital infidelities, and personal disaster do occur; but would any point in any of her novels be made clearer or more effective by violent gesture or the raising of voices? She was brought up in a rectory, the emotional centre of its parish, where the ordinary duties of a clergyman's daughter must have acquainted her with all classes. But is it any virtue in a novel that it should be about dukes or about dustmen? The restriction to the middle class to which she belonged at least saves her from the condescension or discourtesy to servants and the 'lower classes' we dislike in Thackeray, and from Hardy's uneasiness

in the presence of aristocrats. And is there any point in any of
the novels at which servant or peasant could enter, much more
influence the action? So also with the place of men in her work.
She had no special illusions about men, and saw them coolly,
unlike Charlotte Brontë and even George Eliot, who are always
a little flustered when a man enters the room. It has often been
remarked that she has no scenes among men. None of her
stories are about men. Also, each of her novels, as the title-page
of *Sense and Sensibility* says, is 'by a Lady'. Ladies do not intrude
on the privacy of gentlemen, and wise ladies know that

> men, when their affairs require,
> Must by themselves at times retire,
> And sometimes hunt and sometimes hawk
> And not for ever sit and talk.

Miss Austen provides such evidence about her male characters
as is relevant to her schematic presentation, which prescribes
their appearance always in relation to her female characters,
and especially to her heroines, who—except Anne Elliot—are
young ladies in their teens. They are never shadowy or out of
focus: any man, given this evidence, can make out the rest for
himself, follow John Thorpe to his wine party and Henry Tilney
to his essay society in their colleges, or Captain Wentworth to
his ship, or Mr. Darcy to his boring club; but it would add
nothing to *Northanger Abbey* or *Persuasion* or *Pride and Prejudice*.
   The same argument applies to her silence about contemporary events. She had seen a militia camp, at least from a distance, and followed her brothers in mind wherever the navy
served; she had not seen Walcheren or Trafalgar. Contemporary history can constrain the imagination as much as ancient
history if even imaginative truth is to be guaranteed. And
though the reading of contemporary literature is a sign of grace,
especially in her young gentlemen, literary discussion must be
at conversational level. In Sir Edward Denham in *Sanditon*, the
shallow mind is satirized for intrusive dithyrambics about
poetry, and Miss Stanley disclaims interest in politics and refuses to argue about Queen Elizabeth. It is the inveterate ironist
that writes to her sister, her dear confidant, of the newly
published *Pride and Prejudice* that

> The work is rather too light, and bright, and sparkling; it wants
> shade; it wants to be stretched out here and there with a long

chapter of sense, if it could be had; if not, of solemn specious nonsense, about something unconnected with the story, a critique on Walter Scott, or the history of Buonaparte, or anything that would form a contrast, and bring the reader with increased delight to the playfulness and epigrammatism of the general style. I doubt your quite agreeing with me here. I know your starched notions.

Direct instruction is not part of a novelist's duty. The artist must not be restricted by time and space, but only by such restrictions as she imposes on herself: which she is free to choose. Jane Austen accepted willingly the limitations of life and of the life she knew, and thus attained freedom. For discipline, as her sailor brothers could tell her, is neither subservience nor slavery. The rebel and the outlaw are never free, since their actions are conditioned by external power, and mere selfwill, as Wordsworth knew, is burdened with 'the weight of chance-desires'. So also she limited herself, for freedom's sake, to comedy. Hamlet, Macbeth, Hotspur, are fated; Rosalind, Viola, Portia, work out their own problems; and our mental image of Falstaff, whatever happens to him, remains intact. So likewise Elizabeth Bennet is a true heroine, because the springs of action lie in herself, not in any code nor in reflexes acquired from circumstance or education. She makes her own decisions out of her own honesty and courage. And she was her author's favourite heroine, which means that she embodies the qualities Jane Austen prized most highly. Anne Elliot saves herself from long suffering caused by her having obeyed an external principle—call it duty or prudence or submission to the wisdom of her elders, or what you please: at least it was her own error, and she retrieves it herself. Emma Woodhouse learns that well-poised rectitude is not enough. Jane Austen's characters are never 'reformed'; they remain themselves; only they have—or have not—learned some sense and will be more careful in future. All her heroines are self-deceivers except Anne Elliot and Fanny Price, and the *Young Lady's Entrance into the World* is complete when she is enlightened, not about the world, but about herself. Unlike some young ladies of her contemporary Mrs. Brunton, they are not contrived in order to unmask the world by their clear-eyed innocence. They are figures of comedy, not instruments of satire.

By what experiences Jane Austen achieved her own integrity of spirit we do not know, since her sister Cassandra, with becoming reticence, destroyed her intimate letters. By what processes she achieved her artistic integrity is equally obscure. Her activity seems to divide into two periods, between 1796 and 1798 and between 1811 and 1816, but the dates of publication bear little relation to the composition of the early novels. She wrote *Elinor and Marianne* in Richardson's epistolary form, and left it to write *First Impressions* which was refused by the publisher Cadell in late 1797, and published as *Pride and Prejudice* in 1813. *Elinor and Marianne* was remodelled into *Sense and Sensibility* and published in 1811. *Susan* was accepted by the publisher Crosby in 1803; it was recovered from him after lying unpublished for some years, revised and ready for publication as *Northanger Abbey* in 1816, and published in 1817. There was thus ample time for revisions and for discovering and resolving artistic difficulties. The other three had easier passages. *Mansfield Park* was begun in 1811 and published in 1814; *Emma*, begun in 1814, was published in 1815; *Persuasion*, written in 1815–16, was published with *Northanger Abbey* late in 1817 after the author's death on 18 July. There are progressions that can be observed. *Sense and Sensibility*, worked over the antithetical formula like Mrs. Inchbald's powerful *Nature and Art* and a score of feeble negligibles, suffers inevitably from its conception as a cautionary tale. When a character exemplifies a quality or habit, it must continue to exemplify it, and though the manner and incidence of the consequences may be made interesting, their effect is predetermined. Nor is the balance preserved. Sensibility meets its ironical fate in middle-aged worthiness; sense merely fades into inevitable respectability. Personification and symbol are tied but comedy is free. *Pride and Prejudice* was Miss Austen's own favourite, because in it her imagination worked most freely to produce this her purest comedy. Here also she indulged her turn for satirical exaggeration; and, in spite of some small awkwardnesses, the balance is never disturbed.

We may take it that the order of publication is the order of conception, though the periods of gestation were variable and uncertain. After the logical development, in *Sense and Sensibility*, of a theme embodied in a set of invented characters, and the tight organization of a set freely invented for their own sakes in *Pride and Prejudice*, Miss Austen allowed herself to relax in general observation. *Northanger Abbey* began, we may believe, as a mature version of *Love and Freindship*, a farce like E. S. Barrett's *The Heroine*, playing with the absurdity of taking the fashionable romance as having anything to do with life. But Miss Austen had by now a practical knowledge of what the writing of fiction involves and an interest beyond that of an addict of the circulating libraries, and the farce develops into an essay on the Novel as written by one whose natural mode is story-telling. The book begins with a satirical discussion of novels in general, emphasized by the careful presentation of Catherine Morland as the antithesis of the conventional romantic heroine. In chapter v, when the scene has been set, the satire is broken by the famous defence of the serious novel as practised by Miss Burney and Miss Edgeworth, repeated within the character-set in chapter vii. The vogue of the 'horrid' romance enters in the same way in chapter vi, where it might be a piece of 'manners-painting', or casual allusive satire such as might occur anywhere but is also preparatory to the executive satire which begins in chapter xx, when that evocative word 'Abbey' begins to work on Catherine Morland's too-well-prepared imagination. Miss Edgeworth thought that 'the behaviour of the General in *Northanger Abbey* packing off the young lady without a servant or the common civilities which any bear of a man, not to say gentleman, would have shown, is quite outrageously out of drawing and out of nature'. The defence might be that the game must not be kept up too long, and it was time to bring it to an end; the General does it brusquely, but someone had to do it. Miss Edgeworth's criticism, however, brings out just what makes *Northanger Abbey* vastly superior to *The Heroine*, the suspension of the satire against romance-addiction in favour of manners-painting, the ousting of farce by comedy until it returns in 'those necessary evils, the concluding chapters'. The horrid romance is dead and the sting is out of the satire. It has faded into the general pattern, the behaviour of some young people in a certain social environment in the 1790's, and keeps its place only as a framework within which are exhibited scenes composed by—if such a thing were even remotely conceivable—a ladylike Rowlandson: the groupings in the Upper Rooms, uncomfortable expeditions in gigs, streetscapes, and inset pieces like that in chapter xiv where Miss Morland is introduced to the theory of the picturesque, an essay in pure good-humoured comedy flavoured

with irony but untouched by burlesque or satire or even criticism. Anti-romantic extravaganza is superseded by the complications within the groups of brothers and sisters, Morlands,
Tilneys and Thorpes; and as they move through their country-
dance they somehow engage the sympathy of the onlooker.
Whatever the satirist might intend, the mystery of the story-
teller has supervened. Catherine Morland is built up as the
farcical anti-heroine, ineligible by all the standards of fiction in
vogue and doomed to commonplace experience; and the reader
soon accepts her as a very nice girl. She is only the little sister
of Fanny Price, as Henry Tilney is the younger brother of those
other *honnêtes hommes* Edmund Bertram and Mr. Knightly, but
she exists.

These are people. Part of the miracle lies in the perfect
congruity of tone. The sensational romance is a lighter thing
than the emotional romance, largely French and German,
which Miss Edgeworth attacked in *Leonora*. In that novel a
mother watches anxiously over a daughter, and the reader is
made acutely aware of the presence of two historical generations, and even of a third as the Georgian Lady prophesies that
the appearance in society of the Rousseau–Goethean heroine—
Mary Wollstonecraft and her parody Lady Caroline Lamb?—
will make men desire ignorance in their partners, to the loss of
true moral consciousness; which the Victorian male did, and
the status of women suffered. No shadow of elderly anxiety, or
even tenderness or complaisance, broods over the comedy of
youth which is *Northanger Abbey*. The reader enters the charmed
circle and accepts what he finds. Fanny Price is an anti-heroine
to more serious purpose. Even without the anxieties in Miss
Austen's family, a possible attachment of which we are properly
kept uninformed, the retirement and death of her father,
consequent changes of residence before settlement at Chawton,
and dubious health, a woman between thirty-eight and forty-
one is not the young lady between twenty-one and twenty-
three. Little is lost except high spirits; the sharp observation so
closely allied with the comic sense is still predominant, and
much is added of greater depth and complexity. The specious
appearance of moral disinterestedness has worn thinner, and
Mansfield Park is structurally designed to carry specific morals
after the manner of Miss Edgeworth. Richard Edgeworth's
daughter could not have understood or valued the theme of

clerical ordination like the Rector of Steventon's daughter, her social vision did not include a cheerful midshipman like the one lovingly depicted by Charles Austen's sister, nor would her positive habit of mind create a catalyst-character like Fanny Price; but the reader is back in the region of *Patronage* and *Belinda*, and prepared for 'the anguish arising from the conviction of his own errors in the education of his daughters' that afflicts Sir Thomas Bertram when

He feared that principle, active principle, had been wanting; that they had never been properly taught to govern their inclinations and tempers by that sense of duty which can alone suffice. They had been instructed theoretically in their religion, but never required to bring it into daily practice. To be distinguished for elegance and accomplishments—the authorised object of their youth—could have no useful influence that way, no moral effect on the mind. He had meant them to be good, but his cares had been directed to the understanding and manners, not the disposition.

An Edgeworthian sense of responsibility overclouds the affair of the private theatricals, which at the *Northanger Abbey* level might have produced a chapter of brilliant inconsequence.

It is not that Miss Austen was unaware of evil, but only in *Mansfield Park* does she give her bad characters major parts in her comedy. To maintain the balance of the work of art this stronger moral intention needs greater depth of feeling and also more complete presentation of character. The roughly symbolic use of appearance and manner suffices in romance but not in the novel as she understood it, and here the reader is more happily reminded of Miss Edgeworth in the recognition of mixed character, especially in that of Henry Crawford, the deceiver who is not a mere hypocrite and whose moral irresponsibility is not incompatible with attractive qualities. Even Edmund Bertram, who represents the type Miss Austen could most approve of and is more intimately drawn than its other representative Mr. Knightly, is not a mere piece of Grandisonian perfection, since he was capable of entanglement with Mary Crawford, whom this woman novelist draws in harder lines than her brother. Miss Austen's references to *Mansfield Park* give an impression of anxiety. She has no complaint about the *Quarterly* reviewer of *Emma* 'except in the total omission of *Mansfield Park*. I cannot but be sorry that so clever a man as the Reviewer of *Emma* should consider it unworthy of being noticed.' She was aware that she had put more into it than into the earlier stories and perhaps worked more happily in the even movement of *Emma* and the return to the method of *Pride and Prejudice* by which all motivation is contained within the character-circle. She was now mistress of her craft and could do what she pleased. Beyond its perfect weaving neither she nor any other novelist could go; what we notice in *Persuasion*, the introduction of irredeemably bad characters and the note of tenderness, were already developing in *Mansfield Park*, the novel in which sense and sensibility are unified in the person of Fanny Price.

With such a writer, and in the circumstances, 'development' is a precarious study. The subject of all novels is human behaviour, and human behaviour, for a social realist like Jane Austen, cannot be sited in a cloudland, nor—however closely the attention is concentrated on a particular group—in an insulated *lieu théatral* like Mrs. Inchbald's. As she was careful in the timing of action, so she was in its placing. Criticizing her niece Anna's attempt at a novel, she wrote 'Lyme will not do. Lyme is towards forty miles' distance from Dawlish and would not be talked of there. I have put Starcross instead. If you prefer Exeter that must always be safe.' When action is sited in real places this sense of the time–space problem is obvious enough. Bath and Lyme Regis are not mere names as Harrogate is in Miss Edgeworth's *Belinda*. We can walk where Catherine Morland and Anne Elliot walked before us, and even in London people have their home addresses. Where a place is invented, we cannot make out a map of Jane Austen's country like those of Trollope's Barsetshire or Hardy's Wessex, or identify the originals of Mansfield Park or Highbury for local guidebooks, but we know at least the first figures of the map co-ordinates, and one result is the peculiar ease and security we feel in her novels. Each novel concerns a neighbourhood, with various households within walking or driving distance of one another; for longer journeys we are aware that a road-book or coach timetable is required. She must have visualized neighbourhoods adequately to give the reader, in her economical and unobtrusive way, what is needed to place her people on the ground, and we may assume that the process was useful to herself. It was no accident. When she was engaged on *Mansfield Park* she wrote to her sister, 'I am glad your enquiries have ended so well. If you could discover whether Northamptonshire is a country of hedgerows, I should be glad again.'

Nor was it a question of moving chessmen on a board. The surroundings of her characters are never described with the lavish precision that reduces many of Mrs. Radcliffe's chapters to 'Landscapes with Figures', with the figures reduced in proportion to the landscapes like so many of Claude's. Yet when in *Sense and Sensibility* Mrs. Dashwood and her daughters retire to Devonshire, Miss Austen is at pains to make it clear that Barton Cottage is not a secluded bower in a fashionable romance or drawing-room lyric but a convenient modern residence, and the description of the hills around it, more elaborate than either the story or the mood demands, adds to its solidity. This particularity about the folding and opening of the hills may remind us that in the Memoir prefixed to *Northanger Abbey* we are told that 'She was a warm and judicious admirer of landscape, both in nature and on canvas. At a very early age she was enamoured of Gilpin on the Picturesque; and she seldom changed her opinions either on books or men.' She had recourse to Gilpin in visualizing her most elaborate landscape, the setting of Pemberley in *Pride and Prejudice*. Pemberley is in Derbyshire presumably to ensure that it is 'towards forty miles' from Longbourn and so 'would not be talked of there', which would interfere with the 'first impressions' that are the warp of the plot. She might have heard talk of 'the celebrated beauties of Matlock, Chatsworth, Dovedale, or the Peak', and she certainly would find them in Gilpin's *Observations on Several Parts of England, particularly the Mountains and Lakes of Cumberland and Westmorland*—the original objective of Elizabeth's tour with her relatives. There, in sections xxix and xxx, she found what suited her in the descriptions of Ilam and Kedleston. At one point in Pemberley park, 'the valley, here contracted into a glen, allowed room only for the stream and a narrow walk amidst the rough coppice-wood which bordered it. Elizabeth longed to explore its windings.' In *Forest Scenery*, Book II, section iv, Gilpin explains:

From the copse we proceed to the *glen*. A wide, open space between hills is called a *vale*. If it be of smaller dimensions, we call it a *valley*. But when the space is contracted to a *chasm*, it is called a *glen*. A glen therefore is most commonly the offspring of a mountainous country; tho it is sometimes found elsewhere with it's common

accompaniments of woody-banks, and a rivulet at the bottom. . . .
The path, which winds through it, may run along the upper part, or
the lower.

Other details confirm the suggestion that she had been re-
reading Gilpin for her own purposes. These purposes, however,
lay deeper than mere decoration, or even the mechanics of
action-planning. This carefully contrived landscape is the
scene of the emotional hinge of the whole novel, chapter xliii,
the first chapter of the third volume in the early editions, where
the first impressions are modified and Darcy's pride and Elizabeth's prejudice break down together and their feelings begin
to dominate. Miss Austen did not thrust it on the reader, but
we may well say of Pemberley what Gilpin said of Ilam, 'We
have few situations so pleasingly romantic.' This may well be
an early taste. In *Northanger Abbey* she had smiled over the
solemn orthodoxy of her young people's talk of the Picturesque
—and perhaps over her own. But in the later *Mansfield Park*,
the visit to Somerton is turned to real satire of the 'improvers',
Humphrey Repton and his gentlemen employers, as well as to
another contrast between Fanny Price and Mary Crawford.
Throughout that novel Fanny's sensitiveness to natural beauty
is insisted on. Chapter xi closes one turn of the action, and
closes with a picture of summer night

when all that was solemn, and soothing, and lovely, appeared in the
brilliancy of an unclouded night, and the contrast of the deep shade
of the woods. Fanny spoke her feelings. 'Here's harmony!' said she;
'here's repose! Here's what may leave all painting and all music
behind, and what poetry only can attempt to describe!' [Not Claude,
not Paisiello, but Cowper.] 'Here's what may tranquillise every
care, and lift the heart to rapture! When I look out on such a night
as this, I feel as if there could be neither wickedness nor sorrow in
the world; and there certainly would be less if the sublimity of
nature were more attended to, and people were carried more out of
themselves by contemplating such a scene.'

And Edmund, sympathetic enough to her enthusiasm, leaves
her by the window to join Mary Crawford. More subtly ironical
is the scene on Portsmouth ramparts in chapter xlii, when
'everything looked so beautiful under the influence of such a
sky, the effects of the shadows pursuing each other, on the ships
at Spithead and the island beyond, with the ever-varying hues
of the sea now at high water, dancing in its glee and dashing

against the ramparts with so fine a sound'—an effect partially repeated in *Sanditon*—where also the mood is softened, but the sadness is not lifted. The weather in *Emma*, again, is worth noticing. 'Symbolism' is a crude term. This is something simpler and deeper, the vision of human minds and feelings in a natural world.

Jane Austen, however, like Chaucer, is too tempting a subject of discourse. Our business is history, and the historical point is that Jane Austen was no more insulated than Blake from the influences of the time. There was also something more important. In the year of *Mansfield Park*, *Waverley* rescued time past from ignorant incompetence, and other scenes and other themes were to follow, but—in the words of the author of *Waverley*—the 'talent for describing the involvements and feelings and characters of ordinary life . . . the exquisite touch, which renders ordinary commonplace things and sentiments interesting from the truth of the description and the sentiment' established the essential art as including all dimensions and existing in its own right free from dependence on time, place, morality, learning, or any extraneous consideration.

V

THE INTERMEDIATE GENERATION

THE 'Age of Johnson' was over, and the field open to younger men, past their first youth when the Bastille fell and ready to present mature work to the public. They do not form an established group to supersede the elder one, but carry forward separate existing interests and so could be more readily accepted by many readers than the innovators who, in time, came to be recognized as forming a new 'age', that of Wordsworth. They may have contributed to the later synthesis, but in the early 1790's they were disconnected, and must be treated separately. The order of treatment has no significance.

William Lisle Bowles[1] was a pupil of Joseph Warton at Winchester, and he remained faithful to his master's doctrines but exaggerated them, softening the strain of sentimental melancholy into self-pity and elevating the Wartonian notion of 'Nature' into a dogmatic and exclusive principle. Thus when in 1819 Thomas Campbell criticized Bowles's views set out in his edition of Pope's works (1808), Bowles replied with *The Invariable Principles of Poetry*, which brought in Byron and William Roscoe, Pope's next editor, to whom Bowles retorted in sixteen letters of surprising violence reinforced with all the resources of typography: nor was that the end. The best result of this critical scuffle was the provocation of the piece of Byron's lounging, insolent prose, but it does point to the survival of the simple feeling for natural objects even while Wordsworth's more philosophical principles were finding acceptance. Bowles really owes his place in history to his earliest work, the little anonymous volume of fourteen sonnets published in 1789, not only because of Coleridge's youthful enthusiasm but because, as its republication eight times by 1805 proved, it testifies to an audience prepared by Goldsmith and Cowper to sympathize

[1] 1762–1850. Son of vicar of King's Sutton, Northamptonshire. Educated at Winchester and Trinity College, Oxford; B.A. 1792. Vicar of Bremhill, Wiltshire, 1804; prebendary of Salisbury Cathedral 1804, and canon 1828; chaplain to Prince Regent 1818. Neighbour and friend of Crabbe in later years.

with the sentiments of a melancholy wanderer, obviously sincere and not without a gentle accomplishment. Bowles was not alone in following up the Wartons' revival of the sonnet. Cuthbert Shaw[1] and Thomas Russell,[2] who both died at an early age, though Russell's poems were published only in 1789, and still more Mrs. Charlotte Smith, had gone some way in establishing the sonnet as an appropriate form for the expression of melancholy feeling. Wordsworth's adoption of the form in 1802 was an independent discovery of the wider and deeper values inherited by Milton from the Italians, but Coleridge and Lamb, not to mention many gentlemanly and ladylike amateurs, derive from this concept of its uses. The qualities that carried Charlotte Smith's[3] *Elegiac Sonnets and Other Essays* (1784) through some dozen editions by 1811, with a second volume added in 1797, are the greater immediacy of the positive feelings caused by her unfortunate experiences, and—for contemporaries at least—her share of some common amateur interests of the middle class, notably her translations from Petrarch and her taste for botany, but she displayed an emotional force that cannot quite die with fashion.

Financial success was no doubt welcome to the young Bowles and to Charlotte Smith in their poverty, but they were not merely exploiting a particular public: they were part of it. This public must always be remembered, the central uncommitted public which reads for pleasure, buys the books, and produces occasionally articulate individuals to write them. Of such is William Sotheby,[4] who could afford to amuse himself with translation from Homer, Virgil, and Wieland's version of the romance of Huon of Bordeaux and to produce a handsomely printed quarto, illustrated with aquatints, of his own *Poems* about tours in Wales and elsewhere, combining the tourist fashion with the old landscape fashion of Denham and Dyer, still practised by gentlemen versifiers. Sir Brooke Boothby,[5]

[1] 1739–71. Son of a Yorkshire schoolmaster. Schoolmaster and actor. Poems published between 1760 and 1776.
[2] 1762–88. Winchester and New College, Oxford. B.A. 1784; ordained 1786. Died of tuberculosis.
[3] See Chap. IV, p. 67.
[4] 1757–1833. Officer in dragoons 1774–80. Student of classics and member of the Dilettante Society. *Poems* 1790; various poems and tragedies; translations of *Georgics* 1800 and Homer 1830–4. A bad poet but a good friend of Coleridge and Scott.
[5] 1743–1824. Baronet. One of the Lichfield group and friend of Edgeworth.

whose portrait by Wright of Derby is a monument of this cultural group, could employ Bulmer, the best printer of the time, and Glover, a reputable artist, in a piece of bookish dilettantism, *Sorrows Sacred to the Memory of Penelope* (1796), adding to the sonnets and elegies versions from Horace and a canto of Tasso which indicate some origins of his manner. The dubious question of 'sincerity' need not be raised: if Sotheby enjoyed his tours, and Boothby wished to commemorate the loss of a little daughter, they were entitled to deploy their taste and talent. They are not 'important'; their works are products of a cultured society, not born of innate compulsion either artistic or emotional; but they provide, for the historian, evidence of the cultivated society to which they belonged. The same may be said of Anna Seward,[1] the copious and determined Swan of Lichfield. Her pretensions, unbalanced by her capacities, made her a bore, but at least she exemplifies a useful desire for literature in non-professional provincial society and a useful advertising agency for such writers as she condescended to approve of. The young Walter Scott thought her important enough to send her an inscribed copy of his first publication; whether he welcomed her legacy of the duty of editing her voluminous correspondence is more doubtful.

The most conspicuous and most considerable example of the type is the banker poet Samuel Rogers.[2] His education in the traditions of the dissenters' academies, and his family relations with the serious intellectual society which created such educational institutions, may have given him wider sympathies as well as liberal politics and a place in intelligent commercial circles; in later years his breakfast-table and his purse were open to men of letters of different persuasions. His comparative width of interest in the arts as in politics might be held as symptomatic of the dilettante temper that deprived his own work of the positive impact of strong convictions, so that the final condemnation of his poems, as of those of the type in

---

[1] 1747–1809. Daughter of Thomas S., prebendary of Lichfield. Lived in Lichfield, corresponded with intellectual friends and produced poems between 1780 and 1809, also some prose. Scott edited her collected works 1810. Six volumes of letters published 1811. A well-intentioned but tiresome woman.

[2] 1763–1855. Son of a London banker whom he succeeded. Lived an uneventful bachelor life, except for a stay in Paris and his tours. Knew everybody worth knowing; including himself, since he refused the Laureateship on Wordsworth's death, 1850, leaving it for Tennyson.

general, is that there was nothing in them to which anyone could object, except that they were not quite good enough. At least he did not merely follow prevailing fashions as they arose, as Bowles did in his long life as a respectable parson; for though Bowles's *Spirit of Discovery* is an odd interweaving of modern exploration with the story of Noah's Ark, his later works merely invite classification as dull efforts in the manner of Southey or Scott or village piety. Rogers followed his own interests, which began in the discursive style inherited from Thomson and Akenside, though he lacks both their intellectual scientific armature and positive political faith as well as the positive religion and the satirical admixture that save Thomson and Cowper from sentimental over-sweetness. His feeling for 'nature' reaches little further than a taste for landscape. Yet *The Pleasures of Memory* is a true transitional poem in that it is based on the theory of Association which was so important to Wordsworth and still more to Coleridge until he inflated it to bursting point, but which Rogers uses in the eighteenth-century way, giving an explicit statement of the theory, some heterogeneous reminiscences tinged with something of the pastoral nostalgia familiar to readers of Goldsmith and the drawing-room lyrists with whom Rogers had much in common, some mixed reading, and direct moral reflections after the manner even more prevalent in earlier generations. These arise in turn, heterogeneous matter and heterogeneous illustrations side by side where Wordsworth concentrates and fuses. The discursive poem requires severer control than amateur poets could or cared to exert. Thomson could move easily from his first-hand observations to matter derived from his academic training and his wide reading in travel-books, because his borrowings were always strictly relevant to the theme of the moment. Rogers, like others of his type, had to explain or authenticate his allusions in appended notes, which are always a danger-signal. This method demands little from the co-operative imagination of the reader, little effort at self-adjustment such as comfortable library-subscribers resented when they dipped into Wordsworth, and so it made for popularity, for *The Pleasures of Memory* reached some fifteen editions by 1806.

The desultory form suited one for whom poetry was only a spare-time occupation, and *Columbus* appeared in fragmentary condition (1810) for the same reason; *Human Life* (1819) has at least the framework of birth and death to support some serious moralizing natural in a man of his upbringing. It seems odd to find *Jacqueline*, a simple romance in smooth eight-syllabled verse, sewn in the same boards with Byron's *Lara* (1814), but the section headed *Bologna* in *Italy* records a meeting on easy friendly terms as well as Rogers's admiration of the greater poet. *Italy* (1822; part ii, 1828) returns to the earlier way of conducting a long poem. If Rogers had any model for the arrangement of his memories of a tour from Geneva to Monte Cassino it was *A Sentimental Journey*. Two at least of the prose sections have a distinct tinge of Sterne's style, but it is in the conception of the work that the influence is clear, where a place or a stage recalls a personal experience or a story told by or about someone, Swiss guide or unfortunate woman or Italian gentleman. If there is more description of scenery, more historical and literary allusion and less of the author's own emotions than Sterne indulged in, it is because these were the main incentives to the journey. This tourist does not dramatize himself, as do Goldsmith and Sterne and Byron each in his own way. Some force and literary interest are lost; on the other hand he never inflates his emotions so as to provoke scepticism. Seven passages remain in prose, as if he knew that the imaginative temperature was too low for verse, and he never intrudes himself between the reader and the subject. Mr. Sam Rogers of London is a pleasant, unassuming fellow traveller, never querulous or patronizing or censorious. When he touches, as he rarely does, on public issues, it is to lament the troubles of the Swiss or the political debasement of Italy without the common English touch of superiority. A friendly listener and an easy guest, he makes many acknowledgements of kindnesses and courtesies from people of all classes. Mr. Rogers enjoyed his tour and enjoyed writing about it in easy verse derived, at considerable distance, from Thomson. As in all his poems, the effect varies as his enjoyment communicates itself to the reader, and if that enjoyment is heightened by the addition of Turner's landscape vignettes to Stothard's rather trivial figure decorations in the expensively produced editions of 1834 and after, it is because Rogers was indulging his own tastes first, and then admitted others who might share them.

It is in the Recollections and Table Talk collected by other men, however, that Rogers remains alive. He knew and appreciated artists of all kinds, and they usually found him, as Walter Scott noted in his Journal for 1826, 'exceedingly entertaining, in his dry, quiet, sarcastic manner'. He had a sharp wit, though he kept it out of his poems, and he did not arrogate for himself an undue place in the ranks of literature where he found his best enjoyment. We can believe him when he writes of himself at the close of *Italy*:

>   Nature denied him much,
> But gave him at his birth what most he values;
> A passionate love for music, sculpture, painting,
> For poetry, the language of the gods,
> For all things here, or grand or beautiful,
> A setting sun, a lake among the mountains,
> The light of an ingenuous countenance,
> And what transcends them all, a noble action.
>   Nature denied him much, but gave him more;
> And ever, ever grateful should he be,
> Though from his cheek, ere yet the down was there,
> Health fled; for in his heaviest hours would come
> Gleams such as come not now; nor failed he then
> (Then and through life his happiest privilege)
> Full oft to wander where the Muses haunt,
> Smit with the love of song.
>   'Tis now long since;
> And now, while yet 'tis day, would he withdraw,
> Who, when in youth he strung his lyre, addressed
> A former generation. Many an eye
> Bright as the brightest now, is closed in night,
> And many a voice now eloquent, is mute,
> That, when he came, disdained not to receive
> His lays with favour. . . .

The visitor who strays along these paths will find flowers enough of sentiment, phrase, or description to beguile his steps. What is lacking is power, whether of thought, passion, or expression. A young man could learn here how to write verse, and—despite Wordsworth's indiscriminate outburst about 'gaudy and inane phraseology'—need acquire no vicious habits of style; but he would encounter neither the shock nor the enchantment either of which might make him a poet. We are told that Robert Bloomfield[1] began life as a farm hand, but

---

[1] 1766–1823. Born in Suffolk, but became a shoemaker in London; given small post in Seal Office 1802; failed as bookseller; poor all his life, though achieving some notice as a minor poet.

The Farmer's Boy (1800) might have been written by a sympathetic bystander. The Wartonian mode was predominantly
visual and verbal, and gave Bloomfield no example of how to
communicate physical sensation in direct speech; nor could he
find a way for himself, so that he missed the evocative phrase or
epithet which is often tactile (as in Milton and Keats) and could
only describe. He may have inherited some portion of the
traditional song of the farmlands, and if he had appraised it at
its true value it might have helped him to write of the joys and
sorrows of 'poor Giles'; but whereas Burns could advance himself by his accomplishment in a similar tradition because in
Scotland that tradition was cherished by all classes in society,
Bloomfield would have been unnoticed except in the fields and
the village inn. So he worked in an acquired style. In *Rural
Tales* (1802) also he was unable to subdue the style to his
subject, nor had he the resources of thought or knowledge to
add weight to it. In *The Banks of Wye* (1811) he invokes the
name of Burns in vague and conventional terms; his mention
of Gilpin is more to the point. An unassuming colloquial manner, not untinged with humour, appears here and there, and is
authorized by the examples of Thomas Warton (the younger)
and Rogers, but to exploit it thoroughly would have required
a self-confidence which his insecurity denied him; and one is
uncertain to what extent it is inadvertent in *The Banks of Wye*, iv:

> Your steed prepare,
> Drink nature's cup, the rapture share;
> If dull you find your tedious course
> Your tour is useless —sell your horse.
>
> CANFROME shall from her vaults display
> John Barleycorn's resistless sway
> To make the odds of fortune even,
> Up bounc'd the cork of 'seventy-seven',
> And sent me back to school; for then,
> Ere yet I learned to wield the pen;
> The pen that should all crimes assail,
> The pen that leads to fame—or jail;
> Then steem'd the malt, whose spirit bears
> The frosts and suns of thirty years!

Between the slippery run of the eight-syllable couplet, the
second-hand descriptive style, and the borrowed historical allusions, even an indulgent reader will agree that Bloomfield

deserved no better advancement than he received. The death of Henry Kirke White[1] at the age of twenty-one casts an aura of regret round his name, which it is proper to mention at this point, for though he was twenty-three years younger than Bowles he moved in the same orbit. His is student work; it is unlikely that he would ever have found an individual voice; but he had a nice feeling for metre and phrasing, and might have made a good parson-poet if he had not burned out his consumptive body with overwork to make up for the early schooling his father refused him. Southey encouraged him as he did other struggling aspirants to poetry, but White had nothing that cannot easily be found among minor versifiers and hymn-writers of the eighteenth century. And that century left greater legacies than the School of Nature and Warton.

In terms of strict biographical fact, the Rev. George Crabbe[2] may be included, along with his friend Bowles and many another country parson too lowly for remembrance here, in the category of the leisure poets, and indeed his discretion in restricting himself to a form which could be thoroughly worked up in the time and conditions he could allow for writing proves this as well as his artistic tact. When we turn to his poems, however, we enter a different region of feeling, thought, construction, and style. Here we face power. Yet when we try to comprehend the poetic personality of Crabbe we become involved in negatives. His work falls into two groups: the first, containing the anonymous and unimportant *Inebriety* (1775) and *The Candidate* (1780), *The Library* (anonymous in 1781, acknowledged in 1783), *The Village* and *The Newspaper* (both

---

[1] 1785–1806. Born at Nottingham, son of a butcher. Articled to a lawyer, but, with help of Southey, became sizar, St. John's College, Cambridge. Published poems in periodicals, and *Clifton Grove* 1803. *Remains*, with life by Southey, 2 vols. 1807, vol. iii, 1822.

[2] 1754–1832. Born Aldeburgh, Suffolk, son of the collector of salt-duties. After some schooling at Bungay, apprenticed at age of 14 to a surgeon near St. Albans, then to one in Woodbridge. After unsuccessful practice at Aldeburgh, tried to live by writing in London, 1780, sent poems with a letter to Burke, who saw their merit, introduced him to Reynolds and Johnson, and helped publication of *The Library* and *The Village*. Deacon 1781, priest 1782. Curate at Aldeburgh; chaplain to Duke of Rutland; two small livings from Lord Chancellor, qualifying by LL.B. degree from Archbishop of Canterbury. Married 1783. Curate of Stathen; Rector of Murton, Leicestershire, from Lord Chancellor. Inherited property of his wife's aunt in Suffolk. By bishop's orders resided at Murton 1805–14. Vicar of Trowbridge, Wiltshire. Became widely acquainted in literary circles, where he was more popular than in his parishes.

1783), is the product of his twenties; the second, between the ages of forty-one and fifty-three, begins with *Poems* (1807, a reprint of earlier works with additions) and continues with *The Borough* (1810), *Tales* (1812), and *Tales of the Hall* (1819). The gap seems fortuitous, unlike the similar gap in the career of Milton, for this second group shows little or no evidence of change or development either in spirit, thought, or manner. No inner compulsion seems either to have checked the poet of the successful *Village* or moved him to resume the practice of his craft after twenty-four years in which he published only a funeral sermon and a botanical essay. Milton set aside poetry to rally to a political cause; Crabbe, traditionally the poet of the poor and unfortunate, aged twenty-two at the American revolution and thirty-five at the French, shows no inclination to revolutionary sentiment. The sight of the Gordon riots in 1780 may have shocked him, but indeed his middle-class disapproval of Jacobinism and clerical horror at infidelity signify merely that, like most people in this world, he had no real political convictions of his own or of any consequence. He had neither a philosophical doctrine to promulgate, nor personal complexes to sublimate nor obsessions to discharge, nor any vision to reveal of a spiritual cosmos or the destiny of man; he was not rapt into a poetic fury by any divine enthusiasm and celestial inspiration, nor called to spend laborious nights and days over any art that was long to learn.

He had, of course, the inexplicable capability, the artist's birthright of power to do and desire to do, which we can only remark and accept; and it may be that what seem commonplace incentives are proper to the poet of the commonplace. Much of the force that created *The Village* was generated by plain dislike of his surroundings, then the need to escape from his poverty and the distasteful occupations of a country apothecary and to win a position to marry a brave and devoted girl, slightly above himself in fortune, with whom he was in love. *The Village* was successful, not only in catching the attention of Burke and Burke's literary friends, but in engaging their influence to have its author received into holy orders and beneficed, though sparingly at first, by the interest of the Duke of Rutland. The creative force abated thereafter. Yet the capability was not destroyed: only the incentive was lacking. As a clergyman he seems to have been neither noticeably assiduous nor very well liked, but his offices did open to him a wider view of society, and his parochial functions enforced on him the critical observation of the characters, habits, and fortunes of men and women who lived their ordinary lives in country houses and villages and small towns of the east midlands. His son's biography supplies some hints of incentive to the resumption of his practice of writing: he had considerable leisure, a growing family, and an inveterate addiction to circulating-library fiction.

Crabbe's ministerial experience roused in him no overpowering religious convictions, nor did it compel him into imaginative self-identification with the emotions or aspirations of his parishioners. He observed them as he observed the ferns and mosses of the Vale of Belvoir; and, since men and women did not lend themselves to classification by natural orders, and since his interest in them remained at the level of sympathy and esteem or their opposites—that is, since the emotional forces inhered in them and were not absorbed into himself— his observations formulated themselves, for this novel-reader, in stories rather than in philosophical or religious treatises on the one hand or lyrical effusions on the other. He wrote his stories in verse because he was an old practitioner in eighteenth-century forms, because verse was a more reputable medium for a beneficed clergyman than the slight novels with which he drugged his mind, because even a slight novel demands more complication of plot and interest than he cared to burden himself with—since the merest novel-reader expects explanation and he was content with statement—and because of the strange nature of verse itself: for verse may be an ultimate refinement or it may be a primitive formula, and, either way, a competent craftsman can make it carry the implications, enforce the suggestions, and define the shades and colours of emotion and description more economically and more directly than prose. Also, since he wrote primarily for recreation and then with pleasure in the reputation he had earned and the company it brought him, he probably enjoyed the exercise of verse more than the prose he had to use for sermons and botanical reports.

Crabbe refused all suggestions that he should write a set of stories to illustrate or expound a general theme. His writing was not a vocation, and he had the desultory mind of an opium-addict as well as that of a novel-addict. To dedicate his efforts to a cause or a thesis would mean thinking one out,

and while he had his lessons to convey, his warnings and judgements, he was a preacher, not a theologian. His only principle
of organization is topographical, as in a local Flora, or, in *Tales
of the Hall*, the leisured talk of friends. He sees individuals as
individuals and describes them in their habitat, by virtue of a
direct vision, a pleasure in tracing motives and determining the
precise quality of emotions, and a habit—partly innate, partly
professional—of affirming his own sadness or distaste or amusement as he contemplated the constitutions and behaviour of
people around him. The general character of his stories is
obvious enough. His early trials marked him for life without
perverting him. Having raised himself out of occupations and
an environment he hated, he was decently sorry for people who
failed or declined in society or suffered from their state of
despondency; having an assured status, a good wife and a well-
doing family, he was sorry for lonely men and deserted women;
and his sardonic vein of comedy was stimulated by the spectacle
of people whom prosperity and superiority made arbitrary or
ungracious. But this general character was not thought out,
and it is doubtfully legitimate to select one story or another as
specially significant of his philosophy. His emotional range is
narrow: happiness is such a state as is achieved by the brothers
in *Tales of the Hall*, when fraternal kindness in one and release
from anxiety in the other unite them in a gentle and affectionate
monotony of retired days; misery is the state of the oppressed
underling, the condemned felon, the betrayed woman. Crabbe
inhabited a region of moderate elevations and marshy bottoms,
where the characteristic interest is in its wide and changeable
skies, and the corresponding landscape of his mind contains
little of the deep power of joy, the ecstasy of laughter, or the
generous magnificences of tragedy.

It was a sound instinct that confined him to the compilation
of separate stories. Chaucer had discovered the danger of the
set theme when he abandoned *The Legend of Good Women* for
the free range of *The Canterbury Tales*, and Wordsworth labours
under the burden of the connected series in *The Excursion*.
Crabbe was wise in recognizing his limitations, and criticism is
in turn limited to asking whether one volume contains more or
fewer of his better stories, and why one story is better or less
good than another. The reasons are largely casual. Crabbe
made his collection, and some specimens are intrinsically more

rewarding than others. He selected on the vaguest principle, or, rather, on the realist's principle that selection is itself an improper procedure. Sometimes he comprehended his subject better because it came home to his own experience, and sometimes he happened to be working more intensely or more luckily. He would not be greatly perturbed by the variation of quality any more than he would over the variation in the latest batch of novels from the library. Not that he was not serious; but it was not a thing to agonize over, and he probably enjoyed writing each of them with greater or less pleasure only as they came easily or with difficulty, according as he was 'on his day' or out of form. His Peter Grimes (to take the most obvious instance) appears a tragic figure to some modern minds who suspend him for observation in the medium of a social philosophy developed since Crabbe's day, and are themselves comfortably removed from the oppressive reality from which Crabbe struggled to free himself. The intensity of that story is the intensity of Crabbe's hatred of Aldeburgh, hatred that embraced the character of the landscape and the character of the people whose harsh coarseness is most efficiently projected in this example because Crabbe exploited the symbolic value of environment, which he is so often content merely to describe as accessory to his story. His usual limitations become more apparent when we remember the unfinished sheepfold in Wordsworth's *Michael*, the enveloping sense of the hills around and the enveloping significance of the emotional theme. But we should remember also Wordsworth's long technical struggle with *The Thorn* as well as his deeper purposes. Comparison is scarcely fair, for Crabbe was not an incomplete Wordsworth. His own discovery was the value of the ungeneralized truth, and the hard clarity, the emphasis and validity he gave it by his uncritical application to it of the technique developed by eighteenth-century poets like Young and Johnson to propound their conclusive statements of generalized truth. The discovery was worth making, and its acceptance by his generation proves that it was relevant to the times. He was not a Seeker as Godwin and Blake were seekers each in his own way, but a humanist, and it was for the elemental humanity in him that two great humanists, Charles James Fox and Walter Scott, turned to his poems in their last days—as good a tribute as poet need ask.

Crabbe belonged to the school of Johnson not merely by

following the conspicuous literary exemplar of his youth but through real affinity, sensitiveness tempered in early hardship, moral consciousness and a melancholy sense of human weakness breeding the same kind of satire. Only the merciful power of God can overcome sin, but society has its own weapons, and especially 'the grateful stings of laughter', wherewith to lessen harm and even bring about some reformation. Crabbe's satire is sporadic like that of the novelists, descriptive rather than analytic, the satire of a humanist rather than a metaphysician. He did not study it as an art in itself and does not give his reader the peculiar pleasure of Dryden's ruthless efficiency or the deadly elegance of Pope; but no one else had the aloof astringency that is so great a part of the secret. The satire of Dr. John Wolcot[1] 'Peter Pindar', is a different thing. Peter Pindar was the literary equivalent of those Masters of Fence who fought their challenges at singlestick and backsword in Hockley-in-the-Hole, possessed of unfailing energy, cheerful irreverence, and a good rough trick with a cudgel. His flourishes did nobody much harm or much good, and if his victims were to reform his occupation would be gone. He worked on the level of gossip and no deeper, with no ideals either spiritual, moral, social, or political to propagate, but with none of the butcherly destructiveness of Churchill, producing something analogous to parody rather than to criticism. Any writer with a marked style like Scott was fair game for a score of parodists, and any public figure was fair game for the caricaturists, Burnaby, Rowland-son, Gilroy, and Peter Pindar. The King's mannerisms, the jealousies of 'Bozzy and Piozzi', Sir Joseph Banks's consequence as President of the Royal Society, James Bruce of Kinnaird's strange tales from Abyssinia, were all fish for Peter's net. He knew something about painting—enough to perceive the early promise of John Opie and give him some elementary lessons, and to edit Pilkington's *Dictionary of Painters* (1799)—and his annual Odes to the Royal Academy accompanied its exhibitions as inevitably as its catalogues. Peter Pindar was indeed something of an institution, the English Philistine, too much determined to be nobody's fool but, if sometimes annoying, sometimes tiresome, no great

[1] 1738–1819. A west-country man; studied medicine in London; M.D. Aberdeen 1767. Physician to governor of Jamaica 1767; took deacon's and priest's orders 1769, and continued medicine and divinity there till 1773. Practised in Cornwall and Devonshire. Literary life in London from 1778, producing satires steadily till 1807.

menace to anybody. Peter Pindars have their uses: they help to keep us from getting too solemn, and a little of their cheerful blackguardism is a corrective of oppressive dignity. The noisy coffee-house breaks the monotony of the week so long as we do not stay long enough to be bored—which is the danger of the collected editions. At least Peter is all of a piece whereas the facetiousness of George Colman 'the Younger'[1] seems the feebler for his annotations and quotations from Horace. Such things are bad enough in Mathias; in the weaker man they smack of pretension, or if they are genuine, a man of his intelligence and education should at least write more carefully, and his plays, box-office successes when they were new, were composed of sentiment and farce, those perishable materials. We do not resent Peter Pindar's rough-and-tumble verse: the coffee-house is less boring than the club bar. So also Captain Charles Morris[2] is rightly remembered for his praise of 'the sweet shady side of Pall Mall'; when the custom of after-dinner singing at table died out the rest of his small collection was as deservedly forgotten.

Even with the example of Cowley in mind, it took the impudence of a Wolcot to claim the gorgeous Pindar as an ancestor. Sterne's friend John Hall Stevenson stood in a more direct line, and it was in imitation of his imitation of the 'easy' style of de Fontaine's *Contes* that Holcroft[3] wrote his *Tales in Verse: Critical, Satirical, and Humorous*. This was in 1806, but, as he tells us in his Preface, three of them had appeared in *The Wits' Magazine* in 1783, and he kept to the same outmoded manner in the other ten—irregular rhymed verse with parts in stanzas or eight-syllable couplets. His theatrical interests appear: he did not share the craze for the boy actor Master Betty, but did share the common enthusiasm for Mrs. Siddons and Mrs. Jordan, as early as 1785. The introduction to the passage of eulogistic mock-satire addressed to them is more up to date: an attack on Malthus for his theories on population, and on Bonaparte for his practical support of them. The only direct personal satire has as its object certain *Observations* by Thomas Hope criticizing

---

[1] 1762–1836. Son of dramatist of same name. Educated Westminster School, Christ Church, Oxford, Aberdeen. Published loose comic poems 1797–1816; comedies and dramas in popular style with interpolated songs 1784–1822. Rigid examiner of plays in Lord Chancellor's office 1824–36.

[2] 1745–1838. Captain in infantry 1764, later in Life Guards. Laureate of the Beefsteak Club, and as such received by Prince Regent. Songs collected 1840.

[3] See Chap. IV, p. 63.

Wyatt's designs for the new Downing College in Cambridge. Holcroft's acquaintance among painters, which tempted him to some disastrous picture-dealing, doubtless prompted this rebuke of the intrusion of a gentlemanly amateur in a professional concern; Hope's wealth would not endear him to Holcroft, and politics as much as taste would make him dislike the French 'Empire style' of decoration which Hope admired. This might be a refreshing line, for the self-important dilettante was too conspicuous in the cultural landscape, but Peter Pindar did that sort of thing, as he might say, 'more natural'. Otherwise Holcroft's little tales are generalized moral fables with no great point, nor had Holcroft the lightness of touch to carry off their banality. One is glad to return to Crabbe, or go off, as one can at this unsettled time, in an entirely different direction.

William Blake[1] earned a modest livelihood as an engraver with a reasonable trade connexion, moved among artists who accepted him as one of themselves, and had a few friends who loved and helped him. His annals are so simple that biography seems almost irrelevant, were it not that there is no break between these simple facts and the urgently creative activity within him. His life was a complete unity in which we can recognize only variations of intensity whether in professional business, emotional relations, or philosophic thought. In his family he learned enough of the doctrines of Emanuel Swedenborg to be convinced for ever that man is divisible into separate entities sometimes called body, mind, and spirit, or material form, spectre, emanation in other technical terms; that the spiritual world perceived by spiritual insight is the only reality, to which indeed the material world corresponds in detail though negligible except in that correspondence; and that creation consisted in successive emanations from God, so that each material creature, being separated from God, is a fallen creature and requires a process of regeneration by which it returns into the divine unity after internecine strife and passage through successive states of happiness and sorrow. Readings in Boehme reinforced these doctrines and also the habit of interpretation of all experience out of the terms of material falsehood into those of spiritual truth, so that the libertarian and revolutionary

---

[1] 1757–1827. Born London, son of an Irish hosier (originally O'Neil). Apprenticed to Basire 1771–5. At Royal Academy school; exhibited in R.A. 1780–1808. Printseller 1784–87. At Felpham with Hayley 1801–4, otherwise always in London.

ideas that echoed round him in the group of his acquaintances, so far from being mere political opinions, were powers opposing the hateful dominion which one part of the divided essence endeavoured to impose upon the rest—the spirit of Reason and Law, Urizen who arrogated to himself the ultimacy which can only be in the divine unity, and in doing so prevented those activities by which the reunion in God is accomplished. At the same time he was learning to draw from such prints and monuments as his master Basire, who had a certain practice among antiquarians, set him to, and absorbing the principles of the 'historical' school of painting from current teaching and from the conversation of Mortimer, Flaxman, Barry, Fuseli. Raphael, and especially Michelangelo whose creative strenuousness and emphatic delineation coincided most obviously with his own temper, were for him the only models and ideals; and Swedenborg gave him the habit of expressing all doctrine in anthropomorphic terms. By such association he identified spiritual insight with artistic imagination, and his imagination worked in the visual terms of the school—that is, in images of human figures in action.

It is possible, and useful, to study Blake as artist and as poet and again as philosopher, but such studies can only be fragmentary. The thought of Swedenborg and the imagery of Michelangelo did not constitute two elements in his education nor two cults to which he adhered after examination and comparison, but one fundamental and persistent matter upon which his innate energy exerted itself and through which his concepts, moods, and desires expressed themselves. The orthodoxy of his Swedenborgianism is as irrelevant as the accuracy of his Angelesque figure-drawing. He could be no man's disciple, but took what he required. So also with his reading. He was poet as well as draughtsman—that is, he employed language and rhythm as well as line and composition—and there also he took what he required, a little from Spenser, something from Shakespeare, less than might appear from Milton, something from Chatterton and Macpherson, more from Joseph Bryant the inventor of 'Druidism', still more from the popular verse tradition of his childhood, most from the Bible. His limitations are as significant as his acquirements. He developed early—the *Poetical Sketches*, published in 1785 when he was twenty-six, were written in his teens—and, like many of the type, he was fixed early. He had what he needed for his own satisfaction and his own purposes, and anything that could not be placed within that corpus immediately and without conflict was not merely rejected or despised, but damned. Swedenborg arrived at his scheme after solid and fruitful studies in natural science, and never lost the sense of its reality. Blake accepted Swedenborg's spiritual universe but denied the rest. He had no such experience in the face of beautiful landscape as excited Turner and Constable, no such experience in research into natural phenomena as exalted Dalton or Faraday. These were not merely gaps in his experience, nor neglected possibilities; there are no negatives in Blake: what is not affirmed as good is affirmed as evil. The spiritual alone is real, therefore all attention to natural objects is of the devil; the only way of truth is by the imagination, therefore all reasoning is satanic; the only hope of regeneration is by the satisfaction of desire, therefore all laws are accursed: and Rembrandt, Bacon, Locke, Correggio, Reynolds, Newton, Titian likewise. Nor does intensity of belief imply consistency. Plato's doctrine of the relation of the ideal and natural worlds might be expected to appeal to him, and so might Rousseau's faith in free human impulse: but their names are anathema.

Whatever the imagination received must be true, and any attempt to control it by reason is the sin against the Holy Ghost. The rational inquirer will find much obscurity and contradiction in his work, but then the rational process, however sympathetically applied, is a false process—if the end be understanding. Criticism requires it, but that comes later. It is dangerous at best to assume of any poet that he had, or was trying to make, a permanent and systematic philosophy which he then embodied in verse and which we can extract by patient and ingenious collation of lines and passages from different poems written at different times for different purposes and under pressure of different circumstances. Some fixed ideas, some inveterate moods and desires will naturally recur, and in Blake's work these are so few, so powerful, and expressed in such constant images, that the temptation to schematize detail is strong. Listening to music, we recognize certain progressions, cadences, resolutions as habitual in Handel or Bach; we do not gather them up and argue that they constitute the essential Handel or the lesson of Bach. So also we recognize in Blake certain emblems, certain theories, which reappear in different combinations and relations, the more insistently because of his absolute confidence and extreme tenacity.

He preserved remarkable identity in his successive versions of the same designs in different mediums—we may contrast the *Job* series with Constable's rearrangements of his large landscapes—and preserved a general scheme and an expressive style throughout his working life of poetry for the same reason, that, quite apart from the trained engraver's necessary foresight and decision in every stroke of his tool, no artist who lived an intense inner life was so free from critical introspection. It does not follow that we can clamp an intellectual consistency on every appearance of every image. He invented new techniques in painting—though his antiquarian habit led him to claim his inventions as the recovery of old ones—and learned— from spirits as he insisted—better techniques in engraving that gave him greater freedom of creation. At the same time we can trace the pressures of the world upon him. His general imagery shadows the general activity of his time: revolution, war, industry, forge, loom, plough, mill, the necessary contrast appearing in images of youth, childhood, lambs, and in music and, visually, musical instruments, which gave him personal delight. He was a Londoner, of that London which we can reach most easily in John Thomas Smith's *Book for a Rainy Day* and *Nollekens and his Times*. It is in those streets, those fields and recreation-grounds, and in somewhat the same society, that the Songs of Innocence and Experience were made. In the same way he fuses his own significances into traditional ballads in *William Bond* and *Mary*; and if we could listen to his sweet tenor voice we might expect to hear the old popular tunes, *O London is a fine town* or *Two children sliding on the ice*. He saw the same sights, heard the same news, listened to the same arguments as other men; but where Burke and Paine and Godwin brought principles—real or unreal, true or false—to bear on what they saw and heard, in order to put the world right, Blake saw only verities within which all he saw and heard was but a partial adumbration of reality. The political and scientific discussions of his acquaintances—who were not negligible people—are satirized in *The Island in the Moon*, as if a later Swift were recording, among echoes of street songs, some batlike twitterings of modern polite conversations in an exanimate Laputa. The great issues of the time were for him greater than they appeared in parliaments and on battlefields. America appears constantly as the symbol of Liberty, for he shared that sentiment with so many of his fellow countrymen, and the American revolution had been the political excitement of his formative youth, a sufficient inspiration not to be superseded by other and later excitements. He was not a commentator, and had no need to keep up to date. Of *The French Revolution, A Poem in Seven Books* (1791), only a stray proof copy of Book I exists to show that it was printed. It never was published, presumably because it was too close to mere natural causes—real persons and real actions, as worldly men call them—the events of the few weeks before the destruction of the Bastille, and Blake was more than the poet of political revolution some have made him. He did indeed see the episode as a manœuvring of cosmic forces, but it is imperfectly and unevenly universalized. Two years later, he etched *America*, the political basis of which was a lively memory but no longer a living political issue. It lay in the past, had become part of the greater universe, or—what amounts to the same thing—had lost actuality enough to be a useful symbol for conflicts immeasurably greater than itself. So also, if *Europe* (1794) closes with echoes of the French war, it is beyond all time and space. From *Songs of Innocence* (1789) to *The Song of Los* (1795), Blake was too well occupied in framing his prophetical utterance and finding ways to set it out on copper plate and paper to be helped by new external existences, whatever their mundane importance. Yet the pictures of the Spiritual Forms of Nelson guiding Leviathan and Pitt guiding Behemoth (*c.* 1806) prove that he was not immune from worldly contacts, and that he shared the common view of Napoleon—not that he would think it out; it happened, just as his final condemnation of the classics marks the waning of friendship with Flaxman and Fuseli rather than any progression of thought or learning.

Napoleon, the despotic warlord and patron of scientists, might indeed have been a type of Urizen, but he makes no appearance in Blake's poems, for by the time his name was on every man's lips Blake had retired within the cosmos of his own imagining and did not need to look abroad for significant appearances to enrich an already overfilled mythology. From 1795, during the years when Napoleon was growing in political stature, Blake was deep in *Vala, or the Four Zoas*, personally unhappy, and somehow hindered in his creative activity. *The French Revolution* had been incompletely visualized. He had seen France as a range of mountains, full of fires and fiery colours, but cloudy—there are some thirty cloud-images in 305 lines— and the vision was unsatisfactory to the poet of the sun. And it was printed, the only printed work since the early *Poetical Sketches*. *Vala* never got beyond manuscript. Full activity for Blake involved complete creation in design as well as in words, and also the tangible expression of the whole in engraving, for all was creation, the man was an artist, possessing and possessed by his own technique, and his hands must have their part along with brain and eye: his training might be dismissed as mechanical and his bread-and-butter tasks as mere reproduction, but the complete expression of his free imagination demanded the exercise of that kind of skill along with all his other powers. He was too single-minded to divide himself, despite his theories, and his prophetic books were not things to be scribbled on scraps of paper and consigned to the anonymous mechanics of a printing house. Los had to labour at the forge, not merely dream and organize.

Complete creation began again about 1804, to produce *Milton* and *Jerusalem*, the long and consummate prophecies. The difficulty and confusion of these works grow out of the nature of their creation. What the imagination receives must be true, but 'the' imagination can only be William Blake's imagination, and here the difficulty lies, whether we read the words or examine the pictures—and we must do both—for symbolism depends on knowledge. There is no universal symbolism: we must know the story of the Cross, have seen the sea, clouds, lambs, at least have been told about lions, before their imagery can affect us, and the degree of their effect depends on the importance of their knowledge to us and the degree of our receptivity caused by personal and often temporary circumstances. He began with lyrical poems and one fragment of drama, all strongly coloured by readings in Elizabethan poetry. This youthful work was succeeded by a series of oracular sayings, short gnomic poems, and a few ballads which, rather mysteriously, carry more meanings than the street songs from which they take their form. *The Songs of Innocence and of Experience* combine the lyrical and the gnomic in varying, but everfascinating, proportions. For the promulgation of his developing doctrines, however, Blake required more scope and more than lyrical effusion. Exposition of doctrine normally entails an appeal to reason, the direct mode of winning agreement. Since reason was barred, and the end was not agreement but belief, normal methods of exposition, even if Blake had been capable of them and had held his faith in clear intellectual terms, were irrelevant. For any communication, however, terms of some sort are necessary. Blake's habit and practice being visual, much is conveyed in pictures; but pictures are not explicit, and they are static. We gather much from his images of things —flowers, mountains, trees, and so on—by the intellectual process of symbolic interpretation, but, taught by Wordsworth and Turner among others, we may take more than Blake might be prepared to sanction from these natural objects in their natural entity. His philosophical beliefs and his artistic creed centred alike in the human figure, and his faith in action, in unceasing activity, and therefore, even if the activity were 'mental fight', it was best embodied in figures in action and therefore the appropriate mode of projection was narrative, which forms the ballads and many of the Songs of Innocence and Experience. But narrative also requires connexions and relationships in a quasi-logical process. This difficulty, the conflict between visual image, story, and the direct expression of emotional and credal states, between intuition and exposition, was resolved in the formula of Macpherson's *Ossian*, wherein passages in an unceasing warfare between the powers of Morvern and Lochlann give momentary visions of masculine strength and female beauty in movement, within a setting of wind-blown mists, mountains, and grey stones on the hill-side, all conveyed in suggestions of music—song, the harp, the sounding shell of Selma. Blake needed many more images and figures than the few that sufficed for Macpherson, but those few included all the modes that came naturally to Blake, and did not demand more than was proper for his purposes. Thus the method—if the term may be used—of the long prophetical works is precisely that: active figuration, subsiding at intervals into static imagery, suggesting narrative relations without imposing them on the free movement of the imagination, creating emotional states nakedly and free from strict controls of cause-and-effect. We can, if we like, set our brains to identifying symbols, but we may find ourselves committed to intellectual process and losing the fluidity of aesthetic response. In any case, the historian's business here is not to add more interpretations to the existing confusion but to note that Blake achieved a form admirably fitted to his purpose.

Blake was the one great master of the 'historical' school. Benjamin West horrified the purists when he painted the Death of Wolfe in correct contemporary uniforms as on the Plains of Abraham on 13 September 1759, instead of removing the heroic event by symbolic pseudo-Greco-Roman draperies into an ideal timeless world of imagination. His transfer of 'fact' into 'art' was too direct; but they also had 'facts'—of history, poetry, or traditional concepts like Fame, Sorrow, and the like—to transfer, and their success was to be measured by the lucidity and completeness, as well as by the skill and ingenuity, with which their compositions conveyed the facts to the beholder. The difficulty with Blake is that we have no access to his 'facts', for they were his own and we have no other record. Most of the activities of his commentators are directed to the reconstruction of them, and there is nothing to control the results: which is right and proper, for these efforts are exercises of the imagina- tion and any individual is free to make what he can, for him- self, so long as he does not impose the results on others. We can refer his cosmic vision, to some extent, back to Boehme, Sweden- borg, and the Old Testament. We can understand his concept of *The French Revolution*, because the actions and persons of that poem are—allowing for Blake's faulty information—on historical record, and his imaginative enlargement of them differs only in degree from Carlyle's. But anything that impinged on Blake may be caught up into equal philosophical importance. Thus a personal affair, a commonplace row with a soldier, out of which, thanks to the common sense of the local justices, he emerged with no more inconvenience than a few days' worry, becomes entangled in the great vision of Jerusalem and these real but obscure personages are involved with the spiritual essences whose nature and functions are gradually dawning on our imagination. This is not a failure on Blake's part: these were only figures that obtruded themselves on the universe within him, or new terms of expression added to the old because they were so vividly present to himself, but it is as well that we know the story or the confusion would be even worse. We may read his projection of Britain, London and its streets, Jerusalem, all the towns, counties, countries, and continents he knew by name, as cosmic symbols, though we must not do so too rigidly, for they have their own aesthetic or emotional or associative reality as well as their metaphysical interpretations, are images of things he loved because they were familiar or beautiful, or hated because of their cruelty or their inconvenience to himself or their ugliness or their conflict with his theories of art, not mere cold token currency of intellectual concepts. All modes of judgement are of one value to him. Thus his scathing criticism of Wordsworth's lines:

> All strength—all terror, single or in bands
> That ever was put forth in personal form;
> Jehovah—with his thunder, and the choir
> Of shouting angels, and the empyreal thrones,
> I pass them, unalarmed. . . .

which, he told Crabb Robinson, brought on a fit of illness, was doubtless aroused not only by his general suspicion of Wordsworth's addiction to natural objects and natural piety, but because Wordsworth evokes, and then dismisses, a pictorial vision after Blake's own manner. *Strength . . . terror . . . in personal form, the choir of shouting angels* are too near Blake's own visual habit to make their rejection bearable. In another man this would be noted as an intellectual failure, but Blake's intellect is not in court: his imaginative revulsion suffices, because imaginative power is the one mode of reaching truth and reality. Wordsworth ought to have been alarmed at such a vision; and if Wordsworth did not visualize with such force, or if his vision meant less to him, then the less was he in a state of grace.

It is difficult to isolate the effect of the symbol from the aesthetic and nervous values of line, composition, rhythm, sonority, colour, which are not referable to anything else but exist as realities making their own impact as they occur; and especially in 'romantic' art, moments arrive at which the mysterious creative power irradiating the balanced fusion of thought, knowledge, emotion, and craft begins to weaken and the fused elements disintegrate, or one begins to dominate. Where the craft—the management of the 'realities'—dominates, the impetus of making, the delight of making, carries the artist on, not entirely—or not at all—aware that he has left the rest behind. So Spenser, Donne in the *Anniversaries*, Tennyson, compared with Milton, who is controlled by his great argument as Pope is by his common sense; so Shelley curbs his lyrical impulse at the end of *Hellas*, and Keats struggles for balance as he advances from *Endymion* and wrestles for it in the two versions of *Hyperion*. Blake had a double portion of crafts, and the free-flowing movement of the etching-needle, the pulse of metre, the hypnosis of rhythm may carry him on, all the more since he despised control. We are uncertain whether the imagination is of the mind or of the soul or of the working hand. To him it was all the same. In other artists this may not be serious. As Tasso said, everything in an allegorical poem need not be allegorical, and in other kinds decoration and elaborate pattern may add only pleasure: but in a symbolist the difficulty of recognizing the moment of unbalance may have unfortunate consequences for the diligent exegetist. Anyone can recognize the humanitarian in the couplet:

> A robin redbreast in a cage
> Sets all Heaven in a rage.

We can also recognize the Londoner who shared the 'popular feeling repugnant to the imprisonment, or coercion in any way, of "a robin"', emphasized, with statistics, by Henry Mayhew, sixty years later, in *London Labour and the London Poor*. It is not so easy to interpret the next couplet:

> A dove house full of doves and pigeons
> Shudders Hell in all its regions.

Is it even worse to cage a pigeon than a robin? Or, since Hell abhors it, is it a good thing to do? Or, remembering Blake's equivocal use of 'Hell' as an affirmation of energy and therefore of good, does the couplet mean that it is the acceptance of confinement by the placid doves that is evil? There are other possible interpretations. But the first couplet leads into the second; one bird calls for another; *Heaven* is answered by *Hell* though the force of the terms may be quite different. It may be suspected that the second couplet is a piece of automatic writing, a residuum of the energy generated in the first. So also with places. We know Blake lived and was happy or unhappy in Lambeth and South Molton Street and can therefore understand, in part, what he associates with their names. London Stone the ancient landmark, Tyburn the place of punishment and death, are simple enough; Hampstead and Hackney may have the values of height and level, and personal associations as

places of recreation, at least intermittently. Beyond his personal
orbit, Bath has obvious value as the ancient place of healing,
and Stonehenge as the ancient place of sacrifice. At others we
may guess, but what of 'the thirty-six counties of Scotland and
the thirty-four of Ireland'? They were only names to Blake,
some vaguely coloured with reminiscences of Irish politics, and
though their allocation between the 'Gates', the tribes of Israel,
and half-imagined figures like Hand, Hyle, and the rest has
some schematic significance, it does not invite detailed scrutiny,
and it is likely that the scheme engendered its own excitement
like the excitement of the decorative coloured scroll-work
around them and had to be completed on the map because the
excitement could not be satisfied until the name-lists were
exhausted.

The modes of judgement are uncertain, and so the basic
difficulty returns, that the ultimate reference is to Blake himself
in all his individuality of notion, quality, habit, circumstance,
doctrine, ignorance, prejudice. The traditional mythologies of
Europe and the Near East deify law and government, but there
is no Zeus on England's mountains green, no Jehovah in his
Jerusalem. His is a mythology of desire and action, refusing the
certainty, which most men require, of an ultimate power of
justice and control, and where it has any terms in common with
other mythologies it changes and even reverses their values.
In grappling with concepts necessarily expressed in such individual terms, it is of little help to know that this name is borrowed
from Macpherson or that attitude from Marc Antonio, and the
scholiasts' diagrams are all different and all unsatisfactory. The
rational inquirer must use his reason and his memory—and he
is entitled to do so, whatever Blake may say—must collate lines
and phrases in order to interpret Blake's peculiar language,
must call in the assistance of parallels and analogues from
Bunyan, Milton, the Hebrew prophets, and the poets generally,
to understand how places may be states of soul. But he must not
approach the prophetical books as if they were demonstrations:
he must accept them as experiences. He may be able to give
little account of his experiences, and add little to the rudimentary statements with which we begin; but he may find dawning
upon him some sense of what imagination is, and of its strength
and importance in a world in which—in Blake's time as in
ours—the uncreative investigators of matter claim exclusive

property in truth and a paramount right to consideration, and economists and politicians arrogate to themselves the sole dominion over the minds and spirits and bodies of men.

Blake may be regarded as an adept of ancient mystical doctrine—all the more that like most who claim authority in that kind, he was apt to denounce all other adepts, from time to time, as heretics, for mysticism is an essentially individual experience—or as a case to be analysed according to whatever psychological school the analyst prefers, or as a supreme religious heretic or a profound theological teacher. He has something for all seekers. An historian may best accept him as a furiously creative artist, an extreme example of the emphasis any artist places in the universal complex of art, who, feeling himself isolated in the material universe, over-elaborated as Spenser over-elaborated in his Irish solitude; and again as an English eccentric in the strict sense of the term like Richard Rolle and George Fox, who was confidently affirming the devilishness of reason, the supremacy of imagination, and the sacredness of individual desire about the same time as Godwin was proclaiming the sanctity of reason and individual judgement and Wordsworth was working himself into a nervous breakdown over the discrepancies of political and moral theory and practice, and Miss Jane Austen was writing down her precise formulation of such of the eternal verities of human nature as came within her observation. It is a major fact in our history that these things, and a hundred other things, were happening at the same time.

VI

THE NEW MEN

MEANWHILE the poetic territory of England was in process of occupation by a new tribe. The new generation was growing up. When we are tempted to think schematically of 'the Romantics' as a group and to link their appearance with the French Revolution, it is well to remember that on the day the Bastille fell, while Crabbe and Blake were over 30, Wordsworth was just over 19, Scott close on 18, Coleridge not 17, Southey newly 16, Byron being aged 18 months and Shelley and Keats yet unborn. The men we are now concerned with, Wordsworth, Coleridge, and Southey—for Scott must be considered apart—began their schooling in pre-revolutionary times, grew into young manhood among the agitations of 1789–94, and were making themselves as poets while Bonaparte was maturing into a dictator. Each was orphaned young: Southey was fortunate in his uncle Herbert Hill, but there is nothing in their lives like the relations of Milton and Pope and Browning with their fathers. Forced into forming their own lives without the shelter of a home and the natural influences of an elder generation, alone, and aware of the power within, each grew highly conscious of his own personal individuality, and that in times that were a forcing-house of ideas and excitements. Mere chance twisted those three separate lives together, for good and for evil: to us as their heirs in letters, on the whole for good.

We know too much about these men. Much that passes in talk between people who belong to some community, whether of family or political party or college or office, went down on paper, in letters and memoranda. Coleridge and Southey had the habit of writing, and if it was a physical affliction to Wordsworth, it was not to his sister. Critical judgement is thus disturbed even now by personal feeling instead of resting upon aesthetic and philosophical conviction. The mysterious attraction of the tragic spectacle and the self-pleasing emotion of pity lead some to overvalue Coleridge; Wordsworth's persistent good luck alienates others; and Southey is damned by his virtues. Poems are scrutinized for what they hold of private occurrences. It is natural enough, in the study of such self-conscious individualists; yet Wordsworth and Coleridge doubted the propriety of publishing Coleridge's lines *To a Gentleman* because, as Coleridge told Wordsworth, 'I never once thought of printing them without having consulted you, and . . . I wanted no additional reason for its not being published in my lifetime than its *personality* respecting myself. . . . It is for the biographer, not the poet, to give the *accidents* of *individual* life. Whatever is not representative, generic, may be indeed most poetically expressed, but it is not poetry.' The fact that Coleridge did publish it without consulting Wordsworth is only Coleridge's way; that so many of Wordsworth's poems are concerned with personal experiences—on the larger scale in *The Prelude* and in the smaller in minor poems—merely exemplifies Keats's shrewd phrase 'the egotistical sublime': Wordsworth felt that his experience was 'representative, generic', and therefore both poetical and important. 'The feeling . . . developed gives importance to the action and situation, and not the action and situation to the feeling'; and part of the situation is the man William Wordsworth: 'the poet' is another matter. He refused to arrange his poems in chronological order, for that would betray an 'egotistical' notion that their value lay in recording his successive feelings, not in their intrinsic meaning. This psychological attitude is obscure, and it was dangerous, but it should be understood, for it is that 'generic' quality that has made so many men find in Wordsworth's experience, as recorded in his poems, a revelation and a spiritual support and fulfilment of their own.

This is least true of Southey.[1] His letters, even more voluminous than those of Coleridge, are little concerned with self-analysis, and his poems rarely grew out of personal occurrences. His most self-revealing poem, which is also his best remembered, *My days among the Dead are past*, records the absorbing interest of

[1] 1774–1843. Born Bristol, son of a draper. At Westminster School 1788 where he made good friends but was expelled for a denunciation of whipping in a school magazine 1792; Balliol College, Oxford, 1793; left without a degree 1794. In Bristol with Coleridge 1794–5. Married Edith Fricker Nov. 1795. In Spain with his uncle Herbert Hill 1795–6, London, and Bristol, studying law and writing verse and prose for Reviews and newspapers 1796–1800. In Portugal, where Hill was chaplain to the British embassy, 1800–1; Dublin; Greta Hall, Keswick, Sept. 1803 till death. Began writing at school and continued all his life. Poet Laureate 1813.

his life: 'Never before was so poor a man so rich in books, and never did any man who possessed books enjoy them more heartily.' Though he was the youngest he may come first, because he found his own way of working earlier than the others, and he found it earlier because it was no new departure but a continuation of certain ways of the last generation. He explained it himself in the Prefaces to his collected edition of 1837–8. Like everything in Southey, it is open and explicit. His youthful taste was formed on Hoole's translations of Tasso and Ariosto, on Shakespeare, Beaumont and Fletcher, Spenser, Chaucer, Percy's *Reliques*, the Bible and Homer. 'It was not likely to be corrupted afterwards. My school-boy verses savoured of Gray, Mason, and my predecessor Warton; and in the best of my juvenile pieces it may be seen how much the writer's mind has been imbued by Akenside. I am conscious also of having derived much benefit from Cowper, and more from Bowles.' It seems curious that he does not mention Milton, and indeed he lacked both Milton's formal magnificence and his depth of purpose. No one bred on eighteenth-century verse could escape Milton, but where a Miltonic echo may be caught, it is from the minor poems, and in the manner of the next teacher he mentions, Dr. Frank Sayers[1] of Norwich.

Southey acknowledges his debt to Sayers for the irregular verse unrhymed in *Thalaba* and rhymed in *The Curse of Kehama*. There is more in it than that. Sayers is one of the forgotten links in the poetic tradition. Too tender-hearted to face the horrors of surgery, he lived quietly on his patrimony, content with the society of Norwich and occupied with Greek and English poetry and with literary experiment, exploring the possibilities of Collins's versification and the new sources of imagery which Gray had found in Celtic and Scandinavian tradition. Knowing less than Gray about either, he crossed these second-hand antiquarianisms with the deadly Ossianics of Macpherson and a simplified version of Greek tragic structure in *Dramatic Sketches of Northern Mythology*. Economy and speed make them more readable than the formula suggests. He could appreciate too the Gray of *The Long Story* as well as Gray of *The Bard* and *The Descent of Odin*, amused himself with burlesques and minor erotics after the fashion of Whitehead, criticized by parody, sonnetteered in moderation, subscribed a song to the

[1] 1763–1817. Lived quietly in Norwich, reading and writing at leisure.

anti-slavery campaign, and so on. When added up the whole
comes to much the same in effect as the summation of Southey,
though markedly less in weight and bulk. It is all minor work,
but less boring than the minor work of some better poets. So
when Southey became acquainted with him and his friend
William Taylor[1] in 1798, he found a congenial society that
confirmed his tastes without changing them greatly, for he was
already too absorbed in Spanish and Portuguese literature to
be deflected by Taylor's enthusiasm for German, and had
enough Greek to be inoculated against Sayers's restraining
classicism. Sayers's deliberate approach to the business of
poetry, however, was also Southey's: 'It has long been my
intention to try the different mythologies that are almost new to
poetry. "Thalaba" shows the Mohammedan. The Hindoo, the
Runic and the old Persian are all striking enough and enough
known, of the Runic I have yet hardly dreamt.' He soon
'dreamt of' the Hindoo, in *The Curse of Kehama*, before that, of
Madoc, which combined the Welsh and the Aztec, and, later,
dug *Roderick the Last of the Goths* out of his Spanish researches.
There is some heat in this last, because Southey knew the
Peninsular landscape, and its history was a major interest all
his life, but they all suffer from the same basic weakness.
Southey studied his subjects conscientiously and appended to
his poems the references and extracts from which the reader
could verify his images; since he was a highly competent writer,
they contain passages which any reader can admire and enjoy;
but the subjects are not chosen because they can be made to
express or symbolize any passionate thought of the author.

Southey was eager, ambitious, and skilful; for him poetry
was the noblest of all possible occupations: he never learned
from his master Spenser that poetry 'is not to be gotten by
labour and learning', however well it be 'adorned with both'.

Literary exertion is almost necessary to me as meat and drink,
and with an undivided attention I could do much. Once, indeed, I
had a mimosa-sensibility, but it has long since been rooted out: five
years ago I counteracted Rousseau by dieting upon Godwin and
Epictetus; they did me some good, but time has done more. I have
a dislike to all strong emotion, and avoid whatever could excite it;
a book like 'Werther' gives me now unmingled pain. In my own

[1] See Chap. I, p. 6.

writings you may observe that I rather dwell upon what affects
than what agitates.

He was suffering when he wrote from nervous disturbance
arising out of the same excitability that had made him a
Jacobin and produced *Joan of Arc* and *Robespierre*, and it was to
overtake him at last; he kept it at bay during his working life
by distraction and self-control, not by sublimation. As Coleridge
found refuge in metaphysics, he found it in reading. Miscellaneous information, welcome for its own sake and piled up in his
commonplace books and, with some contributions from Coleridge, who shared the same taste, in *Omniana*, could not become
poetry by the infiltration of factitious excitement and extravagant fancies: the Arabian Nights blighted the oriental as Ossian
did the Celtic. Worse: he did not learn Spenser's other lesson,
that however remote the imagery, the matter of poetry is
always contemporary.

Scott, a sound critic, saw how this inordinate pleasure in
reading was linked with a persistent fault in his prose work:
'Great as Southey's powers are, he has not the art to make
them work popularly; he is often diffuse, and frequently sets
much value on minute and unimportant facts, and useless
pieces of abstract knowledge.' Taylor had observed the same
weakness long before, and that in short poems where it is more
serious: 'If there be a poetical sin in which you are apt to indulge, it is expatiation, an Odyssey garrulity, as if you were
ambitious of exhausting a topic, instead of selecting its more
impressive lines only.' He knew it himself: 'Perhaps it is the
consciousness of a garrulous tendency in writing that impels me
with such decided and almost exclusive choice to narrative
poetry.' The short narrative poems also owed something to
Sayers and Taylor, who discussed with him what Sayers called
'monodrama', and 'ballad', a story-poem in popular verse and
style, too often merely anecdotal, and 'eclogue', by which
Southey meant not the worn-out Virgilian imitation, but the
sketch of manners as practised by Theocritus. These were to
come to fuller growth with the greater Victorian poets, who
were able to enrich without destroying the forms. If he had
exploited his gift of irresponsible fun—one almost says, more
seriously—he might have left more to be remembered; it was
in prose that he infused this gift into his letters, and into miscellaneous collections in that delightful and preposterous farrago

The Doctor; in verse he betrays the insecurity of the second-rate artist by the careful insulation between major and minor, and between poem and poem, which means that his whole self never went into any as Wordsworth's whole self went into the least thing he wrote, and that the materials he gathered were never subjected to the full heat and pressure that fuse them into one new substance as Coleridge fused his in *The Ancient Mariner* which he disliked so much. Southey built his long poems on sound and even noble morality: the expiation of past wrong in *Roderick*, the heroic exaction of retribution in *Thalaba* and *Kehama*, rising to tragic perception in the close of each. He can claim precedence in the adaptation from Ariosto and Spenser of the magic boat—

> The moon is bright, the sea is calm,
> The little boat rides rapidly
> Across the ocean waves;
> The line of moonlight on the deep
> Still follows as they voyage on;
> The winds are motionless;
> The gentle waters gently part
> In dimples round the prow.
> He looks above, he looks around,
> The boundless heaven, the boundless sea,
> The crescent moon, the little boat,
> Nought else above, below.

The Ship of Heaven sails in *Kehama*; and though Shelley made finer things of them, Southey made fine things of them first, and, like Shelley, made poetry of water:

> Wide spreads the snowy foam, the sparkling spray
> Dances aloft; and ever there at morning
> The earliest sunbeams haste to wing their way,
> With rainbow wreaths the holy stream adorning;
> And duly the adoring Moon at night
> Sheds her white glory there,
> And in the watery air
> Suspends her halo-crowns of silver light.

> On that ethereal lake, whose waters lie
> Blue and transpicuous like another sky,
> The Elements had rear'd their King's abode.
> A strong controuling power their strife suspended,
> And their hostile essences they blended,
> To form a Palace worthy of the God.

Built on the Lake, its waters were its floor;
  And here its walls were water arch'd with fire,
And here were fire with water vaulted o'er;
  And spires and pinnacles of fire
  Round watery cupolas aspire,
And domes of rainbow rest on fiery towers;
And roofs of flame are turreted around
  With cloud, and shafts of cloud with flame are bound.
Here too the elements for ever veer,
  Ranging around with endless interchanging;
Pursued in love, and so in love pursuing,
  In endless revolutions here they roll;
  For ever their mysterious work renewing;
The parts all shifting, still unchanged the whole.

Yet taking the poems as a whole, idea and image and inevitable intuition lie side by side: the thing and its meaning are separable. No poet since Dryden wrote such pure clean English so consistently: but the words do not dissolve the whole into rapture.

He had indeed small part in the new poetry. Though his name is inextricably connected with those of Coleridge and Wordsworth, it is by personal relationship rather than by community of ideas. That personal relationship has been sufficiently discussed and the tragi-comedy of the young men, so young and so ignorant of affairs and of themselves, left to themselves to mishandle their lives, need not be repeated. So far as poetry is concerned, Southey issued his declaration of independence in the 1837 Preface:

The advantage arising from intimate intercourse with those who were engaged in similar pursuits cannot be in like manner specified, because in their nature they are imperceptible; but of such advantages no man has ever possessed more or greater than at different times it has been my lot to enjoy. Personal attachment first, and family circumstances afterwards, connected me long and closely with Mr. Coleridge; and three-and-thirty years have ratified a friendship with Mr. Wordsworth. . . . When I add what has been the greatest of all advantages, that I have passed more than half my life in retirement, conversing with books rather than men, constantly and unweariedly engaged in literary pursuits, communing with my own heart, and taking that course which upon mature consideration seemed best to myself, I have said everything necessary to account for the characteristics of my poetry.

He reiterates his adherence to the late-eighteenth-century

tradition, writing to Bowles, 'Your poems came into my hands when I was nineteen and I *fed* upon them. Our booby critics talk of *schools*, and if they had had common discernment they might have perceived that I was of your school.' 'I agree with you entirely upon the invariable principles of poetry: We learned them in the same school, and I was confirmed in them in my youth by seeing them exemplified in your writings.' 'There are three contemporaries, the influence of whose poetry on my own I can distinctly trace, Sayers, yourself, and Landor.' He had reason to refuse Jeffrey's faggoting him with Wordsworth and Coleridge in 'the Lake School of Poetry'—all the more that his settlement at Keswick was none of his choosing, however well he resigned himself to it: when Coleridge died he wrote to Bowles, 'Forty years have elapsed since our first meeting,— and one consequence of that meeting has been that I have re-sided during the last thirty in this place, whither I first came with no other intention than that of visiting him.' During that crucial year 1797–8 he was staying mainly in London and Hampshire, in poor health, only half reconciled with Coleridge and certainly not admitted to the charmed circle. The man who mattered most to him at this time was the 'miraculous' Humphry Davy. *Lyrical Ballads* were as strange to him as to any other reviewer, and *Gebir*, a publication of the same year, both more accessible and more satisfying.

Southey drew the same kind of distinction in poetry that the painters drew in their art, between the 'eclogue' or *genre* and the grand or 'historical' creation that demanded elaborate construc-tion, notebooks full of information, and sustained objective effort of the imagination. He could not follow Wordsworth in the elevation of *genre* into major importance any more than Barry or Fuseli could countenance the elevation of landscape by Turner and Constable: nor could most people for another generation. So it is not surprising that he hailed Walter Savage Landor[1] as a congenial spirit on the appearance of *Gebir* in 1798. This young man brought a passionate imagination and a passionate apprehension of appearances to the service of an

[1] 1775–1864. Son of a doctor. Educated Rugby; Trinity College, Oxford, rusti-cated 1794. Lived Tenby, Swansea, Bath, Bristol. In Spain 1807–8. At Llanthony Abbey, Monmouth, 1811; married same year. After quarrels at Llanthony, in Jersey, and France 1814. In Italy 1815; Como, Pisa, Florence 1821–35. Separated from wife 1835. In Bath 1838–58, Florence till death, living poorly after transfer of estates to his son. See the next volume.

exotic theme and an enlarged conception of construction and style. We can understand too why Charles Lamb dubbed it 'Gebor aptly so denominated from Geborish, *quasi* Gibberish'. Into the framework of an 'Arabian' tale appended to Clara Reeve's *The Progress of Romance* (1786), a second-rate book by a third-rate novelist, Landor crowded reminiscences of the *Aeneid* (especially Book VI), the story of Hercules and perhaps Seneca's tragic version of it, the widespread folk-tale of building interrupted by supernatural forces which demanded to be placated, *Anthony and Cleopatra*, the excavations of the 1780's at Pompeii, the campaigns of Bonaparte whom Landor hated as fiercely as did Coleridge or Wordsworth. The scene is Egypt, but fortunately some fifteen years were to pass before Champollion published the collections of Bonaparte's team of savants, so that only a mention of the Mocattam Hills and casual references to crocodiles and asps give local colour or require annotation. The elaborate apparatus of decoration and allusion is drawn from the Greco-Roman literary tradition familiar to Landor, and therefore, he assumed, to his readers. These varied matters are strung on a double strand: the epic theme of Gebir, the warrior-king from Spain reconquering his ancestral land of Egypt and in love with its Queen, and the idyllic theme of his shepherd brother Tamar whom an enamoured sea-nymph transports—by a somewhat capricious route—through the Mediterranean to eternal bliss in south-western Spain. This comes to a full period at the end of Book VI where

with huge golden bar
Atlas and Calpe close across the sea:

then in the seventh and last book the reader is wrested back to Egypt and the destruction of Gebir by the queen's nurse. His biographer John Forster supplies a moral interpretation, the superiority of love and peace over war and conquest. Landor may have so intended it; few readers would light on it.

There are other difficulties. In his second *Imaginary Conversation* with Southey, Landor extols 'Invention, energy, and grandeur of design—the three great requisites to constitute a great poet, and which no poet since Milton hath united'. But grand conceptions require patience, reflection, and judgement in the working out, and these are just what Landor conspicuously lacked both in life and in art. In his *Imaginary Conversation* with

l'Abbé Delille he proclaims that 'In poetry, there is a greater
difference between the good and the excellent than there is
between the bad and the good. Poetry has no golden mean.'
He was ambitious of nothing less than excellence, which requires intense concentration for prolonged periods, and *Gebir*
is a series of immediate impulses, without the connexion that
carries on a tale or the construction that organizes diverse
matter into a unity that can be grasped and remembered. In
later years Landor confessed that in the attempt at concentration he had 'boiled away too much' of *Gebir*; but indeed the
process was not so much one of simplifying abundance as one
of scamping the less exciting labours of large-scale poetry. Scott
may have had Landor in mind when he wrote:

> Let any one cut out from the *Iliad*, or from Shakespeare's plays,
> every thing . . . which is absolutely devoid of importance and of
> interest *in itself*; and he will find that what is left will have lost more
> than half its charms. We are convinced that some writers have
> diminished the effect of their works by being scrupulous to admit
> nothing into them which had not some absolute, intrinsic, and in-
> dependent merit. They have acted like those who strip off the
> leaves of a fruit-tree, as being of themselves good for nothing, with
> the view to securing more nourishment to the fruit, which in fact
> cannot attain its full maturity without them.

Yet the reader who will yield himself to the recurrent impulses,
who is caught by the sharp precision of images that only accen-
tuate the uneven vagueness of the action, will agree with Lamb
that 'Gebor hath some lucid intervals', and understand how,
as late as 1831, Lamb, 'ever muttering *Rose Aylmer*', was
'always turning to *Gebir* for things that haunt him in the same
way'—such things, probably, as the couplet he quoted from
memory in a letter of 1824:

> In smiling meads how sweet the brook's repose
> To the rough ocean and red restless sands.

The same mind is at work in the tragedies. The legend of
Julian and his part in the Moorish invasion of Spain may have
suggested itself originally as a parallel to the French invasion:
Southey had the parallel in mind when he wrote his *Roderick*,
and it was the theme of Scott's *Vision of Don Roderick*. Landor's
impulsive excursion of 1808 in aid of the Spaniards gave him
some knowledge of the distraction of an invaded country as

well as of landscape, but the titles are significant. Southey thought first of the eighth century, Scott of the nineteenth, but their theme is patriotic resistance to an invader; in *Count Julian* Landor concentrated on the mind and feelings of the traitor and his personal motive of revenge for Rodrigo's betrayal of his daughter. He knew the Spaniards well enough to appreciate the force of the motive, and if he had known himself better he might have seen how much of himself he put into the figure of the magnanimous man trapped in the ruins made by his own furious impulse. Julian became his theme, a second Coriolanus. In a note appended to the first version of *Inez de Castro*, Landor wrote: 'Camoens . . . was not felicitous in the development of character; which, whatever may be talked of and repeated on the beautiful and the sublime, is the best and most arduous part of poetry.' But few readers will find much character in his own *personae*. They express mood and movement of feeling, but not the true development by which the reader comes to understand the moods or how they are proper and inevitable in the individual and produce the actions which make the thing a play and not something else. Landor's notion of economy is partly responsible, and his impatience. A solid tragedy cannot be 'conceived, planned, and executed in thirteen days', and a long series of afterthoughts is no substitute for organization, especially from an author who proclaims that 'My scenes fall in the natural order. What is *plot* but *trick*?'. Landor's plays, and especially *Inez de Castro* and *Hippolito d'Este*, are comprehensible only to a reader who knows the stories. Landor might retort that only such a reader is a 'fit audience', but a poem should carry its own explanations within itself. The full-length plays are not 'imitations of actions' but interpretations of the emotions accompanying passages in actions. Except that Landor presents linked series covering whole actions instead of separate passages from different actions, his method is near to that of Sayers. It is most successful in *Count Julian*, by reason of that portion of himself that is in the character, or in a simple action like *The Siege of Ancona*; in the long trilogy *Andrea of Hungary—Giovanna of Naples—Fra Rupert*, the interest lies in Landor's aristocratic-democratic politics and his inveterate anticlericalism. It was well that Landor discovered the Imaginary Conversation, where persons and actions can be referred to history books and the public press, and commentary is freed from the expectations aroused in the reader by full dramatic form. *Inez de Castro* is better in its original form (as printed among the Additional *Conversations*) than in the heavily textured verse of the later, and the short pieces are constrained dialogues.

All these poems, however, are concerned with people, and are informed with something of their author's stormy experience of human relations. The idyllic *Hellenics* do not catch the reader's attention as they should. Landor is seeking after a static beauty such as he found especially in Theocritus, but except in *The Hamadryad* where the emotions are comparatively violent, the effect is of surface decoration. As such, the *Hellenics* like the dramas contain admirable passages which no one but Landor could achieve; and we are led back to the problem of *Gebir*. The *Hellenics* were originally written in Latin, and *Gebir* was rewritten in Latin, in an attempt to overcome the criticisms it aroused. Why a Latin translation should answer that need is not clear; the difficulty is stifled rather than met by the new interest: but indeed it is an unconscious recognition of fact. From his schooldays at Rugby, Landor had written Latin verse readily and with pleasure. Something in him responded to the delights of adroit adjustment of words, phrases, and syllables, of effort after the stylistic compression and economy that seem to give Horace his precision and completeness of statement, Lucan his weight, Virgil his miraculous suggestiveness. Above all, the practice provided the tension, the delightful sense of concentration of his enormous energy, which he tried to attain in English also, and which generates the curious compulsive power of Landor at his best. It has its dangers. The more concentrated and continuous attention required in reading in a foreign language lends added importance, and sometime factitious value, to what one reads; and so also in writing. When this tension is removed in turning from the Latin to the English *Hellenics*, it is perceived to be adventitious; too much of the virtue is in the reader, as it was in the writer, and too little in the poem. Behind the non-lyrical poems—partly, no doubt, because there are too many of them, for writing became a habit and Landor was long-lived—there looms an imaginary form-master, setting the theme for the week, just as so much of Landor's criticism is that of a form-master scrutinizing lines and phrases, checking loosenesses and inaccuracies. We find ourselves reading in the same spirit, and relishing, very often, felicities for which we pin up his copies on such an honour-board as his Rugby verses hung on. It is just this kind of interest that Wordsworth tried to avoid—not always successfully, for we hoard the Lucy poems along with *Rose Aylmer* and two or three from *Ianthe*, not among the pearls which are perfect secretions but among the diamonds, the singular products of enormous pressures, cut by masters. It was this master, albeit 'in rattling vein', that maintained that Blake was 'the greatest of living poets' and '*Marmion* superior to all that Byron and Wordsworth have written'. Taking these things together, we can safely and happily return to the 'lucid intervals' of *Gebir* and the caverns of *Count Julian*.

Southey and Landor remained friends all their lives, despite extreme differences of temper and circumstance. There are few such tributes in poetry as Landor's to Southey, and we can believe them, because their subject is so clearly the same man that Carlyle—another violent nature full of contrary prejudices—describes in the Appendix to his *Reminiscences*. This sympathy, however, begins as that between two men who found they were working at the same thing separately, not that of two men who arrived at their ideas together. This is what happened with Coleridge[1] and Wordsworth.[2] They could disappoint one another as time went on, both as men and as poets, but their minds were once so united that neither is conceivable without the other. Their meeting seems fated, for they came to it by different roads.

We know more about the young Coleridge than about the young Wordsworth. From boyhood he was what Wordsworth

[1] 1772–1834. Ninth son and thirteenth child of the vicar of Ottery St. Mary, Devonshire, who died 1781. At Christ's Hospital 1782–90; Jesus College, Cambridge, 1791 to Dec. 1794, broken by enlistment in 15th Dragoons Dec. 1793 to April 1794. In Bristol with Southey Jan. 1795–6. Married Sara Fricker Oct. 1795; at Clevedon; at Nether Stowey Dec. 1796. Annuity from Wedgwoods 1798. Germany Sept. 1798 to July 1799; London, Sept. At Greta Hall, Keswick, 1802; tour in Scotland with the Wordsworths 1803. Malta 1804–6. Did not return to his family. In London, and on visits; at Highgate 1816 till death.

[2] 1770–1850. Born at Cockermouth, Cumberland, second of the four sons of an attorney, who died 1783. Educated at Hawkshead 1778–87, lodging in the village. St. John's College, Cambridge, 1787. B.A. Jan. 1791. In London; France Nov. 1791 to Dec. 1792; Racedown, with Dorothy, autumn 1795. Met Coleridge 1795 or 1796. At Alfoxden July 1797. In Germany Sept. 1798 to April 1799. At Grasmere Dec. 1799. Tour in Scotland with Dorothy and Coleridge 1801. At Calais Aug. 1802. Married Mary Hutchinson Sept. same year. Tour in Scotland 1803; met Scott. Distributor of Stamps for Westmorland 1813–42. Poet Laureate 1843.

called him, 'noticeable': he attracted attention, and responded
to it in conversation and letters with long and detailed descriptions of his intellectual, moral, and medical symptoms; and he
lived among boys and men of livelier mind than Wordsworth's
neighbours in Cockermouth and Hawkshead. They were moved
to record their vision of this fascinating, inspiring, infuriating
companion and had the gifts to do it. We know his physical
appearance, his slovenly dress, his abounding and inadequately
controlled vitality of mind and body, the lifelong habit of monologue that left so many hearers uncertain whether they had
been entranced or bored. Of Wordsworth we know what his
adoring sister told her girl friends; his nursing of Raisley Calvert
and Calvert's practical gratitude in an opportune legacy, and
the friendly offices of the Pinneys who housed him in Racedown, suggest a young man with good in him; but no friend or
acquaintance left any description of the young Wordsworth to
set beside the many descriptions of the revered old man of Rydal
Mount. There was nothing strange about him. He joined
naturally in the sports and amusements of his country neighbours so as to be accepted as just one of themselves; neither his
behaviour nor his academic promise would attract the attention
of college authorities for discipline or encouragement, and there
was little show of warmth in his personal relations. His friend
Robert Jones could have told much, but was never moved
either to assist the struggling poet to public recognition or to
claim reflected glory in the years of fame. Yet of the two,
Wordsworth, the less reckless and less enthusiastic, came the
longer way round to their meeting.

Debts, false starts, and plain folly make up most of Coleridge's
early history, alleviated by a lenient college and by intelligent
officers and tolerant comrades during that military episode
whose absurdity he acknowledged by enlisting in a dragoon
regiment as Silas Tomkyn Comberback. A schoolboy affair of
sentiment became serious only when he had made its future
impossible by engaging himself to Sara Fricker during the
mercifully brief fantasy of a communal settlement in America.
Then he was pinned down by Southey's nervous punctilio in
marriage. That marriage seems another false start, but for more
than two years he was quieter and, in spite of occasional short
journeys, more settled than ever before—or after, until premature
old age fixed him at Highgate—living in real affection with his

wife in the only home of his own that he had known since he
was nine years old. He was indeed maturing, but the stabilizing
influences of a household and the friendship of the solid Thomas
Poole assisted the process, and it was in the matrimonial
establishment that he produced poems in which we can
recognize for the first time the individual authentic voice of the
poet Coleridge—*To the Nightingale, The Aeolian Harp, Reflections
on Having Left a Place of Retirement.*

Wordsworth's undistinguished university career had been
unmarked by such positive follies or such bouts of scholarship
as Coleridge had indulged in, and when it was over he had
slipped away, evading the pressure of his uncles, the responsible
family trustees for whom he must have been a problem, to
engage himself in a profession. It is not surprising that a powerful, headstrong, unsophisticated young man, at a loose end
among strangers, in France where social and literary habit
assumed such relations as natural, should be entangled with a
young woman. The episode seems to have been a somewhat
commonplace affair, and it was wound up in conventional
fashion when circumstances permitted. Annette Vallon was the
elder of the two, and had the more experience of the world;
Wordsworth was neither sentimentalist nor philanderer: which
was the captor and which the victim may admit of doubt.
Wordsworth underwent a brief excitement, suffered the complications and accepted the responsibilities it brought upon
him. As one part of his first entry into independent society it
had its importance, but the precise effect is not so easy to estimate. No doubt there was regret and vexation, but we can
trace no symptoms of lasting contrition or afterlonging. Its main
effect was to make him suspicious of irregular passions, which
can disturb so distressingly the flow of individual and family
life. Even without the separation enforced by war, and allowing
that Dorothy's sisterly possessiveness discouraged brooding over
a strange woman who had intruded on a part of her William's
life in which she had no share—she alludes to Annette in letters
to her friends with no trace of feeling for any of the parties
concerned—the episode would have remained without sequel,
past and done with. None of the Wordsworth circle, among
whom it was no secret and who were not conspicuously reticent,
troubled about it any more than they troubled about the
paternity of their friend Basil Montagu; nor did anything in

the works of this most egotistical poet lead his innumerable commentators to make any such deductions as have been made from those of Spenser, Shakespeare, Milton, and a dozen others—not to mention professed womanizers like Burns and Byron—until G. M. Harper found the official records. If Annette Vallon had any marked character or personality, it left no trace in the poems; and if it had penetrated to the central core of Wordsworth's, he would have been unable to pass it off in the fanciful terms of *Vaudracour and Julia*. Still, this violent episode was a rougher introduction to adult life than Coleridge's sighing, however vehemently, after Mary Evans.

Southey and Coleridge, Coleridge and Wordsworth, could easily sympathize over politics. All three traced the common curve of 'ingenuous youth' from revolutionary enthusiasm to solid conservatism, but with characteristic differences. Southey's excitable temperament blew up his instincts of independence and responsibility into a generalized defiance of authority that took shape in *Wat Tyler*. Coleridge's facile emotions engaged him in whatever affair seemed generous and hopeful and stimulated the zestful exercise of his gifts of verse and rhetoric. When the two joined forces in Bristol they supported each other's antipathy to organized power in Church and State, but, as Coleridge told Sir George Beaumont ten years later, 'both Southey and I were utterly unconnected with any party, or club, or society'. Their idealism expressed itself in the limited— indeed negative—terms of Pantisocracy, and their lively interest in public affairs was that of the journalists they were, to some degree, by nature, for whom, however strong the bias or preference, the spectacle is more absorbing than the principle. Southey's ardour seems to have subsided with his visit to Spain. New intellectual interests, the acceptance of facts that independence and responsibility always prompted in him when excitement abated, the plain need to conserve energy to earn a living for his wife and himself when his Jacobinism lost him the fortune that might have been his, all wrought with the progress of events in France to turn a man in his early twenties, without catastrophe or much heart-searching, to the other side. Coleridge's emotional adventurousness lasted rather longer. *Fire, Famine and Slaughter* is good partisan brawling; on the wider scale, he told his own story even more clearly than he knew in *France: an Ode*, written in February 1798. The declamatory rhetoric of the second and third sections, all too reminiscent of such effusions as the *Destruction of the Bastille* which he printed in 1834, betrays the origin of much—though certainly not all—of his Jacobinism in

an ebullient fancy, a flowing utterance, a light and dancing heart, and a disposition to catch fire by the very rapidity of my own motion, and to speak vehemently from mere verbal associations, choosing sentences and sentiments for the very reason that would have made me recoil with a dying away of the heart and an unutterable horror from the actions expressed in such sentences and sentiments—namely, because they were wild and original, and vehement and fantastic. . . .

This might be construed as self-exculpation in writing to the sedate Sir George Beaumont, but its accuracy is attested in the *Apologetic Preface to 'Fire, Famine, and Slaughter'*, less by the turgid argument than by the innocence with which he tells the anecdote of its recitation by Scott, as an anonymous poem, in his presence at a dinner party in 1809, without an inkling that it was a joke at his expense: by now it was just one of his poems, from which everything had evaporated except the aesthetic qualities, which are those displayed in these sections of *France*. The fourth section states the cause of his change of mind, the invasion of Switzerland that disturbed Burns and Wordsworth and many another; but the first and last disclose a deeper reason, the new philosophic import of the concept of 'Nature', which he had played with under the influence of Bowles but was now occupying much more of his mind and was no longer an alternative theme to politics in his fits of versification, but unified with it in a larger concept. He did not hold this long, but he felt it then, and he owed it to Wordsworth.

Wordsworth, and he alone among major writers, saw the French Revolution at close quarters, and its effect on him was the more powerful that, unlike Tom Paine or Helen Maria Williams who had crossed to France out of political sympathy, he had gone with few prepossessions and small understanding beyond the common undergraduate fashion that lent him 'the guise of an enthusiast'. To him France meant 'delight and liberty', the grand experience of the previous July, when he and Jones happened to land at Calais just in time for the first *Fête Nationale* and the pleasure of the festival was superadded to that purest of youthful pleasures, the sense of the long summer and the long roads before them. It was only gradually that he learned the meaning of that festival from conversations with chance acquaintances, and only when his emotions were caught that his pleasure in it changed into something more profound and more active. The 'pleasant exercise of hope and joy' was broken by the realization of the cruelty and suffering involved in the revolutionary turbulence, which brought on the first access of nervous disturbance that was to afflict him all his life. What to Coleridge and the others were ideas for discussion and items in the newspapers, to Blake, emblems of spiritual process, were, for Wordsworth, things that happened in places he had seen, voices he had heard raised in argument and aspiration, the torment and the blood of men he knew and liked. The attempt to solve the discrepancy which Coleridge never perceived, to reconcile these grim realities with the intellectual concepts by which the theorists pretended to comprehend and direct them, defeated him. Meanwhile, he lacked occupation. His two poems, *An Evening Walk* and *Descriptive Sketches*, had to be seen through the press, but they were finished. The democratic cause commanded his support, but he had neither political connexions nor political aptitude—

> Little graced with power
> Of eloquence even in my native speech
> And all unfit for tumult and intrigue.

His mind was too slow and too stiff for journalism either in prose or verse. The scheme for a political journal sketched in letters to his Cambridge acquaintance Francis Wrangham, and the attempt at a modernized version of Juvenal after the Johnsonian model, were ill-judged and short-lived. Wrangham settled down in the Church, to become an enlightened book-fancying archdeacon; Wordsworth had to find something he could do. Friends tided him over the immediate problems of food and lodging, but could not save him from black depression and nervous collapse.

The lucky coincidence of Calvert's legacy and Dorothy's coming of age—released from tutelage of the uncles who had kept them apart and mistress of her share of the Wordsworth patrimony—with the Pinneys' offer of Racedown Lodge, made it possible to cut free. The intellectual problems were no nearer solution; they were deliberately shelved along with the problem of Annette and his financial obligations to relatives. Racedown gave him what his physical conformation required— quietness, wide spaces, and exercise in all the winds of heaven; and, with these, a little mild clerical occupation about the property in lieu of rent. Above all, he found with Dorothy something in which he could have absolute faith, a love that brought peace and confidence instead of storm and trouble. Yet from that disastrous initiation in the active world there remained with him an exaltation too great to be destroyed, too precious to be lost even if it were left only in the memory, so strong that if its immediate occasion had to be slowly and reluctantly abandoned, some greater and remoter cause must exist to justify it.

The sign of recovery was that he was writing poetry again. It was not easy, though he was trying things more within his competence than heavy satire. *An Evening Walk* and *Descriptive Sketches* had been honourable efforts by a young man who had read his Milton, Thomson, Young, Cowper, and so forth, and had looked at scenery for himself. The labour of transferring his visual memories, with the reflections demanded by the landscape tradition, into formal couplets to the length of 446 and 813 lines was salutary exercise. The later revision of the *Sketches* shows what he found wrong. The pruning of over-crowded detail, affected epithets, and cold personifications was a matter of matured technique in writing. To cut out borrowings from l'Abbé Delille, whom he had read in France as he wrote the first version, meant a return to the original, Thomson, but, much more, confidence in himself. A more important and significant change was the replacement of the common Goldsmithian convention of the 'remote, unfriended, melancholy, slow' Traveller by more truthful emotion:

> But doubly pitying Nature loves to show'r
> Soft on his wounded heart her healing pow'r
> Who plods o'er hills and vales his road forlorn. . . . (1793)

> And plods through some wide realm o'er vale and height
> Though seeking only holiday delight. . . . (1849)

> Renewing. . . . Our various journey, sad and slow. . . . (1793)

> With a light heart our course we may renew. . . . (1849)

The damping down, in the later version, of the revolutionary optimism of the first was less candid, but it cleared away some crude rhetoric and brought the poem nearer to a unity. Most of the things that make his poetry lay in *Descriptive Sketches*—visual impression, personal feeling, public interest, literary ambition —but they lay separate, impure and fragmentary. The new labours at Racedown did not produce a new formula; they seemed at the time to produce very little, but if the crop was small the tillage was useful.

Wordsworth learned from his struggle with *The Borderers*. Dramatic form can help a man who is wrestling with ideas, even if he knows little of the theatre, but the ideas must have some consistency, and his changed as he worked. He had 'yielded up moral questions in despair' because he required complete conviction, which must rest upon permanent fundamentals which he could not discover in his books. Godwin's display of logic had promised the comfort of finality—that is the strength and weakness of logic—but Wordsworth was losing interest in Godwin. The figure of Oswald in *The Borderers*, as it emerges from the interesting essay in which Wordsworth sums up what he found in his mind as he worked, is close to that of Falkland in *Caleb Williams*, but the other themes, based on emotional rather than moral phenomena, were bulking larger as he went on, and were seen to lie deeper in human nature than the diagrams of Godwin's social mechanics. Worse, dialectic was not for him. Wordsworth was like his own cloud that 'moveth all together if it move at all'. He could not set one part of himself working against another part to produce a result. Dramatic form, therefore, was less useful to him, all the more that it made its own demands as one of the Kinds whose discrimination and definition, worked out by Renaissance critics, had been so long accepted as to be taken for granted. The critical doctrines that had guided Spenser and Milton and trained their readers only hindered a man who had to find his own way. The abandonment of *The Borderers* was the abandonment of the dominant critical tradition: with all his ambition he never contemplated Epic.

The other occupation of those years was more in his direct line. Both *An Evening Walk* and *Descriptive Sketches* contain an incidental image which was to persist for years: the vagrant woman and children in the former, in the latter a more conventionally picturesque gipsy. A hasty guess might see Annette

Vallon in the forsaken woman, but the image is primarily
visual, involved not only in the recollection of earlier experiences but in images occurring elsewhere, and paralleled by
other recollections of human figures met by chance on the
roads, including the 'hunger-bitten' girl whose appearance
precipitated his fluid emotions into belief in the Revolution.
Apart from the irrelevance of vagrancy and hard weather to
Annette, the correlative idea is not that of unlicensed passion.
In other variants, *The Mad Mother* and *The Complaint of the
Forsaken Indian Woman* in which it vivifies an anecdote from
Hearne's *Journey*, the theme is maternal love; catching up a
well-worn scrap from Langhorne's *Country Justice*—which in
turn suggests that the original experience may have been reinforced by sight of Bunbury's engraving which so affected
Burns—it carries also a political implication, elaborated in *The
Female Vagrant* which after an intermediate stage as *An Incident
on Salisbury Plain* was hammered out with much labour and
alteration as *Guilt and Sorrow*, to be laid aside as unsatisfactory
until 1842. The variants of this, the second abortive attempt at
Racedown, show Wordsworth attempting to develop his image
into significance by combining it with a story like some that
Thomas Hardy was to pick up in the same neighbourhood
seventy years later, heightening that with melodramatic coincidences, and then learning how much complication he could
handle without hindering the development of emotion and
argument—or rather, how little, for he learned now to strip
his story of circumstance as he stripped it of rhetoric.

From these apparently abortive efforts he found that

> The moving accident is not my trade;
> To freeze the blood I have no ready arts,

and, by habit rather than design, let his poems henceforth grow
out of something seen, and often a figure, or two figures, in a
landscape. One other poem of 1795–7, *Lines left upon a Seat in a
Yew-Tree*, looks back to the time and scene of *An Evening Walk*
and like that poem contains what the ambitious failures lack,
the solvent conception of beauty. These were his occupations
when, just as each was arriving separately at his full stature,
a masterstroke of fortune brought him and Coleridge together.
Coleridge indeed had published little of value, and less that
suggested any diversion from the habits and techniques in

vogue. His friends Southey and Lamb, and some lesser men, could do that sort of thing about as well as he could. Cuthbert Shaw, Thomas Russell, Charlotte Smith, had written better sonnets, and indeed there is an occasional clear chime of phrase in those of Lamb which might come—without imitation —from the crisper rhythms of his favourite Burns, while Coleridge was immersed in Bowles, which did not compensate by any force or variety of style for the soft self-indulgent strain it encouraged in him. If we recognize something of Coleridge in *The Destiny of Nations*—for which the incentive came from Southey—and the slowly compiled *Religious Musings*, it is only after grappling with much diffusive declamation and unassimilated lumps of philosophical erudition: the merely journalistic efforts are almost a relief. Yet at Clevedon he began to find himself, and at Nether Stowey he was ready to meet Wordsworth.

Theirs was a wonderful companionship of two men of abounding genius each having qualities the other lacked, and one woman who, without their creative power, possessed in overflowing measure, by gift of nature and through unconditional response to the elements around her, the beginning and end of their search, love and joy. Wordsworth, slow of comprehension and slow of utterance, was uplifted by the fluid swiftness of Coleridge's mind; Coleridge, all too rapid and tangential, was steadied by Wordsworth's tenacity of apprehension and patient determination to work out the precise expression of his thoughts and feelings. Coleridge had the erudition, wide reading in philosophies, and critical discipline learned in a strict school and based on classical precedent; Wordsworth the brooding insight, the direct approach, the firm grasp of basic realities that buttressed his independence. Power was in each, mutually recognized, and equal power, so that neither could dominate and neither sink into discipleship. Together, their power was multiplied like that of opposed blocks in a tackle; when they separated, each was incomplete.

Which of them contributed any particular element to the endless discussions of those ecstatic months neither could have decided afterwards with any certainty. Their statements of conclusions—Wordsworth's in the 1800 Preface to *Lyrical Ballads* and Coleridge's *Biographia Literaria*—do not agree. Neither is more authoritative than the other, but Coleridge was writing in 1817, and by then his main interest lay in philosophy. Also he was, by now, critical, whereas Wordsworth had been explanatory. We may assume that, however personal some of his developments, Wordsworth wrote the Preface on the basis of the discussions of 1797-8, and that the main conclusions—or at least the dominant themes—are resumed in his leading statement: 'The principal object, then, proposed in these Poems was to make the incidents of common life interesting by tracing in them, truly though not ostentatiously, the primary laws of our nature: chiefly, as far as regards the manner in which we associate ideas in a state of excitement.' Wordsworth would hear a great deal about Coleridge's views of the manner in which we associate ideas. Coleridge had been an enthusiastic adherent of the Associationist doctrine as developed by David Hartley to account for all mental process—its attraction may have been its double appeal to his speculative habit and to the interest in physiology he had caught from the medical studies of his brother Luke. With equal enthusiasm he had accepted the necessitarianism to which the theory forced its adherents, for determinism, however arrived at, has a conclusiveness attractive to people at certain stages of development. By 1798, however, the speculative side of his mind, developed by wide reading in metaphysics, asserted itself against this mechanistic conception, and his other interest, poetry, now strengthened by the influence of Wordsworth, demanded some explanation of the phenomena of artistic creativeness. In revising the Preface in 1802, Wordsworth filled out the statement quoted above from the edition of 1800. The principal object now

was to choose incidents and situations from common life, and to relate or describe them, throughout, as far as possible in a selection of the language really used by men, and, at the same time, to throw over them a certain colouring of imagination, whereby ordinary things should be presented to the mind in an unusual aspect; and further, and above all, to make these incidents and situations interesting. . . .

The rest follows as in 1800. Here enter the technical considerations essential to any sound discussion of any art, and the concept of imagination, a faculty as distinct from a mechanism of the mind. The distinction and definition of Imagination and Fancy, on which Coleridge worked so long and hard, seems at first sight a side-issue, but it is a line of attack that presents

itself in the course of criticism. We do observe the difference
between a novel and a yarn, comedy and farce, tragedy and
melodrama, and can enjoy and criticize them without confusing
them; though whether the difference is one of degree or intention or taste remains obscure. Wordsworth also worked over the
same ground, but, like the practical artist he was, carried the
argument no further than was useful to himself. Whether it is
worth carrying further is arguable. For Wordsworth, the value
of the discussion—apart from its forcing him to think, which
was always good for him—lay in its opportunities for meditation
on the nature and significance of poetry. For Coleridge, it
opened up wider issues. The notion that man is an aggregate
of Faculties can be carried to absurd lengths; yet in plain fact
some people can do things that other people cannot, and noticeably in the arts. However dubious and tedious Coleridge's
later theoretical analysis—or invention—of faculties 'esem-
plastic', 'coadunative', and so on, his speculative argumentation
about the nature and significance of poetry—the art he did
know something about—led to consideration of the originative
activity of the individual mind; and in discussion of technical
problems, the inevitable occurrence of such terms as 'to choose
incidents and situations', 'a selection of language', implies
freedom, at least within limits. Thus through the theory of the
arts he was assured of the autonomy of the individual mind
before he read Kant and long before he began to understand
him.

Having escaped from the necessitarian dogma, Coleridge
was soon damning Hartley, Associationism, and everything
bearing any relation thereto, with his usual enthusiasm. Wordsworth had never subscribed to the Associationist system—he
was not easily persuaded into systems—but the fact of associated
ideas, one of the commonest of experiences, was very present
to him, and the theory was useful to him because it supplied,
if not an explanation, at least a reasoned statement of the inter-
relation of different internal processes—perception, feeling,
thought, and so on—and their results as he found them inter-
related in himself. The phrase 'the manner in which we associate ideas' might be ominously suggestive of Hartley, but in
fact it is a convenient device by which to refer to the phenomena
of human activity comprehensively and without suggesting any
primacy among them. For practical purposes of study and

argument it is convenient to separate sensuous and intellectual cognition, will and impulse, reason and intuition, moral and aesthetic judgement, emotional and judicial opinion, and so on indefinitely; but it is impossible to arrive at any conclusion along one line without violence or self-coercion. Such a conclusion never satisfies except as a feat of mental athletics, and in broad and complex questions we reach our conclusions by the conscious or unconscious exertion of the whole self. In the cultivation and application of this total exertion in order to apprehend and project the total experience, the theory of association was useful to Wordsworth since it made him aware of many of his own processes, and awareness gave him some appreciation of them and therefore a measure of control. Further, with a little pressure the theory authorized the extension of felt relationship beyond the individual as having real existence not to be explained as accidental entanglement in the individual mechanism, and it legitimized some of the habits of observation, thought, and feeling which, since he depended on them and deliberately built upon them, may be summarily designated his 'philosophy'.

This concentration of the whole being was not unprecedented. Mark Akenside had gone a long way towards the unification of all the modes of activity within the single act. With a cast back to Plato, but basing his argument on Shaftesbury and Addison and Hutcheson's doctrine that 'the moral sense' and 'taste' are analogous powers operative one in matters of behaviour as the other in aesthetic matters, he found the agent of union in Imagination and the measure of success in Pleasure, the arts being the modes of commemoration, and Nature, created and informed by the Supreme Being, in some undeclared way the sovereign interest. Thus *The Pleasures of the Imagination* could be read as a rough prospectus of the new school; but Akenside argued in generalized terms after the manner of his time and his ideal was the cultivated deist, whereas Wordsworth had had enough of generalized argument and synthetic ideals, and the Supreme Being recalled too much of the artificer of a Newtonian universe, now degraded by Parisian ceremonies. The fundamental conditions of the good life must be common conditions independent of circumstance and contrivance. Having little knowledge of music or painting or architecture and having the habits of a countryman, he accepted all too wholeheartedly the cult of Nature. On the other hand, his ear and eye were acute and in continual exercise. The cult of nature was based, not on a taste for sentimental retirement but on the perpetual delight of things heard and things seen. This cannot be over-emphasized. The external world existed—as Gautier said it must exist for the artist—and the 'things' and 'goings-on' perceived by the vigilant senses were indissolubly associated with the ideas and feelings which originated within the individual: 'nature' included both; and what that meant was a mystery not to be explained in terms of one or the other.

Leaving aside those shifting and elusive discussions, it is time to examine their outcome, the *Lyrical Ballads, with a Few Other Poems* published in 1798. Of the twenty-three anonymous poems, four are Coleridge's, all recent, *The Foster-Mother's Tale* and *The Dungeon* being excerpts from his tragedy *Osorio*, refused by Sheridan but reasonably successful at Drury Lane in 1812 in its revised form *Remorse*. Wordsworth's nineteen poems are a mixture of old and new. *Lines left upon a Seat, Lines written near Richmond* belonging to the days of *An Evening Walk*, and *The Convict*, a piece of melodramatic gloom probably from the dark winter of 1792–3 and wisely omitted from the second edition, presumably constitute, along with the excerpts from *Osorio*, the 'other poems'. Of the Lyrical Ballads proper, *The Female Vagrant, The Mad Mother*, and *The Forsaken Indian Woman* have been mentioned as belonging to that turn in the poet's development that occurred mainly at Racedown, *The Thorn* contains the image of the forlorn woman associated with a natural place-image in Wordsworth's peculiar manner, and *Old Man Travelling* a visual image less developed, part of the image developed in *The Old Cumberland Beggar* but close to *The Sailor's Mother* written in 1802; the rest represent the full growth of the poet's mind reached at Alfoxden. Two poems are singled out by half-titles, *The Rime of the Ancient Marinere* and *The Idiot Boy*, which suggests that they had special significance, for the other half-title, to *The Indian Woman*, is a somewhat clumsy way of setting out an explanatory note. Of the remaining pair, the *Lines written a few miles above Tintern Abbey*, the last poem in the volume, was an addition to the original plan; the other was certainly an afterthought, for a unique copy, once Southey's and now in the British Museum, contains both Coleridge's

Lewti and *The Nightingale* which replaces it in all other copies, and two contents-pages with corresponding entries. Thomas Hutchinson gave as a reason for the cancellation that *Lewti* had been published in *The Morning Post* that April, and though it appeared over a pseudonym its authorship was well enough known to betray the secret of the experimental volume which, like that other experimental volume which inaugurated a new poetic era, *The Shepheardes Calendar*, was strictly anonymous. There may have been other reasons. The appearance of a blank page after *Lewti* in Southey's copy might be due to a technical failure in the making-up of the type or to an earlier change of mind; also *Lewti* is a rehandling by Coleridge of a schoolboy poem of Wordsworth's, *Beauty and Moonlight*, and whether Wordsworth entirely approved of the fanciful elaboration of his lakeland poem into a Circassian Love-Chant we do not know.

Whatever happened, *The Nightingale* is not only a much better poem, but an example of one of Coleridge's two ways of poetry during the part of his life in which he deployed for the first and last time the full equipment of a great poet. For both ways he was indebted to Wordsworth, and in both he showed powers which Wordsworth did not possess. *The Ancient Mariner*, with *Kubla Khan* and *Christabel*, is a mystery of the Muses. Mr. Livingston Lowes mapped the country round the Road to Xanadu brilliantly, and better than Coleridge himself would have done it, but how the road was opened is beyond exposition even in Coleridge's most ingenious word-coinage. In the words of Davenant, '*Wit* is not only the luck and labour, but also the dexterity of thought, rounding the world, like the Sun, with unimaginable motion; and bringing swiftly home to the memory universal surveys.' *The Ancient Mariner* was conceived as a joint enterprise, but once the unimaginable motion began only one wit could continue with it. Wordsworth supplied a suggestion or two and a few lines: his main contribution was his habitual assumption that a piece of work once begun would be carried through. When Coleridge was alone or disturbed by unhappy relations with other men, his endurance was unequal to his wit, and *Christabel* and *Kubla Khan* remained unfinished. The two Wordsworths, however, gave also the lively sense of 'things' and the habit of seeing them. The greatness of these poems lies in their being free exercises of the imagination working in a

medium of clear concrete images. In their earlier works Coleridge had wrought in words and Wordsworth hampered himself
with literary clichés. Now Wordsworth had learned, and taught
Coleridge, that 'things', not general notions, are the essentials
of life, and that, therefore, images of things, not abstract termi-
nology, are the appropriate medium; that in the desperate
battle to express the complex of associations the key to the situation is the 'thing' round which associated thoughts and emotions
cluster. This is the new way of the new school.

It is a powerful and dangerous way. The image evoked in
the reader's mind may satisfy him so as to remain an end in
itself, as has happened to Dyer's *Grongar Hill*, or it may provide
a pleasure separate from the theme like the decoration of an
illuminated page separate from the script, as happens in Tennyson. Wordsworth was all too conscious of this danger, but less
concerned about the danger that a lively image may stir up
associations irrelevant and even inimical to the type of association desired by the writer. Both in writer and in reader the
image is a centre of energy, but of energy precariously controlled. The energy of a symbol is limited by its range of
reference and the reader's transference to the concept for which
he knows it stands. Wordsworth was never a symbolist: the
desolation of Salisbury plain, the alpine terrors, are integral to
the image of the forlorn vagrant, not mere settings or correla-
tives; the beauty of his beggars is inseparable from the mirth
and freedom he prizes even in the absence of moral or social
values. So also the images of *The Ancient Mariner, Kubla Khan*,
and, to a lesser degree because of the poem's general association
with the ballad tradition, *Christabel*, call up 'things', not symbolic references, but 'things' so remote that no reader's mind is
diverted into irrelevant associations or tempted to stray out of
the group of images with which Coleridge presents it; and these
images are so sharp, and so complete in themselves, that the
mind is satisfied with the energy they distil. It may have been
this self-containedness that made Southey dislike *The Ancient
Mariner* and Wordsworth hesitate over it. The orderly mind of
Southey could not receive it into any section of its encyclopaedia, and for Wordsworth it was too remote and too much a
mere artifact. He had had his dreams, but in the introduction
to *Peter Bell* which he was writing at that time he renounced
uncharted flights for the sake of this our earth and its people.

He did not deal in miracles; fortunately for us, Coleridge did. Unfortunately, the magician who steps outside his magic pentagon cannot step back. To say that *Christabel* and *Kubla Khan* are the more miraculous for lacking conclusion is intelligible but sentimental: they 'play tricks with the mind', as Charles Lamb said of *The Ancient Mariner*, but I should like to see more of the tricks they played with Coleridge's mind, which is more interesting than mine.

The other poems of Coleridge's wonderful year are not miraculous, but that does not degrade them: they are different in kind, not in degree. The striking thing about them is their sheer competence. There is no better-conducted poem in the English language than *Frost at Midnight*; and one cannot conceive of that poem, or *The Nightingale*, or *This Lime-Tree Bower my Prison*, in a fragmentary or uncompleted state. Between his own household, the companionship of the Wordsworths, and the neighbourhood of Thomas Poole, Coleridge found an anchorage, temporary but real, among things of earth, the goings-on of living beings around him, and the quietness of the Quantock country. Here only could he feel himself

> The humble man, who, in his youthful years,
> Knew just so much of folly, as had made
> His early manhood more securely wise.

The mood of the time can be caught by comparing *Fears in Solitude* with the *Ode on the Departing Year*, a poem on much the same political theme but couched—though it is a good example —in his old declamatory style, and ending in negation and— the danger-signal—in a pseudo-elevated rhetorical close:

> I unpartaking of the evil thing,
> With daily prayer and daily toil
> Soliciting for food my scanty soil,
> Have wailed my country with a wild Lament.
> Now I recentre my immortal mind
> In the deep sabbath of meek self-content;
> Cleansed from the vaporous passions that bedim
> God's Image, sister of the Seraphim.

The poem of sixteen months later ends with the landscape of Nether Stowey

> Where my babe
> And my babe's mother dwell in peace

and with a positive relation to the world and men—

> all my heart
> Is soften'd, and made worthy to indulge
> Love, and the thoughts that yearn for human kind.

It was in this mood that he was able to look outside himself at the things the Wordsworths taught him to see, to fuse them with his thoughts and feelings into the unity he admired in Wordsworth, and to re-create that unity in poems by strength of what he in his turn taught to Wordsworth, the constructive 'inner logic' which he had learned in Christ's Hospital to be an essential condition in the making of poetry.

The organization of *This Lime-Tree Bower* is comparatively simple, being topographical. The sense of place is admirable: neither the movement of the walkers round Alfoxden nor the immobility of the poet in his Stowey garden usurps the attention of the reader so much as to allow him to lose the relation between them, until they are unified in the close by the sunset and the last rook. The scheme is worked out in concrete images intensely visualized, varied in scale but, being almost entirely images of light and plants, relevant to one another as in their places. The tender emotion lapses only once into the old self-pity in the reference to

> Friends, whom I never more may meet again

which is somewhat extravagant in association with a seven-mile stroll on a June day; but the lapse can be ignored. *Frost at Midnight* uses fewer aids: cold, silence, moonlight outside the cottage, the fire in the room which supplies an association to lead the poet back to his childhood, thence to his hopes for the baby at his side, and the return to the first image—the repetition of the phrase 'secret ministry' a trifle over-emphatic but the full close perfectly managed. *The Nightingale* is called 'A Conversation Poem' so that we may not expect such close articulation. Like all good conversation it is far from desultory, but the transitions are less carefully contrived and there is no circling back to give a formal unity that would be inappropriate here, where the scheme is the progression of talk, not a situation. The nightingale fills the pause before the friends part after their evening walk; the thought of going home brings the thought of the child, a brief restatement of the hopes expressed in *Frost at Midnight*; and 'farewell' makes an easy and natural ending. These poems, and *The Ancient Mariner* with all its shifts and turns, are true compositions, not 'effusions' such as he had indulged in. The same control returns in *Dejection* and *To a Gentleman*, the two poems in which, four years later, he looks back to this best part of his life. Indeed the comparison of the first and final versions of *Dejection* shows how an intensely personal effusion became a more intensely poetical composition by closer organization of the significant images, more equable verse, and firmer structure. It seems as if the exercise of his craft relieved the present stress of emotion and enabled him to regain control; but the intermediate version in which the ode is addressed to Wordsworth instead of Sara Hutchison shows not only the discreet masking of his hopeless love-longing but how the recalling of the Alfoxden days revived by association the skills he had then pursued in company with his brother poet.

Wordsworth's mark is clear on the poems of 1797–8, technically in the reform of Coleridge's early verbalism, still more in his enthusiastic acceptance, for the time being, of the doctrine that the good and happy life is to be sought among natural things and not among human inventions whether physical or philosophical. The measure of it is clearest in the contrast between *To the Nightingale* printed in *The Poems* of 1796 and *The Nightingale* written in April 1798, the disappearance of sentimentality and of the awkward jocosity which Coleridge always mistook for humour, the finer style and conduct, and the recantation—emphasized by quotation in both, to different effect, of Milton's line 'most musical, most melancholy bird'— of the literary commonplace echoed automatically by poets from Ovid to Cuthbert Shaw. The nightingale is now 'joyous' like Wordsworth's green linnet and the nameless birds of *Lines written in Early Spring*. By April 1802, when he wrote *Dejection: an Ode*, Coleridge had changed his mind. Having parted with the Wordsworths he had lost the trick of observation, and all that remained was his old habit of watching the sky. Wordsworth never lost his 'faith that every flower enjoys the air it breathes', for it was grounded on his experience and habits, built up by innumerable associations, and essential in his philosophy of nature. Among the many connotations of that elusive term 'Nature' three are prominent in the tradition of eighteenth-century English poetry: the theoretical Popian Nature which by this time was dying even among painters;

the sentimental Nature—'sentimental' in no derogatory sense—
which afforded quiet retirement to contemplative or wounded
souls, occasional in Thomson, at its best in Cowper, sporadic
among many lesser poets, and handed on by Bowles to young
Coleridge; and the stronger and purer philosophical Nature of
Thomson at his best, of Akenside's none too conclusive thought,
of Wordsworth by 1798, and of Coleridge during 1797–8 only.
In Coleridge it was a passing enthusiasm. It just touched *The
Ancient Mariner*, appeared as the future kindly nurse of the
'babe' of *Frost at Midnight* and *The Nightingale*, ominously and
unconvincingly in the heavy-handed *Dungeon* where it adds
more non-dramatic padding to *Osorio* and *Remorse*, still more
ominously in the ascription to Charles Lamb—of all people—
of his new-found cult—

> thou hast pined
> And hungered after Nature, many a year,
> In the great City pent.

Lamb was not insensible to country enjoyments, but his regret-
ful memories of 'the green plains of pleasant Hertfordshire' are
more concerned with his 'wanderings with the fair-haired maid'
than with any absorption, either emotional or thoughtful, in
Nature as Wordsworth knew it and Coleridge thought he did.

In *Dejection* Coleridge denies—to put it in such terms as he
affected—that 'joy' coheres in objects and declares it to be a
state—apparently an unconditioned state—of the subject in
which the perception of certain objects is a pleasurable activity.
The statement is primarily emotional, but Wordsworth in his
most melancholy moods was incapable of such a phrase as 'that
inanimate cold world'. For him there was no question of subject
and object, for subject and object—himself and his natural
surroundings—were one within a greater unity which is the
theme of all his poetry and the centre of his contemplation.
At Alfoxden he reached a position he was to occupy, with little
addition and less modification, all his life, and he set it out in
the last of the Alfoxden poems, made after *Lyrical Ballads* was
consigned to its publisher Cottle but too important, as a sum-
ming up of the whole content of the volume, to be omitted, the
Lines Written a Few Miles above Tintern Abbey . . . July 13, 1798.
It might be said, without too much exaggeration, that Wordsworth spent the rest of his life expanding, glossing, commenting
upon that poem. At this point it is most apposite to note the

extension of the doctrine of man and nature to lengths to which
Coleridge could not follow him.

> These beauteous forms
> Through a long absence, have not been to me
> As is a landscape to a blind man's eye:
> But oft, in lonely rooms, and 'mid the din
> Of towns and cities, I have owed to them
> In hours of weariness, sensations sweet,
> Felt in the blood, and felt along the heart;
> And passing even into my purer mind,
> With tranquil restoration.

We recall *I wandered lonely as a cloud* and the daffodils that

> flash upon that inward eye
> Which is the bliss of solitude,

and how

> The immortal spirit of one happy day
> Lingers beside that rill, in vision clear

and observe the importance and value of Association. The next
lines are bolder, though the idea is advanced tentatively, for
they relate the vestigial pleasure retained in the memory with
action, which involves ethics—

> feelings too
> Of unremembered pleasure: such perhaps
> As have no slight or trivial influence
> On that best portion of a good man's life,
> His little, nameless, unremembered acts
> Of kindness and of love.

'Feelings of unremembered pleasure' means states caused by
past occasions of which the precise detail and lineament has not
recurred to consciousness: thus 'joy' is not innate or unconditional in the mind or feelings, nor does it end in pleasant
perception. The next section, lines 35 to 48, is, logically, less
difficult. It relates to the same cause a state which Wordsworth
describes directly as an experience. Like other statements of
the same nature in his poems it cannot be reasoned about; but
it is not a unique experience. If the reader comprehends it, he
comprehends it. And it is his ability to state such experiences
so completely and convincingly, in such direct and irreplaceable
terms, that is the final vindication of Wordsworth's right to be

numbered among the very greatest of the poets. A later passage
may have troubled Coleridge even more, as it has troubled
many another.

> And I have felt
> A presence that disturbs me with the joy
> Of elevated thoughts: a sense sublime
> Of something far more deeply interfused
> Whose dwelling is the light of setting suns
> And the round ocean, and the living air,
> And the blue sky, and in the mind of man;
> A motion and a spirit, that impels
> All thinking things, all objects of all thought,
> And rolls through all things.

This again is not peculiar to Wordsworth. To call it 'Pantheism',
the recognized title of a systematic philosophy, is to throw it out
of perspective. If it is to be traced back through other men's
statements, it must be, as always with Wordsworth—with all
but a few English thinkers—through the poets: Akenside,
Thomson, and from the Hymn that closes *The Seasons* back to
the Pythagorean Hymn, always allowing that for each in his
time it was a new and personal revelation, not taken on trust
from any teacher or priest however it may have been corrobo-
rated or formulated in the tradition. In this passage Wordsworth
comes nearest to religion; and, to Coleridge's regret, is farthest
from Coleridge.

Coleridge's religion lay always within the bounds of Christianity as Wordsworth's did not, but, given that each had powerful instincts of piety, reverence, love, the deeper difference
between them was that between the metaphysician and—the
word is used for want of a better—the artist. Coleridge found
faith in theological disquisition. That was his mode of ascent,
and his turnings and returnings on the way of religion as on the
ways of love are those of his suggestible and self-convincing
temperament. At the age when a man has to examine his
beliefs and rebellion comes naturally, he found Unitarianism
canvassed and condemned at Cambridge, and so became a
Unitarian. Later, he argued himself out of Unitarianism into
orthodoxy and out of his Jacobin anticlericalism into belief in
the Church of England as a vital religious organism; and all
this without catastrophic conversion but by the continual working of his subtle intellect over his emotions and his learning.

It is doubtful whether Wordsworth understood or even followed his reasonings. The crucial passage just quoted from *Tintern Abbey* is the climax of a summary recapitulation of his experience up to 13 July 1798, and the spirituality it enshrines is a simple percept, to be understood without any mediacy of argument or erudition and inseparable from the aesthetic, emotional, and moral percepts with which it is associated. This is his plainest and most philosophical statement, formalized no doubt by a year's contagion with the logical mind of Coleridge but not thereby more accurate or more lucid than the many restatements less completely rectified from the physical percepts within which the experience occurs. It is Wordsworth's distinction that he could state such experiences directly, without recourse to literary or ecclesiastical commonplaces, in the vision of the mountain after which

> My brain
> Worked with a dim and undetermined sense
> Of unknown modes of being . . .

the sense of presence—

> for there is a spirit in the woods. . . .

or the more common sensation on the moonlit fells when

> I heard among the solitary hills
> Low breathings coming after me, and sounds
> Of undistinguishable motion, steps
> Almost as silent as the turf they trod. . . .

—which makes Coleridge's use of it, however appropriate in its place, seem almost vulgar 'Gothicism'—

> Like one, that on a lonesome road
> Doth walk in fear and dread
> And having once turned round walks on
> And turns no more his head;
> Because he knows, a frightful fiend
> Doth close behind him tread.

Such experiences have been stated in terms of Pan and the nymphs—the fear and fascination of the solitudes—and, in later ages, of trolls and—before Shakespeare and Drayton killed them—fairies. They had such power in Wordsworth's mind that he could not retain the aesthetic purity they have at first. He had freed 'Nature' from the sentimentalism of the

eighteenth century, but in these intense moments 'Nature'—
or the 'Wisdom and Spirit of the universe', for they become
indistinguishable—assumes the associated emotions as attributes.

> The Being, that is in the clouds and air,
> That is in the green leaves among the groves
> Maintains a deep and reverential care
> For the unoffending creatures whom he loves.

The spirit might be separated from the 'things' but for the
forcible use of the absolute verb 'is'; yet even later, when
Wordsworth had moved from paganism to Christianity, and the
spirit is understood as the Christian God, it is not divorced,
still less contrasted, and least of all set in an adversative aspect.
After 1839, in a retouch to the last revision of *The Prelude*, he
reverted to eighteenth-century orthodoxy:

> Wonder not
> If such my transports were; for in all things now
> I saw one life, and felt that it was joy.

> Wonder not
> If high the transport, great the joy I felt
> Communing in this sort through earth and heaven
> With every form of creature, as it looked
> Towards the Uncreated with a countenance
> Of adoration, with an eye of love.

This might descend from Addison's planets:

> In Reason's ear they all rejoice
> And utter forth a glorious voice,
> For ever singing as they shine
> 'The hand that made us is divine'.

But even at the end of the *Ecclesiastical Sonnets* that record his
return to the Church he sees Christ himself in physical terms
that might be taken from a late Turner:

> The Power who came
> In filial duty, clothed with love divine
> That made His human tabernacle shine
> Like Ocean burning with a purpureal flame;
> Or like the Alpine mount, that takes its name
> From roseate hues, far kenned at morn and even,
> In hours of peace, or when the storm is driven
> Along the nether region's rugged frame!
> Earth prompts—Heaven urges. . . .

The statement in *Tintern Abbey* is explicit. It is implicit, and
not easily discernible by many readers, in *The Idiot Boy*, which,
marked out by its separate half-title, would have been Wordsworth's major contribution to *Lyrical Ballads* but for the afterthought of *Tintern Abbey*. The relation of the two poems lies in
their both being works of art. *Tintern Abbey* is easier, because
the theme arises out of a landscape such as we have been
taught to regard aesthetically—taught, that is, by John Dyer,
Thomson, Turner, Constable, and Wordsworth himself, to
contemplate with all our powers awake, thought and emotion
together. In *The Idiot Boy* it has to be disentangled from social
circumstance, the associations and values of which the reader
imports habitually into any tale about people, and has to be
accepted as Wordsworth felt it, as another example of 'external
nature and the great moving spirit of things' comprehended by
the same disinterested aesthetic activity. The human feelings
are simple: neighbourliness, mother-love, the boy's elation,
anxiety, and relief. The circumstances are slight, and have no
consequences. The whole occurs within a setting which is pure
delight—to be alone on the hills, moonlight, and the owls calling,
all isolated and intensified by the reduction of the boy to a
mere existence. In this the poem began, and the pleasure of it
is the imaginative solution of natural emotions in natural surroundings—the 'music of humanity' and the music of nature in
one strain.

That phrase 'the great moving spirit of things' might translate the first of the Six Canons of Chinese painting; appropriately, since for a European the study of Wordsworth is the
best preliminary to the study of Chinese art, just as a reading
in Blake is a good preparative to looking at Indian; and usefully,
since it may remind us that in defining Wordsworth's religion at
this stage we must not identify religion with Christianity any
more than with theology. It takes much effort to comprehend
the elaborate dignity of Confucian ethics, the metaphysics of
Buddhism, the imaginative fantasy of Taoistic vitalism; but
when, walking alone through the rice-fields, one comes across
a foot-high shrine of dried clay, and in it some oddly shaped
stone with burnt-out incense-sticks before it, one can easily
share the farmers' instinctive sense of the divinity of earth and
the processes of earth, the divinity without which the earth
would be dead and we dead with it. The stone is only a stone,

but it is set up in the field corner as a recognition of that perva-
sive spirit through which—or Whom—everything has its being.
Wordsworth was always seeking to erect such signs of recognition. Elaborate reasonings or fantastic adventures would not
suit. The signs had to be natural and simple, found, not constructed; signs, not symbols which require specific knowledge
and the interposition of the intellect. If they had little form or
comeliness, so much the better. The mother and her idiot son,
the mindless creature lost on the hillsides; the blind child
triumphantly afloat; the sailor's mother with the birdcage; the
cuckoo, the lesser celandine, the old Cumberland beggar:
around these, and so many more, he built his poetic shrines of
native clay, with just so much contrivance as would make them
hold together. The religion may be primitive, but any viable
religion must have some portion of it, and the simplicity and
the humility of the shrine may be preferred at times to the
overpowering complexity of a great temple; and in its stillness
and unity the stone that betokens primal being may mean more,
in certain moods, than Blake's symbolic asseverations of primal
energy.

Within its shrine the token may often have a peculiar beauty.
That beauty only reinforces its power of reference, for the earth
is beautiful and the spirit benign; but, though chosen for some
quality by which it arrests the eye, it must not satisfy by mere
prettiness or curiosity. If it be ingeniously or charmingly sculp-
tured, the danger is that we may prize it for its ingenuity and
charm and not for its significance. This Wordsworth understood only too well. His reasons, as given in the Preface to the
later editions of *Lyrical Ballads*, for choosing his examples from
humble life are entirely legitimate: any artist is entitled to use
such material as he can handle best and as is most convenient
for his own purposes. The choice of rustic life can be allowed
him for the same reasons, even if in his doctrinaire statement
he is at the mercy of his own inveterate and, some might say,
overvalued associations. This over-emphasis, however, distorts
the technical discussion that follows. The basic principle of his
selection of language is logical enough; it is the ancient principle of 'Decorum': as his purpose was 'to trace the primary
laws of our nature', he had to reduce style to common terms.
For the sake of the theme he had to free the matter of his poems
from the habits and customs of London, Cambridge, and Lich-

field, so he had to free his mode of expression from the habitual and customary styles prevalent in such places. His argument is very dubious, and, as Coleridge showed, his notion of language was inadequate. Revolt against the fashions of the older generations is to be expected in a strong mind, but this was more than the normal impatience of the young enthusiast. Wordsworth had just struggled through the conflict between his own experience and the arguments developed within their eighteenth-century political traditions by the older generation, in the course of which he had been forced to discard their intellectual formulas in order to grapple with naked facts. His was not a mere change of taste, but a radical replacement: in style as in thought he tried to get back to the fundamentals. Like every other artist, he had to learn his trade, and he made it harder for himself by refusing the aids the unthinking use of which, as he now saw, had marred his early work. He tried the common story-teller's trick of the imaginary narrator in *The Thorn*, the imaginary audience in *Peter Bell*, and dramatic monologue in *The Indian Woman*. In *Expostulation and Reply* he found a more natural way, speaking in his own voice as in *To My Sister*, or as the first person in an imagined situation; for here the occasion, the 'conversation with a friend who was somewhat unreasonably attached to modern books of Moral Philosophy'—probably Hazlitt, as Hutchinson suggests—is happily reconstructed by combination with an apposite reminiscence: an excellent example of his notion of the function of imagination. In these we hear the Wordsworth in whose conversation Carlyle 'found that no man gave you so faithful and vivid a picture of any person or thing which he had seen with his own eyes'.

This kind of practice taught him more than all his sociological arguments with himself. His opinions on verse grow from the same desires. Any poet who claims that his language and style represent those 'really used by men' saddles himself with the difficulty of explaining why he distorts them by metre. Wordsworth offered the weakest of all possible justifications in his contention that verse is a mere regulative mechanism 'super-added' to thought, emotion, and language in the making of a poem. It might be ignored but for its use as a clue to some of his awkwardness—and thereby a provocation to Coleridge to write some of the best pages of *Biographia Literaria*. Wordsworth could have quoted the excellent examples of Dryden and Pope. If he had read them in the proper spirit he might have become better aware of the value in his own poems of the same tension that Dryden exploits to serious purpose in *Religio Laici* and Pope to humorous and emotional ends in the *Epistle to Arbuthnot*, the tension induced by playing off informality of style against the formality of verse. Dryden and Pope, however, were gods of the gentiles, not to be invoked by Wordsworth. The residual beliefs that survived the intellectual crisis of 1793–5 might be not entirely irrelevant, if not greatly helpful, to the consideration of style and language, but what had the moral and political philosophers to do with versification? Wordsworth was divided against himself. His instincts were right, but his theoretical realism fought with his genuine feeling for language, each in turn gaining control and thus producing the 'inconstancy of style' of which Coleridge rightly complained, and by an illegitimate extension in reason, though by a natural consequence since the feeling for language and the sense of rhythm are inseparable, inhibited his fine feeling for sound. His native austerity is not in question—his most memorable passages gain by it—but his fear that the pleasure it is his duty to give his reader might be adventitious pleasure and therefore harmful to his purpose. He was indeed extremely sensitive to sound, delighted in 'the sounding cataract', in echoes, and bird-song and the noises of the wind and water, and—the ultimate test— in silence and the delicate indefinable sounds that thread the silences. He was fifty-eight when he wrote *The Power of Sound* and thought it one of his best. In that poem he has to touch on music, but can only fall back on Pythagoras. The pleasures it celebrates run through all his poems from first to last, and so does the deficiency apparent in it, for Wordsworth's other references to music are almost entirely literary. In *The Power of Music* the popular jig-measure is manifestly appropriate, but appropriate to the street rather than the dance itself, since he uses it also for the companion street-scene *Star-Gazers*. The jig is only one of the street noises; he does notice it, but he is never happy in such metres. We may well ask of the Solitary Reaper 'Will no one tell me what she sings?' for no echo of a highland air comes through to us. In these earlier years he might have dismissed music as a sophistication of natural pleasure, but in fact he had little opportunity for that intimate knowledge of music which might have woven it into his web of associations.

He was born on the wrong side of the Pennines and the Solway
to receive any real body of local song in his birthright, his
family does not seem to have had the habit of singing or playing
instruments, and he lived all his life isolated from musical
society, without a friend to interest him in music as Sir George
Beaumont interested him in pictures. Thus when, retailing the
conventional catalogue of the Kinds of poetry, he notes 'The
Lyrical:—containing the Hymn, the Ode, the Elegy, the Song,
and the Ballad: in all which, for the production of their *full*
effect, an accompaniment of music is indispensable', the emphasis on *full* implies a reservation. He did not feel the need of
it in his own: when describing 'the powers requisite for the
production of poetry' the power of organizing sound for the
purposes of expression appears only in a footnote added twenty-
one years later: 'As sensibility to harmony of numbers, and the
power of producing it, are invariably attendants upon the faculties specified, nothing has been said upon those requisites.' Yet
the physical realities of sound are as inherent in his art as those
of line and colour in Blake's; and just as he kept retouching the
language of his poems in successive editions, so, according to
Carlyle, 'When he spoke of poetry he harangued about metres
and so forth.' In these early days he might not harangue about
it, but it is through the power of the rhythms—the placing of
the long syllables—that we are satisfied with rudimentary
images in such a verse as this

> There is a blessing in the air,
> Which seems a sense of joy to yield
> To the bare trees, and mountains bare,
> And grass in the green field.

So also in the *Ode: Intimations of Immortality* the argument may
not convince, but consolation and reconciliation come clear to
us in the splendid rhythms of the last stanza. He does not con-
descend to discuss the cultivation of the faculty of producing
harmony, but the faculty was there; and the poets whose
phrases haunted his mind are the musically instructed poets,
Spenser, Milton, Gray.

As Coleridge said, it was when he forgot his theories that he
wrote best—when, as a competent and complete artist whose
faculties and experiences all converge in one creative act, he
worked like Kuo Hsi's ideal painter 'with eyes unconscious of

silk and hands unconscious of brush and ink . . . with utter
freedom and courage'. This state he achieved in 1798. *The Idiot
Boy* 'was composed in the groves of Alfoxden, almost extempore
. . . in truth, I never wrote anything with so much glee'. 'No
poem was composed under circumstances more pleasant for me
to remember than' *Tintern Abbey*, made in four days and 'not
a line of it was altered, and not any part of it written down till
I reached Bristol'. Much more was done then, and though
he was not so uplifted as to imagine it was all easy or perfect—
he kept *Peter Bell* by him for twenty-one years—he had made
himself and stood master. The same elation possessed Coleridge,
with results less uniformly happy. Having changed his ways in
poetry, he could not refrain from damning his old poetic creed
as he damned religious and political creeds he discarded; unfortunately the errors he parodied in *Sonnets Attempted in the
Manner of Contemporary Writers* were not all his own. This, and
other exhibitions of tactless superiority of which the details are
fortunately lost, estranged Southey, antagonized his quondam
collaborator Charles Lloyd[1] who, though a poor creature, was
not worth the inveterate hatred Coleridge conceived for him,
and, worse, alienated Charles Lamb. The relation between
Coleridge and Lamb[2] had been that of the Christ's Hospital
Grecian and his admiring junior who submitted perforce to the
editing and alteration of his contributions to *Poems on Various
Subjects*, 1796 and 1797, not without protest and not without
reason, for the lesser genius had the better taste, and in these
small things taste is essential. In the tragic hours of Mary's
frenzy and his mother's death, Coleridge's letters had brought
comfort and were rewarded with devotion; but these events,
and the resolution with which he faced them and the dark
future he foresaw, also matured Lamb's character so that their
relation became less unequal. Lamb was soon criticizing more
profoundly and with greater assurance. In his sorrow he had
renounced poetry, and though the mood did not last long, he
turned to prose in the curious rudimentary novel *Rosamund
Gray*, a shadow of Richardson with a flavour of Henry Macken-

[1] 1775–1839. Lived with Coleridge 1796–7. A difficult person who became insane later in life.

[2] 1775–1834. Born in London. Educated at Christ's Hospital 1782–9. Clerk in
South Sea House 1789–92; in India House 1792–1825. Visited Coleridge at Nether
Stowey and met Wordsworth 1797. His sister Mary (1764–1847) stabbed her
mother while insane 1796, and was subject to recurrent fits ever after.

zie, of no great importance, but exemplifying that limpidity of style shown in his early verse and never lost even when he played with mannerism in later years. In the June of 1797 he visited Nether Stowey; early in 1798, in loneliness of spirit, he wrote his best-known poem *The Old Familiar Faces*, and he was still in need of delicate handling when, probably through the mischief-making of Charles Lloyd, things went wrong. The lofty moral tone and the insufferable Christian charity of Coleridge's letter—if it was ever sent—might be offence enough, but the provocation must have been great that roused Lamb to strike so savagely with his *Theses Quaedam Theologicae* in May 1798. There was perhaps no time for the breach to be healed before Coleridge and the Wordsworths sailed for Germany in September; it lasted for nearly two years, and when it was closed for ever, Lamb was still admiring and affectionate, but independent. *This Lime-Tree Bower my Prison* appeared in Southey's *Annual Anthology* for 1800, and 'your satire upon me' aroused some touch of the old irritation. Lamb was not flattered at being addressed in public as 'my gentle-hearted Charles'; he was too shrewd to enjoy the faint patronage with which participation in Coleridge's newly acquired enthusiasm for Nature was ascribed to him, and the condolence for city up-bringing felt by Wordsworth for Coleridge transferred by Coleridge to himself, and with it something of the spiritualistic inflation he had criticized four years earlier. By now he could carry it off with a humour that indicates his freedom; but the whole estrangement sheds an unhappy light on Coleridge's state of mind: he was far from having learned the humility he professed, and that Lamb had enjoined upon him time and time again.

II

Whether his ten months in Germany did Coleridge much good, apart from his learning the language, is a difficult question. Certainly the Wordsworths' eight months' sojourn was neither comfortable nor profitable, but for them it was less important. They had to live somewhere, Dorothy only wished to be with William, and William was still working off the poetic energy generated at Alfoxden, embarking on the great philosophical poem he had planned with Coleridge—or which Coleridge had laid upon him as his task in life—by writing parts of what was to become *The Prelude*, and also composing some lesser pieces and notably the 'Lucy' poems which commentators have found so enigmatical. Lucy has been identified as a boyish love, as Mary Hutchinson whom he was to marry, as Dorothy; it is most probable that in surroundings which had no associations for Wordsworth, and were not so attractive as to induce associations, his imagination—the combining faculty as Coleridge defined it—was for once working freely. Something of boyish memory, of his ripening love for Mary, of Dorothy, went to the creation of Lucy; and, since Lucy was imagined as dead, possibly a subconscious echo of the love that had died, his love for Annette; but also the memory of a song *Lucy Gray* by a Carlisle poet, Robert Anderson (1794), about a girl who was loved but died young. It is their imaginative isolation that gives these little poems their purity, free of time and place and personality. That independent activity was different from the power that went into the autobiographical poem that was to be his greatest, to take six years of work and forty more of intermittent revision. The weakness of the theory of associated ideas, and the danger of it when assumed as practical method— which is what it meant to the practical artist Wordsworth— is that everything depends on the past. That is the justification of *The Prelude* and the meaning of the title: the poet was to give an account of himself before imposing on the reader any philosophical system he could construct. Wordsworth did it magnificently, but by that very process trained himself out of independent intellectual habit and out of that mysterious creativeness we call independent poetry, of which the Lucy poems, like *Tam o' Shanter, The Ancient Mariner*, and *Proud Maisie*, are examples. Back among the familiar sights and sounds of Grasmere, Wordsworth could never get away from himself and recover that independence. It is not a thing to complain of, for splendid things were to come by the other way, but it leaves the Lucy poems in a different category from the rest.

For him the German expedition was an episode; for Coleridge it was an end and a beginning—the end of his wonderful year of poetry, the beginning of a new philosophical direction and of his unhappiness. His experience of a household of his own was too short—some 14 months at Clevedon and 21 at Nether Stowey—for him to learn to live in it, for the small

duties and daily responsibilities to become habitual and easy
and thus to provide the training in the acceptance of duty and
responsibility which he badly needed. Sara Fricker was not the
woman to train him, but the Wordsworths did not help her.
Moral judgements are out of place at this late date; the historical fact is that Coleridge's affection lasted, perhaps increased
by absence that authorized the emotional luxury of homesickness—for any emotion makes a morbidly introspective person
like Coleridge more interesting to himself—but once he had
resumed the homeless existence to which he had been accustomed since childhood the slender filaments were broken and
could not be re-knit. Also he found in Germany interests which
the Wordsworths missed. During four months in the University
of Göttingen he studied—a truly Coleridgean curriculum—
Germanic philology, physiology, and theology, and in various
places he collected material for a book on Lessing, a work for
which no man was better fitted. The urge for poetry was gone.
The only original poems he wrote in Germany were expressions
of his homesickness, and only the *Lines written in the Album at
Elbingerode* contain anything of interest. The view from the
Brocken demanded commemoration; but though the memory of
Tintern Abbey provides the formula, Coleridge is no longer
thrilled by 'things':

> I moved on
> In low and languid mood: for I had found
> That outward forms, the loftiest, still receive
> Their finer influence from the Life within.

The 'Life within', however, is merely the personal emotions
associated with things seen, and no advance on Dyer's rumina-
tions in *Grongar Hill*. It is interesting that Coleridge's homesickness breeds patriotic feeling, like Bruce's at the source of
the Nile, but generalized. On the other hand, while he does
not deny Wordsworth's concept of the spirit, he restricts it to
humanity and to orthodoxy—

> nor will I profane,
> With party judgment or injurious doubt,
> That man's sublimer spirit, who can feel
> That God is everywhere! the God who framed
> Mankind to be one happy family
> Himself our Father, and the World our Home.

The allusion to *Tintern Abbey* and the anticipation of *Dejection* are obvious. For practice in the language, he translated a dozen German poems, of no consequence. It was after his return that he translated the first two of Schiller's three plays on Wallenstein, a commission from Longman—who lost heavily on it—and a cause of many groans, though he looked back upon it afterwards with some complacency, not unjustified. The most notable result of his readings in German poetry appeared in 1802, the *Hymn before Sun-Rise, in the Vale of Chamouni*. As Mr. H. W. Garrod says: 'It is to be noticed that Coleridge says far less in the [*Lines written in the Album*] about the Brocken, which he *had* seen, than in the lines on Mont Blanc about that mountain, which he *never* saw.' The original impulse, however, came from an ascent of Scafell on 5 August 1802. He tells that very minor poet Sotheby, 'I involuntarily poured forth a hymn in the manner of the Psalms, though afterwards I thought the ideas, etc., disproportionate to our humble mountains.' This means no more than that the impulse was powerful and was such as could best transfer itself in poetry, but not powerful enough to 'give importance to the action and situation'. The force that brought the experience of Scafell into being, gave it direction and form, was a poem by one Friederike Brun, which Coleridge translated, expanded, and vastly improved. He was better able to write about Mont Blanc because he had never seen it: of Scafell there remained a general sensation, free from insistent detail; Friederike Brun's Thomsonian effusion gave him the inspiration of words, an inspiration more potent than 'things' could give him, and a medium more plastic and more native to him than the bare images that sufficed for Wordsworth. The fusion of a visual experience and a verbal experience—the sight of Scafell and the reading of Friederike Brun's poem— inspired a splendid piece of writing; no further emotion is involved, and the thought goes no further than any eighteenth-century religious poet might have taken it. It was a psalm that Coleridge 'poured out' on Scafell—Psalm 148 is the relevant model. The *Hymn* is none the worse for that, but it contradicts what he was impressing on Sotheby in a letter written at the time with the same experiences in mind. Criticizing Bowles, whose limitations he has at last discovered, he goes on:

Never to see or describe any interesting appearance in nature without connecting it, by dim analogies, with the moral world proves faintness of impression. Nature has her proper interest, and he will know what it is who believes and feels that everything has a life of its own, and that we are all *One Life*. A poet's heart and intellect should be *combined*, intimately combined and unified with the great appearances of nature.

This was Wordsworth's creed, now recalled to his mind by renewed contact; he did not believe in it when he wrote the *Lines written in the Album*, and it does not appear in the orthodox *Hymn*. In fact he was uncertain of the authority of poetry itself. In the second edition of *Lyrical Ballads* he called *The Ancient Mariner* 'A Poet's Reverie', as if to warn the reader against taking it too seriously; and that rambling piece *The Picture*, made by the same process as the *Hymn*—memories of the Scafell expedition crossed with memories of Gessner's prose-poem *Der Erste Schiffer*, which he despised but which Sotheby was urging him to translate—with all its neat decorations, comes from the surface of his mind.

His mind indeed was too much distracted for any serious work. The book on Lessing, which might have been a solid base for future thinking, was forgotten, if it was not already lost, in a brilliant idea:

If I do not greatly delude myself, I have not only *completely extricated the notions of time and space*, but have overthrown the doctrines of association, as taught by Hartley, and with it all the irreligious metaphysics of modern infidels—especially the doctrine of necessity. This I have *done*; but I trust that I am about to do more—namely, that I shall be able to evolve all the five senses, that is, to deduce them from one sense, and to state their growth and the causes of their difference, and in this evolvement to solve the process of life and consciousness.

So it was to continue all his life, one project starting up so brightly that it seemed consummate and only awaited time or health or freedom for the mechanical business of writing it down; and being obliterated by a new project. Among these the completion of *Christabel* was prominent, but since poetry demanded even more exertion of all the faculties, and even more continuous attention, it was even more hopelessly sunk in moral failure. The passage quoted, however, contains hints of other complications. The idea seems reminiscent of Erasmus Darwin's biological theory of the unitary origin of life; but Darwin was dismissed as a materialist, and Coleridge's explanation was metaphysical or psychological. He never distinguished

between the two studies—in which he was probably right in
the end—for his method was purely introspective. Self-analysis
was his strength, and over-indulgence in it was his weakness. If
he had indeed been reading Darwin's *Zoonomia* he would find
in the medical section not only a wide selection of pathological
symptoms but also prescriptions which invariably included
opium. Exactly why and when Coleridge began to take opium
is of little importance. Like Burns, he suffered from rheumatic
fever early in life and never freed himself from the sequels and
the palliatives, and suffered more torments from the latter than
from the former; also, having been interested in his brother
Luke's medical course, he studied his ailments with assiduity,
examined his body as he examined his mind, and experimented
with both. Self-doctoring is proverbially foolish, and unregu-
lated curiosity worse: he wrote to Thomas Wedgwood, a confirmed drug-addict, with dangerous zest, 'We will have a fair
trial of *Bang*—Do bring down some of the Hyoscyamine Pills,
and I will give a fair Trial of Opium, Henbane, and Nepenthe.'
Wordsworth was right: body, mind, emotions, and morals are
interwoven first and last; he proved it in poetry, Coleridge by
exemplifying the fact that playing tricks with one spells weakness and suffering in all. There we may leave the wretched
subject.

There were other distractions. The need of Wordsworth's
moral and intellectual support took him to Greta Hall near
Keswick. Bickering with his wife drove him from it. If Sara
Coleridge had been accepted by the Wordsworths, still more
admitted into the circle of Dorothy's intense but narrow affections—which no woman was, except childhood friends and the
family—she would not have been unworthy; and she would
have added a touch of comedy that might have done them
good, even if William might not share Southey's enjoyment of
the *Lingo Grande* in which she anticipated James Joyce. She had
a shrewd enough mind of her own—if she had been a fool or
a trollop the situation would have been easier—and too much
spirit to sustain the role which Coleridge required of her more
in the fashion of Milton than of one who, he said, sought only
love. It was not so much his wife that vexed him as the con-
straints of household living. Pressing Southey to live at Greta
Hall, he wrote,

Loved and honoured as you will be, by some very good and

pleasant people at Keswick, I should be sorry that such impressions should be blended with the feelings, which your brother will inspire not when he is by himself, but from his disrespectful and unbrotherly spirit of thwarting and contradicting you. Indeed, I cannot help saying that I have not for a very long time met a young man who has made so unpleasant an impression on my mind.

Southey and his sailor brother Tom were on the best of terms and constantly helpful to one another; Coleridge, who was on no terms at all with his brothers, did not recognize normal brotherly behaviour. The final distraction, and the one that matters now, since it brought him back to poetry, was his love for Mary Hutchinson's sister Sara whom he met in 1799. Fortunately, or unfortunately, Sara Hutchinson, a steady warm-hearted north-country woman like her sister, did not return his love. If she had, it would have given her a claim on Coleridge, and that would have been fatal. As it was, it involved Coleridge in no obligations and made no demands on him, but remained like his old love for Mary Evans, *desiderium*, love-longing, the stronger for its impossibility, the more to be cherished that it was confined within that endlessly interesting object of inspection, himself. Thus the great love-poem addressed to her was easily rearranged as a confidential address to Wordsworth, because it was about neither of them, but a piece of self-analysis. Something has been said about *Dejection: An Ode*. The relevant passage here is stanza VI. 'Fruits and foliage, not my own, seemed mine' can only be an acknowledgement of his debt to Wordsworth, for he was a good enough critic to realize that his poems of 1797–8 were different from anything he had written before, and better, and his letters at this time were full of Wordsworth's praise. The rest of the stanza reflects his uncertainty as to what he should be doing, poetry or metaphysics, and the recognition that his poetic powers were waning, that in any case the loss of 'joy' meant that the emotional content of poetry could be only painful whereas intellectual activities, which did not involve emotion, could be continued. The obscurity of the passage must be felt even in the attempt to understand, for the obscurity is caused by his distractions and they are the most prominent things in his life at the time.

His life from his return from Germany in July 1799 until he settled down in the care of Dr. Gillman in April 1816 was indeed one long uncertainty. The one positive occupation was his return to journalism for the most positive of reasons, the need to earn his living. Coleridge professed journalism in two capacities: as projector of his own periodicals, *The Watchman* in 1796, containing political and miscellaneous articles in prose and verse, and *The Friend*, mainly philosophical and critical, in 1808; and as miscellaneous contributor mainly of verse from 1797 until he went to Germany and thereafter till 1802 as what in a modern office might be called leader-writer, on *The Morning Post*, and casually in *The Courier* about 1808–11, under Daniel Stuart, the most competent and most tolerant of editor-proprietors, and his strictly businesslike partner Street. Both employments broke down for the same cause. Coleridge's confidence in his own powers was not balanced by any aptitude for business, and that weakness was intensified by his lifelong failing, the nervous resentment of any kind of tie to person, place, occupation, or time-scheme. He had many qualifications: interest in public affairs, penetration, a fluent pen, occasional liveliness so long as he did not attempt humorous epigrams—if he had not had possibilities Daniel Stuart, who knew his business, would not have engaged him on easy conditions at a good salary—but as Stuart said, 'He never could write a thing that was immediately required of him. The thought of compulsion disarmed him.' In *Biographia Literaria* Coleridge lamented that he had 'wasted the prime and manhood of my intellect' on the newspapers. He exaggerated the quantity and importance of his contributions; but he wrote better under Stuart's eye than in his own periodicals. *The Watchman* contains some good violent prose; *The Friend* is heavier, more involved, and duller. Poole helped him out in *The Morning Post*, Wordsworth in *The Friend* with an Essay on Epitaphs as heavy as the tombstones from which it came; Southey collaborated in *The Devil's Walk*, the most noticed and only remembered contribution to *The Morning Post*, just as in 1796 he had done in *The Fall of Robespierre*, a hurried catchpenny half-way between Drury Lane and Fleet Street—for if Wordsworth steadied Coleridge, Southey energized him. The prose piece which Stuart notes as attracting attention was the Portrait of Pitt, hard hitting at the time, in short straight newspaper sentences, but valueless afterwards by reason of its monotonous negation, for Coleridge hated Pitt as he hated Mackintosh, Bonaparte, Hazlitt. There is more warmth and dignity in his rebuke to Charles James Fox for appearing at Bonaparte's levées in Paris in 1802, for both motives and feelings are more varied and better natured. But it is not there that we look for Coleridge. We can find more of him in the lectures, for, as Stuart found, 'though he would talk over everything so well . . . he could not write daily on the occurrences of the day', whereas in lecturing he could improvise as in conversation, and often had to, through failure to prepare, so that he could be dull, or repetitive, or extremely brilliant, disappointing or exceeding the expectations of such good friends as Crabb Robinson who attended with trepidation, and delighting or perplexing or annoying the general public.

When we return to Wordsworth the old contrast becomes almost tiresomely obvious. The pursuit of poetry, and the theme of human life within a natural environment, sufficed for this single-minded and determined character. In Germany he had worked out the last of his variations on the image of the forsaken woman in *Ruth*; as he had to combine it with exotic detail borrowed from Bartram to produce a deliberately contrived tale, the visual image was evidently fading. On his return, the question was whether he should settle in Coleridge's countryside or Coleridge in his. The instinct to seek inspiration in his native region—and probably Dorothy's addiction to familiar places and people—led him to Grasmere, and he never lived more than five miles away in the fifty years that remained to him. Here he found stories to embody 'the primary laws of our nature' among people whose motives and emotional habits he understood, and scenes appropriate in their simplicity and satisfactory in their austere beauty. The characteristic poems are *The Brothers* and *Michael*, both written in 1800, the latter the best handled of these 'eclogues', plain and quiet in style and verse, and completely realized. He still drove on with the great work, but the force that had carried him on since 1797 was abating somewhat, and he read widely and usefully in Chaucer, Drayton, Daniel, Milton, and the English poets at large—he was never erudite like Southey, but, like most poets, was well read. By 1802 he had generated a new supply of poetic energy: in March he wrote the first four stanzas of the *Ode: Intimations of Immortality*, in May, *Resolution and Independence* and the *Stanzas Written in . . . Thomson's Castle of Indolence*. The first two were written by the moody creature described in the last-named. The elation of *The Idiot Boy* and *To My Sister* had subsided, and the balance between the delight of external beauty and the sobriety bred of his experience of humanity—which is the theme of *Tintern Abbey*—seems disturbed by his melancholy. These first sections of the *Immortality* Ode have nothing to do with immortality but repeat, in a heightened lyrical style enriched by his recent reading, the statement in lines 65–85 of *Tintern Abbey*. He was thirty-two, he had come through much, had come to terms with life and himself, had written what he knew were good poems, and had arrived in a peaceful settled home: a lament over the lost joys of childhood seems ungrateful; but this arrival was an end as well as a beginning, like that other long ago and clouded with the same melancholy—

> Loth to believe what we so grieved to hear,
> For still we had hopes that pointed to the clouds,
> We questioned him again, and yet again;
> But every word that from the peasant's lips
> Came in reply, translated by our feelings,
> Ended in this,—*that we had crossed the Alps.*

The paragraph that follows these lines in *The Prelude* contains much of the same mood and thought, though differently orientated. It is the melancholy of achievement, such as made Walter Scott, gazing on that best-loved scene in the moonlight at a gay dinner-party in his new Abbotsford, call on his piper to play *Lochaber No More*. Wordsworth did not know quite what it meant, and the poem stopped there for two years, with the admonition to fight off these depressed moods. Then followed the sharper self-rebuke and the resolution to face the world with the stoicism of the leech-gatherer.

More was to come before the year ended. As before, private and public affairs coincided: the 'mad' Lord Lonsdale died, and his executors paid his debts, including those to the Wordsworths' father; and the Peace of Amiens opened the Continent. Wordsworth regularized his position by meeting Annette Vallon and their daughter at Calais, introducing them to Dorothy, and making the correct financial settlements. On the way back to Grasmere he married Mary Hutchinson. This stir of movement and emotions produced a new access of poetry. The public occasion seems more in his mind than the personal one, but, as before, the public occasion was a personal experience also. Economy of time and money was reason enough for halting at Calais when all the world was hurrying to Paris, but the contrast between 1802 and 1791 struck deep into Wordsworth's mind. The 'pleasant exercise of hope and joy' had brought not only the Terror, which could be discounted as a passing frenzy, but a series of aggressive wars, and now a dictatorship. The old memory was vivid

> Jones, as from Calais southward you and I
> Went pacing side by side—

Recalling the same scenes in *The Prelude*, he uses the same verb:

> I paced, a dear companion by my side,
> The town of Arras—

There is no other verb for the unhurried rhythmical step of the long-distance tramp: Wordsworth remembered not only what he had seen but—a more powerful thing—what he had felt in his body. All the emotions followed. Bonaparte had betrayed the Revolution, and the French were not worthy of it. If freedom was desirable, there was more of it in England than anywhere. He still held the old principles were right, but that alienated him no longer. The many things he criticized and deplored could not prevent his reconciliation with his own land, and the return brought comfort and confidence. These commotions could not help the making of long poems; the moments of impression and reflection on Calais sands, on the Channel crossing, on landing in Kent and passing through London, ran better into sonnets, for, apart from their appropriate brevity, strict forms are useful in abstracting the mind from the accidents of the day. Their basic unity is proved by the fact that through all the arrangement and rearrangement of his poems, these sonnets are kept together in the same order except for the transfer of the Killiecrankie sonnet, which is a literary reminiscence, a comment rather than a direct experience, to the *Memorials of a Tour in Scotland*. Wordsworth's Italian studies at Cambridge had acquainted him with the Petrarchan school—indeed his first printed poem, in 1787, was a bad sonnet —and he had discovered a new interest in the sonnets of Milton, whose example shows in his formal practice and, more importantly, in his rescuing the sonnet from sentiment and using it for comment on public situations. He lacked, however, Milton's discretion: while the sonnets of August and September 1802 have the urgency of strong associations and direct contacts, the thing became a habit, too often a matter of notes and remarks, and, in sequences after the Italian fashion, a way of working over subjects which interested him enough for desultory treatment but not so deeply as to command heavy labour. The minimum time was required for recollection in sufficient tranquillity: when the experience was forcible, the response is a fine sonnet, but a sonnet of sorts could be made out of a feeble or feebly recollected experience.

This access of energy lasted till *The Prelude* was drafted in the summer of 1805. Seen against this great philosophical task the *Poems in Two Volumes* of 1807, work done since 1799, seemed minor affairs

> Posterius graviore sono tibi Musa loquetur
> Nostra: dabunt cum securos mihi tempora fructus

says the title-page motto; but the great Ode which closes the second volume has its separate motto: *Paulo majora canamus.* This magnificent restatement of the central doctrine that material and spiritual, human and non-human, are intimately and indissolubly related, after lying by for two years, was set moving again by importing the concept of pre-existence, which neither arises from the lament with which the poem began nor leads to the consolation with which it ends. Coleridge's logical sense fastened on the 'mental bombast' of the eighth stanza— much the sort of thing that Lamb complained of in himself. The cause of it is the strain imposed by bringing a concept of secondary value into a statement of primary emotion. In the Fenwick note Wordsworth says,

> I think it right to protest against a conclusion, which has given pain to some good and pious persons, that I meant to inculcate such a belief. It is far too shadowy a notion to be recommended to faith, as more than an element in our instincts of immortality. . . . When I was impelled to write this Poem on the 'immortality of the Soul', I took hold of the notion of pre-existence as having sufficient foundation in humanity for authorising me to make for my purpose the best use of it I could as a Poet.

There is nothing shadowy or vague about the rest of the poem, which is a direct statement of Wordsworth's experience. It is unlike Wordsworth to work on two levels in this fashion, and to leave his reader uncertain whether he is or is not offering philosophical argument; but it is one way of expressing the

inexpressible. Also he had to reply to *Dejection*. A more natural
and stronger concept is contained in the *Ode to Duty* and illustrated in *The Happy Warrior*, the concept of discipline, the
willing acceptance of duty, more earthbound, but thereby more
native to an earthbound poet. Behind both, it may be, is
Wordsworth's favourite poem *The Faerie Queene*, especially
Book III, canto vi, and the two cantos of Book VII, with vaguer
memories of Book V, canto ii. The *Ode to Duty* is the active
counterpart of the contemplative *Ode: Intimations of Immortality*,
and the core of it is in the seventh stanza,

Stern Lawgiver! . . .
Flowers laugh before thee on their beds;
And Fragrance in thy footing treads;
Thou dost preserve the Stars from wrong;
And the most ancient Heavens, through Thee, are fresh and strong.

This may seem an illegitimate extension of a term of human
ethics into the physical world; but indeed Wordsworth could
not say, with Kant, 'Two things fill me with unutterable awe,
the starry heavens above me and the moral law within me.'
He was filled with awe, but by one thing, not two things. This
is what the years had brought to his philosophic mind: just as
he had become reconciled to the constitution of his country, so
he was reconciled to the constitution of the universe. This
conception of cosmic unity is something that goes back through
Spenser, through Boethius, to the ancient world. It was none
the less his own. It does not lend itself to argumentation so
readily as the German systems that came to dominate European
thought; it is difficult; it is none the less valid. It is as 'true' as
any other philosophical concept; and it gave us the poetry of
Wordsworth.

Meanwhile Coleridge was less reconciled than ever. In April
1804 he sailed for Malta and Sicily, whence he returned, after
a visit also to Rome, in August 1806. A fragmentary journal
remains, of observations such as Dorothy Wordsworth had recorded for them all at Alfoxden, but neither in verse nor prose
have we any evidence that this scholar, poet, journalist, theologian received any deep impression from the experience. The
whole affair was negative: except for a notion that the climate
would be good for his health, the motive was escape from what
was, rather than the attraction of what he would find. Thomas
Wedgwood, a most dangerous friend for him, had encouraged

the idea of foreign travel as well as the drug habit, and the two
were of the same nature. Wordsworth's hopes were futile, and
he returned in worse shape than ever. His one decision was to
separate from his wife. Separation from Wordsworth also, to
the extent at least that the old cross-influences had lost their
power, became evident. Already in 1803 the Alfoxden trio had
set out to explore Scotland, only to part company, Coleridge
bored, he said, by Wordsworth's melancholy moods, Wordsworth bored by Coleridge's hypochondria. To judge by the
symptoms detailed in his letters, what Coleridge was suffering
from was deprivation of opium. The loss of sympathy showed
again during a visit to Coleorton in 1807; Wordsworth lamented
over it in *A Complaint*. Yet that visit was painful to Coleridge for
deeper reasons: the reading of *The Prelude* brought home to him
not only the contrast between what Wordsworth had accomplished and his own barrenness, but the plain fact that he had
fallen away by his own defect, and the realization that he could
never reinstate himself. It wrung from him his last great poem,
the tragic lines *To a Gentleman*. When he stayed with the
Wordsworths again at Grasmere in 1810, the relationship was
one-sided: he was to be settled and steadied, to produce *The
Friend* for which Stuart had supplied some capital. The enterprise was hopeless, and the personal relationship broke down
in a miserable quarrel that lasted three years, into which we
need not enter but the background of which can be found in
Dorothy's letter to Mrs. Clarkson, of 10 April. Though it was
patched up and they could meet and travel together, they met
only as old friends; the partnership of mind and art had died in
Scotland, if not in Germany four years earlier.

What the estrangement cost Coleridge is difficult to estimate,
for his days as a full creative worker in either of his two arts,
poetry and metaphysics, were over. In 1813 *Remorse* was successful at Drury Lane, and in 1815–16 he gathered his *Sibylline
Leaves*. These were old things, and his piece of new writing,
Biographia Literaria, begun as an introduction to *Sibylline Leaves*,
was about the old arguments. *Zapolya*, an attempt to follow up
Remorse, was a failure. What the estrangement cost Wordsworth
is easier to see. His task was to produce the great philosophical
poem *The Recluse*, and though fortunately he did not heed
Coleridge's expostulations about wasting his time on small
poems, he drove on with his usual determination. But how does

one set about writing a great philosophical poem? He had triumphantly concluded the first part, for which his own life supplied the material and the sequence. Now, to use the old critical terms, he had to set himself to Invention and Disposition. He could not invent, and dispose in logical form, a construction of abstracts like the great metaphysical artists, St. Thomas Aquinas and Kant; nor was he sustained by a body of formulated thought like Lucretius or Dante. The philosophical precedent might be Plato, who had to adopt some methods of the imaginative artists to carry his thoughts beyond logic and to his hearers; but Wordsworth was no Platonist. A poetic precedent certainly was *The Faerie Queene*, the one attempt to write an original philosophic poem; but that unfinished effort was warning enough, and Wordsworth had neither Spenser's researching habit nor his varied experience nor his continuous contact with active business. As for method, allegory was impossible and, as we have said, Wordsworth did not work in symbols: everything in his poems is there for its own value, not for its referential utility. In the passage quoted in the 'Advertisement' to *The Excursion* he pays graceful tribute to the epic tradition by announcing his subject and invoking the Muse in correct fashion, but in doing so he renounces myth, and so emphatically as to alarm that great mythopœist William Blake. As ever, he had to get down to fundamentals, and these he could find only in that complex of associated ideas, himself. His worldly self he dealt with in *The Prelude*; the next stage involved the creation and projection of an imaginative self, the Recluse, and that was invented at Alfoxden with Coleridge, and perhaps largely by him, if he then assigned to his friend 'the contemplative position, which is peculiarly—perhaps I might say exclusively—fitted for him. His proper title is Spectator ab extra.' It suited Wordsworth in 1798, when he was still rejoicing in his recovery from his first adventures; the age of twenty-eight was too early to assume it permanently. Separated from Coleridge, then, and settled in Grasmere, he accepted it all too happily. When *The Excursion* was published in 1814, Coleridge sent Wordsworth a long outline of the poem he ought to have written. It is a metaphysical argument such as Wordsworth would not and could not have written at any time, a reflection of Coleridge's own mind and evidence both of the proprietary interest he took in the great work and of the extent to which he had lost touch. But agreement is unimportant: what matters is the intellectual turbulence, the thrust and recoil of the mind engaged with a master logician. Even if the old equality was impaired, though Coleridge was moving restlessly between London and the country, living largely on his friends and leaving Southey to shoulder as many responsibilities as that generous soul could meet, he was still producing, in talk and lectures and innumerable notebooks, spurts of critical and philosophical matter of the mos⁺ animating and penetrative force; and Wordsworth missed it.

Left to himself, he returned to his old themes. The Preface to *The Excursion* announces 'a philosophical poem, containing views of Man, Nature, and Society; and to be entitled, The Recluse; as having for its principal subject the sensations and opinions of a poet living in retirement'. The verses attached 'as a kind of *Prospectus* of the design and scope of the whole Poem' relate 'Man, Nature, and Society' together in the same way as *Tintern Abbey*, and the first Book contains the final version, written about 1806, of a tale first drafted at Racedown ten years earlier, one of the series of variations on the image of the forlorn woman who enshrines the undying spirit of love. The circumstances are reduced to the simplest elements, with none of the violence of *Guilt and Sorrow*, the mystery of *The Thorn*, or the exotic romance of *Ruth*, but the theme is realized by the intensely visualized detail,—old images perhaps reinforced by the scene described by Dorothy in her Journal of the Scottish tour, August 20th, 1803—the well-conceived and well-developed imaginary narrator, the Wanderer, and the provision of an audience in the first person, the 'I' of the whole poem, positive but neutral. The invention of the Wanderer is crucial. The imaginary narrator of *The Thorn*, the retired 'Captain of a small trading vessel', of whose existence the reader is not warned, existed merely as a technical device to set the style and diction. For this greater purpose Wordsworth required a mind as well as a tongue, a *persona* intimate with nature but not a hermit, and this he found in the pedlar, a useful member of society whose business kept him in the remoter regions of the country. Through this figure he could express his own 'sensations and opinions' not only because he could construct it from men he had known but because it satisfied, as no other could, his own contradictory instincts of wandering and housekeeping. The

projection of himself, even if only partial, into a retired man
of over sixty, when he himself was thirty-six at most, is less
happy. *The Excursion* is usually underrated because it lacks the
lyrical intensity of *Tintern Abbey* and the *Ode: Intimations of
Immortality* on one hand and the personal emotion of *The Prelude*
on the other; but it should be read as what it is, a discursive
meditation on the same themes. Discursive poetry—as distinct
from argumentative or homiletic—is rare and difficult. Wordsworth attempted it by combining *exemplum*, in the appropriate
form of the 'eclogue', and discussion, in the dramatic *personae*
of the Wanderer, the Solitary, and the Parson, within scenery
which is not a mere setting or decoration but an essential part
of his whole theme. The first Book, apart from the development
of the Wanderer which has to bulk larger than it might in
preparation for the other Books also, is a simple 'eclogue' displaying this unity of human and nonhuman, for the life of
Margaret is seen as part of the 'goings-on' of the universe, from
the politics and economics that broke up her home to the sheep
and the weeds and the weather that make the ruined cottage
what it is to see. The third and fourth Books contain the medita-
tive expression corresponding to the two parts of the *Ode*,
Resolution and Independence, and the *Ode to Duty*. The rest is a
series of 'eclogues' interspersed with description and moralizing,
handled with skill and 'decorum', but suggesting deliberate
arrangement of selected specimens. Wordsworth has given
'views', 'sentiments and opinions' worthy in themselves and
skilfully presented. The poem is full of admirable things; the
doubt remains whether it is a poem. It does not contain within
itself the reasons for its size and conduct. In the Preface Wordsworth declares, 'It is not the Author's intention formally to
announce a system: it is more animating to him to proceed in
a different course; and if he shall succeed in conveying to the
mind clear thoughts, lively images, and strong feelings, The
Reader will have no difficulty in extracting the system for himself.' This is very right, but the oppressive idea of the philosophical poem has hindered the artist's freedom. The Solitary,
the sophisticated man uprooted by the passing excitements of
the day, is obviously contrived to introduce certain subjects for
discussion; as in *Guilt and Sorrow* the main theme is obscured by
the multiplication of incident, and the story is left in the air.
The monologues lose some of their value if the reader allows

himself to be carried on by the narrative. That is the difficulty
of discursive poetry: it must be read as it is written, in fragments. They might be more effective standing by themselves.
After the fourth Book the poem becomes what Crabbe might
have planned if he had accepted his friends' advice to link up
his tales in a continuous poem; he was the lesser poet, but in
this he was the wiser. The tale of Margaret is too complete
and balanced for what follows. After *The Excursion* Wordsworth
revised *Peter Bell* (1819), and it is tempting to think what might
have happened if he had set that violent figure beside the
elegiac figure of Margaret. *The Waggoner*, the other early poem
published just after *Peter Bell* at Lamb's insistence, would be
more difficult. It is the longest of the 'eclogues', a picture of
manners too featureless to bear juxtaposition with others, moving slowly like the wagon itself and requiring several readings
before it discloses its very real charm; but it has two features
not so fully displayed in any other poems of Wordsworth's: the
picture of the travelling entertainer, for whose counterpart we
have to go to George Borrow—no admirer of Wordsworth—
and the sympathetic zest of the drunken catastrophe, which
would seem quite out of Wordsworth's character but for the
Letter to a Friend of Burns. The general sense of neighbourhood,
the regret for the familiar wagon merely because it was familiar,
and the factual telling of the tale without criticism or moralizing, give it high place artistically if not philosophically or
spiritually. Lamb's pleasure in its dedication is easily understood; and this quiet tale, suffused with unobtrusive humour,
is more truly philosophical than some of the conscientious insertions in *The Excursion*. Coleridge's influence had its dis-
advantages.

The scheme of *The Excursion*—views of man and society in
mountain country—required description on a larger scale than
Wordsworth usually allowed himself. With some help from
Dorothy's diaries and the notes dictated to Miss Fenwick, we
can place most of his poems. We return the images to their
origins in the known scene, and forget how little Wordsworth
needed for his purposes: trees, water, daffodils; a man beside
a bare pool; some tumbled stones on a hillside. After these
economical designs the large landscape and cloud effects of *The
Excursion* seem like gallery pictures. Wordsworth indeed did not
wholly escape the connoisseurship in scenery that has been a

local disability in the Lake District since Gray's time: his acquaintance with Payne Knight and Uvedale Price brought him perilously near the amateur Picturesque, and his friendship with Sir George Beaumont gave him acquaintance among Sir George's artist friends and the droves of water-colourists for whom a tour in the Lakes had long been almost a professional requirement. He needed less than most poets to be taught to see, and the connexion did him no harm except to give him the occasional airs of an art expert. At least his approach was empirical where Coleridge's was metaphysical, but some hardening of the aesthetic arteries is apparent in the sonnet-sequence on the River Duddon. The idea—the poetic equivalent of a Chinese scroll-painting—is pleasant, but the fixed form tactless and incongruous with the nature of a hill stream. There are pretty things in the sequence, but only the splendid closing sonnet saves it. This deliberate approach to the large set piece is right, however, for *The Excursion*, and for more reasons than its length: the view of Grasmere is composed round the church tower, which not only provides a neat transition to a new figure and a new turn in the discussion, the Pastor and official religion, but presents them in their proper aspect.

The Racedown story of Margaret had contained nothing specifically Christian until Wordsworth inlaid one passage in the edition of 1845, but any view of Society must include institutional religion. Wordsworth had laboured to formulate his spiritual experience, and that experience was outside the Church. The later modifications and insertions of orthodox ideas here and there have the appearance—it is a hard saying but cannot be shirked—of conventional conformity. He was no theologian, and as he suffered no sense of sin there is no record of conversion. It is an undogmatic religion that the Pastor argues, and he represents Society as much as doctrine, for he is shown in his family as well as in his churchyard, the pastor in his parish and not the priest at the altar. It is one of the rediscoveries of England that Wordsworth made after his reconciliation in 1802. 'National Independence and Liberty', to which he dedicated a whole section of his poems, rested on national duty and virtue, and in the Church of England he saw the best agency for the promotion of both. On the doctrinal value of service and sacrament he has little to say, but much on their humane and emotional values. Their continuity from season to season, binding generation to generation in the slow passage of time, standing witness to the permanent things above all shifting desires and fleeting agitations, endeared them to one who had lost the 'pleasant exercise of hope and joy' and had grown into the past through dependence on association and habit. Association suffused with his spiritual intuition bred his share of the piety that is the religious emotion most characteristic of the English and therefore of their poets. He had come to value what Spenser called 'the seemly form and comely order of the Church' and could understand at least some things in George Herbert. In the Church—though not only here— the 'Wisdom and Spirit of the Universe' manifests itself in tenderness and beauty. Resolutely opposed to the Roman organization as to all dominating powers, he sympathized late in life with the Oxford Movement. Coleridge would have been pleased, but by then Coleridge was dead.

In politics as in philosophy Coleridge held his latest opinions as absolute truths and never worked out his most original and important observation, that freedom and servitude are made, on the individual scale, more by conditions of employment than by constitutional politics; his most conspicuous opinions were the anti-Pittite and anti-Bonapartist feelings he shared with Daniel Stuart and Wordsworth and thousands more. In *Humanity* Wordsworth expresses feelings for the wage-slave akin to Coleridge's, but deriving also from his general thought: he regarded factories as unnatural and ugly, and opposed, therefore, the kind of freedom for which Cobden and John Bright were to contend. His old revolutionary ideas were another matter. He never departed from them intellectually. Of that there is abundant evidence, but once more the diarist Farington may shed his cold light on it. On 17 June 1806 John Taylor 'found Him strongly disposed towards Republicanism. His notions are that it is the duty of every Administration to do as much as possible to give consideration to the people at large, and to have *equality* always in view; which though not perfectly attainable, yet much has been gained towards it and more may be.' His Toryism was indeed a form of political scepticism: after what had happened in France, any constitutional change seemed a dangerous movement towards incalculable ends. Wordsworth had seen the Parisian mob. Popular uprising, which to Scott was the mere restlessness of west-country

weavers whom his volunteer Light Horse would scatter cheer-
fully, might end in such massacre as had shaken him in his
youth.

This was the Wordsworth who in later years opposed almost
every attempt at legislation from the Reform Bill to Erskine's
bill for the prevention of cruelty to animals, for all action was
illusory and only states of being mattered—the eternal human
virtues and the unchanging life of the peasant. Yet Wordsworth, and Southey who wrote *Espriella's Letters from England*,
retained in their Toryism something of the old Jacobin. Scott's
atavistic sentiment held nothing for the future; a new generation of Tories found the concept of 'the two nations' in Coleridge; Wordsworth and Southey—whose Laureate odes could
be charitably forgotten with the rest of their kind but for Byron's
Vision of Judgment—are the first of the Tory Radicals. With less
aloof superiority they might have made common cause with
William Cobbett; but Cobbett was too exuberantly committed
to the rough business of day-to-day political action for their
taste. According to Carlyle, Southey approved of his *French
Revolution*. Memory is a selective mechanism, and Southey's
boyish excitement was revived by this zestfully horrified picture
of a grandiose scene of destruction. Wordsworth disapproved.
The Revolution had meant too much to him. He did not confuse the Revolution and the Terror. The 'benignant spirit'
had been stifled by new tyrannies: better no action, it seemed,
than such humiliation: but it had been abroad, and the failure
to construct a logical explanation of it all did not tempt him
into intellectual or moral nihilism nor into a cult of despair or
a search for easy compensations. If in his retirement he could
not grasp the full realities of action in Spain or Westminster,
he was honourably concerned about it. If he was unable to
meet the new men on their own ground or solve the problems
created by the new industrial society that was growing too
rapidly for control on the old principles, he saw that the problems existed and that they were human problems. If, like later
inhabitants of his native district, he approved of enterprise and
invention only so long as they did not interfere with his favourite
walks, that is human nature. We must not expect too much. He
could not go on to build 'Jerusalem', but the benignant spirit
had only changed its scene; it led him to 'the grand human
principle of pleasure', which is a 'Beulah' more intelligible and

accessible to more men than Blake's. 'At the University', says Traherne, 'there was never a tutor that did expressly teach felicity, though that be the mistress of all the other sciences.' Wordsworth is our tutor. And he is indispensable because he embodied so much that is valuable and permanent in the English nature. He is part of our experience, to be accepted as he accepted his experience in his time, an Anglo-Saxon in direct descent from Cynewulf and the authors of *Beowulf* and *The Seafarer*, with recognizable ancestors in all generations since their day and a share in the making of every later generation; to be neglected at our peril.

If Wordsworth had cast off earlier the burden that Coleridge helped to lay upon him of creating in poetic form a complete and systematic philosophy, and trusted more to the artistic common sense visible in the *Lyrical Ballads* Preface, he might have organized his observation and experience in new forms invented or adopted each for its purpose with a free mind, as he did in *The White Doe*, the *Song at Brougham Castle*, and *The Power of Sound*, and so contributed more happily and more philosophically to our inheritance. Yet the persistent phantom of *The Recluse* and the anxious revisions of the *Prelude* testify to his constancy. He was as incapable of careless or unfinished work as of logical architectonics. Once more the contrast with Coleridge is forced upon us. As he confessed in *Dejection*, Coleridge's creative power dwindled away and he became wholly the student and commentator, philosophic by nature and habit but incomplete as philosopher since the 'shaping spirit of Imagination' is necessary to any construction, aesthetic or intellectual. Even the more consecutive pieces like *Biographia Literaria* and the longer essays break up under examination. Working through the enormous mass of notebooks, annotations, marginalia, and omniana, notes of lectures and reports of lectures, the student begins to expect that, some time or other, a complete doctrine will emerge. Coleridge felt, often enough, that it was about to do so; but it never did, and the wise reader must resist the temptation to select and organize. To gather the limbs of Osiris is a pious occupation, but when we have achieved an articulated body we cannot be sure whether it is Osiris or a god of our own making in our own image; and here we are engaged not with a dismembered unity but with matter that was never anything but fragmentary. It may be possible to

build up a system of metaphysics or theology or aesthetic, but
may we call it Coleridge's? Yet the student will become conscious that he is growing into contact with a mind, and—while
remaining on his guard against the exhilaration induced by the
process—that the experience is more enlightening than any
logical conviction.

The critical remains are not only the most relevant to us here
but the most developed—for fragmentary metaphysic is a contradiction in terms, and any legacy in religion was seminal
rather than doctrinal and correspondingly slow in effect. The
nature of Coleridge's power becomes apparent when we turn
back to such a treatise as the *Essays on the Nature and Principles
of Taste* (1790) in which Archibald Alison elaborates in two
volumes

a Doctrine that appears very early to have distinguished the Platonic
school; which is to be traced, perhaps (amid their dark and figura-
tive language), in all the philosophical systems of the East, and which
has been maintained in this country, by several writers of eminence,
by Lord Shaftesbury, Dr. Hutcheson, Dr. Akenside, and Dr. Spence,
but which has nowhere so firmly and so philosophically been maintained, as by Dr. Reid in his invaluable work 'On the Intellectual
Powers of Man' . . . that matter is not beautiful in itself, but derives
its Beauty from the expression of Mind.

This is no great harm; but, as befitted an orthodox Prebendary
of Sarum trained in Edinburgh, he attempted a complete
rationalization in formal style of the accepted agencies and
categories: the Sublime and Beautiful which appear so ubiqui-
tously at this time that the student begins to curse the very name
of Burke, Association, Fitness, Proportion, and so on. Alison is
not stupid; he tempts his reader to argue with him, but only
for the pleasure of argument. He convinces us even less than
most other aestheticians that he is trying to comprehend a
passionate experience, or even that he has had one. It is not so
with Coleridge, nor with Charles Lamb. They, like Wordsworth,
directed their criticism at the active mind of the reader, without
attempt at legislation. Lamb compiled his extracts and annotations to share with his readers his passionate experience in
reading Burton, Fuller, the older dramatists, and to uphold
their memory who provided it for him. As a clerk in the East
India Company's Office he was efficient and trustworthy,
which was all that was required for regular promotion to an

adequate salary; the energy and interest which another man might have put into his professional work was reserved for his private pursuits. What he lacked was time: he resented the long days in the office which he could have spent more happily in the British Museum or at his own desk instead of the Company's. In such broken study he could do little but record his moments of appreciative enjoyment, and of those he had plenty, so that he is complementary to the 'blackletter dogs' and hunters of factual details whom Mathias mocked at, Steevens and Malone and the rest, in keeping alive—or prominent, for their zeal has its infective quality also—the real reason of their labours, the values in art and humanity that make these old things worth working over. It is a limited service, confined to personal taste and accident. Yet his taste is so sure, and the communication of his own pleasures so lively, that we would not give even his dubious passages for a wilderness of Alisons.

This same power of reception and communication is the life of Coleridge. After all, he had been a poet, and he knew and treasured the experience. His first virtue is that he was aware of all the forms of criticism, from metrics to speculative aesthetics, that must be deployed to cover the complex activity of the artist. To control this multifarious effort was too much for his limited concentration and resolution. It is easy to pick holes. His view of literary history was wider than his knowledge, and was limited by prejudice and personal feeling as well as by taste. He knew that music existed, but that was all, and his theories of painting were based only on the work of his friend Allston. No man could keep all the elements in the complex balanced all the time; an attractive intellectual sequence could always lead him off, and once his mind was set in motion he assumed that he had nothing more to learn. He treats Shakespeare, for instance, too much as a pure intelligence, a spiritualistic philosopher and moralist. It is easy, on the other hand, to admire indiscriminately. His general discursions can be so valuable and so fascinating, that the reader feels that light is being shed for him. It is right to allow oneself to be drawn from criticism into metaphysics, from pleasure in seventeenth-century prose styles into theology, from generalization on evidence into the invention and arrangement of categories, so long as we withdraw at proper intervals. We do not read Coleridge's criticism so much as listen to it, and we do this discursive table-talker most justice—as well as ourselves—if we read rapidly, intermittently, and often, so that the main ideas and processes solidify gradually, and we come to know his mind as we know that of a friend, less by reception of dogma or selection of this or that or formulation of fixed principles, than by acquaintance with how his mind works. Then we can accept strength and weakness together, without uncritical devotion or forced initiation into an order. The life is more than principle, and if there is little felicity there is no stagnation.

VII

NORTHERN LIGHTS

IT is profitable to consider Scotland separately, since conditions there differed, and that significantly. The period 1770 to 1830 is still regarded as her Golden Age, when the harvest of a century's hard labour in agriculture, commerce, manufactures, and thereafter in letters and the arts, was made manifest. London still attracted Scottish journalists, publishers, architects, surgeons, and ambitious lawyers, but it was possible to make a career at home, and, in so doing, earn a reputation abroad. Scottish philosophers, historians, and scientists brought lustre to the north and attracted both students and dilettanti, and in due course Scottish men of letters were to make themselves and their country conspicuous in the eyes of all Europe.

Two literary phenomena in particular forced themselves on men's notice beyond the bounds of Scotland: *The Edinburgh Review* and, more widely, Walter Scott. Taken together they represent the dual and contradictory nature of their people. Long before Macpherson projected its misty landscape into the European imagination, Ariosto had heard of the faraway land where anything might happen, and long before Adam Smith was born, French kings and universities knew the touchy breed of fighting men and theologically minded logicians. The whole history of Scotland in the eighteenth century reinforced each side of the duality, with all the power of an astonishing burst of energy in which the country reorganized itself with increasing momentum until by 1800 the transformation stood clear to see. That unique compilation *The Statistical Account of Scotland*, 1791–9, organized by Sir John Sinclair, and its sequels the *County Reports*, 1795–1814, are there to testify that this was no unconscious trend, but a real movement. *The Edinburgh Review*, fruit of the practical side, came first in time, but the 'romantic', identified particularly with the name of Scott, was fostered by the same set of circumstances, the tension between the growing effectiveness of that energy in the most diverse fields and its frustration in politics. For the Golden Age of Scotland was an

age of political degradation. In 1745 Scotsmen were still capable
of political action, in that some fought for the Stuart dynasty
and some against—crude action, but positive. Thereafter the
government in Westminster arranged that neither body should
be allowed the possibility of action. Scotland was managed
through the Lord Advocate by the exercise of patronage,
bribery, and repression as required, with just so much show of
politics as to admit Scottish members of Parliament to be
merged in the English parties.

Scottish Toryism meant belief in Kingship, partly out of
a sound but unfortunately vague notion that the supremacy of
Parliament is unconstitutional in Scotland, more out of the
resistance of the greater families to any threat to their heredi-
tary power; that the direct exercise of that power was no longer
possible made it the more important to cling to what was left
of it. Jacobitism, the desire to change the person on the throne,
was politically dead. As a sentiment, however, it was strongly
alive. The northern idiom of attaching the definite article to
date-years survives familiarly only in 'the '15' and 'the '45',
because these years were vividly remembered and often recalled.
In a way incomprehensible to one of—for instance—Coleridge's
upbringing, the '45 formed a coloured background to the
present: to many, the adventure of their youth, on one side or
the other; to more, the realized folk-tale of the young prince
seeking his inheritance, the folk-memory of a way of life loved
or feared but worthy of its elegy in any case; and ultimately
the sorrowful song of youth's defeat—whether the Prince's
youth or the singer's, no matter. It also gave a vent for the
obscure resentment of national impotence, and the constant
irritation at the massive self-complacency of the 'English states-
men, who, wisely and judiciously tenacious of the legal practice
and principles received at home, are proportionally startled
at the idea of any thing abroad which cannot be brought
to assimilate with them'. Politically, Jacobitism was a Tory
principle; the sentiment was not confined by party. Scott's
Jacobitism, very equivocal at best, was not inconsistent with
his enthusiastic organization of George IV's visit to Scotland in
1822. Here at last was a King in Scotland again, the natural
counterbalance not only to the presumptuous Whigs but to
the parliamentary bigwigs and the encroaching lawyers of
Westminster: if the notion was illusory, it was not irrational.

Sentiment, however, was not enough; and Jacobitism was a Tory sentiment and the Tories were in power. Opposition to political corruption and debasement had to ally itself with the official opposition, which was Whig, and though the management of Scotland was originally a Whig technique and any attack on the system would affect Westminster only for its usefulness there—the impeachment of Melville was hailed in Scotland as the downfall of the resented manager but in London as a blow at his friend Pitt—the appropriate watchwords were the Whig ones. As the current of native energy rose high enough to lap against the barrier of political negation, it flowed naturally into Whig channels, and when the Whiggism that had sympathized with the American revolutionaries received its reinforcement of excitement and optimism from revolutionary France, it enlisted the native sentiments. Thus in the early 1790's an unsophisticated Pittite, Robert Burns, disillusioned by his glimpse of the facts of political life in Edinburgh, could be Jacobite and Jacobin at the same time.

The French inspiration, however, brought more modern feelings into play, feelings less easily dissipated in historical controversy over Mary Queen of Scots or nostalgic elegies on Bonnie Prince Charlie. There were Friends of the People in Scotland also, new movements with fresh ideas, linked with and corresponding with those of the south but less fortunate in their circumstances. No Scottish mob existed as a permanent and ready tool of the politicians like that of London, but when Thomas Muir of Hunterston was arrested in 1793 he came before judges who were mere instruments of government, and found no protection such as the Westminster juries afforded to Horne Tooke and his friends in the following year. Yet his ideas were more logically and constitutionally formed than theirs, for they grew from sources less picturesque than Lochaber or Whitefriars, slower in action and effect, but none the less real. After 1793 Dugald Stewart, a cautious man in a conspicuous university chair in Edinburgh, might be less inclined to quote his friend M. de Condorcet, but the old alliance with France of the Enlightenment had its influence, government could not suppress philosophic Whiggism, and Muir's best teacher of radical principles had been the Professor of Law in insubordinate Glasgow, John Millar, a master of clear argument and trenchant prose. It might be less pleasing that the Irish rebellion in 1798 was the most dangerous rising because it was stiffened by the Ulster presbyterians many of whose leaders had attended Millar's university, but that was accidental. What was not accidental was *The Edinburgh Review*.

Why the *Edinburgh* Review? Diffused energy and Whig self-assertion were not confined to Scotland: other differences from England have to be noticed. The population was small, and so, with all the striking variations it contained, Scottish society seems more closely knit than that of England, and more conscious of its common task. At every turn, whether it be the recording of traditional poetry or the improvement of agriculture or trade or manufactures, we meet peers, judges, merchants, professors, tenant farmers, ministers, lairds, and tradesmen sharing the same enthusiasms. This society was ministered to by a Church which, though established, was independent of the Crown and governed by its whole body meeting annually in its General Assembly of parish ministers and lay elders; and by universities whose place and power differed sharply from those held by Oxford and Cambridge in England. Their conscious purpose was to serve in all its activities the society of whose life and energy they partook and which was represented in their classrooms in all its variety. Universities and students were alike poor, but they gained strength from their close relation with the community at large. St. Andrews indeed was isolated, like Oxford and Cambridge, in a small town, and it was in a low state; the other three were situated where the native energy was most concentrated and most effective. The vigorous local culture and character of Aberdeen bred hard thinkers, mainly in the abstract sciences, for local activities did not suggest such positive direction as they did in Glasgow. There all through the eighteenth century the College harboured lively academic minds which, while they maintained the very independent status of their foundation, profited by friendly relations with the lively commercial minds of a thriving city whose horizons lay across the Atlantic. In Edinburgh the university gained in influence and public notice what it lost in independence by its official subjection to the city authorities and its position in the capital, the headquarters of the law and the church and the focal point of governmental control. Less self-contained than the English, the Scottish universities thus evolved and offered a less specialized faculty of Arts, as well as being responsible for more of the legal and medical education. They could not have produced a Porson, but where Dalton, Davy, Faraday, were supported by private institutions, they had place for the scientists within, and contributing to, their society and their regular curriculum.

What they did produce was a school, not so much of philosophy as of philosophically directed education adapted to the needs of the time. The Scottish School, built up throughout the eighteenth century, consolidated by Thomas Reid in Aberdeen and Glasgow, and propagated in Edinburgh by the less original and less consistent Dugald Stewart, derived its character from the old habit, which academic England lost in the eighteenth century, of regarding the world as one. Philosophy was divisible into 'natural', 'mental', and 'moral', history into 'natural' and 'political'; whatever bias a man might take, the business of teacher and student was philosophy. Thus Adam Ferguson, in Edinburgh, moved from the Chair of Natural Philosophy to that of Moral Philosophy; his successor Stewart began as deputy for his father, the professor of Mathematics, and taught Natural Philosophy in a vacancy. Reid's early duties in Aberdeen required him to teach natural history, physics, and mental philosophy in rotation. Progress in any branch demanded, of course, the abandonment of this Renaissance versatility, but the habit of mind persisted. After his translation to Glasgow in succession to Adam Smith, Reid attended, at the age of fifty-five, William Cullen's notable class of chemistry; young Thomas Carlyle 'sat under' the inventive mathematician John Leslie whose favourite recreation was history, and Robert Jamieson who interspersed his zoological lectures with quotations from 'Dante and other odd fellows'. The basis of the Scottish philosophy was, accordingly, neither classical scholarship—though they all had some share of it, it was not an end in itself—nor any one received metaphysical system, but, as Reid called it, common sense, which meant observation of relevant facts, applied to the mind and its movements and consequences in action.

It was indeed the minor offspring, as the French Encyclopaedia was the major, of the early Royal Society before Newton imposed specialization upon it, and, true to national tradition, the Scots kept direct contact with the French masters of the greater Enlightenment without becoming their disciples: the

decline of the Scottish School might indeed be dated from the
eclipse of the Enlightenment by the Terror and its betrayal
along with the Revolution by the Emperor Napoleon. With
less genius, bred in the classroom rather than the salon and the
château, nearer to earth in a poor and struggling country, theirs
is an eclectic system, looking back beyond Locke to Bacon, not
sceptical but wary in speculation since Hume had broken the
links of Cause and Effect; chary of pressing any idea, however
valuable in itself, beyond its due bounds as Hartley had pressed
the idea of Association; less concerned to construct a complete
closed system or metaphysical model of the universe than to
awaken and strengthen the mind to examine itself and in that
light to observe and comment upon the world at large. Its
printed records are less impressive than the spoken word seems
to have been. The success of Dugald Stewart[1] was in great part
one of personality: it was none the less a success that earned the
lasting enthusiasm and gratitude of so many intelligent hearers,
English and American as well as Scots. His *Outlines of Moral
Philosophy* are laid out for his students, to ensure that the
sequence of instruction was kept in view, and his other works,
*Elements of the Philosophy of the Human Mind, Philosophical Essays,
Philosophy of the Active and Moral Powers*, built round the armature of the *Outlines*, lose not only the voice and presence, but
the variety of disquisition and illustration that, we are assured,
brought the young men to his feet.

Moral philosophy, then, as outlined by Stewart, begins with
observation of the kind now called psychological, moves to
discussion 'of the active and of the moral powers of man' which
includes 'the duties which respect the Deity' based on a 'preliminary inquiry into the principles of natural religion', and
'the duties which respect our fellow-creatures' and ourselves.
Another section, which grew into a complete course, concerns
'man considered as the member of a political body', opening
with observation of an historical nature, and closing with notes
on constitutions, political duties, and international relations.
Between these comes political economy, for *The Wealth of
Nations* was written by the former professor of Moral Philosophy
in Glasgow; nor is it easy to see why the actions and relations

---

[1] 1753–1828. Educated at Edinburgh and Glasgow. Professor of Moral Philosophy, Edinburgh, 1785. Met Burns 1786, and was helpful to him. 'He was the
great inspirer of young men' (Cockburn).

of men in matters of commerce should be, as claimed by modern economists who arrogate to themselves the independence and irresponsibility of science, exempt from the moral considerations to which their other relations are habitually subjected. To such studies the young man, having received his modicum of Latin and Greek literature, progressed, rather than to making verses and weighing textual variants or grammatical subtleties; though even if he did not attend the course on Rhetoric—another of Adam Smith's topics—the aesthetic qualities of the mind came under purview and both ancient and modern literatures served for evidence and copious illustration throughout. Along with the mathematics, physical and natural science, and logic, which were part of the normal curriculum, they bred the prag-matical Scot of the satirists, and trained many a useful servant of Church and State. It was the weakness of the Scottish school that, while it encouraged width of interest, it discouraged the young mind from the free-ranging speculation in any one direc-tion that, however inconclusive in itself, is the necessary condi-tion of future growth. Something was passed on through Thomas Hamilton, and by the elder Mill to his son John Stuart Mill, but seeking minds and uneasy temperaments like the young Carlyle failed to develop such possibilities as the School offered, and enrolled themselves in the German schools which provided the aesthetic satisfaction of architectonic struc-ture along with uninhibited indulgence of the metaphysical imagination.

Thus the capital city, however truncated its political struc-ture, contained a society already mature and aware of itself, small enough for solidarity and large enough for variety, in close touch with the country, with an intellectual focus for all kinds of interest in the university, and, in the law courts, em-ployment to keep good minds at home. It was a centre of printing, and its publishers—Nelsons (1798), Oliver and Boyd (1801), Blackwood (1804), A. & C. Black (1807); in Glasgow, Blackie (1809), Collins (1819), to note a few survivors still in the same kind of trade—were exploiting the expanding market for educational works and reprints. This was the city that pro-duced the *Encyclopaedia Britannica*, now in its third edition in 1802 and preparing its fourth. The weight and momentum of *The Edinburgh Review*, as compared with *The Monthly Magazine, The Monthly Review*, and their like, came first from the solidity and

thrust of a group, not superior, man for man, to the best contributors to *The Monthly Review*, nor more convinced in political
opinion, but united by social proximity and by the common
possession of an education that accepted and taught as of
official importance a range of studies that elsewhere were
scattered as personal interests, individual tastes and private
pursuits. Phillips of the *Magazine* and Griffiths of the *Review*
had to gather their contributors from different quarters; here
in Edinburgh was a formed body—formed but not enclosed in
a literary coterie or a sectarian connexion.

The original suggestion came from Sydney Smith.[1] That
Anglican clergyman was not in Edinburgh by accident: he was
bear-leading a young Englishman who, like many others, was
sent to find in Scotland something of the varied intellectual
contacts which the wars made it inconvenient to seek on the
Continent. The suggestion was thrown out to young Whigs
who were typical products of Scottish education, Jeffrey[2]
(who had already written for *The Monthly Review*), Horner,[3]
Brougham,[4] J. A. Murray, who hoped, as Brougham said, 'to
receive help from such leviathans as Playfair, Dugald Stewart,
Robison, Thomas Brown, Thomson'—two successive occupants
of the Chair of Natural Philosophy, two successive occupants
of that of Moral Philosophy, and an authority on legal history,
all to be met within a ten-minute walk. The distinctive mark
was that the conduct of the *Review* was not to lie with the
publisher but with these accepted members of Edinburgh
society, on a level with the public they addressed, and independent of booksellers. No attempt was made to cover, still
less to announce, like *The Monthly Magazine*, current production; the first number contains short notices, but these disappear, and the distinctive principle is established, that each

[1] 1771–1845. Educated at Winchester and Oxford; in orders 1794; vicar of
Foston, Yorks., 1808; canon residentiary of St. Paul's 1831.

[2] 1773–1850. Born in Edinburgh, son of a lawyer. Educated at Glasgow and
Edinburgh Universities, and (briefly) Oxford. At Scottish bar 1794; Lord Advocate
1830–4; M.P. 1831; judge in Court of Session 1834. Edited *The Edinburgh Review*
1803–29. A friendly, clever man if no great lawyer, and a born reformer.

[3] 1778–1817. Educated at Edinburgh. At Scottish bar 1800, English bar 1807.
M.P. 1806; a politician with views on economics. Died at Pisa, much regretted,
before the Whig revival.

[4] 1778–1868. Educated at Edinburgh; at Scottish bar 1800, English bar 1808;
M.P. 1810; defended Queen Caroline 1820; legal reforms 1828; Lord Chancellor,
and Baron, 1830. A founder of London University, F.R.S., &c. Valuable in politics and law, but disliked personally by many.

article must be a solid work of some magnitude, bringing knowledge and thought to bear on a subject meriting serious treatment by its good or bad qualities or its possibility of public interest. Subject to the editor's control, a reviewer might choose his subject or refuse one for which he felt himself unfitted—Brougham would refuse little on that account. At least no bookseller might dictate what should or should not be included, and gentlemanly dilettantis were not encouraged. The quality of the reviewer and the quality of his work were ensured by adequate payment—a minimum of ten guineas a sheet, soon raised to sixteen, and up to twenty-five if necessary, as against six paid by Phillips for contributions to *The Monthly Magazine*. This decision established new economic standards of authorship. A little later Southey could maintain his own family, and largely those of Coleridge and Lloyd, on his earnings as reviewer for the *Quarterly*; but even the beginners in *The Edinburgh Review* would have been insulted by such payments as 14*s*. or 36*s*. 6*d*., accepted by William Taylor, a self-educated scholar, and, though claiming some choice of subjects, a good miscellaneous handyman in the monthlies. None of the young founders had any capital, but Archibald Constable was ready for a speculation—too ready for his own and others' comfort in later years—and when John Murray, less flamboyant than Constable but equally venturesome, produced *The Quarterly Review* in 1809, he had to work to the same scale or rather better.

So in October 1802 *The Edinburgh Review* was launched. As Jeffrey said, it stood on two legs, politics and literature. Politics is only incidentally our concern; it is relevant to ask what Jeffrey and his friends understood by 'literature'. It meant the tastes and interests of the educated public, and the immediate success of the *Review* attests the accuracy with which it supplied them. It certainly did not mean only *belles-lettres*, though they were an essential part of it. Taking the contents of the first ten years, and judging by the number of pages allotted, travel and the sciences, including medicine, bulk largest, then the political subjects—politics, history, political economy, public questions like the slave-trade and education—pure literature, mainly English with some French and by southern standards disgracefully little Greek and Latin, coming in third, and well behind. Of philosophy and religion there is less than might be expected, of the arts very little—less than in *The Monthly Magazine*. When in 1809 the Tory *Quarterly* opposed itself to the Whig *Edinburgh Review*, the opposition was entirely political. Opinion might vary with the persons engaged, but the subjects were much the same, except that science claimed less space and religion rather more. The planning of *The Edinburgh Review* was thus unintentionally vindicated, and, equally unintentionally, the general relevance of the training given by the Scottish universities to the founders and closely reflected in the content of the *Review*.

It is a tribute to the permanence of literature, as compared to scientific writing which exists only to be superseded, that the critical opinions of the reviewers alone attract the interest of later generations, but their critical attitude can be understood only in the context of the Reviews as a whole. After the death of Burns—who did not belong to this society of lawyers, scientists, and philosophers in any case—until the rise of Scott, creative literature was not conspicuous in the social landscape, so that personal interests were not excited. Thomas Brown, indeed, wrote intelligent and cultivated verse, decidedly not that of 'a Lake poet' as Sydney Smith called him, but of the intermediate type of Akenside—very respectable for a metaphysician, but minor: Brougham thought it a waste of Brown's time. These young men had other things to occupy them: outside law and politics Jeffrey's first interest was in science. Polite literature was a part of life, but of the leisured part. The motto Sydney Smith proposed, *Tenui musam meditaris avena*, in his interpretation 'on a little oatmeal', might be rejected as uncomfortably near the truth; whether Horner's substitute *Judex damnatur dum nocens absolvitur*, if it referred only to *belles-lettres*, was accepted in complete seriousness, might be doubted. Quite apart from the temperamental lightheartedness of Jeffrey and the levity of Smith, and with all their airs of superiority, they were not judging major criminals. Yet the judge implies the existence of the law; they had a critical code, neither new nor original, but that of the vast majority of their contemporaries. In his condemnation of Wordsworth and all his tribe Jeffrey was not misleading a neutral public but expressing the common orthodoxy of the world to which he belonged; his charges of puerility, false simplicity, and vulgarity were just what the kind of people who read the *Review* were saying everywhere. While his failure to make the effort to comprehend the new poetry might disappoint, it was caused by a genuine sense of responsibility. When he condemned *Marmion*, he was not deflected by his liking for Scott; he knew what he was doing, and expected his brother advocate to understand. The gravamen of his offence, especiálly in the eyes of such single-minded men as Wordsworth and Southey whose whole faith was in poetry, lay in the unconfessed levity of approach, made more irritating by the authoritative didactic tone caught from the professors. The idea of a standard of poetry, taken with the attitude and tone— reflex of classroom and profession—might account for the discrepancy between Jeffrey's public denunciation of 'the Lakists' and his private liking for some of Wordsworth's poems: as reviewer he assumed a public situation, not insincerely but without involving his deeper feelings or his inmost thoughts. The procedure of the Scottish courts, also, laid great stress on written pleadings and judgements. The young advocate was taught to take example from the admirable expositions of great practitioners, and his training inevitably affected his attitude, tone, and process when he sat down to write. Jeffrey's sometimes deplorable conduct was that of a clever young advocate, seizing too quickly on what seems to be the one issue in the case, and enjoying the arguing of it too much, to admit the broad and deliberate consideration proper to the judical office he was too ready to assume. Thomas Brown wrote with somewhat finicking academic elaboration, from a definite standpoint but without the advocate's determination to carry his point, aiming at thoroughness but not at the finality of the judge. The greater ease and humanity of Scott's contributions to the *Review* reflect his lack of forensic ambition, and even interest; his manner grows out of social intercourse, where his genius lay, rather than from professional practice for which he never competed.

Until he revolted against Whig defeatism, Scott[1] could contribute to *The Edinburgh Review* because he belonged to the same society, with the same educational and professional environment as its projectors. Where he differed from such alert worldlings as Jeffrey, Smith, and Brougham, was in belonging —in sociological phrase—to a different sub-group, that of the historians and antiquaries, less conspicuous but equally numerous and industrious. His academic interests were few. His

---

[1] 1771–1832. At Scottish bar 1792; Sheriff-depute, Selkirk, 1799; clerk in Court of Session 1806. Married 1797; bought Abbotsford 1812. Baronet 1820. Died at Abbotsford.

anxious father, suspecting perhaps the business weakness on
which all his sons were to founder, restricted his university
attendance to such classes as he judged to be of professional
utility. Scott regretted afterwards the neglect of philosophy and
science, but it left him the more free—though nothing could
have stopped him—to indulge his inborn love of history and
poetry. His rudimentary Greek soon vanished; Latin he read
naturally and unpedantically, and so too the Italian of Boiardo
and Ariosto, the Spanish of the ballads, old French romances,
Anglo-Saxon and old Norse, with a scholar's erudition in none
of them and more than an antiquary's delight in all. About
1792–3 he caught the prevalent vogue of German, and translated two of Bürger's horror-ballads, Goethe's *Erl-King* and one
or two more, and about 1799 Goethe's *Goetz von Berlichingen*.
The vogue did not last long, nor did the translations catch
public attention; *Goetz* meant so little to him that he left the
publication to Matthew Lewis—so completely that his name
appeared on the title-page as 'William Scott', and he declared
afterwards that he never even saw a copy. Bürger, however,
stimulated him to write three original poems in the same vein:
The Fire-King, *Glenfinlas*, and *The Eve of St. John*, which appeared,
with two versions from the German, in the first volume of
Lewis's *Tales of Wonder*, 1801, among some fifteen efforts by
Lewis, seven by Southey, one by John Leyden, and a few others.

At the same time he was engaged on healthier work, for the
valuable outcome of his non-professional pursuits during these
years is found in the *Minstrelsy of the Scottish Border*, 1802, and
the edition of *Sir Tristrem*, 1804. In these pursuits he was no
lonely eccentric: all through the eighteenth century Scotsmen,
reacting consciously or unconsciously to their reduced nation-
hood and the changing ways of life, had been collecting the
traditional literature and music of their country and com-
municating with English antiquaries who, lured by the romantic
sense of distance and inhibited by the increasing separation of
classes, neglected the treasures of their own countryside. Ballads
were the articles most patronized by English collectors, partly
through the impetus given by Bishop Percy but also for their
quality as antiques—for a good story is always delightful—and
because a ballad, being a story, is a less intimate thing; and it
can more easily be divorced from its music, which requires
special skill in the collector, and, in the listener, freedom from

contemporary fashion. Scott had a conspicuous precedent in David Dalrymple, Lord Hailes, who sent ballads to Shenstone and edited a selection of poems from the Bannatyne Manuscript, and fellow enthusiasts in Bishop Percy, the doyen of them all, David Herd, John Leyden, James Jamieson whose collection was forestalled by the *Minstrelsy*, and a dozen others. While editing *Sir Tristrem* from the Auchinleck Manuscript—like the Bannatyne owned by the Advocates' Library in which both Lord Hailes and Scott had a professional interest—he corresponded with Francis Douce, George Ellis, Joseph Ritson whose peculiarities did not blind the tolerant Scott to his erudition. To go further would be to compile a long register of friendships and a bibliography of contemporary scholarship. Nor was Scott alone in exemplifying his own theory of the authorship of the Romances: 'Whatever individual among a class, whose trade it was to recite poetry, felt the least degree of poetical enthusiasm in a profession so peculiarly calculated to inspire it, must, from that very impulse, have become an original author, or translator'—substitute 'hobby' for 'trade' and 'profession', and you have James Jamieson and John Leyden, collectors, translators, and original writers, and Scott himself, with this distinction that he went beyond the mere production of imitation ballads.

Translation and imitation were early and short-lived fancies; editing occupied him more and brought greater returns. Scott's editorial methods can be criticized, but where there is no valid exemplar a strict scholar can only print the text he judges, on literary grounds, to be the least faulty, or, like Child, all available texts, leaving the rest to the reader; whereas Scott was working, not as a textual scientist but as a lover of ballads who desired for his readers the same delight he found in them himself. Whether his eclectic method was the correct one or not, the editorial exercise forced him to critical consideration of the qualities of narrative poetry. Annotation, in which he followed the methods of Bishop Percy, widened his research into history and its sources in public, legal, and family records, in which he had the help of such learned friends as Fraser Tytler and such repositories of odd information as Charles Kirkpatrick Sharp. From his famous expeditions in the Borders, when, as his companion Shortreed said, 'He was making himself all the time', he brought home not only ballads and stories and 'routh o' auld nick-nackets', but detailed knowledge of country and wide acquaintance with people whose minds and characters retained much of the old fashion.

Thus his capacious memory was stored with the European tradition of romance, the native tradition of song and ballad, English and Scots letters from Chaucer, Spenser, Shakespeare to Fielding, Burns, Wordsworth, history in its most factual and most human records from the chronicles of the twelfth century to the reminiscences of his family and friends, and a horseman's knowledge of country. He had played with ballad, but without satisfaction. In the Introduction to the *Minstrelsy* he is paying a characteristic compliment to John Leyden when he writes 'Upon my ideas of the nature and difficulty of such imitations, I ought in prudence to be silent; lest I resemble the dwarf, who brought with him a standard to measure his own stature'; but the 'ideas' are there. He had supplied fifteen stanzas to *Sir Tristrem* in place of the conclusion missing in the Auchinleck Manuscript, not impeccable in philological detail, but a spirited pastiche. His dissatisfaction is described in the Introduction to *The Lay of the Last Minstrel* in the 1830 *Poems*: the ballad quatrain 'had become hackneyed and sickening', and was too rigid; the 'measured short line' of the romances was too facile. Association with Lewis, 'a martinet . . . in the accuracy of rhymes and of numbers', taught a negative lesson: *The Fire-King*, written as a companion piece to Lewis's *Cloud-King*, fails as Lewis's verses fail—and sometimes Byron's—by the incongruity of metre and sentiment; but he was to use the measure to better purpose in *Lochinvar*. Dr. John Stoddart's recitation of the unpublished *Christabel* did for him what the blank verse of the theatres did for Milton, and listening to Milton's sonnets did for Wordsworth: the form fulfilled the first function of form, which is to act as a catalyst for the surcharged imagination.

Scott said, 'It is to Mr. Coleridge that I am bound to make the acknowledgment due from the pupil to his master', but the form was the only lesson he learned. He admired Coleridge and Wordsworth, and knew that their poetic range was too high for him, so he never dreamed of trying to reach it. In any case, he had superabundantly, by nature and habit, one gift from which all his work arises and of which they were devoid: the sense of the continuity of human life, which is the historical instinct. Both Coleridge and Wordsworth had glimpses of the time-stream in relation to the Church as an institution, but only there. Wordsworth indeed celebrated the Church in *Ecclesiastical Sonnets*, a painstaking historical sequence that would have been better if he had had more sense of history or any historical imagination. The values and insights of *The White Doe of Rylstone* and the *Song at Brougham Castle* are not historical. Pious conservatism made him understand some of the motives of the Rising in the North, and he himself

thought there was a stronger fire of passion than was elsewhere to be found among [his poems] in that lyrical burst near the conclusion of *The Song at the Feast of Brougham Castle*:

> Armour resting in his halls
> On the blood of Clifford calls;—
> 'Quell the Scot', exclaims the Lance—
> Bear me to the heart of France
> Is the longing of the Shield.—

That 'fire of passion', however, is not the motive of the poem, any more than the motive of *The White Doe of Rylstone* is the commemoration of the Rising in the North. The themes are the recurrent ones: in the *Song*, 'the Influence of Natural Objects' in the forming of character, in *The White Doe*, as in the first Book of *The Excursion* and (by reverse) in *Laodamia* which belong to the same years, patient endurance and love among sorrows. Wordsworth's references to history point always to philosophic or emotional conclusions, which are permanent and timeless. The only action he had seen having been disastrous, he had withdrawn himself, and he took little part in affairs for their own sakes even in the present, and, having little time-sense, less in the past. Accident of birth may have contributed. Unlike Walter Scott who could not look out of his window without being reminded of a story and a song, he was brought up in a strategic backwater. The comparison with Scott is forced on us, because Wordsworth had it very much in mind as he wrote *The White Doe*, and so had Coleridge when he criticized the first draft of it. These two, and also Southey, received *The Lay of the Last Minstrel*, *Marmion*, and *The Lady of the Lake* with what would have been resentment and jealousy if Scott had been a man they could have disliked. Coleridge wisely refused to allow any public claim to his priority in the invention of the

free-running adaptation of romance-verse which Scott exploited
so heartily, but he often spoke of it in private. Even apart from
that professional grievance, partly discounted by Scott's ready
acknowledgement of his debt, there were deeper reasons. Here
was a man who took poetry light-heartedly, gave the public
something it liked, was well paid for it, and was quite un-
ashamed. Wordsworth, naturally resentful of the reviewers'
injustice to the 1807 *Poems* and still more, perhaps, the general
neglect—current in Farington's Diary where ordinary opinion
is so usefully reflected—never mentioned Scott's poems without
slighting them, though Scott never spoke of Wordsworth's
without admiration: they were both honest men. There was
cause for Wordsworth's fears of comparison. *The White Doe*
appeared five years after *The Lady of the Lake*, and anyone reading one might remember the other:

> It soothed us—it beguiled us—then, to hear
> Once more of troubles wrought by magic spell;
> And griefs whose aery motion comes not near
> The pangs that tempt the Spirit to rebel—
> > (*The White Doe*, Dedication 33–36.)

> Harp! we have been full long beguiled
> By vague thoughts, lured by fancies wild;
> To which, with no reluctant strings,
> Thou hast attuned thy murmurings. . . .

> But, Harp! Thy murmurs may not cease—
> A Spirit, with his angelic wings,
> In soft and breeze-like visitings,
> Has touched thee—and a Spirit's hand—
> > (*The White Doe*, 324–31.)

> Yet once again farewell, thou Minstrel harp! . . .
> Much have I owed thy strains on life's long way,
> > Through secret woes the world has never known,
> When on the weary night dawn'd wearier day,
> > And bitterer was the grief devour'd alone. . . .

> Hark! as my lingering footsteps slow retire,
> > Some Spirit of the Air has waked thy string!
> 'Tis now a Seraph bold, with touch of fire,
> > 'Tis now the brush of Fairy's frolic wing.
> Receding now the mountain breezes scarcely bring
> > A wandering witch-note of the distant spell—
> And now 'tis silent all—
> > (*The Lady of the Lake*, Epilogue.)

Resemblances are probably adventitious, but solemn theses
have been built on less, and Wordsworth would be all the more
anxious to distinguish his serious teaching from mere frivolity
like Scott's, whose parting wish at the end of *Marmion* was

> To thee, dear schoolboy, whom my lay
> Has cheated of thy hour of play,
> Light task and merry holiday!

Nor let this necessity of producing immediate pleasure be considered as a degradation of the Poet's art. It is far otherwise. It is
an acknowledgment of the beauty of the universe, an acknowledgment the more sincere, because not formal, but indirect; it is a task
light and easy to him who looks at the world in the spirit of love;
further, it is a homage paid to the native and naked dignity of man,
to the grand elementary principle of pleasure, by which he knows,
and feels, and lives and moves.

Scott would be the first to recognize the gulf between Wordsworth's philosophical concept and his own humbler office of
providing pastime for his neighbours; but he would not be
abashed by Wordsworth's deliberate rebukes in the Dedication
of *The White Doe*:

> He serves the Muses erringly and ill
> Whose aim is pleasure light and fugitive—

and Wordsworth lost by his nervous withdrawal of the hem of
his garment. The action of *The White Doe* is obscure—and was
apparently worse in the first draft, to judge by Coleridge's
comments—because Wordsworth, once more, was afraid of
producing the wrong kind of pleasure and thereby detracted
even from his own serious purpose, for the reader's mind is
clouded by the difficulty of following the story and is not made
to feel that the Nortons matter greatly, and is therefore less fit
to enter into the desired sympathy with Emily and to understand the lesson that Wordsworth is trying to convey. When
Coleridge wrote, 'Of Sir Walter Scott's poetry I cannot speak so
highly, still less of the Poetry in his Poems', he meant by 'the
Poetry', presumably, the spiritual and philosophical meanings
which were no part of Scott's intention, but he was too good
a critic to miss his real virtues—'though even in these the power
of presenting the most numerous figures, and figures with the
most complex movements, and under rapid succession, in *true
picturesque unity*, attests true and peculiar genius'. Wordsworth

refused the 'picturesque' and lost the unity, for the powerful visual image of the lady with the white doe is left unbalanced.

The difference was more than artistic. Coleridge sought for metaphysical, Wordsworth for spiritual absolutes. They could not stop to consider that the sense of time, the intuition of relativity, and the intuition of vitality expressed in Scott's images of action, might also be philosophical concepts—not that Scott ever formulated them: that was not his mode of thought. On the other hand, he was never outside the field of ethics, where he and Wordsworth shared the stoicism that prevailed among poets as among men at large in these strenuous days until Shelley sounded the note of a milder generation. Never having retired from the world of affairs, Scott was more concerned with ordinary ethics, which, for him, were based on inherited standards and habits of behaviour, both in personal matters and on the larger scale of behaviour which is politics. It is in the novels, however, with which we are not concerned in this volume, that his ethics and politics become interesting; in earlier days they were unthinking and aesthetic, and enter little into his poetry. The epistle to William Stewart Rose with which *Marmion* opens is a dignified piece of verse, not to be compared for depth and power with Wordsworth's Lines in expectation of the death of Fox, but more on the political level; for Scott could write on the level of society as Wordsworth could not, and, as is obvious on comparing the *Marmion* epistles with the Epistle to Allan Cunningham, the garrulous Southey could not. Scott's poems, indeed, which reflected his pastimes rather than his thought, prepared the public to see little in the novels except the 'romantic' picturesque, so that his more serious and complex reflections passed—and pass—with little remark and little attempt to weigh their various elements; not unreasonably, since they were not the main object of his communications with the public at large. His tales are neither myths like Wordsworth's, nor allegories like Bunyan's, nor symbolic structures like Blake's, but just stories, with as much incidental reflection as comes naturally in stories about people.

Scott's first three romances are strung on well-worn *motifs*: the lovers and the family feud, the disguised avenger, the honest outlaw. Vague memories of *Romeo and Juliet*, *As You Like It*, *Cymbeline*, *Clarissa* might be traced, rather unnecessarily. Other strands, 'supernatural' and historical, may be traced more legiti:nately in the introduction and notes to the *Minstrelsy* and in the personal experiences associated with it. Scott freed himself gradually from the gross German hobgoblins. He had no 'philosophy of the supernatural'; neither had Coleridge, but he was a better poet. In the *Lay* Scott exploited three different modes: the irrelevant River and Mountain Spirits, the mischievous Goblin (with whom indeed it had unfortunately begun), and the Magic Book. In *Marmion* the spectre-knight took shape finally on the very dubious authority of Surtees of Mainsforth, who imposed on Scott more than once. In *The Lady of the Lake* the incidental 'superstitious' element has only historical import, and the air is the fresher for it. When in *The Monastery* Scott returned to the time and place of the *Lay*, association brought back the unexorcised spirit in the disastrous White Lady of Avenel, and when he resuscitated Marmion and de Wilton in Brian de Boisguilbert and Wilfred, the heathen nonsense of Ulrica brought a waft of the old fog into *Ivanhoe*. The historical element in the *Lay* shows how easily Scott moved in time: it was neither ignorance nor confusion that introduced, into a tale dated about 1555, the old pupil of Michael Scott who died about 1289, Wat of Harden, then aged five but already the white-haired father of five grown sons, and 'Belted Will' Howard who was not born till ten years later. All he needed in *The Lady of the Lake* was the traditional anecdotes and songs about the wanderings of James V in disguise, and his breach with the Douglases. When, however, he placed *Marmion* in time by its climax in the battle of Flodden, he engaged himself in genuine emotion. Out of its depth and reality rises the surge of eloquence that makes the sixth canto the finest battlepiece in poetry. The motive is alive: the tune of *The Flowers of the Forest* puts philosophy out of countenance.

Around the historical figures of the *Lay* are grouped those timeless folk which Jeffrey, with true bourgeois gentility and Whiggish correctness, objected to as vulgar: Wat Tinlinn and his wife, whose later descendants were called Dandie and Ailie Dinmont, the bluff English troopers who reappear in *The Lady of the Lake* and have a later representative in *The Two Drovers*. Scott would have shaken his head at the radical Professor Millar's contrast of the honest English carter and the obsequious Highland gillie, but his innate scepticism of the '45 is betrayed in his description, based on John Home's memoirs and probably the stories of eyewitnesses, of the ill-armed conscripts in the Jacobite army; *Waverley*, chapter xliv: for him the 'simple' folk mattered as well as their 'gentle' leaders. The general historical feeling in all three romances is entirely sound; but what is truly solid is the topography. Scott sited his Germanic Tales of Wonder in places he knew: Glenfinlas, his grandfather's farm of Sandyknowe, the Esk valley just south of Edinburgh; and whatever is invented or distorted in the romances, Deloraine's ride from Branxholm to Melrose, James's route to and from Stirling and his scrambles about the Trossachs, Marmion's journeys in Lothian, can be followed on the Ordnance Survey maps and on the ground. This is not for the sake of fashionable decoration or topography or the Picturesque, but grows out of the 'local attachments' which Dorothy Wordsworth noticed in a letter to Lady Beaumont in May 1805—the natural love, which inspired him as it inspired Crome and Constable, and Wordsworth himself. The beginnings of failure, from *Rokeby* on, appear when Scott begins to look for subjects, and finds them in places he knew only as a visitor. The various places around his friend Morritt's house are correctly oriented, the action moves from point to point, but the cross-country feel of the ground is missing. *The Lord of the Isles* and, still more, *Harold the Dauntless*, are the work of a tourist. The same test may be applied to the novels. Scott lacked the 'romantic' love of remoteness. It saved him from the false remoteness of *Thalaba* or *Gebir*, and if it lost him the entranced remoteness of Coleridge and Keats and Shelley, it gave him enchantments of his own. The rootless Coleridge mocked at the plethora of place-names, the habit which Sir Alexander Boswell parodied pleasantly in *Sir Albon*, 1811. Wordsworth would understand up to a point, but his place-names—Blencathra, Glaramara, Helvellyn—though not evocations of distance like those of Milton and Thomson, were incantations of space and solitude. Scott's landscapes, like Thomson's, are inhabited, for his is social poetry, about the behaviour and interactions of people, and for social reading. A lad can have queer sensations after dark in Teviotdale or Lammermuir, or when snaring woodcock on a Lakeland fellside; in later life he can interpret them metaphysically or psychologically, or he can accept them as part of life's experience and tell stories to his friends.

Of the first three romances, *The Lady of the Lake* is the most successful. Though making few demands on the reader's mind and the very reverse of metaphysical, it is all relevant to human life. It is in perfect keeping throughout; and there is no substitute for it. But by the age of thirty-nine, he was ready to go on to something else. In *Rokeby* there is an abortive novel, like *Woodstock* but better; there is some good writing in *The Lord of the Isles*, but one cannot return to it after Barbour's *Bruce*. Whether through lack of ambition and lack of faith in his own powers, or, as with Jeffrey, a notion that *belles-lettres* was a secondary affair, Scott did not put much effort into the romances. As a social being, he was reticent about his deepest thoughts and feelings. The melancholy that endeared *The Vanity of Human Wishes* to him was not for the public; society needed rather such antidotes as he found useful to himself. It was when dramatic values in romance or novel could be enhanced, as he learned from Shakespeare, by song, that he forgot himself and *belles-lettres* and the reading public, and, intent on the scene and the singer, reached beyond time and place and thought into poetry.

The romances occupied only a part even of his off-duty attention. The rest was given to editing. The common notion of Scott is that he was a Jacobite and medievalist; in fact he was no Jacobite, and his medieval studies, though extensive and pleasurable, were desultory. The time he knew best was from the reign of James VI to that of George II; and that knowledge was acquired while editing Dryden, Swift, and the Somers Tracts, which, with auxiliary memoirs like those of Robert Carey, Herbert of Cherbury, and Count Grammont, kept him employed from 1805 to 1814—from the completion of the *Lay* to the writing of *Waverley*. His notion of editing was like Malone's, extensive. Thus he acquired his intimate acquaintance with the politics, society, personalities, and literature of the modern world up to the point at which they were still living and controversial and required different dealing. He embarrassed the finances of Ballantyne and Constable by insisting on the publication of unsaleable editions by his assistants, and was a stout supporter of the clubs which existed to reprint historical and literary documents. The advent of Byron, therefore, does not explain his abandonment of verse romance, though with his usual courtesy he gave that as his reason, but rather the inadequacy of the form. He began and abandoned *Waverley* in

1805; when in 1813 at the age of forty-two he resumed it, his mind was full of the stuff of life to be discharged in the greater form of the novel. All this does not mean a plan of preparation: he resumed *Waverley* as casually as he had dropped it. It might well be ascribed to his deep-seated melancholy. His sense of the brevity of life and the vanity of human wishes drove him into a passion for conservatism, in politics, in society, and in his own circumstances. Men must die in the flesh, but he would do what he could to ensure that their actions and personalities should not vanish from the world, not because he yearned to live in the past—he had too much common sense to yearn after either the past or the future—but because the present would be so much poorer without them. His father's family had not come to much, so he had to see that his branch of it should achieve a permanent place among the families of Scotland; and his own life had to be a full one. Inevitable annihilation could be forgotten in constant activity, reading, publication, tree-planting, building, and strenuous exercise on the hills, and above all in friendly human intercourse. He always drove himself too hard —the feverish labour of his later years was only an exaggeration —and he paid the penalty in his body, for he had little with which to tax his conscience.

These then were the new things in the north when Blake was wrestling with the transformation of *The Four Zoas* into *Milton* and *Jerusalem*, Wordsworth preparing the *Poems in Two Volumes*, and Jane Austen, with *Northanger Abbey* lying idle in the publisher's office, working intermittently on *Sense and Sensibility*, the years from the Peace of Amiens to the opening of the Peninsular Campaign. When *The Quarterly Review* appeared in February 1809 the reader could not fail to measure it against the *Edinburgh*, for reviewing on this scale was now an established craft with Jeffrey as its master. The tone was hardened by the deliberate political collision, and by the choice of editor it dictated. The value of William Gifford to his employers lay in his professional equipment as satirist and his record as editor of *The Anti-Jacobin*. Toughened by his early struggle for formal education, he was never on equal terms with his contributors and therefore less happy than Jeffrey in his treatment of them: when Southey called reviewing 'the ungentle craft' he was lamenting his subordination to the ex-shoemaker editor, though indeed others had more reason to complain. But for politics, he might have been more at ease with Jeffrey, the editor *primus inter pares*, and, like Scott, have found *The Edinburgh Review* men pleasanter company than those of his own party. What neither Jeffrey nor Gifford could give was positive critical direction. However much later poets might disagree with Coleridge and Wordsworth, they have had to take account of their principles as well as their example; Jeffrey merely regulated the apprentice poet, and Gifford intimidated him. Jeffrey was a shrewd judge of detail—his summaries of evidence, that is of the work he is examining, and his choice of quotation, are admirable—but his eighteenth-century conformity gave him only 'taste', 'refinement', and similar criteria to work with—standards rather than principles, for which, in his Whiggish self-assured way, he saw no need to fight. Gifford could not keep from fighting, but had no better cause to fight for.

This may not have mattered much in England; Scotland, with narrower resources, suffered more from the lack of a body of ideas to advance from. The Scottish school of philosophy was no nursing mother of poets. Though Scott was a sound critic whose opinions grew from the best possible soil, a catholic enjoyment of life and literature, and while he elated and energized his countrymen by his example, he was all too ready to disclaim anything more profound than good literary manners and love of his country and its traditions of song, ballad, and story. If people enjoyed reading what he enjoyed writing, it was a fair bargain and there was no need to argue about it. Burns, the other and greater exemplar, deceived later Scottish generations even more by his pose of the Inspired Ploughman. Even the astute Jeffrey found it a hindrance in his claim that Burns must be placed among major poets and criticized without condescension; and simpler men, accepting at its face value the common pose that should never mislead an artist, did not notice that

> I never drank the Muses' stank,
> Castalia's stream an' a' that

is the commonest cliché in European poetry, inherited by scholarly poets like Spenser and Ronsard and Ovid, or that the motto 'Woodnotes Wild' is a quotation from Milton. A few might realize that Scott's easy style depended on an unusual range of knowledge; but too few realized that while episodic parody of the romances is easy, full-scale emulation is not. Of those who entered Scott's personal orbit, John Leyden[1] sailed for India in 1803, two years before *The Lay of the Last Minstrel* was published, and died in Java in 1811, before *The Lady of the Lake* can have reached him. He was then absorbed in Indian studies, and, in any case, his verses indicate strength rather than subtlety—the strength by which he devoured ancient, modern, and oriental languages, walked eighty miles to find the complete text of a ballad, and acquired enough knowledge of medicine to qualify as an East India Company surgeon at short notice. Beyond his imitations of ballad, which owe what quality they have to that rude force exercised on forms he knew from his childhood in the Border, he wrote sonnets after the manner of Warton and Bowles, *Scenes of Infancy*, a series of disjointed sketches which looks back to Goldsmith and Cowper, and translations from an astonishing variety of languages, among which, not surprisingly, the best are from the warsongs of Tyrtaeus. If he had lived he might have written more occasional verses in the vein of the comic apology for his dancing signed 'The Bear', and, when more deeply touched, of the Ode to Scottish Music in Scott's *Minstrelsy*, which needs only the excision of five or six stanzas; in any case this born scholar had something to bring to his own verses as well as to the editing of ballads and of *Scottish Descriptive Poems*, 1803. James Hogg[2] was in a more perilous situation, who, a year older than Scott and surviving him for three years, encountered all the fashions and chances of the time and place.

Hogg claimed precedence over Scott as 'King of the mountain and the fairy school' with his usual lack of manners, but he had some right on his side. He had the advantage of being practically illiterate until he was seventeen, and brought up by his mother in a pure tradition, if such a thing existed anywhere. He was fortunate in hearing, first of modern literature, some pieces of Burns. But he had the disadvantage of the self-taught, in being at the mercy of whatever chanced to come to hand, and losing self-criticism in the pride of conquest. The fruitful meeting of traditional and booklearned culture is a precarious business, if only that the techniques and critical values of a culture received

[1] 1775–1811. Educated in Edinburgh. Assistant surgeon at Madras 1803; in Calcutta 1806; died in Java.

[2] 1770–1835. 'The Ettrick Shepherd': first printed verse 1800; in Edinburgh 1810; farmed in the Borders. 'Christopher North's' Shepherd in *Noctes Ambrosianae* is a caricature, but apparently not too unjust.

casually and almost unconsciously are taken for granted and insufficiently studied, and understanding of the critical values of the deliberately-acquired culture comes late, and often after good work has been spoiled by contamination with what has little to recommend it but the prestige of print. Only a master of both cultures can strike out a new line by combining elements which he rightly judges or divines to be compatible. Burns at his best could do it, but even he, who was far from illiterate, was too easily influenced by inferior poets; and Hogg was defenceless. The situation was complicated further by the eighteenth-century cult of 'simplicity', which may be 'artless' or may be the final achievement of concentration and the remorseless application of skill; the 'artlessness' may be the product of mastery in an artistic mode which is not analysed in the prescribed textbooks, and high simplicity may deceive the uninitiated into thinking its virtue grows out of negations. The confusion hampered Scottish literature for a hundred years. Scott, Hogg, and many others could not proclaim their love for traditional tunes without denouncing the ridiculous complexities and fantastic Italian tricks which drew fashionable audiences to listen to Haydn, Mozart, Beethoven, and suchlike modern impostors—an attitude that would not have appealed to Dunbar, or indeed to any Scottish poet before the eighteenth century. Behind this lies the long political and social history already alluded to, which—more importantly—worsened the linguistic complex present in Gawain Douglas's mind three centuries before; by now the writing of vernacular Scots implied peasant manners or antiquarian curiosity. So far as men of letters accepted their bilingualism they could turn it into an advantage by using it in writing, as they would in speech, to extend the range at least of their pastimes or, more privately, to express tenderness too intimate for their formal English. Thus a solid journalist, John Mayne, following the precedents from *Christ's Kirk on the Green* and *Peblis to the Play* to Fergusson's *Leith Races* and Burns's *Holy Fair*—though Burns had infused Popian satire into that—wrote in the local dialect, *The Siller Gun*, a Breughel picture of a Dumfries festival. In 1811, William Tennant, who was to end as a sober Professor of Oriental Languages in St. Andrews, published *Anster Fair* in English with a strong Scottish accent, a fantastic medley of rustic humours fittingly presided over by King James V, and combining his reputed work with the Italian comic style—a mixture as original as Scott's but of different ingredients, foreshadowing Frere's and Byron's. Scott, who had a shrewd notion of the difficulties, avoided rather than solved them, since they scarcely intruded on him as he followed his fancy. In his ignorance and vanity, James Hogg fell into them all.

His first venture in 1801, *Scottish Pastorals, Poems, Songs, etc.*, is crude work for a man of thirty-one, but in content very much what might be expected: two pleasant Burnsian pieces, a poem and two songs in Allan Ramsay's 'pastoral' style, a vilely inflated elegiac *Dialogue within a Country Church Yard*, and a modern tragedy badly told in ballad quatrains. In *The Mountain Bard* six years later he ranges from bad Allan Ramsay, through fair efforts in the school of Burns, to effusions which only need compression, and ten imitation ballads which—since like the others he was writing for readers, and so lacked the discipline which the old ballad-makers would gain from listeners who would demand dramatic force and reject *longueurs*—are too equable in movement, but, being untainted by German extravagance or antiquarian erudition, are better offshoots of the pure tradition he had learned in his boyhood than any of Scott's or Leyden's. Here the Ettrick Shepherd stood on his own ground; but when he trusted his poetic gift to make him free of Scott's, he began to outrun both his knowledge and his strength. He was indeed capable of learning, or at least of mimicry, as he showed in *The Poetic Mirror* (1816) when, being baulked in a somewhat impudent scheme of enlisting greater poets in a publication for his benefit, he wrote Byron's, Scott's, Wordsworth's, Coleridge's, Southey's, and Wilson's contributions for them—not without malice, but as imitations, not as parodies. The same gift may explain the solidity of *The Private Memoirs and Confessions of a Justified Sinner*, a work of remarkable strength compared with his other prose writings. It is one of a group of novels in which Galt, Lockhart, and some lesser Scots exploited a vein of black melancholy. *The Confessions* indeed make one suspect the hand of Lockhart; Hogg was vain, but not too proud to accept of unacknowledged assistance. In *The Queen's Wake* of 1813 he proved that he could learn to some purpose, and he created too—whether he knew it or not—two fresh personal things. Out of his family inheritance of legend and the strange influences of his native hills he made new poetry in

Kilmeny, where the strain of moral preaching cannot break the enchanted stillness of a fairy-tale that is neither a museum-piece nor a Shakespearian prettiness. Out of two Scottish folk-themes, witchcraft and the village humours of the ill-used husband, he made *The Witch of Fife*, saved by the comic tradition which is the best safeguard not only against sentimentality and false refinement but even against lapses of style and invention. When he tried to elaborate the theme of *Kilmeny* with attempts at philosophy in *Pilgrims of the Sun* he broke down, nor could he carry through continuous narrative in *Mador of the Moor* and *Queen Hynde*. From such as these, and even from a competently handled anecdote like Sir Alexander Boswell's *Clan Alpin's Vow*, one returns to *Marmion* or *The Lady of the Lake* with heightened appreciation of Scott's originality, variety, and tireless elasticity of rhythm.

Yet even in these there are gleams of unsophisticated poetry; and singing came naturally to the Ettrick Shepherd as it did not come to Scott, so that, if it came too easily to force him to distil so much into few lines, and if he could never distinguish between authentic tradition, ephemeral popular ditty, and professional organ-grinding, he added to the floating body of Scottish song. *The Forest Minstrel* of 1810 is his own addition, with a little help from three other rhymers, to the long series of collections of popular song, and therefore not for continuous reading or close examination. Passion could be achieved by the intensity and the artistic self-criticism of Burns, and elevation of feeling in the return to cavalier sensibility by Scott and once by Graham of Gartmore in *If doughty deeds my lady please*; Hogg had none of these gifts, yet at least he has more fire than Robert Tannahill who had a pretty lyrical sense and little else; and humour occasionally saves him as it just saves Alexander Wilson, another discontented Paisley weaver who, having the instinct for scientific collecting and a gift for drawing, eventually earned respect by his *American Ornithology*, and as it gives Sir Alexander Boswell his small niche with the rest. Hogg found his proper level when he drew upon Jacobite sentiment for his theme. Into the hard fighting and the desperate tragedy of the '45 he had little penetration, but like all his countrymen, in whom, whatever their political opinions, obtuseness at Westminster and the brutality of the Duke of Cumberland and his generals cancelled any elation they might have felt at the defeat of the Rebellion, he felt sympathy and admiration for Highland courage and loyalty; and now that the clans had ceased to be dangerous, they were perceived to be picturesque, as the Covenanters, whose strength and endurance Hogg also remembered, were not.

Jacobitism provided an emotion, the Highlands a scene; the reception of influences from Gaelic into English literature was another matter: if any influence passed, it was in the opposite direction. The 'Ossianic' impress lasted for another generation, enfeebled by the dubiety engendered by the equivocal proceedings of James Macpherson. A writer of Mrs. Anne Grant's[1] stature, however sympathetic her prose *Letters from the Mountains* (1803) and *Superstitions of the Highlands* (1811), could not suggest in the limping couplets of *The Highlanders* or the conventional prosody and diction of her translations either the formal or the spiritual qualities of Gaelic poetry, while to recommend its elaborate art by the equally conventional plea of 'rustic simplicity' merely obscured the issues. Thomas Campbell's[2] family kept nothing of Gaelic culture, and for him as a young tutor the Island of Mull and his ancestral Argyll were places of exile.

Nor, on the other hand, did he acquire in Glasgow much more of the lowland inheritance than a Scottish accent and a love of song. In the University he learned Greek, liberal politics, and the accepted principles of English poetry, like Jeffrey before him, and to these he remained faithful all his life: whence Byron's approval and modern neglect. They all appear in his first publication in 1799 when he was living in Edinburgh on the hackwork that was to be his portion thenceforth. Without a profession, and without rich friends like those whose subsidies gave Wordsworth, Coleridge, and Southey time to work out their poetic principles, he faced the young poet's problem, never so obvious as in the late eighteenth century—what to write about and therefore in what form to write. The method of Rogers's *The Pleasures of Memory* offered a solution; the young Campbell, having neither money nor prospects, solaced himself

[1] 1755–1838. Born in Glasgow, daughter of Duncan McVicar, an army officer. In America 1758–68, married James Grant, minister of Laggan, Inverness-shire, 1779. He died 1801. From 1810 she lived in Edinburgh by taking boarders, and had many friends, including Henry Mackenzie and Scott.

[2] 1777–1844. Born in Glasgow and educated there. One of originators of London University. Died at Boulogne.

with *The Pleasures of Hope*. The discursive poem brought its own problems, for which he was not well prepared. The verse runs sweetly, and, though a modern reader checks at some conventional epithets, the phrasing is neat. The transitions are inadequately managed, partly through lack of skill but mainly because there is no thematic sequence in the poem; nor can there be, since Hope was not a true idea but only something to write about and the poet had no depths of thought or experience to draw upon. His generalized treatment is merely stylistic and not philosophical, and his illustrations, upon which generalized discourse depends for its vitality, are mere literary reminiscences. Hope inspires the sailor, exemplified from John Byron's *Narrative* and, in Part II, Falconer's *Shipwreck*, which seems unnecessary in a man from Clydeside. References to Schiller, *The Rambler*, and the history of Charles XII of Sweden illustrate Part II. Even his thoughts on India came from Burke's speeches against Warren Hastings; yet there his ruling passion strengthens the verse. The disciple of Professor Millar who had walked to Edinburgh and back with 4*s*. 6*d*. in his pocket to see the trial of Thomas Muir and his associate Joseph Gerrald and was so moved by Gerrald's eloquence that his friends remarked the change in him, remained a lifelong enthusiast for liberty. So when the hopes of science, Greek philosophy, and poetry have led into sympathy with poverty, maternal love, and childhood, there follows the hope of improvement in savage regions and hope for the freedom of Poland, an attack on the slave-trade and on English behaviour in India. Part II surveys the arts without coming to any positive conclusion, which would be improper to the theme of Hope. Campbell does not dwell too long on any of his episodes; he may have learned his discretion, very noticeable in a garrulous age, from his classical studies, of which some specimens follow *The Pleasures of Hope*. He had won college prizes for Greek translation, and if tragic choruses can be translated into eighteenth-century verse, he could do it as neatly as anyone.

From these and the three songs that close the little volume, a reader might well rise with hope: this sensitive young artist might do greater things as he matured. He did indeed become more skilful, but that was all. In later years he spent much of his time and his scanty resources in helping Polish refugees, and, as a Whig journalist, wrote well for his chosen cause, in

prose and in satirical verse that occasionally makes one regret
that he did not indulge his humour more freely; but he had not
self-confidence enough to allow either his lighter fancies or his
deeper emotions to take charge, and the burden of ill-paid job-
work for publishers and magazines, which he was too proud to
acknowledge, constant anxiety about money, and domestic
sorrows, left him little time to broaden his thought. He suffers
as Southey does, from the restraint self-imposed on an excitable
temperament, and so cannot rise above pathos into tragedy in
Gertrude of Wyoming. In his review of this poem, Jeffrey diag-
nosed Campbell's weakness:

> It seems to us, as if the natural force and boldness of his ideas were
> habitually checked by a certain fastidious timidity, and an anxiety
> about the minor graces of correct and chastened composition. . . .
> We wish any praises or exhortations of ours had the power to give
> him confidence in his own great talents; and hope earnestly that he
> will now meet with such encouragement as may set him above all
> restraints that proceed from apprehension; and induce him to give
> free scope to that genius, of which we are persuaded the world has
> hitherto seen rather the grace than the richness.

The weakness, however, was inherent. On 29 June 1826 Scott
noted in his Journal, in words which reflect back on his own
poetry as well as Campbell's:

> I often wonder how Tom Campbell, with so much real genius,
> has not maintained a greater figure in the public eye than he has
> done of late. . . . Somehow he wants audacity, fears the public, and,
> what is worse, fears the shadow of his own reputation. He is a great
> corrector too, which succeeds as ill in composition as in education.
> Many a clever boy is flogged into a dunce, and many an original
> composition corrected into mediocrity. Yet Tom Campbell ought to
> have done a great deal more.

Jeffrey could approve, for there was nothing to surprise or per-
turb the cultivated reader, none of 'the babyism or the antiquarianism which have lately been versified', 'the elaborate
raptures and obscure originalities of these new artists'. A
Canadian admirer, quoted by Beattie in his *Life of Campbell*
(ii. 324), summed it up:

> Whatever particular beauties of description and striking delinea-
> tions of character are to be found in the 'Lady of the Lake', or the

'Corsair', it is evident, from their peculiar structure, that it requires a peculiar taste to admire them as poems—while 'The Pleasures of Hope', on the contrary, must receive unqualified praise so long as the verses of Pope and Goldsmith continue to be read with pleasure.

This shrinking from peculiarity—from local poetry like Scott's and personal poetry like Wordsworth's—is the outward sign of the inward timidity that weakens *Gertrude of Wyoming*. Campbell understands and depicts the emotions of his characters, but identifies himself with none of them; the reader therefore watches the action—and may well do so with pleasure—but does not enter into it.

There are feelings, however, which must be expressed in general terms because they are held in general, and Campbell could voice communal feeling in his songs on contemporary happenings. A nine-months visit to Germany, overlapping Coleridge's by a few weeks, did not produce the Literary Tour in Germany that was planned; Campbell called on literary men, including Klopstock by whom he was naturally more impressed than was Wordsworth, and wrestled with the works of Kant—a hard task for a disciple of the school of Reid—but caught no great enthusiasm for German literature. On the other hand he was caught up by the war between the French and the Austrians. His political opinions made it easy for him to be on good terms with the French garrison of Ratisbon; he had known Hungarian troops well enough to translate some of their songs: the poem on the battle at Hohenlinden is a poem about fighting by a man who had watched a battle from the walls of Ratisbon, not about the cause on which either side was engaged. So also when, inevitably, he wrote about the '45, *Lochiel's Warning* is neither a piece of fashionable Jacobite sentiment nor the Hanoverian triumph-song that might be expected from Glasgow and Clan Campbell, but grows from the general Scottish opinion that the rebellion was an unnecessary business, disastrous for all concerned. Campbell, however, was in Altona when the British fleet bombarded Copenhagen— on his way home his ship was chased into Yarmouth by a Danish privateer—and there is no detachment in *The Battle of the Baltic* or *Ye Mariners of England*. These, and *The Irish Harper* which appeared with *The Pleasures of Hope* in 1799, are so familiar to us from childhood that they are apt to pass without examination; but the lucid, direct, positive statement of *Hohen-*

linden, in the lineage of John Byrom and Scott of Amwell, is neither artless nor accidental. The metres and rhythms of the others are sufficiently complicated, but always within the range of song. Here, as in the longer poems, Campbell eschewed the vice of inflation, whether commentary or irrelevant description. He cut *The Battle of the Baltic* from 27 stanzas to 19 in the published version, not without sacrificing some good lines. The same immediate impact that comes from controlled power gives effect of deeper imagination to *The Last Man*, in which the fusion of scientific and humane makes fine sombre poetry that calls for illustration by Martin rather than Turner, in whose designs he speculated to carry off later editions of the long poems. Campbell remembered enough from the astronomy classroom in Glasgow at least to coax interesting conversation from Sir William Herschel when they met. Like Jeffrey again, he was a sound factual critic, and along the same lines. It is both pleasant and salutary to return to the *Specimens of British Poetry* that rises above his anonymous hackwork, and meet a sensitive practitioner who had an eye for good writing as for a fine ship, and remembered that each is the result of science and skill as well as creative intuition. Thomas Carlyle may have kept some regard for the poet who had given him the first thrill of poetry; it is something that one who praised with difficulty should include the *Specimens* in a short list of 'Books Worth Reading' with the note 'Good, both *criticisms* and pieces'. Looking back, one can regret Campbell's over-scrupulous treatment of his own work and his adherence to the general view of the new poetry of Wordsworth; one can regret also that his perpetual struggle for a livelihood forbade the development of his own ideas, breadth of interest, generosity, and artistry, and the provision of a sufficient counterbalance to the easy romanticism into which later Scottish generations so readily fell.

James Grahame[1] harked back to Thomson in the *Rural Calendar* (1797) not only for his subject, the lowland scene and weather, but for his verse and style. This was dangerous. Dr. Johnson said of Thomson that 'His mode of thinking, and of expressing his thoughts, is original. His blank verse is no more the blank verse of Milton, or of any other poet, than the rhymes of Prior are the rhymes of Cowley. His numbers, his pauses,

[1] 1765–1811. Lawyer, then episcopal clergyman.

his diction, are of his own growth, without transcription, without imitation.' Few of Thomson's followers, and certainly not Grahame, took warning: blank verse demands strong personal impulse to give it life. When Grahame wrote words for the Scots airs he loved, he, like every song-writer, was borrowing life from the tunes and the voice of the singer; in his other poems there could be no voice but his, and it was not a strong voice. His best-known poem *The Sabbath* (1804) continued a Scottish strain which is the converse of the *Christ's Kirk on the Green* tradition in which Tennant and Mayne worked, a strain of gentle and pious quietness which might be traced back to Henryson, gives its grace to Alexander Hume's *Of the Day Estivall*, and darkens into the gloom of Blair's *The Grave*. It appears occasionally in Thomson, and Burns tried to achieve it in *The Cottar's Saturday Night*, but his crossing of Fergusson and Shenstone was not a viable hybrid. Burns was quite sincere, but his genius lay in the other kind, and this spirit cannot be commanded at will. Grahame possessed it, but not the individual utterance. There is dead wood in *The Sabbath*. *The Rural Calendar* and *Sabbath Walks* are short and almost entirely descriptive. *The Sabbath* is that delusive form once more, the discursive poem. The themes are proper and honourable: the day of rest for the labouring man and 'the toilworn horse', for the poor townsman's respite of pure air and the sight of the fields, for worship and meditation and peace. It may have been his deep sense of compassion that turned Grahame from the law to the church. He pities the poor, the aged, the imprisoned debtor, grows indignant at England's part in the slave-trade and especially at the business men who hired others to do the dirty work and pocketed the profits, laments the forced emigrant, the castaway, the pressganged sailor, remembers his country's history and especially—though he became a priest in the Episcopal Church—the sufferings of the Covenanters in his native west. Such themes recur in *The Birds of Scotland* (1806) along with glimpses of scenery and criticisms of landscape gardening based on Uvedale Price, nature-notes verified from Pennant and Bielby, reminiscences of boyhood and the local lore that held plover and yellow-hammer accursed. Bewick's *Birds* may have given the first suggestion—his woodcuts of landscape and *genre* are almost epitomes of passages and episodes in the ruralist poets—otherwise Grahame can stand with, if well below, Thomson and Cowper, an unexciting kind Christian who wrote in truth and love, but, foreseeing an early death, in unfortunate haste.

Such gentle pieces of observation, reminiscence, and piety, minor examples of the school of Cowper and Bewick, could be appreciated locally, but they were neither new nor forceful. Nor could anyone rate highly such vernacular pieces of morality as those in which Hector Macneill and others declaimed against war and strong drink. Morally they might be justified, but as counterblasts to Scott and Burns they are negligible. Something remained to be done in the novel, in journalism, and in scientific writing, but Scotland had little to contribute to philosophy or poetry for many a long day. The new question appears in John Wilson.[1] Young, rich, clever, an exuberant athlete, he settled in Westmorland to sit at the feet of Wordsworth. *The Isle of Palms* (1812) has much of Southey in it, with something of Coleridge, Byron, and Campbell, but Wordsworth is predominant especially in the shorter poems in the same volume. For *The City of the Plague* (1816), in dramatic form though not a play, like *The Convict* published with it, he found material in Defoe's *Journal of the Plague Year*, and makes a macabre picture even more macabre by placing it in indefinite time so that it might be a prophecy rather than an historical allusion. In that the aim is thus ideal and not historical it may derive from *The White Doe*, from which also might come the radiant figure of Magdalene. All his poems, even lyrics and songs in Scots, derive from the same double impulse, an inexhaustible flux of sentiment and of words. With all his discipleship to Wordsworth, and the patient counsel in Wordsworth's letters to him, he never learned the disciplines of the elder poet, the discipline of art and the discipline of thought. When having lost his fortune he took to journalism in the guise of 'Christopher North', this more than Southeyan garrulity was let loose in prose where it could do less harm, and when he was jobbed into the Chair of Moral Philosophy in Edinburgh his rhetoric seems to have fascinated—or engulfed—at least some of the young men; but there was little behind it, and the gush of emotion, enthusiasm, and uproarious high spirits is now mainly tiresome. In

[1] 1785–1854. Born in Paisley; educated in Glasgow and Oxford (M.A. 1810). At Scottish bar 1815. On *Blackwood's Magazine* staff 1817. Professor of Moral Philosophy in Edinburgh 1820. A roaring Tory.

instalments it may amuse, and Wilson seems to have been well enough liked, but he may be remembered here as a cautionary figure, a warning of what could happen when self-conscious 'romanticism' loosed the controls. It is well that Byron swore by Pope and that Shelley found life hard.

VIII

REOPENING

IT is a commonplace, and something of a mystery, that the vitality of the time fails in one field, that of Drama. Its prestige was high, the theatres were thronged in the provinces as well as in London, the social status of the actors was higher than ever, and, since success in the theatre brings immediate rewards in money and reputation, playwrights by the score were eager to 'catch the luck of the town'. Yet there is singularly little to show for all the bustle. In 1814–15 John Galt attempted a salvage operation with *The New British Theatre*—a title which his publisher Colbourn wisely preferred to Galt's *The Rejected Theatre*. The best commentary on the four numbers which appeared is Galt's own, in his *Literary Life* (1834). He had believed, like many other people,

that such was the want of taste in the managers of the great playhouses, that there would be abundance of rejected pieces to supply and maintain a very respectable publication. But a short trial convinced me that this, like many other vulgar errors, was a fallacy. There was perhaps, indeed, no lack of dramas as to number, but in general such stuff! Many of the authors did not appear possessed of the commonest rudiments of education, and were equally low in conception and literature. The only good that I am aware the publication did, was in vindicating the managers. . . . No doubt, from the mass of trash sent to them, they may have been obliged to adopt a rule which has led to the rejection of several good plays; but no person of common sense, who saw 'such sights' as came before me, could for a moment hesitate to infer that the managers were not to blame, but the genius of the age.

This may be characteristic over-statement. These were rejected plays—and for that matter, Galt included a dozen of his own. The real mystery is not that there were so many bad playwrights but that there were so few good ones and none approaching greatness.

The explanation is usually sought in the theatres. A theatre is a heavy and complicated affair, so loaded with capital assets and liabilities and human bodies and tempers in administration, production, performance, and audience, that much of its weight is dead weight at best. To keep it going at all means expense of effort; to vitalize it requires specialized genius in more than one department. The great playhouses were expensive in every way. Walpole's Act of 1737 had made the old monopoly even more rigid than before, and managers and proprietors were jealous guardians of their privileges. As rebuilding became necessary in Drury Lane in 1791 and again after a fire in 1809, and in Covent Garden in 1792 and—also after a fire— in 1808, the proprietors were tempted to aggrandize their holdings, until Drury Lane held 3,110, and Covent Garden little less. The Opera House (or King's Theatre) in Haymarket, with a similar history of fires and rebuildings, held 3,280. With such overhead commitments, any new play was a greater gamble than ever, especially when such crowds, turbulent by cherished tradition, could with small provocation turn into mobs. Actors and playwrights could have little chance to work up a play that showed promise, and still less chance to experiment. Those vast spaces must have been destructive of the intimacies of comedy and the subtleties of tragedy, and fully responsive only to such resonant instruments as Mrs. Siddons and J. P. Kemble. Lamb says, in his Prologue to Coleridge's *Remorse*,

> There are, I am told, who sharply criticise
> Our modern theatre's unwieldy size.

His defence is specious enough, and the critics were justified.

Physical conditions, however, cannot be held entirely accountable. The weakness lay in the dramatists as well. Active drama is a social phenomenon, and the best minds were working in comparative isolation even from each other, inspired and guided by forces which could not be represented on any boards. The more ambitious thought of drama too much as a branch of literature, and of dramatic literature too much in terms of Shakespeare. Shakespeare was valuable to the Germans for whom he was new and distant, and their hybrid was useful to Coleridge. The large dramatic scale of Schiller and the agitation of Kotzebue suited large audiences, and declamatory style, if it came all too easily to Coleridge for the good of some of his poems, suited his Germanic *Remorse*. Men who wrote in Shakespeare's own tongue accepted verse, style, and construction as conventions where for him they had been the exploitation of the social and physical conditions of his theatre. An appropriate dramatic verse, again, had to be created in German. English blank verse had been created for—and by—the living voice of the actor. In recreating it for the silent reader, Milton had compensated for the loss of intonation and gesture by continuous musical figuration, and later generations, attentive to the two supreme poets, inevitably contaminated the modes. No one thought of new modes for the new age and the new theatres until Byron, and he only in exile. Anyone who tried would probably have been damned out of hand; but no one did.

James Grahame, for instance, compiled one 'dramatic poem' on the almost inevitable subject of Mary Queen of Scots. It would interest a student of the history of style, less for the strained emotional flights and episodes inserted on the analogy —rather than the imitation—of old plays than as an example of contemporary failings in the transference of historical narra-tive into high dramatic speech. The first scene especially, a poetized version of Melville of Halhill's report of his interview with Queen Elizabeth, is almost comic as a stylistic period-piece compared with the crisp original. The weakness is not only Grahame's; it can be found everywhere, in novels as well as in plays. One can account for the contemporary reputation of Joanna Baillie[1] only by this acceptance of what a modern reader refuses. She published some eighteen tragedies, eight comedies, two 'dramas' and two 'musical dramas' in verse, not to mention tragedies and comedies in prose: the number is remarkable in itself, for no Scottish writer has ever approached it. Miss Baillie lived a quiet comfortable life in respectable professional circles, as daughter of a Glasgow divinity professor and niece of the famous surgeons William and John Hunter, who had launched her brother into good medical practice in Hampstead. Some of her 'fugitive verses' are pleasant things; indeed in such little pieces as *The Shepherd's Song* she went near to creating a native pastoral form out of the lowland song to which she herself made two or three authentic additions. She was brought up in that tradition, and worked securely inside it. Her knowledge of the theatre was entirely that of a spectator, as her stage directions show at a glance. She took delight in writing and had evidently little taste for novels, and, having

---

[1] 1762–1851. Born in Hamilton; lived with brother and sister after their father's death in 1778.

little else to do, discharged the warm human interest that endeared her to many friends in volume after volume—1798,
1802, 1804, 1812, three in 1836. Miss Baillie was a sensible and
intelligent woman. If she had found, or had tried to invent,
like Mrs. Radcliffe, a formula that suited her talents, she might
have been as happy and more memorable; but she had a taste
for the theatre, and worked to the formula of Shakespeare as
seen through the medium of John Home and the eighteenth
century. In more than her ear for the familiar talk of servants
and street crowds she is of the same breed as Walter Scott, but
the pressure of thought and the urgency of emotion are not
there. No real dramatist would deliberately sit down to write
a whole series of *Plays on the Passions*. It is an odd and not
unsympathetic spectacle, but—however her friends and the
patients of her well-loved brother might admire it—it is not
drama.

Charles Lamb ought to be an exception. The great playhouses were conspicuous in the London scene that was his
native element and the object of his loving delight. He was a
keen playgoer, with some acquaintance among actors and a
long love for one actress, Fanny Kelly, and only his objection
to being hurried kept him from regular employment as a newspaper critic. He was more than well read in the older English
dramatists; one of the joys of retirement from the East India
Company's office was the long day in the British Museum over
the Garrick collection of plays. What his criticism lacks is the
technical interest which is the mark of the creative artist such
as Dryden. He never discusses a play as a constructed entity
but always as a source of individual characters, moments of
emotional power, bursts of poetic expression, and happy
touches of wit or nature. He describes—and none better—the
manners of individual actors—Bannister, Munden, Bensley—
and how they took individual parts, but never the tone and
balance of a whole production. And the theatre was too much
of an enchantment. The busy street, the bustle of arrival, the
happy anticipation, made a prologue; the raising of the curtain
transported him from the commonplace world into the delect-
able regions of Arden or Illyria or London of the Restoration.
In his critical essays the two enthusiasms mingled. His famous
and misleading character of Malvolio occurs significantly in the
essay *On Some of the Old Actors*; it does not grow out of a study

of Shakespeare's intention, but out of pleased recollection of a performance which had excited him in his teens, nearly thirty years before. The essays *On the Tragedies of Shakespeare* and *The Artificial Comedy of the Last Century*, identical in spirit though so disparate in subject, and full of delicate feeling and fine strokes of appreciation, are, like all his essays, deliberate exploitations of *parti pris*; and they help to explain the failure of *John Woodvil*. In creating his tragedy, Lamb's mind had to inhabit a Devonshire manorhouse and Sherwood forest just after 1660; it also had to be, at the same time, behind the scenes in Drury Lane in 1798. For though characters, speeches, passions, and scenes are figments of the imagination, the play, the artifact, the thing that has to be so contrived as to be intelligible, delightful, and absorbing to people sitting watching it, and is so only if it employs profitably the minds and muscles of actors, scene-painters, stage-hands and managers—that artifact is real. Diderot should have written a Paradox on the Playwright to go with his *Paradoxe sur le Comédien*. Lamb could not balance the factors in the paradox. *The Borderers* fails because Wordsworth's Godwinian theme was too overpowering, *John Woodvil* because the general theme was too weak to control the conduct of the tragedy. Matthew Lewis, again, could win box-office success because his coarser horrors played on the nerves of his audiences. Lamb, who found Shakespeare's tragedies too powerful to see acted, shrank from straining his fragile nervous organization and so would arouse little response. To judge by his letters, what he was proudest of was the speech about life in the forest, and the whole play breaks up into speeches and scenes. It seems absurd that Lamb should waste bright familiar dialogue in his farce, *Mr. H*, and still more that he imagined that such a trifling whimsy could make out two acts—though indeed we wonder at Scott's amusement at James Beresford's *Miseries of Human Life*; but the vagaries of humour are a mystery. The real weakness is suggested by Hazlitt's report, in his essay *On Great and Little Things*, that an actor, 'Gentleman' Lewis, 'said, that if he had had it, he could have made it "the most popular thing that had been brought out for some time"'. The professional saw that what was lacking was the professional touch. After all, Lamb was only a reader and playgoer; as such, he is an obvious instance of a general weakness.

Lamb resented any kind of reality as an intrusion on the

dream-world of the theatre. When in his essay *On the Artificial Comedy* he declares 'We have been spoiled by—not sentimental comedy—but a tyrant far more pernicious to our pleasures which has succeeded to it, the exclusive and all devouring drama of common life', he means the comedy, part original, part borrowed from French and German, of such practitioners as Holcroft and Mrs. Inchbald. It is not quite true of them that 'the moral point is everything', but it sets the themes; and the rest is 'common life'. The recipe is indeed that of the contemporary novel. It could be argued that it is just that intrusion of common life that saves a few plays for a modern reader, but it must also be observed that these same plays are those that have something of the professional touch. Holcroft[1] had been an actor at one turn of his varied career, and Mrs. Inchbald[1] had not only acted but had edited two large collections of plays. Yet of Mrs. Inchbald's twenty dramatic pieces the one remembered is *Lovers' Vows*, an adaptation from Kotzebue, and that for the sake of *Mansfield Park*. Thomas Morton's[2] *Speed the Plough* (1800), nearer to the novels of Charlotte Smith—a violent plot, with passages of rustic humour—gave later generations the name of Mrs. Grundy. It is a parable that this, the only theatre-name of the time which passed into current allusion, is that of one who never appears in the play, and that the references to her do not warrant her later perversion into a catchword for sanctimonious moralizing. In this modified realism there might have been some hope, but though Charlotte Smith might sneer at Mrs. Inchbald as 'a modern Centlivre', what all of them lack is just what Mrs. Centlivre shared with all her generation, the spring of comic inventiveness, which survived only in the short farces of such old theatre hands as O'Keefe.[3] It is not only that the time produced nothing that has lasted; it produced nothing that promised life in the future. The drama was dead. It is a mystery of the Muses, and we can only conclude that drama, like music, was an early victim of the general artistic collapse of the social arts that occurred in the 1830's.

[1] See Chap. III, p. 63.

[2] 1764?–1838. Student in Lincoln's Inn. Wrote ten comedies, besides farces and music-dramas, between 1792 and 1830.

[3] 1747–1833. Actor in Dublin. Settled in England 1780 and until 1798 produced comic operas and farces enjoyed by Lamb. Became blind in later years. Some of his songs survived.

When we turn to the different field of history, we find the same activity. Again there is no masterpiece to record, but here the ground is being prepared for greater things to come. The last generation had perfected the long majestic march of classical Historiography. William Robertson, the last of them, had written in that high style, on such knowledge as was available to him, and with humanity and wisdom. Southey, with greater knowledge at least of Spanish history and more austere tastes, disapproved; but with all his range of reading, his skill in narration, and admirable prose, he made little advance in method. For him, history was a branch of literature, enjoyed as he enjoyed all literature and especially such as occupied him in the collection of multifarious facts. Natural good humour and humane sympathy adapted these gifts and tastes to biography and, with abundant new materials and added insights from his brother's naval experience, produced a masterpiece in the *Life of Nelson* (1813); but he worked always among his books. Great modern historians have concurred in crediting Sir Walter Scott with the change in the spirit of history from the Olympian surveying of human action as a panorama of crime, abuse, and oppression shot with gleams of virtue and heroism, to the effort at imaginative comprehension; but, as we have seen, Scott's humane imagination fed on solid documentation, and he was by no means alone. It seems as if the human interest that the drama had lost was finding a new outlet. Standards of good and evil may be held as permanent and universal, but the forms and modes by which men have acted and judged of action may change under the needs and pressures of circumstance. In technical terms this half-conscious shift was one from historiography based on chronicle to historical inquiry into documents.

Several movements may be noted, all converging towards the imaginative comprehension of the human past. Antiquarians advanced slowly from curio-collecting to the handling of objects with emotions resembling those long accepted as appropriate to scenes of famous action—'upon the plains of *Marathon* . . . or among the ruins of *Iona*'—and so to their study as evidence. This was not new. Joseph Strutt's[1] *Sports and Pastimes of the English People* (1801) may be his best remembered work, but his

---

[1] 1749–1802. Artist and engraver and antiquary. Scott completed his unfinished novel *Queenhoo Hall* 1808.

greatest, 𝕳𝖔𝖗𝖉𝖆 𝕬𝖓𝖌𝖊𝖑-𝖈𝖞𝖓𝖓𝖆𝖓 or *A Compleat View of the Manners, Customs, Arms, Habits &c of the Inhabitants of England*, was published in 1774–6. Strutt may have strengthened the growing recognition that people had lived their lives through all the vicissitudes of politics, and, by his careful copies from medieval manuscripts published in these books and in *Dresses and Habits of the English People*, 1796–9, helped historians and novelists to visualize their stories. He has never been given credit for his perception of the permanent intrinsic values of medieval art. He had little imagination, but if he did not make new spiritual emblems, as Blake did of the tombs in Westminster Abbey, it is something to have acclaimed the 'elegance and taste' of Gothic drawing in the 1770's. His works, however, are not readable. They are for reference or browsing, which restricts their interest to people of like taste. The example of 'the industrious and useful Strutt' and his years of poring over manuscript collections in London and Cambridge, may have encouraged Sharon Turner[1] to neglect his legal practice for similar immersion in early English manuscripts: with this difference, that his ambition was to write history. Turner has been censured for his Gibbonesque style. He probably felt—and justifiably—that a survey carried out from a base-line other than that of Athens–Rome might incur the charge of tasteless barbarism, and he wished to give the neglected history of his own land the dignity of classic historiography.

The deficiencies of Turner emphasize his originality. He saw that a true history demanded analytic study of documents, not only English but also Scandinavian and Celtic. Few of the documents, however, had been published. The Danes had done something, the Welsh and Irish were just stirring, but the old school of Rymer and Wanley had lost impetus. He had to work from manuscripts, and that without the instruments of criticism slowly forged by later generations. That Tyrwhitt's work on Chaucer, coeval with Strutt's *Compleat View*, was neglected while Horne Tooke's dogmatic theorizing about philology was widely accepted, proves how isolated individual scholars were. Turner suffered from the isolation of the pioneer; and though the central subject of his explorations in laws, literature, annals, and registers, the consolidation of the politico-geographical

---

[1] 1768–1847. Attorney. Studied old Norse literature published in Denmark, and old English, but dependent on the few translations for Welsh material.

entity called England, was an enduring thing, the bulk of his work—and indeed much of the spirit of it—had the character of archaeology. Valuable, even necessary as it was, it concerned things that were dead and gone, too ancient to contribute even to the fictions of the common lawyers. In *The Antiquities of the Anglo-Saxon Church*, on the other hand, John Lingard[1] had a subject of enduring life, since the Anglo-Saxon Church meant the Roman Church of which he was a priest, and that living principle informed his later *History of England* which he carried down to 1688. Lingard is more immediately successful in being more readable. His sentences are heavily loaded, but they are short. Still more, he is attractive by his secure and candid devotion. He pleased neither his ecclesiastical superiors nor his Protestant critics, but may have helped to create the frame of mind that made Catholic Emancipation a feasible policy, as well as to contribute to the historical bias in the Oxford Movement.

There were other converging forces. Local interests vivify the work of regional historians like the brothers Daniel and Samuel Lysons,[2] even when the material is dug up from manorial rolls and family records. Commentators on Shakespeare and Pope, inspired by the permanent interest of living literature, had to find and use original documents, and methods of use were well exemplified by biographers. Mason's *Life of Gray* taught Hayley[3] how to compile those of Cowper and Romney, and William Coxe[4] had learned the technique when he wrote the *Memoirs of Sir Robert Walpole* (1798) and the *Life of Marlborough* (1816–19).

[1] 1771–1851. Student at Douai. In orders, and vice-president of Crookhall College, Durham, 1795–1811. Created D.D. and LL.D. by Pius VII 1821, but balked of promotion by hierarchy in England.

[2] (1) Daniel 1762–1834. Educated at St. Mary Hall, Oxford; M.A. 1785. Held several livings. Published *Environs of London* 1792–6. (2) Samuel 1763–1819, his brother. Barrister, Inner Temple, 1798. Keeper of Tower of London records 1803. F.R.S. 1797, vice-president and treasurer 1810. Professor of Antiquity, Royal Academy 1818. Published *Reliquiae Britannico-Romanae* 1801–17. They collaborated in *Magna Britannia*, a series of county histories (ten counties completed) 1806–22.

[3] 1745–1820. Educated at Eton and Trinity Hall, Cambridge. For his principal poem *The Triumphs of Temper*, see Vol. VIII. Blake lived with him at Felpham, Surrey, engraving plates for *Ballads Founded on Anecdotes of Animals* 1805. Life of Milton 1796, Cowper 1803, Romney 1809. An interesting psychological case, but had his virtues.

[4] 1747–1828. Educated at Eton and King's College, Cambridge. Held several livings; Archdeacon of Wiltshire 1804. Published various works of travel and tourism between 1779 and 1801 as well as of history and biography.

Coxe, however, is a dull writer. It is probably true that the pedestrian techniques had to be infused with the imaginative power of Scott before new and greater historians could arrive.

This contrast of a dead branch and a growing shoot summarizes what has been slowly emerging during our survey. Art depends on experience, which includes everything from education and reading to the smallest public and social event and the most intimate personal involvement; on the nature of the individual artist, which includes everything from his most casual tastes to his creative power (which is a mystery) and the equilibrium or disorder of his physical and nervous organization; and on the modes of expression, which come from both. These must work together and upon one another, and success depends on the extent to which they are finally unified in the work of art, allowing for occasional preponderance of one or another according to circumstance and individual bias. The new men have their new experience and their unique personalities, and have to make their own modes. The natural self-assertion of any new generation discounts the conclusions of its immediate elders, and is often slow to allow for the permanent and universal conditions which must be observed if the work of art is to have lasting validity. At this time the need for change was the greater because so much of the experience of the last century, as preserved in its works of art, was exhausted. So we see the historians abandoning the chronicles to search for basic material in that portion of experience which they take pleasure in exploring, the knowledge of the past, and Wordsworth turning from the social life in which the eighteenth-century men had found their main interest, to explore the basic facts of humanity and its basic relation to the non-human universe.

The painters were the happiest, because the technical element of their art is so important. They came to the world with fresh vision and found in it new delight, but in deploying their individual instincts they were saved from extravagance by the physical qualities of their medium and the ineluctable fact of the rigid rectangle of the canvas within which they had to deploy their findings, each according to his individuality, and the permanent elements, ultimately reducible perhaps to mathematics, of relative space, position, and rhythm. Thus Turner, Constable, Bewick could indulge their emotions and interests, and Blake could find appreciation for his without

compelling anyone to accept the intellectual conclusions into
which his adventures in language tempted him. A man can
work only within limitations, and too much experience was
thrust upon that generation. The excitable Southey had to
retreat among his books. Coleridge, torn between his volatile
responses to experience, the desire to create, and a restless and
ambitious intellect that could not be content to labour like
Wordsworth over the facts of life and art but ran ahead to
construct systems of generalizations before the time was ripe,
had to deaden himself with opium. Lamb tried to work
within the terms of dramatic conventions devised to exploit the
experience of earlier generations and weighted with technical
conditions which he could not translate into criticism, and
found himself only in new developments of the essay, a form of
comparatively simple techniques which was satisfied with such
portions of his experience and response as he cared to expose.
Wordsworth was able to work out an experience in which public
and private affairs had curiously coincided and to create appropriate terms and modes for the purpose, and so unify all into
works of art; but only by retiring into seclusion at an early age.
Jane Austen achieved that final unity by dint of the resolute
common sense that refused to stray beyond the limits of her
womanhood and the natural society of family and neighbourhood; but these limits were drawn well within the range of her
experience, and few writers could be content with what sufficed
for her. And, as always, people in general, less concerned—
wisely or stupidly—with their responses to experience especially
in such violent and wildly changing times, with little desire to
formulate experience and response in new creations whether
political or artistic, had difficulty in accepting those awkward
individuals who insisted on so doing, to the disturbance of
habit and inherited belief. The new could be incorporated in
time; but it needed time.

Meanwhile, once more a younger generation was growing
up, whose formative experience was different and in many
ways simpler. For them the Revolution was a legend. Their
realities were the repressions and privations of the war against
dictatorship, the economic breakdown that followed the peace,
and the anticlimax of the reinstatement of decrepit monarchies
all over Europe. But, unlike the earlier generation who hated
both Pitt and Bonaparte, they had to face only one way, nor

did they live to be forced into drastic reconsideration of their first opinions. The political revolution lay at a distance. On the other hand the literary revolution was too near. Hazlitt saw something of it, but, out of both personal and political prejudices, would not admit that its effects were permanent. He had made two false starts, as philosopher and painter, before he found himself at the age of twenty-eight. The change is marked by the early age at which the younger men could produce significant work. The two volumes which Byron published when Wordsworth had only *An Evening's Walk*, *Descriptive Sketches*, and *Lyrical Ballads* to his name might be little enough, but by 1815 he was well established in public regard as a writer of poetical romances to rival Scott's and a travel-poem which, though shot with a blacker melancholy than the Goldsmith tradition warranted, wandering further afield than the average tourist, and infected with the savagery of war-time, was, like the romances, of an understood and indeed popular kind. It was after 1815 that his thoughts and styles became difficult. Shelley was known, if at all, as the youthful author of some subversive pamphlets which might have been more effective twenty years earlier, a lurid prose romance, and a poem, *Queen Mab*, which belied its fairy title by strange and none too comprehensible philosophizing.

In prose, Leigh Hunt, after some feeble verse, was a dramatic critic who was embarking on Whiggish journalism. His first periodical *The Reflector*, begun along with his brother in 1810, is noticeable mainly for its contributions by Charles Lamb. Since the *Specimens of English Dramatic Poets* of 1808, Lamb had been occupied along with his sister mainly with books for children. The revival of the periodical essay which was to flourish is a theme for a later volume, in which Elia will take his place. This was no real deflection of Lamb's ways, but other men were changing theirs. *Waverley* appeared in 1814. In Thomas Love Peacock, three years older than Byron, and a poet in the style that descended from Milton's minor work through Collins and the Wartons, objective in purpose and very loyal in politics, the love of technical neatness and quiet English scenery shown in *Palmyra* (1806) and *The Genius of the Thames* (1810) scarcely foreshadowed the satirist of *Headlong Hall* (1816). No direct line from Coleridge and Wordsworth is traceable. Their powers worked at levels too deep for immediate effect, and there was still strength in the older schools. 'The Age of Wordsworth', if it ever was, was not yet.

Our history has been of twenty-five years, years of great events, great upheavals, great beginnings, but in the arts, no endings: for in their history there may be revolutions, conquests, and even empires, but no Waterloo.

Date	Public Events	Literary History
1789	Pitt Prime Minister (1784–1806). France: States-General met, May; National Assembly, June; Fall of Bastille, 14 July; King brought to Paris, Oct.	Wordsworth at St. John's College, Cambridge; Coleridge at Christ's Hospital; Lamb in South Sea House; Southey at Westminster School; Scott studying law in Edinburgh. Burns in Dumfries. Cobbett in army (Nova Scotia).
1790	Death of B. Franklin	Deaths of Adam Smith and Thomas Warton. Pye poet laureate. Wordsworth and Jones walking on Continent, July–Oct. Turner's first exhibit in Royal Academy.
1791	French king's flight and capture at Varennes (21 June). Many French emigrate. Death of Mirabeau.	Wordsworth B.A. (Jan.); in London; in Paris (Nov.) and Orleans. Coleridge in residence, Jesus Colledge, Cambridge. Priestley's home wrecked by Birmingham mob; he moves to London. Burke finally separates from Fox and supports government.
1792	Warren Hastings acquitted. Austria declares war on France (Apr.); allies invade (Aug.); battle of Valmy (Sept.), Jemappes (Nov.). Capture of Tuileries; imprisonment of royal family (Aug.). Massacres of 4 Sept. National Convention (Sept.); rise of parties. Monarchy established (21 Sept.).	Wordsworth in Orleans, Blois till Oct., Paris Oct.–Dec. Lamb in India House. Cobbett in France and then in Philadelphia. Death of Sir Joshua Reynolds. West President of Royal Academy. Birth of Shelley and Keble.
1793	Board of Agriculture founded. Trial and execution (21 Jan.) of Louis XVI. Committee of Public Safety (Apr.) (The Terror). Conscription in France. Risings in la Vendée, Lyons, Toulon. Fall of Girondins. Murder of Marat. Execution of Queen Marie Antoinette;	Wordsworth in London. Coleridge enlists in Dragoons (2 Dec.). Marriage of Fanny Burney and Gen. d'Arblay. Landor at Trinity College, Oxford. Birth of J. Clare.

Verse	Prose
Darwin, *Loves of the Plants*. Blake, *Songs of Innocence*; *Book of Thel*. Russell, *Sonnets*. Bowles, *Sonnets*.	Bentham, *Principles of Morals and Legislation*. White, *Natural History of Selborne*. Gilpin, *Observations on the Highlands of Scotland*. Radcliffe, *The Castles of Athlin and Dunbayne*.
Sayers, *Dramatic Sketches of Northern Mythology*. Blake, *Marriage of Heaven and Hell*. Baillie, *Fugitive Verses*.	Burke, *Reflections on the French Revolution*. Bruce, *Travels*. Bewick, *General History of Quadrupeds*. Turner, *History of the Anglo-Saxons*. Alison, *Essay on Taste*. Radcliffe, *A Sicilian Romance*. Smith, *Ethelinde*.
Burns, *Tam o' Shanter* (in Grose's *Antiquities of Scotland*). Cowper, Translations of *Iliad* and *Odyssey*. Ritson, *Ancient Popular Poetry*.	Malone, edition of Shakespeare. Ellis, *Specimens of the Early English Poets*. Burke, *Letter to a Member of the National Assembly*; *Appeal from the Old to the New Whigs*. Mackintosh, *Vindiciae Gallicae*. Priestley, *Letters to Mr. Burke*. Paine, *The Rights of Man*. Williams, *Letters from France* (vol. iii, 1796). Bentham, *Panopticon*. Boswell, *Life of Johnson*. D'Israeli, *Curiosities of Literature*. Inchbald, *A Simple Story*. Radcliffe, *The Romance of the Forest*. Smith, *Celestina*. *The Observer* founded.
Darwin, *Economy of Vegetation*. Blake, *Song of Liberty*. Rogers, *Pleasures of Memory*.	Burke, *Collected Works*. Wollstonecraft, *Vindication of the Rights of Women*. Young, *Travels in France*. Bligh, *Voyage to the South Seas in the Bounty*. Gilpin, *Essays on Picturesque Beauty*. Stewart, *Philosophy of the Human Mind*. Bage, *Man as he is*. Holcroft, *Anna St. Ives*. Smith, *Desmond*. Holcroft, *The Road to Ruin*. Aikin and Barbauld, *Evenings at Home* (miscellany for children).
Thomson's *Select Scottish Airs* (songs of Burns). Blake, *The Gates of Paradise*, *A Vision of the Daughters of Albion*, *America*. Wordsworth, *An Evening Walk*, *Descriptive Sketches*. Ritson, *The English Anthology* (completed 1794).	Burke, *The Conduct of the Minority*. Godwin, *Political Justice*. More, *Village Politics*. Young, *The Example of France*. Dr. Moore, *Journal during a Residence in France*. Stewart, *Outlines of Moral Philosophy*. Smith, *The Old Manor House*.

Date	Public Events	Literary History
	of Girondins (Oct.); and many more. Retirement of Danton; Robespierre in power. France declares war on Britain (1 Feb.), Britain on France (11 Feb.). Expedition to Dunkirk. British fleet in Toulon; Toulon recaptured; first notice of Bonaparte.	
1794	Trial and acquittal of Horne Tooke, Holcroft and Thelwall. Danton executed (Apr.). Robespierre executed (28 July). End of the Terror. The Directorate. Death of Dauphin (10 June). Howe's naval victory, 1 June.	Coleridge discharged from Dragoons (April); returns to Cambridge; meeting with Southey in Oxford (June): Pantisocracy planned; engagement to Sara Fricker; left Cambridge without a degree (Dec.), as Southey left Oxford. Landor rusticated. Priestley in United States. Death of Gibbon. Drury Lane theatre rebuilt.
1795	Bonaparte in Italy.	Death of Boswell. Birth of Keats, Carlyle. Wordsworth meets Southey and Coleridge in Bristol; at Racedown (autumn). Coleridge married (Oct.), and Southey (Nov.). Southey in Spain and Portugal.
1796		Death of Burns and Macpherson. Birth of Hartley Coleridge. Mary Lamb kills her mother in insane fit (Sept.). Coleridges at Nether Stowey (Dec.).
1797	(Oct.) Treaty of Campo Formio (Venice handed over to Austria). Mutinies at Spithead and the Nore. Battles of Cape St. Vincent (Feb.) and Camperdown (Oct.). Bank of England suspends payment.	Death of Horace Walpole (Earl of Orford) (Mar.); Burke (July); Mary Wollstonecraft (Godwin) (Sept.). Lamb's visit to Coleridge at Nether Stowey (July). Wordsworths

Verse   *Prose*

Blake, *Songs of Experience* (*Songs of Innocence and Experience*); *Europe*; *The Book of Urizen*. Coleridge, *Monody on Chatterton*; with Southey, *The Fall of Robespierre*. Southey and Lovell, translations of Bion and Moschus. Payne Knight, *The Landscape*. Mathias, *Pursuits of Literature*. Gifford, *The Baviad*. Ritson, *Scotish Songs*. Wolcot ('Peter Pindar') Collected Works.

Paine, *The Age of Reason*. Darwin, *Zoonomia*. Uvedale Price, *Essay on the Picturesque*. Paley, *Evidences of Christianity*. Hayley, *Life of Milton*.
  Godwin, *Caleb Williams*. Holcroft, *Hugh Trevor*. Radcliffe, *The Mysteries of Udolpho*. Smith, *The Banished Man*.

Blake, *Book of Los, Book of Ahania, Song of Los*. Gifford, *The Mæviad*. Landor, *Poems*. Nacneill, *Scotland's Skaith*. Lloyd, *Poems*.
  Ritson, editions of Minot and Robin Hood Ballads.

Coleridge, *Conciones ad Populum*. D'Israeli, *Essay on the Literary Character*. More, *Repository Tracts*. Paine, *First Principles of Government*. Williams, *Letters*.
  Radcliffe, *Journey through Holland and . . . Germany*. Lewis, *Ambrosio, or The Monk*. Smith, *Montalbert*.
  The Morning Post bought by Daniel Stuart.

Coleridge, *Poems on Various Subjects*; *Ode on the Departing Year*. Southey, *Joan of Arc*. Scott, *The Chase*, &c. (from Bürger).

Burke, *Letter to a Noble Lord, Letters* (i and ii) *on a Regicide Peace*. Cobbett, *Life and Adventures of Peter Porcupine*. D'Israeli, *Miscellanies*. Roscoe, *Life of Lorenzo di Medici*. Strutt, *Dresses and Habits of the English People*.
  Bage, *Hermsprong*. Burney, *Camilla*. Edgeworth, *The Parent's Assistant*. Moore, *Edward*. Smith, *Marchmont*. White, *Original Letters of Sir John Falstaff*.
  Colman, *The Iron Chest*. Holcroft, *The Man of Ten Thousand*.
  The Courier bought by Daniel Stuart.
  Coleridge's periodical *The Watchman* (March–May).

Southey, *Poems*. Coleridge, *Poems*, 2nd ed. with additions by Lamb and Lloyd.

Burke, *Thoughts on French Affairs*; *Letter* (III) *on a Regicide Peace*; *Letter on Affairs in Ireland*. Southey, *Letters written in Spain and Portugal*. Sir Joshua Reynolds, *Works* (ed. Malone).
  Lee, *Canterbury Tales*. Radcliffe, *The*

Date	*Public Events*	*Literary History*
		at Alfoxden (July). Marriage of Scott. T. N. Longman succeeds to family business.
1798	French in Egypt. Battle of the Nile (Aug.). Nelson in command in Mediterranean.	Coleridge given annuity of £150 by T. and J. Wedgwood (Jan.). Wordsworth and Coleridge in Germany (Sept.). Constable begins publishing in Edinburgh.
1799	Bonaparte unsuccessful at siege of Acre; returns to France. Directorate ejected. The Consulate—Bonaparte First Consul. Religious Tract Society founded.	Wordsworths return from Germany (Apr.) and Coleridge (July). Wordsworths at Sockburn; at Dove Cottage, Grasmere (Dec.). Coleridges in London (Nov.). Scott appointed sheriff-depute of Selkirk.
1800	Battles of Alexandria, Hohènlinden, Marengo. Act of Union with Ireland. Highland Clearances.	Coleridges at Greta Hall, Keswick (July). Southey in Portugal. Campbell and Crabb Robinson in Germany. Death of Cowper, Joseph Warton, Hugh Blair.
1801	Pitt resigns on King's refusal to assent to Catholic emancipation (Mar.). Addington Prime Minister. Danish fleet seized at Copenhagen (Mar.).	Death of Bage. Blake at Felpham with Hayley.
1802	Peace of Amiens (Mar.). Bonaparte First Consul for life (thenceforth took name of Napoleon). Reoccupation of Switzerland by French (Oct.).	Wordsworths at Calais (Aug.). Marriage of Wordsworth (Oct.). Death of Darwin. *The Edinburgh Review.*
1803	War renewed (Apr.).	Southey in Greta Hall (Sept.). Wordsworths and Coleridge tour in Scotland (Aug.). Meeting of Wordsworths and Scott.

Verse

Prose

Italian. John Walter, the younger, joint editor of *The Times.* Godwin, *The Inquirer.* Cobbett, *Porcupine's Gazette* (New York). *The Anti-Jacobin.*
Bewick, *History of British Birds.* Blake, Illustrations to Young's *Night Thoughts.*

Wordsworth and Coleridge, *Lyrical Ballads.* Landor, *Gebir.* Coleridge, *Fears in Solitude, France, an Ode,* and *Frost at Midnight.* Lamb and Lloyd, *Blank Verse.* Rogers, *Epistle to a Friend.* Cowper, *On the Receipt of my Mother's Picture* and *The Dog and the Water-lily.* Baillie, *Plays on the Passions,* vol. i. Inchbald, *Lover's Vows* (from Kotzebue). Lewis, *The Castle Spectre.* Morton, *Speed the Plough.*

Malthus, *Principles of Population.* Coxe, *Memoirs of Sir Robert Walpole.* Godwin, *Memoirs of Mary Wollstonecraft.* Edgeworth, *Practical Education.* Gilpin, *Picturesque Remarks on the West of England.* Vancouver, *A Voyage of Discovery.* Lamb, *The Tale of Rosamund Gray.* Roche, *The Children of the Abbey.* Smith, *The Young Philosopher.* Lloyd, *Edmund Oliver* (satire on Coleridge).

Campbell, *The Pleasures of Hope.* Lewis, *Tales of Terror.* Scott, Translations from Bürger. Southey and Coleridge, *The Devil's Thoughts* (in *Morning Post*). Southey (and Coleridge, &c.), *The Annual Anthology,* i.

Turner, *History of England to the Norman Conquest.* Darwin, *Phytologia.* Park, *Travels in the Interior of Africa.* Godwin, *St. Leon.* Lewis, *The East Indian.* Sheridan, *Pizarro* (from Kotzebue). Scott, trans. Goethe, *Goetz of Berlichingen.*

Coleridge, *Poems;* Trans. of Schiller's *The Piccolomini* and *The Death of Wallenstein.* Wordsworth and Coleridge, *Lyrical Ballads* (revised preface): Southey (and others), *The Annual Anthology,* ii. Bloomfield, *The Farmer's Boy.* Moore, Translations of Anacreon; Sotheby, of *Georgics.* Hogg, Songs. Gifford, *Epistle to Peter Pindar.*

Dibdin, *History of the English Stage.* Edgeworth, *Castle Rackrent.* Moore, *Mordaunt.*

Bowles, *Sorrows of Switzerland.* Hogg, *Scottish Pastorals.* Hunt, *Juvenilia.* Lewis, *Tales of Wonder.* Moore, *Poems by Thomas Little.* Southey, *Thalaba.*

Strutt, *Sports and Pastimes of the People of England.* Stoddart, *Remarks on Local Scenery and Manners in Scotland.* Williams, *Sketches of Manners and Opinion in the French Republic.*
Edgeworth, *Moral Tales, Belinda, Early Lessons.* Opie, *Father and Daughter.*

Scott, *Minstrelsy of the Scottish Border.* Landor, *Poetry by the Author of Gebir.* Bloomfield, *Rural Tales.* Gifford, Translation of Juvenal (incl. Autobiography). Ritson, *Bibliographica Poetica.* Baillie, *Plays on the Passions,* vol. ii, Lamb, *John Woodvil.*

Edgeworth (R. and M.), *An Essay on Irish Bulls.* Paley, *Natural Theology.* Sibbald, *A Chronicle of Scottish Poetry.*

Darwin, *The Temple of Nature.* Campbell, *Collected Poems.* Bowles, *The Picture.* Sir A. Boswell, *Songs, Chiefly in the Scottish Dialect.* Leyden, *Scenes of Infancy.* Sayers,

Bentham, *A Plea for the Constitution.* Hayley, *Life of Cowper.* Cooper, Letters. Godwin, *Life of Chaucer.* Repton, *Theory and Practice of Landscape Gardening.*

Date	Public Events	Literary History
		Murray London agent for Constable. Walter sole editor of *The Times.*
1804	Resignation of Addington; Pitt Prime Minister (May). Napoleon proclaimed Emperor (May). Camp at Boulogne. End of Holy Roman Empire.	Death of Wilkes, Priestley, Kant. Coleridge to Malta (Apr.). Blake returns to London. Scott at Ashestiel.
1805	Napoleon at Boulogne (Aug.). Battles of Trafalgar (21 Oct.), Ulm (Oct.), Austerlitz (Nov.)	Coleridge leaves Malta (Sept.) for Italy. Death of Jane Austen's father; move to Bath. Death of Paley, Schiller.
1806	Death of Pitt (Jan.). Ministry of 'All the Talents'; Grenville Prime Minister. Death of Fox (Sept.). Battle of Jena. Decree of Berlin.	Coleridge returns to England (Aug.). Austens at Southampton. Scott clerk in Court of Session.
1807	Battles of Eylau and Friedland. Treaty of Tilsit (June). French invasion of Spain and Portugal. Abolition of Slave-Trade. Resignation of Grenville over Catholic question. Duke of Portland Prime Minister.	Wordsworth reads *The Prelude* to Coleridge at Coleorton (Jan.). Austens at Chawton.
1808	Spanish rising (May); surrender of Dupont at Baylen (July). Joseph Bonaparte enters Madrid as King (July). Wellesley lands at Corunna; and at Oporto; army landed at Montego Bay (July). Battles of Roliça and Vimiero; Convention of Cintra (Aug.). Moore in com-	Coleridge's first public lecture, Royal Institution (Jan.). Wordsworths at Allan Bank. Hazlitt married. Crabb Robinson at Corunna as *Times* correspondent. Hunt editor of *The Examiner.* Byron sails for Mediterranean.

Verse

Nugae Poeticae. Southey, translation of *Amadis of Gaul.*

Blake, *Jerusalem*; *Milton, a Poem.* Hayley, *The Triumph of Music.* Bowles, *The Spirit of Discovery.* A. and J. Taylor, *Poems for Infant Minds.* Grahame, *The Sabbath.* Peacock, *The Monks of St. Mark's.* Baillie, *Miscellaneous Plays.*

Scott, *The Lay of the Last Minstrel.* Southey, *Madoc.* Lamb, *The King and Queen of Hearts.* Hayley, *Ballads on Anecdotes of Animals.* Anderson, *Ballads in Cumbrian Dialect.*
   Cary, Translation of Dante's *Inferno.* Ellis, ed. *Early English Metrical Romances.* Gifford, ed. of Massinger.

Scott, *Ballads and Lyrical Pieces.* Landor, *Simonidea.* Holcroft, *Tales in Verse.* Bloomfield, *Wild Flowers.* Roscoe, *The Butterfly's Ball and Grasshopper's Feast.* Byron, *Fugitive Pieces.* Moore, *Epistles, Odes, and other Poems.* Peacock, *Palmyra.*
   Bowles, editions of Pope. Jamieson, *Popular Ballads and Songs.*

Wordsworth, *Poems in Two Volumes.* Crabbe, *Poems.* Kirke White, *Remains.* Sotheby, *Saul.* Smith, *Beachy Head.* Logan, *Poems.* Hogg, *The Mountain Bard.* Grahame, *Poems.* Tannahill, *Poems and Songs.* Heber, *Palestine.* Dorset, *The Peacock at Home.* Byron, *Stones of Idleness*; *Poems on Several Occasions.* Moore, *Irish Melodies.*
   Southey, *Specimens of Later English Poets.*
   Barlow, *The Columbiad.*

Reliques of Burns. Scott, *Marmion*; ed. of Dryden. Cowper, translations of Milton's Latin and Italian Poems. Hemans, *Poems.*
   Colman, *The Battle of Hexham.* Lamb, *Specimens of the English Dramatic Poets.*

Prose

Burney, *History of Discoveries in the South Seas.*
   Porter, *Thaddeus of Warsaw.*

Seward, *Memoir of Erasmus Darwin.* Smith, *Conversations.* Gilpin, *Coasts of Hampshire, Sussex, and Kent.* Holcroft, *Travels from Hamburg.* Thornton, *A Sporting Tour.* Larkington, *Confessions.*
   Edgeworth, *Popular Tales, The Modern Griselda.* Lewis, *The Bravo of Venice.* Opie, *Adeline Mowbray.*

Hazlitt, *The Principles of Human Action.* Knight, *Principles of Taste.* Sayers, *Miscellanies, Antiquarian and Historical.* Brydges, *Censura Literaria.* Roscoe, *Life of Leo X.*
   Godwin, *Fleetwood.* Owenson (Morgan), *The Novice of St. Dominick.* Collins, *The Adventures of a Picture* (with Life of Morland).

Cobbett, *Parliamentary History of England.* Hazlitt, *Free Thoughts on Public Affairs.* Edgeworth, *Letters.* Forbes, *Life of Beattie.* Lingard, *The Antiquities of the Anglo-Saxon Church.*
   Webster, *A Compendious Dictionary.* Edgeworth, *Leonora.* Owenson (Morgan), *The Wild Irish Girl.* Opie, *Simple Tales.* Inchbald coll., *The British Theatre.*

Southey, *Letters from England by Don Espriella*; Translation of *Palmerin of England.* Malthus, *Letter . . . on Poor Laws.* Hazlitt, *Reply to Malthus.* Sydney Smith, *Letters on . . . Catholics, by Peter Plymley.* Coxe, *History of the House of Austria.* Pinkerton coll., *Voyages and Travels.* Douce, *Illustrations of Shakespeare.* Cumberland, *Memoirs.* Lamb, *Tales from Shakespeare*; *Mrs. Leicester's School, Mr. H.*
   Maturin, *The Fatal Revenge.* Porter, *The Hungarian Brothers.* Godwin, *Faulkner.* Washington Irving, *Salmagundi.*

Fox, *History of the . . . Reign of James II.* Clarkson, *History of the Abolition of the African Slave Trade.* Ackermann, *The Microcosm of London.* Dalton, *A New System of Chemical Philosophy.* Wilson, *American Ornithology.* Hunt, *Critical Essays on . . . the London Theatres.*
   Hamilton, *The Cottagers of Glenburnie.*

Date	Public Events	Literary History
	mand (Sept.). Napoleon in Spain (Nov.). Moore's retreat (Dec.).	
1809	Battle of Corunna; death of Moore (Jan.). Coronation of Joseph Bonaparte in Madrid (Jan.). Defence of Saragossa (Jan., Feb.). Wellesley in command in Portugal (Apr.). Napoleon beaten by Austrians at Aspern (May). Walcheren expedition (July). Wagram (July); Austria makes peace at Schönbrunn (Oct.). Resignation of Portland; Perceval Prime Minister (Oct.).	*The Quarterly Review* (ed. Gifford). *The Watchman* (Coleridge) June–Mar. 1810. Covent Garden and Drury Lane theatres burned and rebuilt. Death of Anna Seward, Paine, Holcroft, Porson. Birth of Poe, Tennyson, C. Darwin, Lincoln, Gladstone.
1810	Lines of Torres Vedras	Coleridge's lectures on Shakespeare. Death of Dugald Stewart.
1811	The Regency. Luddite Riots. Capture of Java.	Shelley expelled from Oxford; his marriage. Byron's return from Mediterranean.
1812	Murder of Perceval. Liverpool Prime Minister. Capture of Ciudad Rodrigo (Jan.), Badajoz (Apr.); battle of Salamanca (July). War with America. Napoleon's invasion of Russia (June); Retreat from Moscow (Oct.).	Death of Malone and Horne Tooke. Landor at Llanthony Abbey; his marriage. Roxburghe Club founded. Scott at Abbotsford. Shelley in Ireland. Birth of Browning and Dickens.

Verse

Prose

Lewis, *Romantic Tales.* Maturin, *The Wild Irish Boy.*
Southey, Translation of *The Cid.*

Lamb, *Poetry for Children.* Campbell, *Gertrude of Wyoming.* Byron, *English Bards and Scotch Reviewers.*

Wordsworth, *The Convention of Cintra.* Cobbett, *Collection of State Trials.* Hayley, *Life of Romney.* Blake, *Descriptive Catalogue.* Godwin, *Essay on Sepulchres.* Dibdin, *Bibliomania.* Hope, *Costumes of the Ancients.* Gilpin, *Counties of Cambridge,* &c. Hobhouse, *Travels through Albania.*
Edgeworth, *Tales of Fashionable Life.* More, *Coelebs in Search of a Wife.* Owenson (Morgan), *Woman, or, Ida of Athens.* Inchbald coll., *The Modern Theatre, A Collection of Farces.*
Adams, *American Principles.* Irving, *Knickerbocker's History of New York.*

Scott, *The Lady of the Lake.* Southey, *The Curse of Kehama.* Crabbe, *The Borough.* Rogers, *The Voyage of Columbus.* Hogg, *The Forest Minstrel.* Shelley, *Original Poetry by Victor and Cazire; Posthumous Fragments of Margaret Nicholson.* Peacock, *The Genius of the Thames.* A. and J. Taylor, *Hymns for Infant Minds.*
Chalmers coll., *English Poets.* Weber ed., *Metrical Romances.* Cromek coll., *Select Scottish Songs; Nithsdale and Galloway Song.*
Baillie, *The Family Legend.*

Stewart, *Philosophical Essays.* Southey, *History of Brazil.* Wordsworth, *Topographical Description of the Country of the Lakes.* Clarke, *Travels.* Brydges, *The British Bibliographer.*
Brunton, *Self-Control.* Porter, *The Scottish Chiefs.* Shelley, *Zastrozzi.*

Scott, *The Vision of Don Roderick.* Lamb, *Prince Dorus.* Bloomfield, *The Banks of the Wye.* Barbauld, *Eighteen Hundred and Eleven.* Hunt, *The Feast of the Poets.*

Ricardo, *On the High Price of Bullion.* Stewart, *Biographical Memoirs of Reid,* &c. McCrie, *Life of John Knox.* Lamb, *On the Tragedies of Shakespeare* (in *The Reflector*). Shelley, *The Necessity of Atheism.*

Crabbe, *Tales in Verse.* Colman, *Poetical Vagaries.* Tennant, *Anster Fair.* H. and J. Smith, *Rejected Addresses.* Combe, *Tour of Dr. Syntax in Search of the Picturesque.* Heber, *Poems and Translations.* Montgomery, *The World before the Flood.* Hemans, *Domestic Affections.* Byron, *Childe Harold* (I and II); *The Curse of Minerva.* Wilson, *The Isle of Palms.* Peacock, *The Philosophy of Melancholy.*
Cary, Translation of Dante's *Purgatorio* and *Paradiso.*
Baillie, *Plays on the Passions,* iii. Landor, *Count Julian.*

Nichols, *Literary Anecdotes of the Eighteenth Century.* Southey and Coleridge, *Omniana.* D'Israeli, *Calamities of Authors.* Shelley, *Address to the Irish People,* &c.
Edgeworth, *Tales of Fashionable Life.* Maturin, *The Milesian Chief.* Opie, *Temper.*

Date	Public Events	Literary History
1813	Battle of Vittoria (June); Wellington in Pyrénées. Battle of Leipzig (Oct.).	Southey poet laureate. Leigh Hunt in prison.
1814	Battle of Toulouse (Apr.). Fall of Paris (Mar.). Abdication of Napoleon (Apr.). Treaty of Ghent ends American War (Dec.).	Landor in France. Shelley on Continent with Mary Godwin.
1815	Napoleon leaves Elba (26 Feb.); The Hundred Days (19 Mar.–22 June); Waterloo. Napoleon's surrender (15 July).	Marriage of Byron (2 Jan.). Landor in Italy. *The North American Review.*

Verse

Scott, *Rokeby*; *The Bridal of Triermain.*
Hogg, *The Queen's Wake.* Byron, *The
Bride of Abydos*; *The Waltz*; *The Giaour.*
Shelley, *Queen Mab.* H. and J. Smith,
Horace in London. Moore, *Intercepted Letters.*
Coleridge, *Remorse.*

Wordsworth, *The Excursion.* Southey,
Roderick. Byron, *Ode to Napoleon, The Corsair, Lara.* Rogers, *Jacqueline.*
Cary, Translation of *Divina Commedia*
complete.

Wordsworth, *The White Doe of Rylstone*;
Poems. Scott, *The Lord of the Isles*; *The
Field of Waterloo.* Hogg, *Pilgrims of the
Sun.* Bowles, *The Missionary of The Andes.*
Byron, *Hebrew Melodies*; Collected
Poems. Moore, *National Airs.* Tannahill,
Collected Works. Combe, *The English
Dance of Death.*

Prose

Southey, *Life of Nelson.* Northcote,
Memoirs of Reynolds. Coxe, *Memoirs of
the Kings of Spain.* Owen, *A New View of
Society.* Shelley, *Vindication of a Natural
Diet.* Reresby, *Travels and Memoirs.*
   Austen, *Pride and Prejudice.* Barrett,
The Heroine. Opie, *Tales of Real Life.*

Malthus, *Observations on the Effect of the
Corn Laws.* Stewart, *The Philosophy of
the Human Mind.* Coleridge, *An Essay on
the Fine Arts.* Scott, *Border Antiquities*;
Essays on Chivalry and Romance; edition
of Swift. Turner, *History of England.*
D'Israeli, *Quarrels of Authors.* Brydges,
Restituta. Hawker, *Instructions to Young
Sportsmen.* Shelley, *The Refutation of
Deism.*
   Scott, *Waverley.* Edgeworth, *Patron-
age.* Austen, *Mansfield Park.* Morgan
(Owenson), *O'Donnel.* Brunton, *Disci-
pline.*

Malthus, *Inquiry into Rent; Importation of
Foreign Corn.* Ricardo, *On the Low Price
of Corn.* Wraxall, *Historical Memoirs.*
Scott, *Paul's Letters to his Kinsfolk.*
   Scott, *Guy Mannering. The Military
Adventures of Johnny Newcome.*

BIBLIOGRAPHY

SELECTION here is drastic, because the body of commentary, discussion, and 'interpretation' is so enormous, and still more because it is a battleground of temperaments, opinions, prejudices, and habits, in which every man fights single-handed, and more by instinct than he always recognizes. The order is:

I. General Bibliographies and Works of Reference
II. Political and Social History
III. Literary History
IV. Arts and Sciences
V. Individual Authors

Abbreviations

CBEL	*Cambridge Bibliography of English Literature*
CHEL	*Cambridge History of English Literature*
DNB	*Dictionary of National Biography*
E & S	*Essays and Studies of the English Association*
E.L.	Everyman's Library
EML	English Men of Letters
H.U.L.	Home University Library
JEGP	*Journal of English and Germanic Philology*
M.H.R.A.	Modern Humanities Research Association
M.L.R.	Modern Language Review
MP	*Modern Philology*
OP	*Oxford Poets*
OSA	*Oxford Standard Authors*
PMLA	*Publications of the Modern Language Association of America*
PQ	*Philological Quarterly*
RES	*Review of English Studies*
R.S.L.	Royal Society of Literature
WC	*World's Classics*
WW	*Writers and their Work*

I. GENERAL BIBLIOGRAPHIES AND WORKS OF REFERENCE

For biographical information the mainstays are *DNB* and the *D. of American B.*; for handy reference *The Concise DNB* or

Everyman's D. of Literary Biography, by D. C. Browning, revised ed. 1960. *Chambers's Cyclopaedia of English Literature*, new ed. by David Patrick, 1903, is still of use, especially for minor authors. For books, *CBEL*, ed. F. W. Bateson, with Supplement ed. G. Watson 1957, is invaluable; also the British Museum Catalogue (new ed. in progress); The Library of Congress Catalog (with supplements at intervals); the Subject Index of the London Library.

For the period in general, H. V. D. Dyson and John Butt, *Augustans and Romantics*, 2nd ed. 1950, in the Introductions to English Literature Series, includes useful sections on philosophy, art, and economics. More exclusive in subject, but more critical and extremely useful, is *The English Romantic Poets: a Review of Research*, 2nd ed., chapter i, by Ernest Bernbaum. Critical bibliographies are published annually by the English Association in *The Year's Work in English Studies*; by the *PQ*, *English Literature, 1660–1800*, and *The Romantic Movement*, which includes other literatures. More complete lists, without criticism, are published by M.H.R.A. in its *Annual Bibliography of English Language and Literature*. For quick chronological reference, use *Annals of English Literature*, Oxford, revised ed. 1961; for general reference, Paul Harvey, *The Oxford Companion to English Literature*, 3rd ed. 1946 and reprints, and for a wider range, Laurie Magnus, *A Dictionary of European Literature*, 1926.

For Drama, Allardyce Nicoll, *Late Eighteenth Century Drama*, 1927, and *Early Nineteenth Century Drama*, 1930, reissued as vols. iii and iv of *A History of English Drama*, 1955, are indispensable. For the Novel, Andrew Black, *The English Novel, 1740–1850*, 1939. D. Blakey, *The Minerva Press*, the Bibliographical Society, 1939, gives an excellent view of one large commercial affair. A. M. Summers, *A Gothic Bibliography*, is specialized and curious. For Travel see E. A. Cox, *A Reference Guide to the Literature of Travel*, 3 vols., Seattle, 1949.

II. POLITICAL HISTORY

John Steven Watson, *The Reign of George III*, 1960, and Sir E. L. Woodward, *The Age of Reform*, 1948, rev. 1954, both in the Oxford History of England Series, are reliable authorities. See also Richard Pares, *George III and the Politicians*, Oxford, 1953. On a smaller scale, J. H. Plumb, *England in the 18th Century*,

Pelican History of England, vol. 7, 1950, is comprehensive and balanced, though weakest on literature; it contains a bibliography. Sir Arthur Bryant's popular and picturesque *The Years of Endurance*, 1942, *Years of Victory*, 1944, and *The Age of Elegance*, 1950, are concerned largely with military history; they make good use of individual memoirs and reminiscences, of which useful lists are given. See *The Debate on the French Revolution*, ed. A. Cobban, 1950; F. J. C. Hearnshaw, *Social and Political Ideas of . . . the Revolutionary Era*, 1930. More will be found in biographies such as J. Holland Rose, *William Pitt and the Great War*, 1911, *Pitt and Napoleon*, 1912, *William Pitt and National Revival*, 1911; A. Cobban, *Edmund Burke and the Revolt against the 18th Century*, 1929; Christopher Hobhouse, *Fox*, 1934; and many more, to be chosen according to special interests. Contemporary gossip, valuable as revealing emotions, attitudes, and ignorances, may be gathered from the many memoirs, diaries, and collections of letters, and from such as J. G. Alger, *Englishmen in the French Revolution, Paris in 1789–94*, and *Napoleon's British Visitors and Captives*.

SOCIAL HISTORY

Consult G. M. Trevelyan, *English Social History*, 1944; E. Halévy, *Histoire du peuple anglais*, Paris, 1912, tr. E. I. Watkin and D. A. Barker, 1924; and Ackerman, *The Microcosm of London*, 1808–10; J. T. Smith, *A Book for a Rainy Day*, 1845, ed. W. Whitten, 1905, and *Life of Nollekens*, 1828, ed. E. Gosse, 1894. Dip into, for example, Henry Angelo, *Reminiscences*, 1828–30, ed. H. L. Smith, 1904; *The Farington Diary*, ed. James Greig, 1922 and after; *The Torrington Diaries*; the annual *Public Characters*, published by Phillips; *The Annual Register*; and the obituaries, &c., in *The Monthly Magazine* which Southey called 'the Nonconformist Necrology'; also Betty Rogers, *Georgian Chronicle*, 1958, for this cultural interest, important but too elusive for proper treatment in our text. Also, for example, D. A. Winstanley, *Unreformed Cambridge*, 1935, Sir C. Mallet, *Modern Oxford*, vol. iii, 1927, also official university and college histories. Lord Cockburn, *Memorials of his Time*, 1856, gives a picture of Edinburgh so strong that Edinburgh has never escaped from it; even a poor creature like R. P. Gillies can help in *Reminiscences of a Literary Veteran*, 1854, and Mrs. Eliza Fletcher in her *Autobiography*, 1875—a grim, humourless Yorkshire Whig, but acquainted with society. For the rest of Scotland see *Ayrshire in the Time of Burns*, Ayrshire Archaeological Soc., 1959; better still, compare a few parishes in the Statistical Account, 1791–9. For Ireland Sir Josiah Barrington, *Personal Sketches of his Times*, 1827, gives a useful entrance into Irish society and politics.

III. LITERARY HISTORY AND CRITICISM

Consult vols. xi and xii of *CHEL*, and the relevant portions of G. Saintsbury, *History of Nineteenth Century English Literature*, 1896; of E. Legouis and L. Cazamian, *History of English Literature*, revised ed. 1948; and that ed. A. C. Baugh, New York, 1948. C. H. Herford, *The Age of Wordsworth*, 1897, is valuable, though tending to confuse the generations; Oliver Elton, *A Survey of English Literature, 1780–1830*, 1912, is an admirable series of studies, with useful references among the Notes to each volume. See also Ernest Bernbaum, *A Guide through the Romantic Movement*, 2nd ed. 1943. Of contemporary writings, Hazlitt's *The Spirit of the Age*, 1825, and the last of his *Lectures on the English Poets*, 1818, must be read, always allowing for his personal and political bias; and above all *My First Acquaintance with Poets*, published in his *Literary Remains*, 1836, vol. ii. De Quincey's *Reminiscences of the Lake Poets* must be read with caution. For Crabb Robinson's see under individual authors, p. 281. John Wain collected *Contemporary Reviews of Romantic Poetry*, 1953. There is much also in such works as *Archibald Constable and his Literary Correspondents* and G. Festing, *J. H. Frere and his Friends*, 1899. Much later criticism is tangled in the concept of 'Romanticism', valid elsewhere but useful to the historian of English literature mainly as a vague descriptive-chronological reference—'pre-Romanticism' is a positive hindrance. One might begin with A. C. Bradley, *The Long Poem in the Age of Wordsworth* in his *Oxford Lectures on Poetry*, 1909; W. P. Ker, *The Terms Classical and Romantic as Applied to Literature*, then *Romance* and *Imagination and Judgment* in his *Collected Essays*, 1925, vol. ii; followed by his pupil B. Ifor Evans, *Tradition and Romanticism*, 1939. See Annie E. Powell (Mrs. Dodds), *The Romantic Theory of Poetry, an Examination in the Light of Croce's Aesthetic*, 1926; M. H. Abrams, *The Mirror and the Lamp*, New York, 1953; C. M. Bowra, *The Romantic Imagination*, 1950; Albert Gérard, *L'Idée romantique de la poésie en Angleterre*, Paris, 1956; Bernbaum's

chapter in *The English Romantic Poets* (above) is (unintentionally) enough to show how the concept crumbles in the hand on
examination. J. W. Beach, *The Concept of Nature in Nineteenth
Century Poetry*, 1936, inclines one to the older, outdoor, tradition
of such as Veitch. Douglas Bush, *Mythology and the Romantic Tradition in English Poetry*, 1937, is perceptive as usual. D. G. James,
The Romantic Comedy, 1948, poised between literary criticism,
philosophy, and theology, is an honest wrestle with the difficulties.

On critical ideas consult G. Saintsbury, *History of English
Criticism*, 1922, extracted and revised from his large *History of
Criticism . . . in Europe*; René Wellek, *A History of Modern
Criticism*, 1955, vol. ii, erudite if limited. On German influences
see A. C. Bradley, 'English Poetry and German Philosophy' in
his *Miscellany*, 1929; F. W. Stokoe, *German Influence in the English
Romantic Period*, 1926; V. Stockley, *German Literature as known in
England*, 1929; René Wellek, *Kant in England*, 1931. On politics
see Cobban, above; Clive Brinton, *The Political Ideas of the
English Romanticists*, Oxford, 1926. A. O. Lovejoy, 'On the
Discrimination of Romanticisms', *PMLA*, xxxix, 1924.

Drama. Allardyce Nicoll's introduction to the bibliographies
noted above will suffice for this barren field. For first-hand
theatre talk see the *Memoirs* of Richard Cumberland, John
O'Keefe, and Thomas Dibdin; also those of Charles Dibdin
the Younger, ed. George Speaight, Soc. for Theatre Research.
See also W. J. Macqueen Pope, *Theatre Royal, Drury Lane*, 1945.

Novel. Consult the relevant sections of Sir Walter Raleigh's
and George Saintsbury's histories; of E. A. Baker's, 1935,
also E. Birkhead, *The Tale of Terror*, 1921; A. M. Killen, *Le
Roman terrifiant*, Paris, 1923; J. M. S. Tompkins, *The Popular
Novel in England, 1770–1800*, 1932; Montague Summers, *The
Gothic Quest*, 1938; D. Blakey's Introduction to *The Minerva
Press* (above); C. N. Parkinson, *Portsmouth Point: the Navy in
Fiction, 1793–1815*, 1948. For a succinct satirical picture see
Scott's Introduction to *Waverley*.

For *Satire* Hugh Walker, *English Satire and Satirists*, 1925,
may suffice. See also George Kitchin, *A Survey of Burlesque and
Parody in English*, 1931.

Periodicals. A few important ones may be listed. Among older
monthlies still vigorous were *The Gentleman's Magazine*, founded
1731, ed. at this period by John Nichols; *The Scots Magazine*,

1739; *The Monthly Review*, 1749, ed. by the publisher Ralph Griffiths and then his son G. E. Griffiths; see J. W. Robberds, *Memoir of . . . William Taylor*, 1843; B. C. Nangle, *The Monthly Review, Second Series, 1790–1818*, 1955, gives complete indexes of contributors, with useful biographical summaries, and of articles. *The Critical Review*, 1756; *The European Magazine*, 1782, ed. James Perry. Founded in this period were *The British Critic*, 1793, ed. by W. Beloe and R. Nares, the literary antiquarians; *The Monthly Magazine*, 1796, ed. John Aiken; see his *Life*. More specialized were *The Anti-Jacobin*, 1797–8, ed. W. Gifford; contributors George Canning, George Ellis, J. H. Frere, *The Poetry of the A.-J.* being frequently republished, latest ed. L. Rice-Oxley, Oxford, 1924; see various *Lives* of contributors, Gifford (below). The unimportant *Anti-Jacobin Review*, 1798, should not be confused with it. For Science note *The Botanical Magazine*, 1787, ed. W. Curtis; *The Repository of Arts and Manufactures*; *The Philosophical Magazine*, 1798. Also *The Sporting Magazine*, 1793; *La Belle Assemblée*, 1806, notable for its fashion-plates.

Quarterlies were *The Edinburgh Review*, 1802, ed. Jeffrey; see under his name; J. A. Greig, *Jeffrey of the Edinburgh Review*, 1948. John Clive, *Scotch Reviewers*, 1957, is good on some points but weak on the intellectual situation in Scotland. See also *Archibald Constable and his Literary Correspondents*, Edinburgh, 1873. *The Quarterly Review*, 1809, ed. W. Gifford; see under his name. S. Smiles, *A Publisher and his Friends*, 1891, on John Murray; also Owen E. Holloway, 'George Ellis, the *Anti-Jacobin* and the *Quarterly Review*', *RES*, x, 1934.

Newspapers. See A. Aspinall, *Politics and the Press, c. 1780–1850*, 1949; *The History of 'The Times'*, vol. i, 1935, especially ch. vi.

IV. ARTS AND SCIENCES

Painting. James Barry's Royal Academy Lectures were collected, along with his *Account of a Series of Pictures* painted by himself for the Society of Arts, 1783, and his violent *Letter to the Dilettante Society* attacking the R.A., 1798, in his *Works*, 1809; those of Opie in 1809; those of Fuseli in his *Life and Writings*, ed. John Knowles: all three are reprinted in Bohn's Scientific Library, 1848. For Fuseli see Paul Ganz, *The Drawings of Henry Fuseli*, 1949; Eudo L. Mason, *The Mind of Henry Fuseli*, 1951;

both rather over-laudatory; and Ruthven Todd, *Tracks in the Snow*, 1946. For less formal writings see *The Artist*, edited by Prince Hoare; Martin Archer Shee, *Rhymes on Art*, 1805, and *Elements of Art*, 1809; Hazlitt's *Conversations with James Northcote*, 1830; J. R. Smith, *Nollekens and his Times*, 1828; and *The Farington Diary*, ed. James Greig, 1922 and after. William Collins, *Memoirs of a Picture*, 1805, is a rambling satirical romance of the picture trade, but vol. ii contains a memoir of his friend George Morland. Thomas Bewick's delightful autobiography was edited by his daughter, 1862, and is the basis of Montague Weekley, *Thomas Bewick*, Oxford, 1953. C. R. Leslie, *Memoirs of the Life of John Constable*, 1843, has the same intimate quality. For Constable see *inter alia* the Catalogue published by H.M. Stationery Office. The standard *Life* of Turner is by A. J. Finberg, revised ed. 1961; and Ruskin's *Modern Painters* centres in him. See also Laurence Binyon, *John Crome and John Sell Cotman*, 1897; R. H. Mottram, *John Crome of Norwich*, 1931; A. P. Oppé, *Thomas Rowlandson: the Drawings and Watercolours*; A. Bury, *Rowlandson Drawings*, 1949; A. P. Oppé, *A. and J. Cozens*, 1952. More general works are: Richard and Samuel Redgrave, *A Century of British Painters*, 1866 and 1890; the edition by Ruthven Todd, 1947, is convenient and has a useful bibliographical index; Laurence Binyon, *English Watercolours*, 1933 and 1944, is brief and lucid. W. T. Whitney, *Artists and their Friends in England, 1700–1799*, and *Art in England, 1800–1820*, are invaluable. Col. H. M. Grant, *The Old English Landscape Painters*, revised ed. 1957, is a mine of information, as also are J. R. Abbey, *Travel in Aquatint and Lithography, 1760–1860*, 1957; *Scenery of Great Britain and Ireland*, and *Life in England*, 1953. Note also J. Grego, *James Gillray*, ed. T. Wright, 1873, and the great British Museum Catalogue of Caricatures. A succinct introduction to this subject is F. D. Klingender, *Hogarth and English Caricature*, 1944. See also his *Art and the Industrial Revolution*, 1947. His obvious political bias does no great harm to either.

Landscape and the picturesque. The important works are: W. Gilpin's *Observations* on the River Wye, 1782; on the Mountains and Lakes of Cumberland and Westmoreland, 1786; on Several Parts of Great Britain, particularly the Highlands of Scotland, 1789; on the Western Parts of England, 1798; also *An Essay upon Prints*, 1768; *Remarks on Forest Scenery*, 1791; and *Three*

Essays: on Picturesque Beauty, on Picturesque Travel, and on Sketching Landscape, 1792. See also *Samuel Rogers and William Gilpin* by C. P. Barbier, 1959; W. A. Templeman, *The Life and Work of W. G.*, Urbana, 1939; W. P. Ker in *On Modern Literature*. R. Payne Knight published *The Landscape, a Didactic Poem*, in 1794, and Sir Uvedale Price *An Essay on the Picturesque*, 1794–8, and *A Dialogue on the Picturesque*, 1801; his *Letter to H. Repton, Esq.*, criticizing Repton's practice in landscape gardening, produced a reply *A Letter to Uvedale Price, Esq.*, 1794, and Repton continued in *Sketches of Hints*, 1795, and *Observations*, 1803, and *An Enquiry into Changes of Taste in Landscape Gardening*, 1806. Modern studies on the subject are E. W. Mainwaring, *Italian Landscape in 18th Century England*, New York, 1925; Christopher Hussey, *The Picturesque*, 1927. H. F. Clark, *The English Landscape Garden*, 1948, will probably suffice for the general reader. C. B. Tinker, *Painter and Poet*, Cambridge, Mass., 1938, is useful; also Sir Kenneth Clark, *The Gothic Revival*, 1928; *On the Painting of English Landscape*, Brit. Acad. 1935, and particularly *Landscape into Art*, 1948. For architecture, Sacheverell Sitwell, *British Architects and Craftsmen*, 1946; Donald Pilcher, *The Regency Style*, 1947. For domestic architecture, John Gloag, *The Englishman's Castle*, 1944, may be adequate. There are curious points in James Laver, *Taste and Fashion*, revised ed. 1945, and E. F. Carritt, *A Calendar of British Taste*, 'a Museum of Specimens and Landmarks'.

For reasons suggested in the text, Science bulks less large than might be expected. Only individual scientists may be relevant at intervals, and such general studies as Charles Singer, *A Short History of Science*, Oxford, 1941, may indicate what kind of work was going on. Klingender's *Art and the Industrial Revolution* (above) may be helpful for views of laboratory and workshop.

There is curiously little also to record in Philosophy. The Scottish School occupies the gap between Hume and the impact of the all too powerful Germans. For a brief general survey see Henry Sidgwick, *Outlines of the History of Ethics*, 1886; also Basil Willey, *The Eighteenth Century Background*, 1940. For the Scots, see A. S. Pringle-Pattison, *Scottish Philosophy*, 1885; A. S. Grave, *The Scottish Philosophy of Common Sense*, Oxford, 1960. Bentham and Coleridge become relevant in the next two volumes of this series.

V. INDIVIDUAL AUTHORS

JANE AUSTEN, 1775–1817

The reliable modern editions are those of R. W. Chapman, 1923–54. Chapman's illustrations and commentaries are invaluable. The World's Classics editions are well introduced.

A memoir (by her brother Henry) was prefixed to *N.A.*, 1818. This was followed by a *Memoir* by her nephew, J. E. Austen-Leigh, 1870, and that by a *Life and Letters* by later generations, William and R. A. Austen-Leigh, 1913. Lord Brabourne had edited *Letters* in 1884; the definitive edition is R. W. Chapman's, 1932. Chapman's *J. A.: Facts and Problems*, 1948, is succinct and complete, with useful chronology, bibliography, and brief critical notes; a model, all the better for Chapman's obvious pleasure in the work. See also F. Warre Cornish, *J. A.*, E.M.L., 1913; W. P. Ker in *On Modern Literature*, ed. Spenser and Sutherland, 1955; (Miss) C. Linklater Thomson, *J. A.*, *A Survey*, 1929; Mona Wilson, *J. A. and Some Contemporaries*, 1938, which presents her in a background of notable women; E. Jenkins, *J. A., a Biography*, 1938. Criticism is mostly, and appropriately, at modest length. Scott began it well (*Prose Works*, 1849, vol. 18), and A. C. Bradley followed in the same vein (*Essays and Studies*, ii, 1911), and Lord David Cecil (Leslie Stephen Lecture, Cambridge, 1935). The remarks of practising novelists can be illuminating: Virginia Woolf (in *The Common Reader*, 1925); Elizabeth Bowen (in *The English Novelists*, ed. D. Verschoyle, 1936); Elizabeth Jenkins (1948); E. M. Forster (in *Abinger Harvest*, 1936); Sheila Kaye Smith and G. B. Stern's *Talking of J. A.*, 1943, and *More Talk of J. A.*, 1950. Mary Lascelles, *J. A. and her Art* (revised ed. 1941) is full-length criticism, almost too clever, but penetrating and subtle and not likely to be superseded. Q. D. Leavis, 'A Critical Theory of J. A.'s Writings', in *Scrutiny*, 1942 and 1944, is smaller but in much the same class. See also M. Sadleir, *The Northanger Novels*, English Association Pamphlet 68, 1927, and an essay (with bibliography) in *WW*, by S. Townsend Warner, 1951. For the views of a philosopher, see S. Alexander in the *John Rylands Library Bulletin*, 1928. Sir Geoffrey Keynes published a *Bibliography* in 1929, and R. W. Chapman, *J. A.: A Critical Bibliography*, revised ed. 1955. *A Jane Austen Dictionary*, by G. L. Apperson, 1932, is useful as an index.

ROBERT BAGE, 1728–1801

Mount Henneth, 1782; *Barham Downs*, 1784; *The Fair Syrian*, 1787; *James Wallace*, 1788; *Man As He Is*, 1792; *Hermsprong*, 1796; the second, fifth, and sixth are most relevant. See also under Godwin, below.

JOANNA BAILLIE, 1762–1851

Dramatic and Poetical Works, 1851, 1853. *Fugitive Verses*, 1790; *Plays on the Passions*, vol. i, 1798; vol. ii, 1802; vol. iii, 1812. *Miscellaneous Plays*, 1804; *The Family Legend*, 1810; *Metrical Legends*, 1821; *Poetical Miscellanies*, 1822; *The Martyr*, 1826; *The Bride*, 1828; *Dramas*, 3 vols., 1836.

M. S. Carhart, *The Life and Work of J. B.*, New Haven, 1923, includes a bibliography. On her friendship with Scott see D. Carswell, *Sir Walter*, 1930; V. G. Plarr in *Edinburgh Rev.*, 1912 and 1913, prints letters exchanged between them. For comment, see A. Meynell, *The Second Person Singular and Other Essays*, 1921, and M. Norton, 'The Plays of J. B.', *RES*, xxiii, 1947.

WILLIAM BARTRAM, 1729–1823

See E. H. Coleridge in *Transactions of the R.S.L.* xxvii (1906); Lane Cooper in *Methods and Aims in the Study of Literature*, 1915; and the *Cambridge History of American Literature*.

SIR JOHN BARROW, 1764–1848

Travels in China, 1804; *Travels into the Interior of South Africa*, 2 vols., 1801–4; *Voyage to Cochin-China*, 1806. The *Memoir of Sir J. B.*, ed. J. Barrow, 1852, is largely autobiography.

WILLIAM BECKFORD, 1759–1844

Beckford produced nothing in these years and accordingly is not discussed, but it may be well to note here S. Sitwell, *Beckford and Beckfordism*, 1930; J. W. Oliver, *The Life of W. B.*, 1932; Guy Chapman, *Beckford*, 1937; H. A. N. Brockman, *The Caliph of Fonthill*, 1956; *Life at Fonthill*, 1807–22, ed. Boyd Alexander.

JEREMY BENTHAM, 1748–1832

Works, ed. Sir John Bowring, 1838–43; *Life* in vol. x. See A. V. Dicey, *Law and Public Opinion in England*, 1905; *The*

Philosophical Radicals, 1907. No more need be noted here for reasons suggested in Chap. I, *ad fin.*

WILLIAM BLAKE, 1757–1827

The only literary works 'published' were *Poetical Sketches*, 1783, the two Catalogues, or rather manifestoes, referring to his exhibition in 1809, and the two prospectuses of the Canterbury Pilgrims engraving, 1809. The first book of *The French Revolution*, 1791, was printed but only one copy exists. The rest were multiplied, if at all, by his own processes, and, since he did not regard them as marketable commodities, it is better to say they were 'produced' as follows: *There is no Natural Religion, c.* 1788; *All Religions are One*, about 1788; *Songs of Innocence*, 1789; *The Book of Thel*, 1789; *The Marriage of Heaven and Hell*, 1793; *To the Public*, also *Visions of the Daughters of Albion*, and *America*, in the same year; *Europe*, *The First Book of Urizen*, and *Songs of Innocence and Experience*, 1794; *The Book of Ahania*, *The Book of Los*, and *The Song of Los*, 1795. Thereafter there is a pause, while he wrestled with *Vala* about 1797 which became *The Four Zoas*, parts of which were used in *Milton*, 1804–8, and *Jerusalem*, 1804–20. *For the Sexes: The Gates of Paradise* was engraved about 1818, and the Laocoon engraving with its complicated letterings about the same time. Two small works, *On Homer's Poetry and on Virgil*, about 1820, and *The Ghost of Abel*, 1822, came last. Facsimiles of 13 of the shorter works were ed. William Muir between 1884 and 1890; *Poetical Sketches*, 1890, 1926, and New York, 1934; *Songs of Innocence and of Experience*, 1893, 1923; *Songs of Innocence*, 1926; *Songs of Experience*, 1927 (Benn). Ellis and Yeats's text (below), vol. iii, was useful for its reproductions of text-pages; all are surpassed by the splendid Blake Society series which may one day be complete.

There are many partial editions from 1874 on; the *Poems* were edited by E. J. Ellis and W. B. Yeats, with *Memoir and Interpretation*, 1893, and by Ellis in 1906. John Sampson ed. *Poetical Works* (shorter poems, with textual notes), Oxford, 1905, and added to it in 1913. The first and greatest ed. is by Geoffrey Keynes, 1925, in 3 vols., also in one vol., 1927, and in successive editions which add letters and other scraps as discovered. A complete ed. of the *Prophetical Writings*, ed. D. J. Sloss and J. P. R. Wallis, Oxford, 1926, contains good notes and a valuable symbol-concordance. Max Plowman ed. *Poems and Prophecies*, 1927, in E.L. H. M. Margoliouth edited the difficult *Vala* in masterly style, Oxford, 1956. The student must remember that, all his life, Blake was drawing, painting, and engraving, of which last the two large pieces are in Young's *Night Thoughts*, 1797, and *The Book of Job*, 1825. For the latter see Laurence Binyon, 1906, and Benn's ed., 1927, and J. H. Wicksteed, *Blake's Vision of the Book of Job*, 1910, revised 1924. In general, A. G. B. Russell, *The Engravings of William Blake*, 1912; *The Drawings and Engravings of William Blake*, 1922, and *The Engravings of William Blake*, 1926; Darrell Figgis, *The Paintings of William Blake*, 1925; Keynes, *Pencil Drawings*, 1927; *Engravings*, 1950, and a selection of coloured reproductions in the Faber Gallery series, 1945; Sir Anthony Blunt, *The Art of William Blake*, Warburg Institute, 1938, and Columbia, 1960; Kathleen Raine in Publ. Warburg Institute, 1958. Of the great designs reproduced—by processes far removed from his—since his death, note those for Gray's poems, published with an essay by Sir Herbert Grierson, for Milton's Poems, 1926, and for Dante, his last work, a few of which are reproduced also in books noted above. It is instructive to compare with the *Night Thoughts* and *Job* the set for Blair's *The Grave*, frozen by being engraved by the 'skilled professional' hand of Schiavonetti. The woodcut illustrations to Thornton's *Virgil* are reproduced, ed. Keynes, Nonesuch Press, 1935.

There are bibliographies by Keynes, Grolier Club, New York, 1921; B. Jagaku, Grolier Society, Kobe, 1929; Kathleen Raine (with essay), *WW*, 1950.

Alexander Gilchrist's *Life*, 1863 and better in the revised ed. 1880, ed. W. Graham Robertson, 1906 and Ruthven Todd, E.L. 1942, is the first full biography. Vol. i of Ellis and Yeats's ed. contains a biography. The best is by Mona Wilson, 1926, revised 1932. T. Wright's *Life of William Blake*, Olney, 1929, gives some details. Arthur Symons, *William Blake*, 1907, includes reprints of earlier notices. See also the *Life* of Blake's friend John Linnell, by A. T. Story, 1892; G. E. Bentley Jr., on Thomas Butts in *PMLA*, 1956; and the *Lives* of the disciples Samuel Palmer by A. H. Palmer, 1892, and Edward Calvert by S. Calvert, 1893, also Binyon's *The Followers of William Blake*, 1925. Keynes's valuable *Blake Studies*, 1947, touch on biography, art, and ideas.

Swinburne's *William Blake, a Critical Study*, 1868, deserves much honour and there is much good sense in Pierre Berger's *William Blake, mysticisme et poésie*, Paris, 1907, tr. D. H. Connor, 1914 and republished 1936, and in the introductions to his translations of *Premiers Livres prophétiques*, Paris, 1927, and *Seconds Livres prophétiques*, 1930. These are pioneers. There are many others, some of which reveal more of their authors than of Blake; with that proviso, some of the following may help different minds—where the title is omitted it is merely *William Blake*—Ellis and Yeats, vol. ii, but see A. J. Ellis, *The Real Blake*, 1907; Arthur Symons, 1907; J. H. Wicksteed's *Blake's Vision of the Book of Job*, 1910; and *Blake's Innocence and Experience*, 1928; also his commentary to the Blake Society's facsimile of *Jerusalem*; T. Sturge Moore, *Art and Life*, 1910; H. L. Bruce, *William Blake in this World*, 1925; Harold Jenkins, *William Blake Studies*, 1925; Oswald Burdett, E.M.L., 1926; M. Plowman, *An Introduction to the Study of William Blake*, 1927 (to be noted); Denis Saurat, *Blake and Modern Thought*, 1929, and *Blake and Milton*, 1935; A. F. Clutton-Brock, 1933; J. Middleton Murry, 1933; M. R. Lowery, *Windows of the Morning*, Yale, 1940; J. Bronowski, *A Man without a Mask*, 1944; Ruthven Todd, *Tracks in the Snow*, 1946; Northrup Frye, *Fearful Symmetry*, Princeton, 1947; J. G. Davies, *The Theology of William Blake*, 1948; Bernard Blackstone, *English Blake*, 1949; D. G. James, *The Romantic Comedy*, 1948, H. M. Margoliouth, Oxford, 1957; D. V. Erdman, *Prophet against Empire*, New York, 1954; William Gaunt, *Arrows of Desire*, 1956; *The Divine Vision*, a symposium, ed. V. de S. Pinto, 1957. The debate continues.

ROBERT BLOOMFIELD, 1766–1823

The Poetical Works, 1835. *The Farmer's Boy*, 1800; *Rural Tales*, 1802; *Good Tidings*, 1804; *Wild Flowers*, 1806; *The Banks of Wye*, 1811; *May Day with the Muses*, 1822; *Remains*, 1824. A selection by R. Cant appeared in 1947.

HENRY PETER BROUGHAM, LORD BROUGHAM AND VAUX, 1778–1868

We need note here only the sections of his *Works* in 11 vols., 1855–61, containing Rhetorical and Literary Addresses, and Historical Dissertations; Contributions to *The Edinburgh Review*, 1856; and *Life and Times written by Himself*, 1871. He is discussed mainly as politician in more formal *Lives*.

JAMES BRUCE, 1730–94

Travels to Discover the Source of the Nile, Edinburgh, 1790. See Edward Ullendorff, Scot. Hist. Rev. xxxii, 1953.

MRS. MARY BRUNTON, 1778–1818

Self-Control, Edinburgh, 1811; Discipline, Edinburgh, 1814; Emmeline, with some Other Pieces, Edinburgh, 1829, with a memoir by her husband.

EDMUND BURKE, 1729–97

See vol. viii. The important works of this period are Reflections on the Revolution in France, 1790; latest ed. by H. P. Adams, 1927; A Letter to a Member of the National Assembly, 1791; An Appeal from the New to the Old Whigs, 1791; A Letter . . . on the Roman Catholics of Ireland, 1792; A Letter . . . to a Noble Lord, 1796; Two Letters . . . on the Proposals for Peace with the Regicide Directory, 1796, with a third, 1797, and a fourth only published in 1812; collected works from 1792, latest in 1910–16 and ed. W. Willis and F. W. Rafferty, WC, 1906–7. The early standard biography is by Sir J. Prior, 1824. See also J. Morley, Burke in E.M.L. 1879; W. P. Ker in On Modern Literature; T. W. Copeland, E. B., Six Essays, New Haven, 1949; Alfred Cobban, E. B. and the Revolt against the 18th Century, 1929; D. C. Bryant, E. B. and his Literary Friends, St. Louis, 1939; A. M. Osborn, Rousseau and Burke, 1940, refer mainly to earlier days; see the previous volume in this series.

THOMAS CAMPBELL, 1777–1844

Campbell began with The Pleasures of Hope, Edinburgh, 1799, which reached its 9th (but not last) ed. in 1807. Two small volumes of Poems appeared shyly in 1803 and 1805, then Gertrude of Wyoming in 1809; its 9th ed. was in 1825; Theodric in 1824; Miscellaneous Poems, 1824; Poland, 1831; The Pilgrim of Glencoe, 1842. The Collected Poems were published in Edinburgh, 1828, and with illustrations by Turner in 1837; the latest is the Oxford edition, 1907. Specimens of the British Poets appeared in 1819, biographies of Mrs. Siddons, 1834, and of Petrarch, 1841. Letters from the South, 1837, records impressions of a tour on both sides of the western Mediterranean, none too lively. Campbell edited The New Monthly Magazine from 1820 to 1830, and The Metropolitan (Monthly), 1831–2. He left much journalistic hack work, unidentified or doubtful. The *Life and Letters* by W. Beattie, 1849, gives useful views of the times; add to it Cyrus Redding, *Literary Reminiscences and Memoirs of Thomas Campbell*, 1860, by another journalist. Glimpses of him in Scott's diary, Byron's life, and works as S. C. Hall's *Retrospect of a Long Life*, 1883, show his position in working society. See G. Saintsbury, *Essays in English Literature*, 2nd series, 1895; A. M. Bierstadt on *Gertrude of Wyoming* in *JEGP* xx, 1921; and W. Macneile Dixon's commemorative *Thomas Campbell: an Oration*, Glasgow, 1928.

HENRY FRANCIS CARY, 1772–1844

Cary began with verses, largely on public affairs, but having produced his blank verse translation of the *Inferno* in 1805, occupied himself till the whole *Commedia* appeared in 1814; it is still the best-known of the many translations. From Greek he translated Aristophanes' *The Birds*, 1824, and Pindar, 1833, evidently with pleasure in technical difficulties, and *The Early French Poets*, in the *London Magazine*, 1821–4; collected, 1846. A *Memoir* by H. Cary appeared in 1847, and a likeable one, *The Translator of Dante*, by R. W. King, 1925. See P. Toynbee, *Dante in English Literature*, 1909, and his centenary article in *MLR*, 1912.

WILLIAM COBBETT, 1762–1835

His American journalism is voluminous, but interesting (as literature) mainly to the student of the art of invective; much the same might be said of *The Political Register*; his greater works belong to the next volume of this series. The one well worth mention here is the *Life and Adventures of Peter Porcupine*, 1796, a prize for collectors of human characters; it was edited by G. D. H. Cole, 1927, who also wrote a *Life*, 1924. See Saintsbury, *Essays in English Literature*, 2nd series, 1895.

SAMUEL TAYLOR COLERIDGE, 1772–1834

The first publication was *The Fall of Robespierre*, Cambridge, 1794, Act I (II and III were Southey's). Then *Poems on Various Subjects*, Bristol, 1796, and 1797 with poems by Lamb and Lloyd; *Ode on the Departing Year*, Bristol, 1796; *Sonnets from Various Authors*, 1796 (four by Coleridge); *Fears in Solitude* (with *France, an Ode*, and *Frost at Midnight*), 1798; *Lyrical Ballads* (with Wordsworth), Bristol, 1798; *Wallenstein, a Drama in Two Parts*, 1800 (translation of Schiller's *Die Piccolomini* and *Wallensteins Tod*); *Remorse, a Tragedy*, 1813 (revised version of *Osorio*, finished in 1797); *Christabel, Kubla Khan, The Pains of Sleep*, 1816; *Sibylline Leaves*, 1817; *Zapolya*, 1817. Many poems appeared in periodicals: several in *The Morning Post*, 'This Lime-tree Bower my Prison' in *The Annual Anthology* for 1800, collected by Southey.

Collected *Poetical Works* appeared in 1828 and 1829. The ed. by J. Dykes Campbell, Macmillan, 1893 and reprints, is prized especially for its notes and the biography prefixed; that of E. H. Coleridge, Oxford, 2 vols. 1912, is the only complete ed., with full textual and bibliographical notes. Simplified versions are in *OP* and *OSA*. A very useful ed. is the Nonesuch, ed. Stephen Potter, 1933 and reprints, giving the poems, *Biographia Literaria*, and a good selection of the literary criticism, less of the philosophical, notebooks, table-talk, and letters, in one handy volume, with a chronological table and introduction by the editor. A type-facsimile of the proofs and MSS. of some poems, ed. J. Dykes Campbell, 1899, is an interesting curiosity.

The first prose publication was *A Moral and Political Lecture*, Bristol, 1795, then *Conciones ad Populum* in the same year; *The Watchman* (periodical), Bristol, 1796; *The Friend* (periodical), Penrith, 1809–10, revised and augmented 1818, ed. H. N. Coleridge, 1837 and reprints; *Omniana*, 1812 (with Southey, who edited it); *The Statesman's Manual*, 1816; *Biographia Literaria*, 1817, best edition by J. Shawcross, Oxford, 1907, also ed. by A. Symons, E.L., 1906, and the critical chapters ed. G. Sampson, Cambridge, 1920; *On Method*, in *Encyclopaedia Metropolitana*, 1818, and separately, also ed. A. D. Snyder, 1934; *Aids to Reflection*, 1825; also some small ethical and political pamphlets. Posthumous collections began with H. N. Coleridge's *Specimens of the Table-Talk*, 1835; *Literary Remains* in 4 vols., of which the Notes and Lectures on Shakespeare and others were reprinted 1849, with additions, as were the Notes on English Divines, and Notes Theological, &c., 1853. *Essays on His Own Times* were collected by Sara Coleridge, 3 vols., 1850, as a supplement to *The Friend*. J. P. Collier's print from his own notes of *Seven Lectures on Shakespeare and Milton*, 1856, contributed to such reprints as the *Essays and Lectures on Shakespeare*, &c., E.L., 1907; *C.'s Literary Criticism*, ed. J. W. Mackail, 1908; and most important of all, T. M. Raysor, *C.'s Shakespearian Criticism*, Cambridge, Mass., 1930, and *Miscellaneous Criticism*, 1936. In 1895 E. H. Coleridge selected *Anima Poetae*, not very interestingly, from the unpublished notebooks; Miss Kathleen Coburn published *C.'s Philosophical Lectures*, 1949; *Inquiring Spirit*, a selection from the same, 1951. Vol. i of her herculean complete edition of the notebooks appeared in 1957, vol. ii in 1962, and publication continues.

Letters were collected in *Memorials of Coleorton*, an interesting set of letters to Sir George and Lady Beaumont, ed. W. Knight, 2 vols., Edinburgh, 1887; *Letters from the Lake Poets to Daniel Stuart*, 1889; *Letters*, ed. E. H. Coleridge, 1895; *Unpublished Letters*, ed. E. L. Griggs, 1932. A complete collection by E. L. Griggs is in progress, 4 vols., 1956–9 (to 1819). See also Stephen Potter, *Minnow among Tritons*, 1934 (letters of Mrs. S. T. C.).

The 'sketch' in *The Observer*, Bristol, 1796, is slight and satirical, but convincing; T. Alsopp's *Conversations and Recollections of S. T. C.*, 1836, is a disciple's picture of the last phase, surveyed by L. E. Watson in *Coleridge at Highgate*, 1925. Between these there is much first-hand evidence: Joseph Cottle's *Early Reminiscences*, 1837, 2 vols., revised as *Reminiscences*, 1847 in one, inaccurate in detail but valuable; Hazlitt's *My First Acquaintance with Poets*; Mrs. Henry Sandford's *Thomas Poole and his Friends*, 1888; Daniel Stuart's reminiscences and *Letters from the Lake Poets*, and the letters of Lamb, the Wordsworths, and anyone who ever met him. The sequence of events is given with admirable clarity in J. D. Campbell's *Memoir* prefixed to his ed. of the Poems, 1893 and reprints, and in E. K. Chambers's *S. T. C., a Biographical Study*, 1938. See also the Life by L. Hanson, 1938. There is more comment and opinion in Stephen Potter, *Wordsworth and S. T. C.*, 1936; G. Whalley, *C. and Sara Hutchinson*, 1955 and *C. and S. H. and the Asra Poems*, 1955; H. M. Margoliouth, *Wordsworth and Coleridge*, H.U.L., 1953, all worth attention.

More general studies are H. D. Traill, E.M.L., 1884; Walter Pater in *Appreciations*, 1889; J. Charpentier, *C. le Somnambule Sublime*, Paris, 1927; H. W. Garrod in *The Profession of Poetry*, 1929; *C., Studies by Several Hands*, ed. E. Blunden and G. M. Harper, 1939; Humphrey House, *Coleridge*, 1953. For his aesthetics, see J. Middleton Murry in *Aspects of Criticism*, 1920; I. A. Richards, *C. on Imagination*, 1934; Basil Willey, *C. on Imagination and Fancy*, British Academy, 1946; Wilma L.

Kennedy, *The English Heritage of C. of Bristol*, New Haven, 1947; Herbert Read, *C. as Critic*, 1949. In *The Road to Xanadu*, 1927, revised 1930, J. Livingstone Lowes analysed the elements of *The Ancient Mariner* and *Kubla Khan*; A. H. Nethercot followed with *The Road to Triermaine*, Chicago, 1935, on *Christabel*. See also, among many, the *Essays in Honor of G. M. Harper*, ed. E. L. Griggs, 1939.

Writers on Coleridge's philosophy are divided between two schools: those who give him credit for originality and those who dismiss him as parasitic on the Germans. The distinction is clearly made by René Wellek, the most emphatic of the latter school, in his chapter in *The English Romantic Poets*. Note T. H. Green, *Spiritual Philosophy, founded on the Teaching of C.*, 1865; J. H. Muirhead, *C. as Philosopher*, 1930; J. F. Danby, *S. T. C. Anima Naturaliter Christiana*, 1951.

Bibliographies are T. J. Wise, Bibliographical Soc., 1913, and Supplement, 1919, descriptive; W. V. Kennedy and M. N. Barton, *S. T. C.*, critical; T. M. Raysor and René Wellek in *The English Romantic Poets*.

George Crabbe, 1754–1832

His first productions were the inconsiderable *Inebriety*, 1775, and *The Candidate*, 1780; his real career began with *The Library*, 1781, and his power with *The Village*, 1783. *The Newspaper*, 1785, added little. Then, in 1807, he began again, with matured force, with *Poems*, 1807; *The Borough*, 1810; *Tales in Verse*, 1812; and, after a longer pause, *Tales of the Hall*, 1819. A few unpublished poems appeared after his death, and even up to 1900?, in *New Poems by George Crabbe*, ed. Arthur Pollard. His few prose writings need detain no one, except that his sermons betray his commonplace religion. Crabbe collected his poems in 1816, and again in 1822 and 1823, and his son added a memoir to an 8-volume edition in 1834. The best modern edition is that by Sir A. W. Ward, Cambridge, 1905–7; another, by A. J. and R. M. Carlyle, is in *OSA*, 1908. His son's pleasant memoir is in *WC* with introduction by E. M. Forster, and in a Cresset Press ed., with one by Edmund Blunden, 1947: both good. The full and valuable *Un Poète réaliste anglais, George Crabbe*, Paris, 1906, by R. Huchon was translated by F. Clarke, 1907; it contains an excellent bibliography. *The Poems of George Crabbe*, by J. H. Evans, 1933, contains topographical details of some interest. *The Poetry of Crabbe* by L. Haddakin, 1955, is an honest survey. See also A. C. Ainger, *George Crabbe*, 1903, E.M.L.; P. Elmer More, *A Plea for Crabbe*, in *Shelburne Essays*, ii, New York, 1905; W. P. Ker in *On Modern Literature*, ed. T. Spencer and J. R. Sutherland, 1955; Ian Gregor, *Crabbe the Last Augustan* in the *Dublin Review*, 1955.

ERASMUS DARWIN, 1731-1802

The poetical works are *The Loves of the Plants*, 1789, which reappeared as Part II of *The Botanic Garden*, 1791, Part I being *The Economy of Vegetation*. *The Golden Age, a Poetical Epistle to T. Beddoes, M.D.*, 1794, has the interest of an 'association', and *The Temple of Nature*, 1803, is described in its sub-title, *The Origin of Society*. There was a collected edition in 3 vols., 1807. The prose *Zoonomia, or, The Laws of Organic Life*, 1794-6, carries on the argument; as does *Phytologia*, 1800, though it is more informative in intention if not in effect. Writers on Darwin are divided into those who take him seriously and heavily, from Anna Seward in her *Memoir*, 1804, to J. V. Logan, *The Poetry and Aesthetics of Erasmus Darwin*, Princeton, 1936; those interested in theories of evolution, like his grandson Charles, who wrote a *Life*, 1887, and Samuel Butler in *Evolution Old and New*, 1879, to which R. B. Crum's less argumentative notice in *Scientific Thought in Poetry*, New York, 1931, may be added; and those who enjoy curiosities, like Hesketh Pearson in *Doctor Darwin*, 1930, and (the best general appreciation) A. Pryce-Jones in *The London Mercury*, 1929.

MARIA EDGEWORTH, 1767-1849

B. C. Slade published *M. E., a Bibliographical Tribute*, in 1937; the children's stories, being published in sections, present a bibliographical question by themselves. They begin with *The Parent's Assistant* in 1795 or 1796, and continue, in *Harry and Lucy* (Part I of *Early Lessons*), 1801, *Moral Tales for Young People*, 1801, *Continuation of Early Lessons*, 1814, *Rosamund*, 1821, *Frank*, 1822, and *Harry and Lucy Concluded*, 1825. Adult novels begin with *Castle Rackrent*, 1800, and *Belinda*, 1801; *Popular Tales*, 1804; *Leonora*, 1806; *Tales of Fashionable Life*, 1809, with its 2nd series, 1812; *Patronage*, 1814; *Harrington* and *Ormond*, 1817; *Helen*, 1834. She also ed. along with her father, *Practical*

Education, 1798, and *An Essay on Irish Bulls*, 1802, and *Essays on Professional Education*, 1809.

For her life, her own edition and continuation of her father's *Memoirs*, 1820, is necessary; it can be supplemented by *The Black Book of Edgeworthstown*, ed. H. J. and H. E. Butler, 1927. The first biography was a privately printed *Memoir* by her latest stepmother and the family, 1867; the first important one was the *Life and Letters* by Augustus J. C. Hare, 1894; the latest, containing new documents, is *The Great Maria* by E. Inglis-Jones, 1959. For contemporary notices consult K. G. Pfeiffer, *PQ* xi, 1932. Later studies are largely biographical, critical studies being few and slight; but see Lady (A. T.) Ritchie, *A Book of Sybils*, 1883; Padraic Colum, 'Maria Edgeworth and Turgenev' in *The British Review*, 1915; Virginia Woolf in *The Common Reader*, 1925; and A. N. Jeffares, introduction to *Castle Rackrent*, Nelson's Classics, 1953.

WILLIAM GIFFORD, 1756–1826

Gifford wrote (*a*) Satires in verse; *The Baviad*, 1791; *The Maeviad*, 1795; *Epistle to Peter Pindar*, 1800. They were frequently reprinted. (*b*) Translations: Juvenal, 1802 (containing the autobiography); Persius, 1821. (*c*) Editions of Massinger, 1805; Ben Jonson, 1816; Ford, 1827. (*d*) Journalism: especially as editor of *The Anti-Jacobin*, 1797–8, and *The Quarterly Review*, 1809–24. His anonymous political and critical writings in prose have not been, and need not be, collected. See C. W. Previté Orton, *Political Satire in English Poetry*, Cambridge, 1910; Hugh Walker, *English Satire*, 1925; J. Longaker, *The Della Cruscans and William Gifford*, Philadelphia, 1924; R. B. Clark, *William Gifford*; New York, 1930 (with bibliography); Kenneth Hopkins, *Portraits in Satire*, 1958.

GILPIN: see under Arts, above.

WILLIAM GODWIN, 1756–1836

Godwin's works fall under various heads.

A. Politics and Society: *An Enquiry concerning the Principles of Political Justice*, 1793, 'corrected' ed. 1796; ed. H. S. Salt, 1890, and abridged by R. A. Preston, 1926; ed. F. E. L. Priestley, Toronto, 1946; *The Enquirer*, 1797; *Thoughts occasioned by Dr. Parr's Spital Sermon*, 1801; *Of Population* (An Answer to Malthus), 1820; *Thoughts on Man*, 1831.

B. Biography and History: *The Life of Chaucer*, 1803; *Lives* of Edward and John Phillips, 1809; *History of the Commonwealth*, 1824–8; *Lives of the Necromancers*, 1834.

C. Novels: *Things as They Are* (*Caleb Williams*), 1794; *St. Leon*, 1799; *Fleetwood*, 1805; *Mandeville*, 1817; *Deloraine*, 1833.

D. Tragedies: *Antonio*, 1800; *Faulkener*, 1807. E. Essays: *Six Sermons*, 1784; *An Essay on Sepulchres*; some unpublished essays, ed. C. Kegan Paul, 1873. Also hack work under the pseudonyms of Edwin Baldwin and Theophilus Marcliffe. C. Kegan Paul, *W. G., his Friends and Contemporaries*, 1876, is important also for Mary Wollstonecraft, Holcroft, Bage, and the whole group. For a sympathetic study, see H. N. Brailsford, *Shelley, Godwin, and their Circle*, Home Univ. Lib., useful also for Paine, Holcroft, and others. See also F. K. Brown's *Life of W. G.*, 1926, and with bibliography, R. G. Grylls, *W. G. and his World*, 1953.

MRS. MARY (WOLLSTONECRAFT) GODWIN, 1759–97

Her *Posthumous Works* were ed. by her husband, 4 vols., 1798, the year also of his *Memoir*; there are editions of the latter by W. J. Durrant, 1927, and J. Middleton Murry, 1928. Her *Vindication of the Rights of Woman*, 1792, is her most notable work. Her *View of the Origin and Progress of the French Revolution*, 1794, does not add much to history. *Letters written . . . in Sweden, Norway, and Denmark*, 1796. Her letters to her betrayer Gilbert Imlay were published by C. Kegan Paul, 1879, and by Roger Ingpen, 1908, with a biographical introduction. Studies, mainly laudatory, are by G. R. S. Taylor, 1911; F. Routen, 1923; H. R. James, 1932; G. R. Preedy, *This Shining Woman*, 1937; R. M. Wardle, Kansas, 1952.

JAMES GRAHAME, 1765–1811

Grahame produced *Poems in English, Scotch, and Latin*, Paisley, 1794; *The Rural Calendar*, Paisley, 1797; *Mary Stewart*, 1801, *The Sabbath*, 1804, *Biblical Pictures*, 1806, *The Birds of Scotland*, 1806, all at Edinburgh; *Poems*, Glasgow, 1807; *British Georgics*, Edinburgh, 1809. His collected poems, ed. G. Gilfillan, were published, with memoir and notice, in Edinburgh, 1850.

MRS. ANNE GRANT, 1755–1838

Poems on Various Subjects, 1803 (including *The Highlanders*); *Eighteen Hundred and Thirteen*, 1814, both at Edinburgh. Her prose *Letters from the Mountains*, 1806, is more worth attention. A memoir and collection of letters, ed. J. P. Grant, 1844, commemorates this admirable lady.

ELIZABETH HAMILTON, 1758–1816

Besides tracts on education, she wrote *Letters of a Hindoo Rajah*, 1796; *Memoirs of Modern Philosophers*, a satire on Godwinism, 1800; *Memoirs of the Life of Agrippina*, Bath, 1804; and *The Cottagers of Glenburnie*, Edinburgh, 1808, her best remembered work. There is a memoir by E. O. Benger, 1818.

JAMES HOGG, 1770–1835

(a) Verse: *Scottish Pastorals*, 1801; *The Mountain Bard*, 1807; *The Forest Minstrel*, 1810; *The Queen's Wake*, 1813; *The Pilgrims of the Sun*, 1815; *The Poetic Mirror*, 1816; *Mador of the Moor*, 1816; *Queen Hynde*, 1825, and various smaller pieces, including songs, some of the best known of which appeared in the *Jacobite Relics of Scotland*, 1819–21. (b) Prose, less interesting. Though a social historian might glean from *The Brownie of Bodsbeck*, 1818, *Winter Evening Tales*, 1820, and *Altrive Tales*, 1832, Hogg is remembered as a story-teller mainly for the *Confessions of a Justified Sinner*, 1824, ed. T. E. Welby, 1924, which gained publicity (and little else) from an introduction by André Gide in an edition of 1947. All these were published in Edinburgh. His *Domestic Manners of Sir Walter Scott*, Glasgow, 1834, was ill advised. He contributed his name, and a memoir, to an ed. of Burns, Glasgow, 1834–6, the useful editing being by William Motherwell. There are many collected and selected editions, from 1822 on. *Memorials*, by his daughter Mrs. Garden, appeared in Paisley in 1887; a biography of 'The Ettrick Shepherd' was published by H. T. Stephenson, Bloomington, 1922, and a good one, with bibliography, by Edith C. Batho, 1927, with bibliography, added to in *The Library*, 1935. Detail is added by Alan Lang Strout in his *Life and Letters of James Hogg*, 1946, which resumes also his articles in periodicals.

THOMAS HOLCROFT, 1745–1809

Holcroft wrote some 22 plays, not all published. The most enterprising was a version of Beaumarchais's *Mariage de Figaro*, memorized from performances in Paris, 1784–5, the most successful *The Road to Ruin*, 1792. His novels were *Alwyn*, 1780; *Anna St. Ives*, 1792; *The Adventures of Hugh Trevor*, 1794; and

Memoirs of Brian Perdue, 1805. The rest is journalism, including his *Travels from Hamburg*, 1804. He also translated from French and German, notably Lavater's *Essays on Physiognomy*, 1789, and Goethe's *Hermann and Dorothea*, 1801. His *Autobiography* was completed after his death by Hazlitt, 1816; ed. E. Colby, 1925; *WC*, 1926; and included in eds. of Hazlitt by Glover and by P. P. Howe. E. Colby produced a bibliography, New York Public Library Bulletin, 1922. For the plays, see also Allardyce Nicoll.

MRS. ELIZABETH INCHBALD, 1753–1821

Her plays number about 18, all comedies and farces, four being versions from French and two, including *Lovers' Vows*, 1798, from Kotzebue's German; on this, see W. Reitzel, '*Mansfield Park*' and '*Lovers' Vows*', *RES*, ix, 1933. Her two novels were *A Simple Story*, 1791, ed. G. L. Strachey, 1908, and *Nature and Art*, 1796. After 1805 she published three large collections of plays: *The British Theatre*, 25 vols., 1808 (annotated); *Farces*, 7 vols., 1809; and *The Modern Theatre*, 10 vols., 1809. There is a bibliography by G. L. Joughin, Texas Univ. Stud., 1934. James Boaden published *Memoirs* in 1833, and there are studies by S. R. Littlewood, *E. I. and her Circle*, 1921; and W. McKee, *E. I., Novelist*, Baltimore, 1935.

FRANCIS JEFFREY, LORD JEFFREY, 1773–1850

He reprinted 4 vols. of his contributions to *The Edinburgh Review* in 1844. There is a selection, with a useful introduction, by D. Nichol Smith, Oxford, 1910. His other works are mainly on current politics, but Lord Cockburn's *Life*, Edinburgh, 1852, is of wide interest. See also Carlyle's *Reminiscences*, 1881, and Jeffrey's letters to Ugo Foscolo, ed. J. Purves, Edinburgh, 1934. Studies are by Merritt Y. Hughes, 'The Humanism of F. J.', *MLR*, 1921; J. M. Beatty, 'J. and Wordsworth', *PMLA*, 1923; R. C. Bald, 'F. J. as a Literary Critic', *Nineteenth Century*, 1925. See also Sir W. Raleigh in *On Writing and Writers*, ed. George Gordon, 1926. James A. Greig, *Jeffrey of the Edinburgh Review*, 1948. John Clive, *Scotch Reviewers*, 1957.

CHARLES LAMB, 1775–1834

His first ambitions lay in poetry, in association with Coleridge. Four sonnets were included in Coleridge's *Poems on Various Subjects*, 1796, and added to in the 2nd ed., 1797. He contributed one poem to Charles Lloyd's *Poems on the Death of Priscilla Farmer*, 1796, and collaborated with him in *Blank Verse*, 1798. *John Woodvil* was printed with the pastiche of Burton in 1802; *Mr. H.* only in Philadelphia, 1813. *Album Verses*, 1830, collects some small pieces. The Essays belong to the next volume, but we may note here *Rosamund Gray*, Birmingham, 1798; *Mrs. Leicester's School*, 1807; *Tales from Shakespeare*, 1807, with his sister; and *Specimens of English Dramatic Poets*, 1808. Lamb collected *The Works of C. L.*, 1818, in two vols., the first containing poems (six of them Mary's) and *John Woodvil*, the second, Essays and *Mr. H.* The poems were collected in 1836. The notable eds. of the complete works are those of P. Fitzgerald, 1875; A. Ainger, 1878; and with a *Life* in 1899; and T. Hutchinson, 1908. The standard ed. is E. V. Lucas's, 1903–5, in 5 vols., *plus* two of Letters superseded by the separate 3-vol. edition in 1935. Selection of letters in E.L., 2 vols., 1945. Anonymous contributions to periodicals remain to be identified but probably would add little; e.g. verses appear in *The Poetrical Recreations of 'The Champion'*, ed. J. Thelwall, in 1822.

The standard *Life* is also Lucas's, 1905; revised 1921. There are many reminiscences, well represented in Edmund Blunden's *Christ's Hospital, a Retrospect*, 1923; *C. L. and his Contemporaries*, 1923; and *C. L. Recorded by his Contemporaries*, 1934. See also F. V. Morley, *Lamb before Elia*, 1932; K. G. Anthony, *The Lambs*, 1948: *C. L. and Elia*, ed. J. E. Morpurgo, Penguin, 1948. Much else has been written, mostly sketches or annotations, and too often sentimental. See Raleigh in *On Writing and Writers*; Blunden's essay and bibliography in *WW*. Another bibliography is in Hutchinson's ed., and a section on Lamb in T. J. Wise's Ashley Library Catalogue.

WALTER SAVAGE LANDOR, 1775–1864

He is noticed here only in part, since we are concerned only with poems, and mainly with early ones. He suppressed a vol. of *Poems*, 1795, and reappeared with *Gebir*, 1798, revised in 1803 and 1831, translated as *Gebirus*, 1803. There followed *Poems from the Arabic and Persian*, Warwick, 1800, original and not translated; *Poetry by the Author of Gebir*, 1802; *Simonidea*, Bath, 1806; *Count Julian*, 1812. A collection, with *Gebir* and *Count Julian*, 1831, appeared after the first two series of *Imaginary Conversations*. *Idyllia Nova*, Oxford, 1815, and *Idyllia Heroica*, Pisa,

1820, are in Latin. The tragedies *Andrea of Hungary* and *Giovanna of Naples*, 1839, were made into a trilogy by *Fra Rupert*, 1840. The large collection, *The Hellenics*, 1847, was added to in 1859. *Poemata et Inscriptiones*, 1847, contains old and new work as does the second vol. of *Works*, 2 vols., 1846. John Forster published the *Works* in 8 vols., 1876, with a shorter version of the *Life* he had produced in 1869. C. G. Crump's ed., 1891–2, contains a selection of poems. The standard ed. is by T. E. Welby and S. Wheeler, 1927, in 16 vols.; the Poems separately in 3 vols., Oxford, 1937.

For Landor's life, after Forster see Malcolm Elwin, *Savage Landor*, 1941, and *Landor: a Replevin*, 1958, and R. H. Super, *Landor*, New York, 1954. For criticism, Sidney Colvin, E.M.L., 1881; E. W. Evans, *W. S. L.*, New York, 1892; Saintsbury in *Essays*, series 2, 1895; W. Bradley, *The Early Poems of W. S. L.*, 1914; S. T. Williams in *PMLA*, 1921, on *Gebir*; Raleigh in *On Writing and Writers*; A. H. Mason, *W. S. L., Poète Lyrique*, Paris, 1924; Sir G. Rostrevor Hamilton, *WW*, 1960, with bibliography, for which also see T. J. Wise and S. Wheeler, Bibliographical Soc. 1919, and Wise's *A Landor Library*, 1928. R. H. Super's *The Publication of Landor's Works*, Bibliographical Soc., 1954, is admirable.

MATTHEW GREGORY LEWIS, 1775–1818

Lewis began with *The Monk*, 1796. Later eds. were expurgated, but the first was ed. L. F. Peck, New York, 1952. Of his plays, *The East Indian*, 1800, is a comedy, six are romantic melodramas with or without music, two tragedies, and two translated from German. His verses appeared in *Tales of Terror*, Kelso, 1799, a publication arranged by Scott, who contributed; *Tales of Wonder* were collected by himself, 1801; *Poems* appeared in 1812. A few verses were published posthumously, also his most attractive work, *Journal of a West India Proprietor*, 1834; ed. M. Wilson, 1929. There is a *Life and Correspondence*, anon., but by M. Baron-Wilson, 1839. Most criticism is of *The Monk*, in E. Birkhead's *The Tale of Terror*, 1821, and A. M. Killan, *Le Roman Terrifiant*. In 'A Note on *The Monk*' in *The Colophon*, 1935, F. Coykendall gives a bibliographical description.

JOHN LEYDEN, 1775–1811

He published *Scenes of Infancy*, Edinburgh, 1803; his *Poetical Remains* were ed. by J. Morton, with a memoir, 1819, and collected, 1875. Leyden ed. *Scottish Descriptive Poems*, Edinburgh, 1803, rather well. Scott's 'Life' in the *Edinburgh Annual Register*, 1811, reprinted in *Prose Works*, iv, 1848, is admirable; but see S. Aiyangar, *An Anglo-Indian Poet, J. L.*, Madras, 1912, and a *Life* by J. Reith, 1923.

CHARLES ROBERT MATURIN, 1782–1824

His novels were *Fatal Revenge*, 1807, 'by D. J. Murphy'; *The Wild Irish Boy*, 1808; *The Milesian Chief*, 1812; *Women*, Edinburgh, 1818; *Melmoth the Wanderer*, Edinburgh, 1820; *The Albigenses*, 1824. His tragedies, *Bertram*, 1816, *Manuel*, 1817, and *Fredolfo*, 1819, were less noticed. He also published sermons in 1819 and 1824. Scott's notice in *The Quarterly Review*, 1818, introduction in the Bannatyne Novels series, is, as usual, sound and sympathetic. There are studies by N. Idman, Helsingfors, 1923, and W. Scholten, Amsterdam, 1933. See Birkhead as under Lewis. In 'M. the Innovator', *Huntington Library Quarterly*, xxi, 1957–58, H. W. Piper and A. N. Jeffares discuss him as a nationalist.

HANNAH MORE, 1745–1833

She began with poems and tragedies, which need not delay us, and became serious in 1791 with *An Estimate of the Religion of the Fashionable World*. Her tracts were contained in *Village Politics, by Will Chip*, 1793, and *Cheap Repository Tracts*, published between 1795 and 1798, when the Religious Tract Society was founded to continue the good work. Her one novel, *Coelebs in Search of a Wife*, 1808, comes between *Strictures on the Modern System of Female Education*, 1799, *Hints towards Forming the Character of a Young Princess*, 1805, and *Practical Piety*, 1811, and *Christian Morals*, 1813, which places it neatly. *Moral Sketches*, 1819, criticizes contemporary manners and morals as she saw them. William Roberts's *Memoirs*, 1834, with letters to and from her, are more interesting; R. Brimley Johnson's *Selected Letters*, 1925, may suffice. There are studies by A. M. B. Meakin, 1911, M. A. Hopkins, New York, 1946, and M. G. Jones, 1952.

AMELIA (ALDERSON) OPIE, 1769–1853

She published a dozen works of fiction between 1790 and 1825, of which *The Father and Daughter*, 1801, *Adeline Mowbray*, 1804, *Simple Tales*, 1806, and perhaps *Temper, or Domestic Scenes*, 1812, made some mark. They were collected in 12 vols.,

1845–79, *Works*, Philadelphia, 1848. She wrote verses, some of which were added to *The Father and Daughter*, but which need detain nobody. Her life was more significant than her imaginative works, and may be read in *Memorials of the Life of A. O.* by C. L. Brightwell, 1854, *A. A. O., Worldling and Friend*, by Margaret E. Macgregor, Northampton, Mass., 1933, and *Amelia, the Tale of a Plain Friend*, by J. Menzies-Wilson and H. Lloyd, 1937. There is a bibliography attached to Miss Macgregor's work.

SYDNEY OWENSON (LADY MORGAN), 1776–1859

Owenson began with *Poems*, Dublin 1801, and wrote a few other verses, but is remembered for *The Wild Irish Girl*, 1806; *O'Donnel, a National Tale*, 1814; *Florence Macarthy, An Irish Tale*, 1818; and *The O'Briens and the O'Flahertys, a National Tale*, 1827. *Woman, or Ida of Athens*, 1809, was successful, her other five less so. In later years she wrote on France, 1817, and Italy, 1821, which had social repercussions, understandable in the light of her *Passages in my Autobiography*, 1859, her *Memoirs*, ed. W. H. Dixon, 1862, and W. J. Fitzpatrick's *The Friends, Foes, and Adventures of Lady Morgan*, Dublin, 1859. She is noticed in 'George Paston's' *Little Memoirs*, 1902; Mona Wilson's *These were Muses*, 1924; and studied at greater length in L. Stevenson's *The Wild Irish Girl*, 1936 (bibliography).

THOMAS PAINE, 1737–1809

His work began in America with journalism. In 1776 he published *Common Sense* in favour of independence, followed by *The Crisis* series of pamphlets. Back in Europe he answered Burke with *The Rights of Man*, 1791, Part II in 1792. There are editions by H. B. Bonner, 1907, and G. J. Holyoake, E.L. 1915, as well as many cheap reprints. There were many such of *The Age of Reason*, Paris, 1794, Part II, London, 1795, as well as editions by M. D. Conway, New York, 1896, and J. M. Robertson, 1905. Conway also ed. *The Writings of T. P.*, New York, 1894–6, and Bonner ed. his *Political Writings*, 1909. There are *Lives* by Conway, New York, 1892, and H. Pearson, New York, 1936. See also A. C. Aldridge, *Thomas Paine*, and H. N. Brailsford's *Shelley, Godwin, and their Circle*, Home Univ. Lib.

MRS. ANN (WARD) RADCLIFFE, 1764–1823

Her novels appeared between 1789 and 1797: *The Castles of Athlin and Dunbayne*, 1789; *A Sicilian Romance*, 1790; *The Romance of the Forest*, 1791; *The Mysteries of Udolpho*, 1794; *The Italian*, 1797. *Gaston de Blondeville* with some verse was published with a *Memoir* in 1826. *A Journey . . . through Holland and the Western Frontier of Germany* was published in 1795, much of it being topical. The novels were collected, 1821, with introduction by Scott, reprinted in his *Prose Works*, vol. iii. See also Montague Summers, *A Great Mistress of Romance*, Trans. Roy. Soc. Lit., 1917, and *The Gothic Quest*, 1938; C. F. MacIntyre, *A. R. in Relation to her Time*, New Haven, 1920; A. S. S. Wieten, *Mrs. R., her Relation towards Romanticism*, Amsterdam, 1926; and in E. Birkhead, *The Tale of Terror*, A. M. Killen, *Le Roman Terrifiant*, Paris, 1923; J. M. S. Tompkins, *The Popular Novel in England*, 1932; A. Grant, *A. R.*, Denver, 1952, and the histories by Baker (vol. v), and by Raleigh and Saintsbury—these two brief but pointed.

HENRY CRABB ROBINSON, 1775–1867

His voluminous papers are in Dr. Williams's Library, London. T. Sadler edited extracts, 3 vols., 1869; 2 vols., 1872. E. J. Morley selected *Blake, Coleridge, Wordsworth, etc.*, Manchester, 1922; *Correspondence with the Wordsworth Circle*, 2 vols., Oxford, 1927; *C. R. in Germany*, Oxford, 1929; *H. C. R. on Books and their Writers*, 3 vols., 1938. She also produced his *Life and Times*, 1935. See also *H. C. R.* by J. M. Baker, 1937.

SAMUEL ROGERS, 1763–1855

He published, anonymously, *An Ode to Superstition* and other verses in 1786, but made a name with *The Pleasures of Memory*, 1792. *An Epistle to a Friend* followed in 1798; *The Voyage of Columbus*, 1810; *Poems*, 1812; *Jacqueline*, 1814; *Human Life*, 1819; *Italy*, Part I, 1822; Part II, 1828. The 1794 ed. of *The Pleasures of Memory* was illustrated by Stothard; *Italy*, 1830, and *Poems*, 1834, by Stothard and Turner. In 1856, Alexander Dyce published *Recollections of the Table-Talk of S. R., with a Memoir*; W. Sharpe ed. *Recollections by S. R.*, 1859; they were combined by G. H. Powell, 1903. P. W. Clayden's *Early Life of S. R.*, 1887, *R. and his Contemporaries*, 1889, give many views of literary society in his time. See also R. Ellis Roberts, *S. R. and his Circle*, 1910; C. F. Harrold, *Portrait of a Saurian*, in the *Sewanee Review*, 1929; J. R. Hale, *The Italian Journey of S. R.*, 1957; and C. P. Barbier's excellent *S. R. and W. Gilpin*, 1959.

WILLIAM ROSCOE, 1753–1831

Roscoe wrote verses, of which only *The Butterfly's Ball*, in the *Gentleman's Mag.*, 1806, is remembered. His real work lies in *The Life of Lorenzo de' Medici*, Liverpool, 1795; *The Life and Pontificate of Leo the Tenth*, Liverpool, 1805; *Illustrations . . . of the Life of Lorenzo de' Medici*, 1822; and his ed. of Pope, 1824. His tr. of Tansillo, *The Nurse*, 1798, helped Italian studies. He also produced works on the Slave-Trade and politics, and various pamphlets. There are Lives by H. Roscoe, 1833; C. S. Jones, Liverpool, 1931; and G. W. Mathews, 1931. *W. R. of Liverpool*, ed. G. Chandler, 1953, contains centenary studies.

FRANK SAYERS, 1763–1817

Sayers published *Dramatic Sketches of the Ancient Northern Mythology*, 1790; *Poems*, Norwich, 1792; a revised edition of these, Norwich, 1803; *Nugae Poeticae*, 1803; also some philosophical, literary, and antiquarian essays, 1793 and 1805. His *Collective Works*, Norwich, 1823, and *Poetical Works*, 1830, contain a biographical notice by W. Taylor, in whose *Life* by Robberds more may be found.

SIR WALTER SCOTT, 1771–1832

His first published work was the anonymous pamphlet, *The Chase, and William and Helen*, translations from Bürger, Edinburgh, 1796; then the translation of Goethe's tragedy *Goetz von Berlichingen*, 1799. The trs. from Bürger reappeared with some imitations in *Tales of Terror*, Kelso, 1799 (with Lewis, Southey, &c.), and six again in *Tales of Wonder*, 1801, mainly by Lewis; *The Eve of St. John*, separately, Kelso, 1800. *The Minstrelsy of the Scottish Border* appeared in 2 vols., Kelso, 1802, and 3 vols., Edinburgh, 1803; the 1810 ed. was revised: an important ed. is by T. F. Henderson, Edinburgh, 1902; *Sir Tristrem*, ed. from the Auchinleck MS., Edinburgh, 1804. And so to *The Lay of the Last Minstrel*, 1805; *Marmion*, Edinburgh, 1808; *The Lady of the Lake*, Edinburgh, 1810. *The Vision of Don Roderick* was first privately printed for a war charity, 1811. The later series is *Rokeby*, 1813; *The Bridal of Triermain*, 1813; *The Lord of the Isles*, 1815; *The Field of Waterloo*, 1815; *Harold the Dauntless*, 1817. *Miscellaneous Poems*, 1820, reprinted earlier work. The Novels began with *Waverley*, 1814, and *Guy Mannering*, 1815; but reviews in *The Edinburgh Review* began in 1803 and continued in the *Quarterly* from 1812. Editing continued, notably of Dryden, 1808, and Swift, 1814, with nine historical eds. and five literary ones between the dates. Since the main work of Scott is dealt with in the next vol., it is necessary to note only the earlier portions of the Lives by Lockhart, John Buchan, and Grierson, and of the Letters, ed. Grierson and others; but see Sir H. Grierson on *The Man and the Poet* in *Sir Walter Scott Lectures*, Edinburgh, 1950; D. Nichol Smith in the *Edinburgh University Journal*, 1950; J. W. Oliver in *Scottish Poetry, a Critical Survey*, ed. J. Kinsley, 1955. A detailed Bibliography of the Poetical Works, by William Ruff, is in the *Transactions of the Edinburgh Bibliographical Soc.*, i, pt. 2, 1937; J. L. Corson's *Bibl. of Sir Walter Scott*, Edinburgh, 1943, is 'a classified and annotated list of books and articles' up to 1940.

MRS. CHARLOTTE SMITH, 1749–1806

Her *Elegiac Sonnets* grew in number from the first ed., 1784 to 1795, a 2nd vol. being added in 1797. *The Emigrants*, 1793, and *Beachy Head*, 1807, are less interesting. Novels began with *Ethelinde*, 1789; thereafter *Celestina*, 1791; *Desmond*, 1792; *The Old Manor House*, 1793; *The Banished Man*, 1794; *Montalbert*, 1795; *Marchmont*, 1796; *The Young Philosopher*, 1798. *Rural Walks*, 1795, inculcating botany, good works, natural history, rural life, and morals, in conversation form, is not the worst of its kind. She does not seem to have attracted much critical attention, though the Sonnets are often mentioned, but see Scott's notice in his *Prose Works*, vol. iv; F. M. A. Hilbush, *C. S., Poet and Novelist*, Philadelphia, 1941; A. D. McKillop, 'C. S.'s Letters', *Huntington Library Quarterly*, xv, 1951–2.

SIDNEY SMITH, 1771–1845

Sidney Smith has survived mainly as a wit, in such selections as *The Wit and Wisdom of S. S.*, 1860, and *The Bon-Mots* ed. W. Jerrold, 1893. His work was in sermons and in periodicals, of which *Extracts from the Edinburgh Review* were reprinted about 1810, and other *Essays from the E.R.* in 1874. The important series *The Letters of Peter Plymley*, 1807, ed. G. C. Heseltine, 1929, with introduction, dealt with Catholic emancipation, and those to Archdeacon Singleton, 1837–9, with ecclesiastical affairs; add various pamphlets on politics and church affairs. The *Elementary Sketches of Moral Philosophy*, 1804, lectures at the Royal Institution between 1804 and 1806, privately printed at the time, were reprinted together, 1850. The *Works* were collected 1839–40. Nowell C. Smith ed. his Letters, Oxford, 1953, and a *Selection* in E.L. There are Lives by S. J. Reid, 1884; O. Saint Clair, 1913; O. Burdett, 1934; and H. Pearson (*The Smith of Smiths*), 1934; and studies by A. Chevrillon, Paris, 1894 (largely political), G. W. E. Russell, E.M.L., 1905. See S. T. Williams, 'The Literary Criticism of S. S.', *MLN*, xxxviii, 1923.

ROBERT SOUTHEY, 1774–1843

He began writing at school; his first adult publication was *The Fall of Robespierre*, Cambridge, 1794, Act I being by Coleridge. Then followed *Poems*, Bath, 1795, with Robert Lovell; *Joan of Arc*, Bristol, 1796; *Poems*, 1797–9; then the long poems: *Thalaba*, 1801; *Madoc*, 1805; *The Curse of Kehama*, 1810; *Roderick*, 1814; *A Tale of Paraguay*, 1825. In 1805 he reprinted his contributions to *The Annual Anthology* which he had edited 1799–1800. His enemies published his early *Wat Tyler*, 1817, as a proof of political apostasy. *A Vision of Judgment*, 1821, is remembered only for Byron's devastating rejoinder. *The Devil's Walk*, originally a collaboration with Coleridge in *The Morning Post*, 1799, was expanded by Southey and printed (as by Porson) in 1830.

His first prose publication was the *Letters written . . . in Spain and Portugal*, Bristol, 1797. The more important *Letters from England: By Don Manuel Alvarez Espriella*, 1807, has been ed. by J. Simmons, 1951. *Omniana*, 1812, was a miscellany in collaboration with Coleridge. The principal historical and biographical works were the *History of Brazil*, 1810–29; *Nelson*, 1813 (and frequently since); *Wesley*, 1820; *The History of the Peninsular War*, 1823–32; *Lives of the British Admirals*, 1833–40. On ecclesiastical affairs, *The Book of the Church*, 1824; and its sequel *Vindiciae Ecclesiae Anglicanae*, 1826. *The Doctor*, a fantastic *Omniana*, appeared anonymously between 1834 and 1847. Collected review articles were reprinted, and hitherto unpublished Tours in the Netherlands, in Scotland, and in Portugal have been printed in 1902, 1929, and 1960. His translating and editing included *Amadis of Gaul*, 1803; *Palmerin of England*, 1807; the *Chronicle of the Cid*, 1808; Malory's *Kyng Arthur*, 1817; *The Pilgrim's Progress*, 1830, with *Life* of Bunyan. The editions, the *Works* of Chatterton, 1803; *Specimens of the Later English Poets*,

1807; *The Remains of Henry Kirke White*, 1808–22; and *Lives of Uneducated Poets*, 1831 and 1836, ed. T. S. Childers, 1925, were works of charity. The editions of Isaac Watts's *Horae Lyricae*, 1834, and the *Works* of Cowper, 1835–7, are sound and solid. The *Minor Poems* were collected in 1815, and the *Poetical Works*, with his own prefaces, in 1837–8. His son-in-law J. W. Warter printed his *Common Place Book*, 1849–51, and *Selections from his Letters* in 1856. The Life by his son Cuthbert also contains many letters. There are more in the *Correspondence with Caroline Bowles*, ed. Edward Dowden, Dublin, 1881; in J. W. Robberds's *Life* of William Taylor, 1843; *Memorials of Coleorton*, ed. W. Knight, Edinburgh, 1887; *Letters from the Lake Poets to Daniel Stewart*, privately printed by Stewart's daughter Mary, 1889; *A House of Letters*, ed. E. Betham, 1905; and a Selection, ed. M. H. Fitzgerald, *WC*, 1902. (The quotations from letters to Bowles in the text are from the originals in the writer's possession.)

The 'sketch' in *The Observer*, Bristol, 1793, is the only admiring one in the set. There are many other Reminiscences, by Cottle, de Quincey, Carlyle, and in Lives of contemporaries and collections of Letters. The original *Life* is his son's, noted above. Modern biographies are by W. Haller, *The Early Life of R. S.*, New York, 1917, with a bibliographical appendix, and J. Simmons, 1945. Criticism is to be found in Coleridge's *Biographia Literaria*, Hazlitt's *Spirit of the Age* (with the usual reservations), and Landor's *Imaginary Conversations*; and in Edward Dowden's E.M.L. volume, 1874; Saintsbury's *Essays*, 1895; E. C. Knowlton in *PQ*, 1928 and 1929. See also H. G. Wright in *RES*, 1932, on the Welsh bard Iolo Morganwg, and 1933, mainly on Madoc. On the reviews see W. Graham in *PQ*, 1923, and E. L. Griggs in *MP*, 1932. For Southey's political views, see A. Cobban, *Edmund Burke and the Revolt against the 18th Century*, 1929, and G. D. Carnall, *R. S. and his Age*, 1960.

JOSEPH STRUTT, 1749–1802

Strutt published four works before 1789, but his later two are the best known: *The Dress and Habits*, and *The Sports and Pastimes, of the People of England*, 1796–9 and 1801. Later editions do not do him justice, especially as an illustrator.

WILLIAM TAYLOR, 1765–1836

Taylor wrote largely for *The Monthly Review*, his periodical summaries of literary production being very competent. He published *English Synonyms Discriminated*, 1813, and *A Historic Survey of German Poetry*, 1828–30. The latter includes translations, and he translated also Lessing's *Nathan the Wise*, Norwich, 1791; Goethe's *Iphigenia in Tauris*, 1793; Wieland's *Dialogues of the Gods*, 1795; and two books of fairy-tales. His most famous translation was that of Bürger, noted in the section on Scott. See J. W. Robberds's *Memoir*, 1843.

GILBERT WHITE, 1720–93

White published *The Natural History and Antiquities of Selborne* in 1789; of many eds., note those by F. Buckland, 1876; Thomas Bell, 1877, with memoir; R. Kearton, 1902; B. C. A. Windle, E.L. 1906; and the (incomplete) *Writings* ed. H. J. Massingham, 1938. R. Holt-White ed. *The Life and Letters*, 1901. See also E. A. Martin, *A Bibliography of G. W. with a Biography*, revised ed., 1934; C. G. Emden in *Oriel Papers* and *Gilbert White in his Village*, 1956; W. S. Scott, *White of Selborne*, 1950.

JOHN WOLCOT, 1738–1819

'Peter Pindar' kept up a running commentary on social affairs, with a few light-hearted excursions on political happenings, from 1778 to 1817; over 70 titles. Collected vols. appeared at intervals, those of 1812 and 1816 including memoirs. More serious works were *Picturesque Views with Poetical Allusions*, 1797; and *The Beauties of English Poetry*, 1804. He also ed. Pilkington's *Dictionary of Painters*, 1799. There are *Selections with Critical Notice* by J. H. P. Hunt, 1890. See H. Walker, *English Satire*, 1925, and especially Kenneth Hopkins, *Portraits in Satire*, 1958.

WILLIAM WORDSWORTH, 1770–1850

He pronounced judgement on *An Evening Walk* and *Descriptive Sketches*, 1793, by reprinting only fragments in 1815 and complete revisions in 1820. He declared himself in *Lyrical Ballads*, 1798, with Coleridge; see facsimiles, 1927, and New York, 1934; ed. Dowden, 1890, T. Hutchinson, 1898 (revised 1920), and E. Littledale, 1911; 2nd ed. 1800 in 2 vols. In *Poems in Two Volumes*, 1807, he began his arrangement of poems in categories, completed in later editions; ed. T. Hutchinson, 1897, and Helen Darbishire, revised ed. 1952. Longer poems follow: *The Excursion*, 1814; *The White Doe of Rylstone*, 1815; *Peter Bell*, 1819; *The Waggoner*, 1819. *The River Duddon* and other poems, 1820, and *Memorials of a Tour on the Continent*, 1822, *Ecclesiastical Sketches*, 1822, augmented as *Ecclesiastical Sonnets*, 1837, ed. A. F. Potts, New Haven, 1922, are sonnet sequences; *Yarrow Revisited*, 1835, contains lyrical work. *The Prelude*, finished in 1805 but continuously revised, was published only in 1850, after his death; ed. Ernest de Selincourt, 1926, with texts of 1805 and 1834, revised H. Darbishire, 1959; the unfinished *The Recluse* only in 1888. Wordsworth collected his poems, in final categories, 1815; ten more eds. appeared between 1820 and 1850. E. de Selincourt used the 1849–50 ed., the last in the poet's lifetime, as basis for the masterly ed., Oxford, 1940–9; a revision is in progress. Note also the eds. of T. Hutchinson, 1895, and revisions, and Nowell C. Smith, 1908.

Prose works were collected by A. B. Grosart, 1876, and W. A. Knight, 1898. A. V. Dicey ed. the tract on *The Convention of Cintra* (1809), Oxford, 1915. W. contributed two articles to Coleridge's *The Friend*, 1809–10. *A Letter to a Friend of Burns*, 1816, is an interesting manifesto. The essay on the *Scenery of the Lakes* finally became *A Guide through the District of the Lakes* in 1842; ed. E. de Selincourt, 1906. *Letters of the Wordsworth Family*, ed. W. Knight, Boston, 1907. The standard ed. of the *Letters of William and Dorothy W.* is by de Selincourt: *Early Letters* (1787–1805), 1935; *The Middle Years* (1806–20), 2 vols. 1937; *Later Years* (1821–50), 1939. Add L. N. Broughton, *Wordsworth and Reed*, 1933; Edith J. Morley, *The Correspondence of Crabb Robinson with the Wordsworth Circle*, 1927.

The 'official' Life was by the poet's nephew Christopher Wordsworth, 1851. Modern studies began well with Emile Legouis, *La Jeunesse de W.*, Paris, 1896, tr. as *The Early Life of W.*, 1897. George McLean Harper, *W. W., his Life, Works and Influence*, 1916, distorted by political opinion but still valuable, revealed the affair with Annette Vallon. Legouis followed in an appendix to the 1921 ed. of *The Early Life*, and printed all available documents in the *Revue des Deux Mondes*, and *W. W. and Annette Vallon*, 1922. E. C. Batho's *The Later Wordsworth*, 1934, is defensive but usefully so. The early life is restudied by E. de Selincourt, *The Early Wordsworth* (English Association Lecture), 1936, by G. W. Meyer, *W.'s Formative Years*, Ann Arbor, 1943, and to 1803 in detail by Mary Moorman, *W. W., the Early Years*, 1957. More opinionative studies are Sir Herbert Read, *W.*, 1930; H. I'Anson Faussett, *The Lost Leader*, 1937;

288   V. INDIVIDUAL AUTHORS: WORDSWORTH

F. W. Bateson, *W., a Re-Interpretation*, 2nd ed. 1956. It is refreshing to return to the brisk treatment of one detail in 'Racedown and the Wordsworths', by Bergen Evans and Hester Pinney,
RES, 1932. B. R. Schneider's *W.'s Cambridge Education*, Cambridge, 1957, contains the facts without the common sense.

General studies may well begin with A. C. Bradley's *Oxford
Lectures on Poetry*, 1909, and Sir Walter Raleigh's *W.*, 1903,
which approach the poems directly; with F. W. H. Myers,
E.M.L., 1881, C. H. Herford, *The Age of Wordsworth*, 1897, and
W., 1930, in spite of his overemphasis on German influences;
H. W. Garrod, Oxford, 1923, rev. 1927, valuable for its
scholarly method; Helen Darbishire, *The Poet W.*, Oxford,
1950; J. C. Smith, *A Study of W.*, 1941, solid and comprehensive; H. M. Margoliouth, *W. and Coleridge*, H.U.L., 1953; J.
Jones, *The Egotistical Sublime*, 1954. Lascelles Abercrombie's *The
Art of W.*, Oxford, 1952, but dating from 1935, is distinguished
as the work of a technically accomplished poet; compare Walter
Bagehot's essay in *Literary Studies*, 1879; *W.'s Literary Criticism*,
ed. Nowell C. Smith, 1905; G. M. Harper, *W.'s Poetic Technique*
in *Literary Appreciations*, 1937; A. F. Potts, *W.'s Prelude, a Study
of its Literary Form*, Ithaca, 1953. Commemorative studies, of
varying merit, reflecting recent opinion, are in *Tribute to W.*,
ed. Muriel Spark and Derek Sandford, 1950, which also reprints contemporary essays; *The Major English Romantic Poets*,
ed. C. D. Thorpe, C. Baker, and B. Weaver, Southern Illinois
U.P., 1957; *Centenary Studies*, ed. G. T. Dunklin, Princeton,
1951. There are many remarks on separate poems: see J. S.
Lyon, *The Excursion, a Study*, Yale U.P., 1950; Helen Darbishire
on *The Ruined Cottage* in *Essays. . . . presented to Sir Humphrey
Milford*, Oxford, 1948; H. V. D. Dyson, *The Old Cumberland
Beggar*, in *Essays . . . presented to D. Nichol Smith*, 1945; J. F.
Danby, *Six Poems*.

Among philosophic studies, Edward Caird's in his *Essays on
Literature and Philosophy*, 1892, is still valid. More modern are
A. Beatty, *W. W., his Doctrine and Art*, Madison, 1922, revised
1927; F. R. Leavis in *Revaluation*, 1936; R. D. Havens, *The
Mind of a Poet*, 1941; N. P. Stallknecht, *Strange Seas of Thought*,
1945; G. Wilson Knight in *The Starlit Dome*, 1941. Any reader
will agree and disagree, and may be helped by occasional
return to the old ways of J. C. Shairp and William Veitch,
who found Wordsworth in the hills as well as in libraries.

Wordsworth's political views require fresh non-partisan study, but see A. V. Dicey, *The Statesmanship of W.*, 1917; Clive Brinton in *The Political Ideas of the English Romanticists*, 1926; A. C. Cobban in *Edmund Burke*, 1929.

For descriptive bibliography see T. J. Wise, *A Bibliography of the Writings . . . of W. W.*, Bibliographical Soc., 1916, and *Two Lake Poets*, 1927; *The Amherst W. Collection*, Amherst, 1936; G. H. Healey, *The Cornell W. Collection*, Cornell U.P., 1957. For critical bibliography see E. Bernbaum's chapters in the invaluable *The English Romantic Poets*, MLA, 1950, and revised in later eds.; also the select list attached to Helen Darbishire's admirable essay, *William Wordsworth*, 1953. Frances Blanchard has listed the Portraits. There is a Concordance by Lane Cooper, 1911.

There are a few verses by Dorothy Wordsworth among her brother's poems. Of her diaries, an invaluable source of information as well as delightful in themselves, that of the 1803 Tour in Scotland was ed. J. C. Shairp, 1874; added to by W. Knight, *Dorothy Wordsworth's Journals*, 1897. The most complete is *The Journals of D. W.*, ed. E. de Selincourt, 1941, revised, 2 vols., ed. H. Darbishire; *WC*, 1952; there is a biography by de Selincourt, Oxford, 1933.

INDEX

Main entries are in bold type; an asterisk indicates a biographical note. Modern authors have initials only. Pp. 242 et seq. are in the Chronological Tables or the Bibliography.